MARTIN YAN'S CHINATOWN COOKING

MARTIN YAN'S
CHINATOWN
COOKING

200 TRADITIONAL RECIPES

FROM 11 CHINATOWNS

AROUND THE WORLD

WM

WILLIAM MORROW

An Imprint of HarperCollins*Publishers*

Grateful acknowledgment is made to Takashimaya New York and Crate & Barrel for generously lending us the merchandise used in the photographs.

Photograph of Martin Yan and Julia Child on page xiii, copyright © 1995 by Constance Brown.

All photographs by Christopher Hirsheimer copyright © 2002, except those on pages: iv, x, xviii, xxxiv, xxxv, 3, 34, 40, 51 (left), 72, 73, 94, 95, 98, 99, 107, 116, 122, 132, 133, 147, 154, 155, 193, 204, 212, 213, 233, 238, 272, 273, 277, 292, 293, 319, 326, 331, 342 (right), 343, 344 (bottom), 348, 349, 351 (top), all by Stephanie Liu Jan copyright © 2002. Photograph of Martin Yan as a young boy on page xvi copyright © 2002 by Yan Can Cook, Inc.

HarperCollins books may be purchased for educational, business, or sales promotional use. For information please write: Special Markets Department, HarperCollins Publishers Inc., 10 East 53rd Street, New York, NY 10022.

FIRST EDITION

Designed by Leah Carlson-Stanisic

Map by Jeff Ward

Printed on acid-free paper

Library of Congress Cataloging-in-Publication Data

Yan, Martin, 1948–
    Martin Yan's Chinatown cooking: 200 traditional recipes from
11 Chinatowns around the world / Martin Yan.—1st ed.
        p.; cm.
    Includes index.
    ISBN 0-06-008475-8
        1. Cookery, Chinese.   I. Title: Chinatown cooking.   II. Title.

TX724.5.C5Y2833 2002
641.5951—dc21   2002021939

02 03 04 05 06 WB/RRD 10 9 8 7 6 5 4 3 2 1

They set out from their native China to find a better life—men, women, and children, who dreamed of prosperity and opportunity, freedom and hope. And amid unimaginable hardship and sacrifice, they found something even more precious: each other. They came together in their adopted lands and formed new families and new communities. They called them "Chinatown."

✳   ✳   ✳

This book is dedicated to those immigrants, whose pioneering journeys would one day enable me and so many others to pursue our own dreams. Their spirit still enriches the communties around them. And all over the world, their food endures as a symbol of family, tradition, and love.

ACKNOWLEDGMENTS

The Chinatowns around the world are amazing communities filled with history, culture, friendship, and, of course, food. And for years I dreamed of creating a television series and publishing a cookbook about Chinatowns and Chinatown cooking so that I could share with everyone what makes these communities so unique. After some years of research and planning, followed by months of travel, my dream has come true. But the dream would not have become a reality without the support of many people around the world. Teamwork is what helped me make this happen, and I am thankful.

Where would I be without the strong support of our sponsors? The people at Waterpik Technologies came on board in support of their new Acquia sanitizing system and were a joy to work with. Alan Chang and Janner Chu at Lee Kum Kee (USA) brought their sauces to us again; and the people associated with Lee Kum Kee from England (Herman Leong) to Japan (Shunji Ohara) to Australia (Bernard Yiu and Alfreda Shun) provided information, contacts, and introduced us to all the local master chefs. The wonderful folks at GE Monogram, Paul Klein, Nolan Pike, and Randall Fong, again supported the show and gave us a brand new kitchen with the best appliances, as well as an appreciation of our cooking. Florence Sheffer and Suzanne Howard of Meyer Corporation joined us again with their Circulon cookware line, which is an invaluable part of our kitchen. Don Ogan, Howard Ong, and Heidi Miklautsch brought Aroma Housewares back as a repeat sponsor of *Yan Can Cook*. With Joe Hernandez and Nancy Eisman, Melissa's/World Variety Produce returned, as did Diamond of California, thanks to Mariam Worsham, Sandra McBride, and Tim Cannon. Cees Talma and Sue Kwon of Unilever Bestfoods helped bring Argo and Kingsford's Corn Starch back. And I didn't get mad, I got very glad that Glad Products, represented by Alan Seidelman and Alyssa Odenburg, became a new sponsor this year.

We visited eleven Chinatowns in seven countries on four continents. We were welcomed and helped by master chefs, restaurateurs, colleagues, and friends everywhere. There were far too many wonderful people helping us to list all of them here. Especially important, though, were the Singapore Tourism Board (Mr. M. Chew) and the Singapore Pan Pacific Hotel, the Macau Government Tourist Office (João Manuel Costa Antunes, Maria Helena de Senna Fernandez), the Australian Tourist Commission (Trish Pascuzzo, Marina Albert, Peter Janssen), Lynn Lee in Honolulu, Shirley Fong-Torres and Bernice Fong in San Francisco, the Marriott Eaton Centre and Chef Professor Bill Wong in Toronto, and the Museum of Chinese in the Americas and Mark and Ellen Lii of Ten Ren Tea in New York.

As we traveled, we had the support of first-rate crews everywhere we went. Dan Dominy, with a keen eye, was especially important in capturing what we saw, and he was ably assisted by Ted Ver-Valen and Aaron Katzman, both of whom seem to have learned to appreciate Chinese food more along the way.

This cookbook is the result of hard work from many dedicated professionals. Coordinating the overall project in my office was the hard-working and incomparable Jeannie Cuan. In the kitchen Chef Drew Gillaspie was on the ball 110 percent and led the way, with chefs Sophie Hou, Anthony Tse, Sandy Rust, Bernice Fong, Suzanne Rocha, Eric Beamesderfer, James Wong, and Damon Barham, who all helped develop and test the recipes in this cookbook. Christopher Styler added clarity to the recipe writing. Word crafting came from my friend the talented John Krich; Jan Nix, Tina Salter and Juan Lai, as usual, provided their valuable expertise. Providing additional support and assistance were Kim Decker, Ginny Bast, Howard Goodman, and Susan Yoshimura. Our editor at William Morrow Cookbooks, Harriet Bell, gave the book a vision, kept it on track, and managed it adroitly. Project coordinator Kathleen Hackett, photographer Christopher Hirsheimer, food stylist Corinne Trang, and prop stylist Michele Michael created the wonderful look we achieved. And thanks also to jacket photographer Brian Smale.

Special mention should be made of Stephanie Jan. She did everything—booked appointments, scheduled our production days, recorded and analyzed recipes, took many of the beautiful on-location photographs, and was invaluable in more ways than I can count. And she did it in English, Cantonese, Mandarin, and a little Japanese when needed.

In-studio production was taped in Toronto at the facilities of Food Network Canada. Special thanks go to Karen Gelbart of Food Network Canada. Behind the scenes we were privileged to have an amazing staff. In particular, producer Anne-Sophie Brieger, director Brian Murphy, and editor Brent Pate were as good as they come, as were the crew members and kitchen staff.

Finally, I want to thank my partners in this exciting project, Nat Katzman and Geof Drummond of A La Carte Communications. They are the best at putting together culinary projects with TV and cookbooks. Geof brought both his food business acumen and his outstanding knowledge of television production to the project. Nat managed it, worried about it, guided it, and watched over it from start to finish. As I told him often, with him around worrying about everything, I can be free to be creative and concentrate on doing my best.

AN APPRECIATION OF CHINESE COOKING AND MARTIN YAN

Julia Child

For almost two years during the second World War, I was a humble but hungry file clerk, one of the dozen or so young women office workers assigned to the Office of Strategic Services in China, first in Kunming, then in Chungking. We were housed in a military compound, where the food was so indescribably dreadful that we ate out at every opportunity. Fortunately our office included a goodly number of American "old China hands," many of whom had been born there, spoke the language, and well knew its customs and, especially, the food.

Although this was wartime and some ingredients must have been scarce, we always ate remarkably well, and to be with friends who knew their way around the restaurants was a rare experience. We were eating the real Chinese food of China, which was nothing like the kind of tourist adaptation—chop suey, or whatever they called it—that I had known back in the States. In fact, just because of that fake food, I did not expect to like Chinese food at all—and was delighted to find that I adored it.

Going to a restaurant meal was always a joyous occasion. At one of our favorites in Kunming, we would sit around a comfortable wooden table, usually next to several large happy families that included grandmothers, mothers, babies, nieces, and friends. Our restaurant, the Hoh-Teh-Fu, was a three-story brown wooden structure built around an open central core. After the waiters had taken an order, they would yell it down the well. Pretty soon a returning yell announced the food was ready, and they would let down their baskets to pull

the food up from the kitchens below. We always had bowls of rice, one per person, and three or four platters of food were set on a big round lazy Susan in the middle of the table. There would be, for instance, beef with Chinese broccoli, chicken and wild mushrooms, and a dish of pork in spicy sauce, as well as pots of tea, and warm rice wine.

We were instructed by our mentors that the rule is you must keep one foot on the floor while you reach into your chosen platter. You picked up a good portion with your chopsticks—we rapidly learned how to use them—and laid it on top of the rice. From there, you popped a bit of it into your mouth. All the while, the rice was sopping up delicious cooking juices, so at the end you had a second pleasure—beautifully sauced rice. If your tea was cold, you threw it over your shoulder onto the floor. Bones and scraps went onto the floor too, where the waiters were constantly sweeping them up. Throughout the meal, appreciative noises and laughter from our table and our neighbors filled the room with a merry buzz.

Every region of China has its own style of cooking, and the food I ate during that period was mostly from northern and southwestern China. Most of the dishes I remember with such pleasure one can now find in many good Chinese restaurants here, including those with mu shu crepes, where you spread the food on one side, roll up the thin little pancake, and hold it in your fingers to eat. Another always welcome dish was steamed or braised whole fish anointed with rich soy sauce and herbs and laid out dramatically on a platter. Peking duck was almost a must, of course, with its strips of crisp brown skin, its frayed scallions dipped in a sweet bean sauce, and, again, its pancakes. An elemental and truly unique flavor that so far I, personally, have never found in Chinese restaurants here, however, is that very special taste of fermented bean curd—hard to describe—somewhat cheese-like, definitely fermented. You would set a small portion on your plate and dip bits of food into it, or mix it into your sauce. I am glad to find it here in this book, because I have missed that, to me, very typically Chinese taste.

I treasure my memories of Chinese meals from that period. They utterly charmed and satisfied my appetite, and military life would have been dreary indeed were they not part of my existence. The subtleties and variety of that creative cuisine actually awoke my palate to new tastes, and really prepared me for the glory of French food, which was, at that point, unknown to me. In fact, if I were forced to choose just one style of cooking for the rest of my life, it would be either French or northern Chinese.

Now, praises be, we have Martin Yan to show us the way. I have enjoyed watching Martin ever since he came on the television, and I have picked up many a pointer on how to eat Chinese when I've shared a meal with him. How do you deal with a large unwieldy bony piece of duck using only your chopsticks, for instance? You take it up and hold it between your teeth while you chew off a satisfactory bite, then you put it down, again with your chopsticks—and go at it again, and again, if need be. Martin cooks and eats with engaging gusto, and he is certainly the premier exponent of Chinese cuisine. He has been researching this ancient art for years, he knows both its classical and modern versions, and, equally important, he knows how to teach. Thanks to this seminal book you are holding in your hands, we now have the best of all China and Chinatowns to savor. How lucky we are to have him here with us.

Come with me through the gates of Chinatown, anywhere in the world. Some gates, like the famed one at the entrance of San Francisco's Chinatown on Grant Street, are squat and imposing, bedecked with jade-colored tiles and fiery, protective dragons. In Vancouver, austere wooden posts topped by a single swirl of Chinese calligraphy quietly greet visitors. Sydney's ceremonial entrance is encircled with dancing fish bringing luck to all those who pass beneath. No wonder I feel their good fortune rub off on me every time I stroll through those gates.

From London to Yokohama, these symbolic doors connect earth and sky, past and future. And while these gates, or *pai lou,* were once barriers to make sure that East and West did not mix, they are now symbols of beckoning welcome. Today the gates of Chinatowns offer easy entry to a once distant culture. They announce to the citizens of the world's cities that an exotic and exciting community has moved in.

But, sometimes, you have to leave home and roam the world before you learn to appreciate the heritage and the resources in your own backyard. That's why I've traveled the globe to discover the value of those nearby Chinatowns. Long before that, of course, I had left my first home in Guangzhou—the southern Chinese city of Canton, as most Westerners know it—when I was thirteen years old. And I've racked up a lot of frequent flyer miles since then: working in kitchens, studying, teaching, eating, cooking, sharing, and trying to be a cultural bridge to Chinese cuisine.

But, unlike many of the nearly one hundred million Chinese who have migrated overseas, I have never lived in a Chinatown. I first crossed the border from China to nearby Hong Kong, a way station to other places for many Chinese, where I apprenticed myself in a restaurant to receive my primary chef's training. From there, I came to America to study food science at the University of California at Davis, near Sacramento, and then moved to the town of Brooks in western Canada, to help an old school buddy, Frank Lee, open a Chinese restaurant. At the time, there were few, if any, Chinese eateries, groceries, or people in that frontier region. The closest Chinatown was in Vancouver, more than a

COOKING IN MY MOTHER'S KITCHEN AT THE AGE OF NINE

day's travel on the transcontinental train that crossed the formidable Canadian Rockies. But all the hours being bounced along those winding tracks were worth it once I arrived in Vancouver's long-thriving, historic Chinese community, where I could immediately satisfy my craving for a bowl of hot *fun,* slippery rice noodles in comforting chicken soup, and other dishes from home. Before getting back on the train, I shopped in Chinese markets to stock up on duck liver sausage, dried shrimp, taro root cakes, and other delicacies that were unavailable in our small western town.

From Canada, where a brief appearance on a local television show led to my first cooking series, I moved to the San Francisco Bay Area. No need to ride the rails here. What a pleasure it was to jump on the freeway and be in San Francisco's Chinatown—the New World's first and most fabled—in just thirty minutes! A lot quicker than getting back to Canton, but just as familiar. From the pressed duck to the bundles of long beans and the many kinds of plum sauce, I found everything a Chinese chef—and fledgling television performer—could want.

But that Chinatown on a hill quickly became more than just a place to buy dried black mushrooms still smelling of the earth. Through frequent visits, I became friends with chefs and shopkeepers, artisans, and association leaders. Grocers shared stories about how their grandparents and other family members had ended up in San Francisco, about ancestral villages they were saving up to visit, about struggling to start family businesses, about the sons and daughters making them proud at college. Strolling from grocer to baker, I passed a Chinese calligrapher who recited Chinese proverbs, sending wishes of joy, prosperity, and long life to all who crossed his path. Passing one of the many tiny pocket parks, I watched a local martial arts troupe of determined kids practice their lion dance routine for the upcoming Chinese New Year parade.

As much as I came to Chinatown to restock my kitchen cupboard, every visit resulted in replenishing my love for all things Chinese. Chinatown renewed my connection with the noisy festivals and solemn rituals that bind Chinese together, no matter where we live. For me, all the Chinatowns I have visited are personal touchstones as well as sources of inspired cooking. There is always something new—a restaurant, a dim sum parlor, a temple, an herbalist—to discover. These Chinatowns of the world have offered this wandering son of China new flavors, new friends, and new memories that I want to share with you.

This book is my way of paying tribute to some of the truly remarkable citizens—and cooks—inhabiting some of the most fascinating neighborhoods on earth. I hope that in trying these very special recipes, from popular favorites like Kung Pao Chicken and Broccoli Beef to banquet dishes like Steamed Whole Fish with Ginger and Green Onions or Flower Drum Crab Baked in the Shell, and, in reading something of the local history and customs, you, too, will be able to experience these microcosms of Chinese culture like an insider—and to distinguish the different cuisines, regions, and customs of the various Chinatowns you visit. I've tried to share not only my rare access to the finest chefs and their unique creations, like Gum-Lo Wontons with Seafood Sweet-and-Sour Sauce or Wok-Braised Lobster Tails in Creamy Rum Sauce, but also the sights, flavors, monuments, and traditions that make each of the world's Chinatowns one of a kind.

Explore and learn. It becomes easier every time. Remember, the key to easy and fast cooking is to be prepared. Become familiar with the basic tools and ingredients; read the "Equipment and Techniques" chapter and the "Chinese Pantry" chapter. If you don't have the exact ingredients, you can use the substitutes I suggest. Be creative and have fun. Be comfortable with yourself, and use both your common sense and your culinary imagination.

So take a walk with me and experience my Chinatowns—and the delights of Chinatown cooking. The streets of any Chinatown are a giant kitchen, a visually exciting classroom offering its secrets to anyone. Explore, take a walk through the hustle and bustle of the main streets and the alleyways and find something intriguing and exciting. When you've reached the end of this global culinary adventure, you'll realize, as I have, that a world tour is just a short distance away. The Chinatowns of the world await your visit and your appetite!

INTRODUCTION
Chinatown History

The history of Chinese all over the world is one of triumph over enormous adversity. Roots that go back five thousand years would aid many in establishing roots in new lands—and not just surviving, but prospering, while remaining loyal to their traditions. Coming after so many miners and sailors, merchants, and doctors who had paved the way, the lure for me was something else: the chance to create wonderful dishes under the best conditions and to teach others about the wonders of Chinese cuisine. In this endeavor, I couldn't help but be inspired by the many examples of bravery that preceded my personal journey. After all, I'm only a "j.o.j." ("just off the jet"), while earlier generations have gone steerage across the entire Pacific. And I knew I had to live up to the standards of excellence set by so many unsung ambassadors of Chinese cooking.

In Singapore, Hokkien traders did wonders with tiger shrimp amid Victorian architecture. In Macau, the relaxed mix of Portuguese ease and Chinese pluck helped cook up what has become one of the world's longest-running fusion foods. Canada, on the other hand, has more recently become a fusion country. Toronto, with the growth of several strong Chinese communities, now competes with Vancouver—sometimes known as Van Kong—over more than fresh air and mounties. In their search for a better life, the Chinese have not overlooked that lucky country "down under," and neither could I. Melbourne's Chinatown is a pristine example of the best goodies Chinese brought at the time of the Gold Rush, while Sydney's newer showcase is a cornucopia of South Seas seafood. London's merry old Soho is made merrier by some outstanding chefs migrated from Hong Kong's farm villages. As for New York City, the Big Apple now boasts the biggest Chinatown of all, but San Francisco, the place that showed the way, still shows its strong Chinese pride on steep hills. And I've introduced two hidden gems: Yokohama, a vast cavalcade of Chinese cuisine stacked on numerous floors and Honolulu, a colorful Pacific melting pot that has come to define East-West cooking. Of course, some would say that Chinatowns were all invented merely to house Chinese restaurants. But the love of their native cuisine binds together Chinese everywhere.

Beijing
Shanghai
Sichuan
Canton

CHINA
CULINARY REGIONS

MONGOLIA
N. KOREA
GREAT WALL
Beijing
SHANXI
S. KOREA
SHANDONG
Yellow Sea
ANHUI
Shanghai
SICHUAN
Yangtze River
HUNAN
East China Sea
BHUTAN
INDIA
FUJIAN
BANGLADESH
YUNNAN
GUANGDONG
TAIWAN
Guangzhou (Canton)
Hong Kong
Macau
MYANMAR
VIETNAM
Bay of Bengal
LAOS
THAILAND
Hainan Island

© 2002 Jeffrey L. Ward

EVEN AMONG THE CHINESE, THERE IS SOME DISAGREEMENT ABOUT THE NUMBER OF MAJOR CULINARY REGIONS, BUT TO MAKE THINGS EASY, THE VARIETY CAN BE NARROWED DOWN TO FOUR: BEIJING, SHANGHAI, SICHUAN, AND CANTON.

How and why did the Chinese end up in these far-flung places? For the same reasons that forced Europeans in the late nineteenth and early twentieth centuries to leave home and seek their fortunes. But the Chinese had a few more reasons. And a lot more people. Especially in southern China, and in the Guangdong province, where I come from, there were simply too many folks farming too few rice paddies. In addition, if locusts didn't wipe out the crops, there were ravaging warlords and foreign powers to do so.

"Water flows downhill, but people flow uphill," goes one Chinese proverb. In the last half of the 1800s, around two and half million Chinese, a drop in the bucket of the population, flowed toward new lands in search of a better life.

Like anyone leaving the only home they had ever known, it wasn't easy for these Chinese to venture to faraway lands. Always patriotic and a tad clannish, my inward-looking ancestors inhabited a place they called the "Middle Kingdom," or *jung gok*—the Chinese name for China. But Confucian tradition encouraged sons to sacrifice their own ambitions in order to honor past, as well as future, generations. It was no shame, but rather an honor, to improve the family fortunes by setting out to climb some faraway "gold mountain," or *gum san,* as America was called. When I was barely old enough to reach the wok in our tiny kitchen, my mom was telling us tales and legends about America and the many mountains there laced with glittering gems.

What lured the Chinese wasn't just rare metals in the hills of California, and Australia, but also steady work on the sugar plantations of Hawaii and at dockside godowns in Singapore, the call of the open seas as merchant marines and stevedores, that led to the docks of London, a modern education in neighboring Japan—and, above all, an escape from plundering armies and constant want. Dropped in Adelaide, Chinese prospectors had to walk for weeks across the blistering desert to get to the gold fields of Victoria. There, they were allowed to pan only among the "tailings" of mines that Australians had left behind. Yet these Chinese were able to send back enough earnings from their finds to finance the first railway across the province of Guangdong. They also left behind enough Chinese culture in this part of Australia that the small town of Bendigo still trots out the longest ceremonial dragon in the world for the Chinese New Year celebration each year.

In the Melbourne Chinatown that was built in the aftermath of the Australian gold rush, in the Limehouse district of London where Chinese sailors settled, or in the Honolulu enclave that was originally home to the Chinese pineapple pickers, family values and so-called family associations helped the Chinese endure—even when they could not build real families. Anti-immigrant laws—exclusion acts—passed in the United States and Australia had reduced the flow of Chinese that started in the 1880s to a trickle by the 1960s. A bachelor society, unable to return home or send for wives, somehow hung on. Thanks to some of the values and rituals mentioned throughout the book—philosophy, religion, design, family associations—these communities grew even stronger and more closely knit. Some experts refer to this vast migration as the Chinese Diaspora, but to me, "diaspora" suggests a forced dispersal, a scattering to the wind, a loss of one's home and identity. Walk down any street in any of the Chinatowns in this book, and you will realize that nothing has been lost, and everything has been gained.

All together, Chinese who live outside China produce far more wealth than their 1.3 billion compatriots in China. The majority of Chinese emigrating in recent times have been programmers and professionals, who have created prosperous, secondary enclaves in the suburbs of large cities. Vancouver has its all-Chinese suburb known as Richmond, while San Francisco now has a bustling enclave that goes by the same name—and numerous bedroom communities in its Peninsula to the south have taken on a decidedly Chinese flavor. New York City has a secondary Chinatown in Flushing, Queens, a third in Brooklyn. Toronto has too many to count. And no study of Chinatowns would be complete without exploring the phenomenon of the so-called "new Chinatowns." These are what I call the twenty-first-century, one-stop Chinatowns, home to the Great Mall (not the Great Wall). In massive complexes, you will find all kinds of Chinese businesses: grocery stores, bookstores, antiques stores, and, of course, restaurants. Refugees from all over Southeast Asia, many of them of Chinese stock, have added further flavor to these pan-Asian enclaves. The new Chinatowns are evidence that Chinese are no longer working on the railroad—now they're working in think tanks. These communities also show that there's a lot more to the cuisine than chop suey.

Still, when it's time to parade with proud banners, honor ancestors, or feast with relatives, we make the pilgrimage to the old neighborhoods. Peek inside, and you will find chambers of commerce members in business suits, congregations worshipping not just in smoky temples but in churches. Kids shoot hoops in noisy playgrounds, street vendors peddle newspapers, drummers practice a martial beat before they head out for a night at the nightclubs. On park benches, couples steal kisses while gray-beards are equally passionate about their chess games. And in the markets, some of the world's most dedicated home cooks comb through mounds of produce, picking out the freshest greens with the world's most practiced sets of eyes. Come for the food, but stay to discover these living, breathing communities.

With my guidance, I hope that you will savor the very best of these samplers of Chinese life and Chinese regions that dot the earth. The restaurants that keep alive so many flavors from my home can become a place where you feel at home too. In these Chinatowns, one of the world's great cuisines has added its unique scents and sensations to many of the world's great cultures. The resulting mix is nothing less than magic in a wok.

Today, the gates of the world's Chinatowns stand high for all of us to honor—and to pass through. With this book, I hope in some small way to help keep those gates open forever.

EQUIPMENT AND TECHNIQUES

EQUIPMENT

Cooking Chinese food requires a few basic pieces of equipment: a wok, a Chinese chef's knife, a chopping board, and a bamboo steamer. You could also add a clay pot to your repertoire.

WOKS

The Chinese wok is the world's most versatile utensil in any kitchen, and it is by far the most important single tool in a Chinese kitchen. Use it to stir-fry, steam, deep-fry, braise, poach, simmer, and even smoke. The key criteria in selecting a wok are size, shape, and material.

Consider how many people you usually feed. To serve a family of four to six, use a 14-inch-diameter wok (measured across the top edge). If you are cooking for one or two people, a 12-inch wok is ideal.

The sides of all woks are round, but some have round bottoms while others are flat.

ROUND-BOTTOMED WOKS are traditional and are best suited to gas burners. Depending on the stovetop, you can place the wok directly over the burner or, for added stability, set it on a wok stand that goes atop the burner. Perforated circular wok stands usually come with round-bottomed woks, and most of them have sloping sides. As a rule, place the stand so that the wok is as close as possible to the heat, exposing the most surface area to the flame.

FLAT-BOTTOMED WOKS are designed specifically to sit directly on the heating elements of electric ranges. These may require a bit of trial and error to find the best heat setting for different cooking techniques. Treat your flat-bottomed wok like a large skillet.

There are a wide variety of materials to choose from. Select the one most convenient for you and your needs.

The latest technological invention in cookware is **anodized aluminum**. Woks made from it are durable, conduct heat well, and often have slightly curved sides and flat bases that function well on both gas and electric stovetops. Some have nonstick coatings, which make for easy cleanup. They're usually ready to go straight from the box, without seasoning. These convenient woks are easy to find in gourmet cookware shops and department stores. Make sure to look for the best-quality brands, such as Circulon or Anolon, with a Dupont nonstick coating label.

Perhaps the most traditional and popular are the age-old **carbon steel** woks. They are strong yet lightweight for easy use and are modestly priced. They conduct heat evenly and quickly. Most Chinese home cooks favor good-quality carbon steel woks. Available in Chinatown hardware stores and from mail-order companies, they're becoming easier to find in other stores too. The one caveat with carbon steel woks is that they require seasoning to prevent rusting.

To season a wok, wash the rust-preventive coating off the new wok using hot water, detergent, and a scouring pad or steel wool. Rinse it well and set it over medium heat to dry for a couple of minutes. Then, keeping the wok over medium- to medium-high heat, and wearing an oven mitt to protect your hand, rub its inner surface with a clean rag or heavy-duty paper towel dampened with vegetable oil. Add ½ teaspoon fine salt as an abrasive and continue rubbing the wok until it starts darkening and smoking, working the oil and salt into the metal's pores. Add more oil and salt whenever the surface starts looking dry, and change the rag as needed. As soon as the rag comes away clean—about 15 to 20 minutes of continuous rubbing—stop rubbing. Let the wok cool, wash it in warm water with a soft nylon pad or brush, and then set it over high heat to dry. The shiny, dark-brown spot that now appears in the center of your wok is the initial layer of seasoning, and the more you cook in your wok, the larger it will grow.

It's important to care for a seasoned wok properly. Wash it first thing after a meal, using hot water and only a minimum amount of soap, if any, so as not to wash away the seasoning. To remove stubborn stuck-on food, rub it away with a little salt. Dry the wok on a warm burner for a minute or two; the heat does a better job than a towel.

Beginner cooks may prefer **electric woks** simply because they have the advantage of a built-in temperature control, which makes for more accurate heat adjustment—a benefit when deep-frying and great for braising and steaming. And because their heating elements are built-in, they free up stove space. You can even take the wok to the serving area and keep foods warm during the course of a meal. However, most electric woks don't reach the high temperatures needed for serious cooks. While the novelty of cooking tableside with an electric wok may be worth the purchase, get a true wok for your daily stir-fries.

For easy cleanup and a wok that requires as little oil as possible, select a wok with a **nonstick coating**. Virtually all types, including electric, are offered in nonstick versions. If treated with care, the coating can last for quite a while. Be sure to use only wooden or plastic utensils and gentle cleansers. However, nonstick coatings vary, and this is one product for which price does reflect quality: spend more, and you get a coating that stands the test of time. A cheaper one will need replacement sooner.

OTHER KITCHEN ESSENTIALS

COOKING CHOPSTICKS These are extra-long wooden or bamboo chopsticks, usually 1 to 1½ feet long. Use them to reach into a pot of boiling water to separate some noodles, or to grab pieces of food from the surface of sizzling-hot oil when deep-frying. Because they're not metal, the heat won't find its way from the water or oil to your fingers.

BRASS WIRE SKIMMER The traditional Chinese skimmer has a long flat bamboo handle and a very shallow wire-mesh basket for retrieving food and allowing oil or hot water to drain off. These baskets let you reach the bottom of the wok to scoop out foods while boiling or deep-frying. The 6- or 8-inch-diameter ones are most functional.

FINE-MESH STRAINER OR SIEVE To pick up the tiny pieces of food that a regular brass wire skimmer might miss, one of these is a plus. They come in a variety of sizes; a basic size to start with is one with a 7- to 8-inch-diameter basket.

WOK LADLE This type of ladle is larger and a little shallower than Western ladles to better fit the curves of a wok. The handle is the same angle as the ladle cup. Using the ladle with a wok spatula gives you the added control of a two-handed approach to toss your food around.

WOK SPATULA This long-handled shovel-shaped tool has a curved blade that fits the curved surface of the wok. Spatulas come in metal, plastic, and wood—the latter two are preferable for nonstick woks.

WOK LID A high dome-shaped or slope-sided lid will transform your wok into a steamer, a braising pot, or a smoker. If your wok didn't come with one, lids can be found at all Chinese hardware and most gourmet stores. Look for one that's slightly smaller in diameter than the wok itself so it will fit just below the wok's edge (for a 14-inch wok, get a 12-inch lid, and so forth).

CHINESE CHEF'S KNIFE

Every chef, from every culinary tradition, will tell you that the most important kitchen tool is a good, sharp knife. The Chinese chef's knife has numerous uses—from slicing, chopping, and dicing to shredding, crushing, even tenderizing, and scooping foods. Do not confuse the Chinese chef's knife with a heavy-duty cleaver, which may look similar but is much heavier and reserved for hacking through bones. Always remember that the sharpest knife is both the easiest and the *safest* to use! A good knife that holds its edge is a must.

A chef's knife should feel comfortable and well balanced. Its center of gravity should be close to where the handle meets the blade. Avoid big knives—they are too heavy and likely to slip out of your grasp. Choose a traditional #3 Chinese chef's knife for all your slicing, dicing, and cutting jobs.

Quality knives are made with a tang. The tang is the part of the blade that sits between the two pieces of the handle material, with three rivets holding them together. Knives with blades stuck into round wooden handles may be less expensive, but the handles are also more likely to crack and separate from the blade.

The cutting blade should not be straight, but have a little "upturn" curve on both ends; this allows the blade to rock as you cut.

Knives made of high-carbon stainless steel have advantages over traditional carbon steel because they don't rust or discolor acidic foods. They also sharpen easily and keep their edge longer.

KNIFE CARE

Don't abuse your knife. It is intended for many things, but it is not a butcher's cleaver, a hacksaw, a hammer, or a screwdriver. Its blade will be harmed if you cut on a metal, ceramic, or other hard surface.

Don't soak the knife too long or put it in the dishwasher. Either will waterlog the handle, possibly causing it to mildew and crack. Instead, wash it in warm soapy water after using it and dry it immediately.

Store your knife properly in a sheath or on a magnetic knife rack. Letting it jostle around in the cutlery drawer can harm the knife's edge; if storing it in a drawer, be sure to protect the blade with a plastic knife guard.

Use a sharpening steel regularly to maintain the knife's edge. With the steel and knife positioned away from your body, firmly grip the handle of the steel. Hold the knife vertically at an 18- to 20-degree angle to the steel. Starting with the heel of the blade on the steel, run the blade lightly along the steel from heel to tip, making sure not to hit any part of the handle. Rely on the weight of the knife itself when sharpening. Repeat this sharpening motion an equal number of times—at least eight to ten times—on each side of the blade.

If you don't have a sharpening steel, you can use the rough bottom of an earthenware bowl. Turn the bowl upside down and, holding the knife blade flat and angled slightly downward, stroke it against the bowl's unglazed "foot."

When the blade eventually becomes dull even with regular use of a steel, use a sharpening stone. You need only to do this on an average of three or four times a year. If you don't feel comfortable doing it, ask your butcher or take it to a cutlery shop. Most of the electric knife sharpeners available in the market are not designed for the traditional Chinese chef's knife.

CHOPPING BOARD

Wooden and plastic boards are available in various shapes and sizes. Choose the right one based on how much counter space you have and how much cutting you will be doing. If you often cook for large numbers of guests, it's better to have larger rather than smaller boards. Always place cutting boards on a flat surface, and lay a damp kitchen towel underneath to provide stability and traction.

The main reason for having two or more boards is that you can reserve one for cutting meat and poultry, to prevent cross-contamination. If you have only one board, be sure to wash it thoroughly with hot soapy water and dry it well every time you switch from raw meat preparation to cutting other foods. Even better, cut the vegetables first, then the meat or poultry. Plastic boards will easily survive the dishwasher. Wooden boards should always be stored with adequate ventilation to ensure that they dry thoroughly. Every so often, rub vinegar or lemon juice into the board to get rid of any lingering odors.

STEAMER

A wok makes an ideal steamer: just add some sort of rack that fits over the water and a lid. Many woks come with stainless steel steaming racks, but you also can simply arrange two pairs of chopsticks in a tic-tac-toe grid 1 to 2 inches above the boiling water. Place the plate of food to be steamed on top, cover with a lid, and you're ready to go.

The round, flat-bottomed handmade bamboo steamers the Chinese have been using for centuries are another option. Bamboo steamers sit in the wok above the boiling water, and you can stack one on top of another to create towers of steaming delights. The steam from the wok will rise through the bamboo slats that form the bottom of each basket. The bamboo lattice of the lid is tight enough to keep most of the steam in, but porous enough to release just the right amount so that condensation doesn't drip back onto the food. You can even carry bamboo steamers right to the table for serving. Look for steamer baskets about 2 inches smaller in diameter than your wok; for example, a 14-inch wok can accommodate a 12-inch steamer. Before you use your bamboo steamer for the first time, soak it in water overnight, then let it air-dry. For general care, dry bamboo steamers thoroughly, and store them in a well-ventilated space to prevent mildew.

As an alternative, aluminum steamer sets work well. They don't require a wok, and they're not prone to mildew or burning.

CLAY POTS

Clay pots are perfect vessels for preparing and serving everything from rice dishes and stews to braises and casseroles. Found in Chinese specialty shops, they come in all sorts of sizes and shapes. Smaller pots will hold two to four servings, larger ones have the capacity to feed large groups. Clay pots may have either a single long handle or loop-like knobs on either side.

Submerge a new pot in water and check for small bubbles rising to the surface—a sure sign that the pot's cracked; if it's cracked, return it. Before you use a clay pot for the first time, soak it and its lid in water for a few hours, then drain and let them air-dry overnight.

Clay pots are durable—made to withstand intense heat—but they are not indestructible. You can set a clay pot of food right over a gas burner, but do not do so with an empty pot. For electric burners, put a diffuser underneath. Warm the pot on the stove before exposing it to an oven's potentially shocking heat. After you have used it, wait until the pot has cooled before putting it in cold water or on a cold, damp surface.

TECHNIQUES

Chinese cooking relies on a surprisingly simple set of cooking techniques. Master them, and you can prepare hundreds of delicious dishes.

BLANCHING (WATER OR OIL)

By immersing foods in boiling water or hot oil for a few seconds to minutes, you blanch them. Blanching in water, the method most common in home kitchens, is also called parboiling. Oil blanching is a more difficult technique, usually limited to restaurant kitchens. Blanching partially cooks food; it is especially helpful in making root and other vegetables tender prior to stir-frying.

BRAISING

The tender texture and intense flavors that develop in foods long-simmered in seasoned liquid is a result of braising. Pieces or chunks of meat are first seared over high heat to brown them, then slowly cooked in seasoned liquid over low heat until tender. The result is tender, flavorful meat. It's an ideal method for tenderizing tough cuts with lots of connective tissue.

DEEP-FRYING

Deep-frying is the technique that allows you to achieve a crispy light texture on the outside while keeping the inside moist and tender. To deep-fry in a wok, add enough oil to come to a height of about 3 inches, or enough to fully submerge the food. Heat the oil to the temperature specified in the recipe: to check the oil's temperature, use a deep-frying thermometer or dip the tip of a long dry wooden or bamboo chopstick into the bottom of the oil; if tiny bubbles surround its tip, the oil is hot enough.

Ingredients to be deep-fried should be at room temperature, so as not to bring down the oil's temperature. Add the ingredients to the wok carefully and in small batches to minimize splashes and maintain a constant oil temperature. As they fry, separate and turn the ingredients with a slotted spoon, Chinese skimmer, or cooking chopsticks for uniform cooking. When they're properly browned or have floated to the surface, retrieve them from the oil and drain them on paper towels or a rack.

You can fry foods in the same oil several times, but don't reuse that oil more than three times. After that point, it begins to break down, or oxidize, darkening and turning murky; also, by that point, it will have taken on the aromas and flavors of whatever you've cooked in it. To store frying oil for reuse, let it cool, then pour it through a fine sieve or strainer to filter out any food particles, put it in an airtight container, and refrigerate. Oil that has been used for fish should be reserved for frying fish because of the strong odor.

MARINATING

Marinades add flavor, tenderize, and/or intensify a food's moisture and flavor. While we usually think of marinades mainly as liquids, such as mixtures of soy sauce and rice wine or vinegar, Chinese cooking also uses dry marinades. A marinade of white pepper and cornstarch, perhaps with a bit of egg white, is used to seal in the food's moisture and flavor.

You don't have to marinate foods for hours. While a long marinating time does make for more intense flavor, it's not always necessary. No matter how long you are marinating something, always do so in a covered nonreactive container (such as glass or stainless steel) in the refrigerator.

PAN-FRYING

A quick comparison of pan-frying and stir-frying reveals some important differences between the two. For one, pan-frying is done in a flat-bottomed frying pan (a flat-bottomed wok will also do the trick). The technique is best for larger pieces of food than those used in stir-frying; you cook them at a lower temperature and for longer. Also, pan-frying generally requires more oil than stir-frying, enough oil to coat the bottom of the pan.

RED COOKING

Red cooking is Chinese-style braising. Like classic braising, it's a way to slowly cook browned meats in a richly flavored liquid, tenderizing and flavoring them in the process, but what makes it truly Chinese are the aromatic ingredients used in the braising liquid: soy sauce, Chinese rice wine, brown sugar or rock sugar, star anise, ginger, garlic, and dried tangerine peel, to name some main players.

ROASTING

Until recently, many home cooks in China were relatively unfamiliar with roasting because the only ovens were in restaurants or bakeries. These usually had large charcoal- or wood-burning ovens that allowed the cooks to hang whole pigs, ducks, pork ribs, and loins on hooks. As the meats roasted, the hot air circulated all around them, creating a crispy, browned surface. In the absence of such generous roasting facilities, you can still get the same effect by roasting meats on a rack in a roasting pan.

SHALLOW-FRYING

The main difference between pan-frying and shallow-frying is about half an inch of oil. Shallow frying requires a bit more—usually enough to *partially* submerge the food.

SIMMERING

Simmering is the gentle cooking of foods in liquid heated to just below the boiling point. A fairly universal technique, it plays an important role in Chinese cuisine.

STEAMING

After stir-frying, steaming is the second most popular Chinese cooking technique.

* Set a steamer rack or basket in a wok or deep pan and add water to come 1 to 1½ inches below the rack or basket's level.

* Bring the water to a full boil.

* Place the food on a heat-resistant dish, such as a glass pie plate, with a diameter slightly smaller than that of the steamer, and set it on the rack or basket. Alternatively, dumplings and buns can go on a rack or steamer basket lined with a damp towel or section of parchment paper to prevent sticking. Cover the steamer.

* Check the steamer occasionally to make sure that it doesn't run dry as the food cooks. If you put a few marbles in the water, they will make noise when the steamer starts to run dry. Keep a pot of water gently simmering on a nearby burner to add to the steamer should it need some.

* Always open the steamer so that the lid directs the steam away from you.

* Carefully remove the food with a towel or oven mitts.

STIR-FRYING

This technique exhibits all the classic characteristics of the quick, efficient Chinese kitchen: small, evenly sized pieces of food are cooked quickly in a wok over high heat. The result is food that stays brightly colored, crisply textured, and vibrantly flavored.

* Before you begin stir-frying, have everything organized and ready. Marinate any ingredients as required and store in the refrigerator until needed. Cut the other ingredients according to the recipe directions, making sure they're uniform in size for quick and even cooking. Prepare the sauce, and have the serving plate ready.

* To prevent the food from sticking, heat the wok for a minute or two before adding the oil.

The wok is ready when your hand feels warm if held a few inches above the surface.

❋ Drizzle a few teaspoons of oil around the wok's sides and swirl to distribute.

❋ Add the ingredients to the wok in batches, with the aromatic ingredients like garlic, ginger, and chilies going in first, followed by any meat, and then the vegetables (the tough ones before the tender). Some recipes direct you to remove the meat to a plate before cooking the vegetables, then return the meat to the wok when the vegetables are done.

❋ Don't overcrowd the wok, or you won't have room to stir the ingredients and they won't brown properly.

❋ Stir constantly; this exposes all the ingredients' surfaces to the wok's heat and enables them to cook quickly, thoroughly, and without sticking.

❋ Right before the dish is finished, add the sauce and stir, to prevent lumps, until it thickens.

❋ Give the dish a taste and adjust the seasoning accordingly.

❋ Place the food on the serving plate, and garnish it.

WOK SMOKING

In Chinese cuisine, smoking isn't so much a way of cooking as it is a way of flavoring food with aromatic ingredients such as tea, brown sugar, spices like star anise and cinnamon, or even raw rice. Fish and duck take particularly well to these flavor characters.

❋ Use a sturdy wok (preferably an older, scruffier one) with a domed lid, to hold in the smoke and give it plenty of room to circulate, and a rack small enough to fit in the wok but large enough to hold the food. Line the wok and its lid with a couple layers of strong aluminum foil, leaving a couple inches of overhang around the edges of both.

❋ First cook the food you are going to smoke.

❋ Turn on the stove's exhaust fan and open the windows before you start smoking.

❋ Sprinkle the aromatic smoking ingredients into the bottom of the lined wok and set the rack 2 to 3 inches above them.

❋ Heat the wok over high heat. When the aromatics and the wok begin smoking, place the food to be smoked on the rack. Immediately cover the wok with the lid and crimp together the overhanging aluminum foil to form a tight seal between the wok and the lid.

❋ Let the smoke permeate the ingredients and infuse it with its aromatic flavor. Sometimes a few minutes are all it takes—follow the recipes for specific times.

BASIC KNIFE TECHNIQUES

You will be amazed at how much your trusty Chinese chef's knife can do for you, but before you cut any ingredient, it's very important that you know how to hold the knife properly. Using your writing hand, grab the handle where it meets the blade, positioning your thumb on one side of the blade and your pointer finger, curled back slightly, on the other. Hold the blade tightly with these two fingers and wrap the remaining ones around the handle. This may feel a little awkward at first, but this grip gives you the best control of the knife.

To cut, hold the food with the other hand, protecting your fingers by curling them under, out of the way of the blade. Rest the flat of the blade against your knuckles and begin to cut: Use a firm, steady downward and slightly forward movement. Keep your fingers curled under, and don't raise the blade higher than the first knuckle. Once you have mastered your grip, these are the basic knife techniques you'll need to know.

SLICING: Hold the food firmly and, with a firm up-and-down motion, raise the knife blade no higher than your knuckles, then lower it down onto the food. Slide the fingers of your noncutting hand back along the food and use your knuckles to guide the blade as you slide it along with them, repeating the up-and-down slicing motion to create evenly sized slices.

MATCHSTICK AND JULIENNE CUTTING: Take a few flat evenly sized slices of a vegetable or other ingredient, stack them, and slice the stack into a bundle of sticks. The main difference between matchstick cuts and julienne cuts is size: Matchstick cutting results in thicker sticks, julienne cutting results in very thin sticks. Sticks about $\frac{1}{8}$ inch thick and 1 to 2 inches long are ideal for stir-fries. Here's a tip: When cutting meats like chicken and pork into matchsticks, chill or lightly freeze them first for 15 to 20 minutes. Chilling makes the meat firmer, and the firmer it is, the less likely it is to get mushy as you cut.

SHREDDING: Slice and stack foods as for julienne cutting, but make the slices paper-thin. Then, as you slice through the stack, make those slices thinner as well.

CUBING AND DICING: First cut matchsticks (see above). Keeping the matchsticks in a bundle, turn them on the cutting board so that their length will run perpendicular to the knife's blade. Slice straight down across them, creating cubes or dice. The only difference between the two is the size, with cubes generally running from 1 inch to $\frac{1}{2}$ inch, and dice usually $\frac{1}{4}$ inch or smaller.

MINCING: Use the shredding technique (see above) to create a bundle of thin strips, then arrange the bundle so it will be perpendicular to the knife's blade and dice the food into very small bits. Alternatively, you can mince food by first dicing the ingredient. Then, holding the knife's handle with one hand and the tip of its blunt edge with the other, use the tip as a pivot around which you raise and lower the blade, moving it from side to side over the food to mince it evenly. To ensure thorough and even mincing, periodically scoop up the minced bits with the knife's blade and give them a turn.

ROLL-CUTTING: This technique is ideal for cutting long cylindrical vegetables like carrots and eggplants into pieces that expose more surface area. To roll-cut, slice off the tip of the vegetable on the diagonal. Give the vegetable a quarter-turn and slice straight down again. Keep on rolling and cutting until you reach the ingredient's stem end.

PARALLEL-CUTTING: Set the piece of food near the edge of the cutting board and place the palm of your free hand on top of it. Holding the knife almost parallel to the cutting board, angling it slightly downward, slice slowly and carefully into the food until you've created two layers, taking care not to direct the knife upward and into your noncutting hand.

BUTTERFLYING: Parallel cutting, but without cutting all the way through the food. You are creating two pieces that are still attached; it resembles an open book.

CRUSHING: Set the ingredient you want to crush near the edge of your cutting board and cover it with the flat of your knife's blade, with the sharp edge facing away from you. Holding the knife's handle with one hand, use the heel of your other hand to whack the flat of the blade good and hard. Mincing approximates the size that crushing achieves—the latter is preferable when preparing aromatic ingredients because it bursts the cellular sacks in the foods, releasing the flavorful oils within.

SCORING: To help food cook faster and more evenly, make a few slightly angled cuts, about ⅛ inch deep, into the surface of the food. Be careful not to cut all the way through it. You can place slices of ginger, herbs, or other flavorings into the score marks to enhance the flavors of your dish. This works especially well for fish fillets.

TENDERIZING: Place the piece of meat you want to tenderize on the cutting board and, holding your knife with its blunt edge down, pound in a crisscross pattern, breaking down some of the meat's tougher fibers.

HOW TO ORDER IN A CHINESE RESTAURANT

"Hunger is the best chef," goes the Chinese proverb. But if you want to have a real Chinese dining experience, rather than just a meal, here are some tips for ordering in a Chinese restaurant.

Ask the waiter for help and suggestions. What are the house specialties? What are their regional favorites? Let the waiter know that you're really open to new ideas and suggestions.

Don't get lost in the translation. Dishes are often translated literally from Chinese to English. Sometimes misspellings make for a good laugh—such as bean "crud" instead of bean curd. The truth is that restaurant menus are often copied so that, when one restaurant makes spelling or translation mistakes, other establishments reprint the same errors.

Try at least one new dish every time you go to a Chinese restaurant. Just as you wouldn't order a hamburger with a steak on the side in an American restaurant, order something other than five stir-fried dishes. A Chinese meal often begins with sliced cold meats, pickled cucumbers, and blanched or golden crisp peanuts for appetizers, followed by a whole fish as a centerpiece, some soup, a vegetable dish, and a rice- or noodle-based dish for the complete dining experience.

Forget one person, one vote. With a group of six or more people, put one person in charge of ordering to keep the menu balanced, or you'll end up with six dishes that are too similar to one another.

Eat with the seasons. Freshness is the name of the game, so order dishes that are made with seasonal ingredients. Asparagus is in season during the spring; Dungeness crab between November and February. And although most Asian vegetables are now available all year round, they are at their peak during the spring and summer months.

Chinese food is regional food. Don't expect a Sichuan chef to be able to prepare Cantonese Steak Kew, or a Cantonese cook to deliver an appropriate spicy meat with bean curd. Ask what area of China the restaurateurs and chef hail from, and order those regional specialties. If they say they can prepare Cantonese, Hunan, *and* Sichuan food, move on to another restaurant.

Keep your balance. Not everything should be cut into cubes and stir-fried. In fact, such dishes are meant to be accompaniments to steamed items like fish or tofu, or items such as braised seafood or meat. Order a selection of dishes that are balanced in colors, flavors, and textures. Chinese cooks often use a variety of ingredients such as water chestnuts, bamboo shoots, wood ears, and cloud ears that have no distinctive flavors but provide textural contrasts.

Categorizing dishes as yin (cold) and yang (hot) doesn't refer to the temperature of the food when it is eaten, but to the temperature that food will create once digested. Chinese believe that every bite we eat is medicine. When people have colds or fever, they need cooling foods like winter melon and watermelon. If the internal fires need stoking, yang foods like lamb or beef

are recommended. Other yin and yang foods include bitter melon, pear, and papaya (all yin) and lychee and lotus root (yang).

Get fishy. The Cantonese word for fish, *yu,* sounds like the word for abundance and plentiful, and since fish were scarce in inland Chinese regions until recent times, a whole steamed fresh fish is often the centerpiece of a special meal. During Chinese New Year and on other festive occasions, fish is served to symbolize abundance and good fortune.

Always order soup. Typical southern Chinese restaurants (such as Cantonese ones) serve soup before the meal or after the appetizer. Northern Chinese have soup toward the end.

Who says it's not polite to point? If you notice an appealing dish on the table next to you, just point and tell the waiter you'd like to try it. Even if the waiter tries to discourage you, keep pointing. And if the waiter says, "You won't like it"? Then insist on trying it! Surprise the wait staff with your adventurous taste buds.

Become a regular. If you find a restaurant you like, visit it frequently to build up friendly relations. Chinese call this practice *guanxi,* the American equivalent of brownie points. The stronger your personal relationship with a chef and a restaurateur, the more they'll understand how serious you are about eating real Chinese food.

SAN FRANCISCO

SAN FRANCISCO CHINATOWN

THE GOLDEN GATE FORTUNE COOKIE FACTORY

San Francisco is the original Chinatown, and it remains the living, beating heart of many Chinese and Chinese Americans. As Americans went West, San Francisco has always looked East. Almost from the early days of the 1849 Gold Rush, this boomtown was the final port for Chinese miners. Portsmouth Square, the center of modern Chinatown, was the first civic green of Yerba Buena, the original name of San Francisco. As fortune hunters streamed in, property values around the square increased at a higher rate than anywhere else in America. And so did the population density in the streets above—especially Grant Street, where the famed gate at the eastern end signals Chinatown's boundary. ✳ Although visitors munch pork buns and scoop up T-shirts everywhere, they are outnumbered by the more than 140,000 Chinatown citizens who still live in small apartment blocks and run businesses, schools, and associations. Seafood markets, vegetable stands, bookstores, and herbalists all cater to the locals. While Grant is the main avenue for tourists, be sure to visit Stockton Street, which runs parallel to it, to see how the locals really shop for the city's freshest produce and the best Chinese snacks. Turn into alleys like Waverley Place, where old churches and temples are found. ✳ After the 1906 earthquake leveled much of Chinatown, along with much of the rest of San Francisco, business interests coveted this prime area so close to downtown. But Chinese community leaders saved the day by hiring non-Chinese architects to rebuild the area with pagoda roofs and exotic iron work. This exaggerated version of the exotic East has been drawing tourists ever since—and Chinatown remains at San Francisco's geographic center as well as the most San Franciscan of sites, with its steep, hilly side streets and great bay views. ✳ If you're visiting San Francisco during Chinese New Year, don't miss the spectacular parade, with decorated floats, martial arts groups, lion dancers, Chinese acrobatics, and the 201-foot-long Golden Dragon, which winds its way from Market and 2nd Streets through Chinatown, ending at Kearny Street and Columbus Avenue.

BOW HON RESTAURANT

850 Grant Avenue

(415) 362-0601

What to order: *yu san (raw fish salad); sun dek clay pot rice; sun dek stuffed freshwater fish*

HARBOR VILLAGE RESTAURANT

Four Embarcadero Center (lobby level)

(415) 781-8833

What to order: *lamb chops with lemongrass sauce; minced chicken; crab with basil*

MING'S HUNAN SEAFOOD RESTAURANT

839 Kearny Street

(415) 956-7868

What to order: *Szechwan peanut chicken; Hunan smoked pork and cabbage stir-fried with spicy sauce; Nanjing beef and shrimp stir-fry*

OLD SHANGHAI RESTAURANT

5145 Geary Boulevard

(415) 752-0120

What to order: *bean curd sheet wonton soup with mung bean noodles; stir-fried fish fillets with fermented rice sauce; braised fish tail Shanghai-style; Shanghai pickled vegetables*

PEARL CITY SEAFOOD RESTAURANT

641 Jackson Street

(415) 362-0601

What to order: *clam soup with Shaoxing wine; beef clay pot rice*

SAM WO RESTAURANT

813 Washington Street

(415) 982-0596

What to order: *any noodle dish; jook*

AN HERBALIST MEASURING INGREDIENTS

A LION ON EACH SIDE OF THE SAN FRANCISCO CHINATOWN GATE GUARDS THE ENTRANCE.

DIM SUM

L et's begin this first chapter with an analogy. Dim sum is to China what hors d'oeuvre are to France or tapas are to Spain. Dim sum is social food, meant to be enjoyed with family, friends, and business associates along with plenty of conversation.

Dim sum has evolved into an art form over the past eleven centuries since its origins in Guangzhou. The majority of Westerners are only now beginning to realize the elegant simplicity of popular dim sum dishes like *char siu bao* and *naw mai gai*.

Before you start touching everybody's hearts with recipes like Surefire Siu Mai (page 4) and Jade Scallop Dumplings (page 13), remember that making dim sum is like kung fu, it takes practice, technique and patience. Don't be frustrated if you make a mistake with dim sum. Chinese master chefs spend years learning and perfecting their dim sum techniques. Some chefs specialize only in the art of dim sum. The ingredients for making many of these recipes are inexpensive, so buy more than you need just in case and make extra because they go quickly. Whatever dim sum is left over, freeze and serve to expected or unexpected houseguests. This cross section of dim sum recipes from Chinatowns around the world will bring the generations of your family and friends together. So, everybody *yum cha* tonight.

DIM SUM DELIGHTS

Here are some of the most popular dim sum items to delight your heart . . . and your stomach. Attempting the Chinese pronunciations might result in some confused looks from the restaurant staff, so I suggest making a photocopy of this page to bring with you.

	PRONUNCIATION/CANTONESE	PRONUNCIATION/MANDARIN
Steamed Delights		
Barbecued Pork Bun	Char Siu Bao 叉燒飽	Cha Shao Bao 叉燒飽
Chinese Chive Dumpling	Gow Choy Gau 韭菜角	Jia Chai Jiao 韭菜角
Chiu Chow Dumpling	Chiu Chow Fun Guok 潮洲粉角	Chao Zhou Fen Jiao 潮洲粉餃
Pork Dumpling	Siu Mai 燒賣	Shao Mai 燒賣
Pork Rib with Salted Black Beans	Jing Pie Gwut 蒸排骨	Zhen Pai Guo 蒸排骨
Rice in Lotus Leaf	Naw Mai Gai 糯米鷄	Nao Mi Ji 糯米鷄
Rice Noodle Roll (Beef, Shrimp, or BBQ Pork)	Churn Fun 腸粉	Zhen Chung Fen 腸粉
Shrimp Dumpling	Ha Gau 蝦餃	Xia Jiao 蝦餃
Deep-Fried Delights		
Flaky Taro Dumpling	Woo Gok 芋角	Yu Jiao 芋角
Glutinous Rice Dumpling	Hom Soi Gok 減水角	Xian Sui Jiao 減水餃
Shrimp Toast	Ha Daw-See 蝦多士	Ciang Su Xia Daw-See 香酥蝦多士
Spring Roll	Chun Guen 春卷	Chun Juan 春卷
Sweet Delights		
Black Sesame Seed Roll	Gee Mar Guen 芝蔴卷	Zhi Ma Juan 芝蔴卷
Egg Custard Tart	Don Tot 蛋撻	Dan Tak 蛋撻
Sesame Seed Ball	Jin Dui 煎堆	Jian Dui 煎堆
Steamed Sponge Cake	Ma Lai Gough 馬拉糕	Xhen Song Guao 蒸松糕
Water Chestnut Cake	Ma Tai Gough 馬蹄糕	Ma Tii Guao 馬蹄糕

DIM SUM

Dim sum are traditional Chinese delicacies meant to be nibbled at and noshed on with cups of tea. In large dim sum establishments, they're wheeled around on rolling carts. Dumplings, like the translucent shrimp *ha gow,* or *siu mai,* flower-shaped pork morsels, are served from stacks of bamboo steamers. Others are portioned out on small plates, heaped into soup bowls, or, occasionally, reheated on hot griddles before they are served. As they make their rounds, the waitresses will stop at your table and lift the lids to show what's underneath; all you have to do is nod your head or point if you want one. (*Dim* means point; *sum* is heart: just point to what appeals to the heart.) Try the stuffed sticky rice noodles (*fun*) topped with dark soy sauce or the steamed chicken wrapped in a lotus leaf. Order some green vegetables with oyster-flavored sauce or some pan-fried noodles. Try the Chinese desserts and snacks, like the gooey glutinous rice balls filled with sweet red bean paste and covered with sesame seeds (*jin dui*), a lightly sweet egg custard tart with a flaky crust (*don tot*), or a savory pastry filled with barbecued pork. The waitress will stamp a form left on your table to indicate how many and the price of each item you've eaten. (They used to total the number of empty dishes until some customers began to hide plates on the floor underneath the table to avoid paying full fare.) ✳ Dim sum teahouses originated in Guangzhou, the Canton region, and there you'll always find huge crowds eating dim sum from early morning to well past midnight. Since most Chinatown immigrants come from Canton, dim sum eateries are located in Chinatowns all over the world. Hong Kong is where dim sum has been refined, perfected, and turned into the late-morning ritual that locals prefer to call *yum cha* (tea drinking), a term heard in Chinatowns everywhere. These gathering places play an important role in the social life of each community. They are the places to see and to be seen. Dim sum are often served in huge banquet halls that can hold hundreds of people. On weekends in particular, dim sum teahouses will be packed with families, often three or four generations at one large table.

SUREFIRE SIU MAI

Makes 25 to 30 dumplings

Siu mai is one of the most popular Cantonese steamed dumplings. Unlike most Chinese steamed dumplings, the wrapper doesn't enclose the ground meat filling completely, but is left open at the top. Look for very thin round siu mai wrappers in Asian markets. Traditionally these are made with shrimp and pork, but for something different I used chicken.

FOR THE FILLING
2 dried black mushrooms
1 pound ground chicken
¼ cup minced bamboo shoots
1 egg, lightly beaten
1 green onion, trimmed and minced
1 teaspoon soy sauce
1 teaspoon salt
½ teaspoon minced ginger
½ teaspoon sugar
½ teaspoon cornstarch
⅛ teaspoon sesame oil
Pinch of ground white pepper

30 siu mai wrappers
3 tablespoons grated carrot
2 tablespoons frozen peas, thawed (optional)
2 lettuce leaves or napa cabbage leaves

Mustard-Soy Dipping Sauce (page 5)

* * *

1. Pour enough warm water over the mushrooms in a small bowl to cover them completely. Let soak until softened, about 20 minutes. Drain the mushrooms, discard the stems, and mince the caps.

2. Make the filling: Stir the ground chicken, bamboo shoots, egg, green onion, soy sauce, salt, ginger, sugar, cornstarch, sesame oil, pepper, and mushrooms together in a bowl until thoroughly combined and spongy.

3. Make the dumplings: Place a heaping teaspoon of the filling in the center of a siu mai wrapper. (Keep the remaining wrappers covered with a damp kitchen towel to prevent them from drying out.) Bring the sides of the wrapper together, bunching them around the filling and smoothing any pleats. (If you like, you can spend a little time making nice, even pleats.) Flatten the bottom of the dumpling by tapping it against a firm surface, and squeeze the sides of the dumpling gently so the filling plumps out of the top. Place a few shreds of carrot and a pea, if using, in the filling. Set the dumpling on a baking sheet and repeat with the remaining wrappers and filling. Keep the formed dumplings covered with a damp kitchen towel to prevent them from drying out.

4. Prepare a wok for steaming according to the directions on page xxvi. Line a steaming basket with the lettuce leaves. Arrange half the dumplings, without touching one another, in the prepared basket. Cover and steam over high heat until the filling is cooked through, about 15 minutes.

5. Transfer the dumplings to a serving platter and cover with foil, shiny side down, to keep them warm while you steam the remaining dumplings. Serve the dumplings warm with the dipping sauce.

❉   ❉   ❉

MUSTARD-SOY DIPPING SAUCE

Paired with Siu Mai (pages 4 and 6) or Tempura Shrimp and Tofu Rolls (page 52), this well-balanced sauce is easy to put together. Stir together 4 teaspoons mustard powder and 4 teaspoons distilled white vinegar in a small bowl until smooth. Add ¼ cup soy sauce, 2 tablespoons plus 2 teaspoons honey, 2 teaspoons rice vinegar, and 1 teaspoon chili sauce, and whisk until smooth. Let stand at room temperature for 30 minutes to develop the flavors. Makes about ½ cup; refrigerate for up to 1 week, and bring to room temperature before serving.

SHANGHAI STICKY RICE SIU MAI

Makes about 60 dumplings

You don't have to travel to Shanghai to discover how different their siu mai is from the classic Cantonese version. It is not surprising that the regional cuisines of China have similar items that are made from different ingredients. This is one such item. Shanghai siu mai is made with sticky rice, or glutinous rice, while the Cantonese version is made with ground meat. This version is from the Shanghai Cuisine Bar and Restaurant in New York City's Chinatown. You can freeze the dumplings before steaming for up to one month.

4 to 6 dried black mushrooms

FOR THE SEASONINGS
1 tablespoon soy sauce
1 tablespoon oyster-flavored sauce
2 teaspoons dark soy sauce
2 teaspoons sesame oil
½ teaspoon sugar

FOR THE FILLING
2 tablespoons vegetable oil
¼ pound ground pork
¼ cup finely chopped smoked ham
2 cups cooked glutinous rice, at room temperature
¼ cup finely chopped bamboo shoots
¼ cup finely chopped water chestnuts
1 green onion, trimmed and finely chopped

One 16-ounce package siu mai wrappers
¼ cup frozen peas, thawed
Cabbage leaves (optional)

*   *   *

1. Pour enough warm water over the mushrooms in a medium bowl to cover them completely. Soak until softened, about 20 minutes. Drain the mushrooms. Discard the stems and finely chop the caps.

2. Prepare the seasonings: Stir the soy sauce, oyster-flavored sauce, dark soy sauce, sesame oil, and sugar together in a small bowl until the sugar is dissolved.

3. Make the filling: Heat a wok over high heat until hot. Add the oil and swirl to coat the sides. Add the ground pork and ham and stir-fry until the pork is crumbly and cooked through, 1½ to 2 minutes. Add the mushrooms, rice, bamboo shoots, water chestnuts, green onion, and seasonings. Cook, stirring, until heated through, about 1 minute. Remove the filling from the wok and let cool.

4. Make the dumplings: Place 1 tablespoon of the rice mixture in the center of a wrapper. (Keep the remaining wrappers covered with a damp towel to prevent them from drying out.) Gather up the wrapper around the filling, pleating it as you go to form an open pouch. Carefully squeeze the sides of the dumpling about halfway up to give the dumpling a "waist," and center a pea on top of the filling. Repeat with the remaining ingredients, keeping the formed dumplings covered with a damp kitchen cloth.

5. Prepare a wok for steaming according to directions on page xxvi. Line a bamboo steamer with cabbage leaves or parchment paper. Place as many dumplings in the steamer as will fit without touching one another. Cover and steam the dumplings until the wrappers are cooked and tender to the touch, 3 to 4 minutes. Repeat with the remaining dumplings. Serve with classic dim sum accoutrements like hot mustard, chili paste, and soy sauce.

CHICKEN JOOK | *Serves 6 to 8*

Jook, or congee, is a thick porridge eaten for breakfast and at other times of the day in many parts of China. I look forward to a steaming-hot bowl when I wake up in the mornings, but it is also a popular late-night snack. In Chinatowns, jook can be ordered in noodle houses throughout the day. Like oatmeal, jook is somewhat neutral in flavor, so it takes well to other flavorings. At the Super Bowl Restaurant in Sydney, I was amazed at the number of condiments offered—seafood, meats, preserved and pickled vegetables, vinegar, chili sauces and pastes, fresh herbs, ginger, and 1,000-year-old eggs. This is truly Chinese comfort food.

3½ quarts water, plus more if needed
2 teaspoons salt
One 3- to 4-pound frying chicken

1 cup uncooked long-grain rice

3 green onions, trimmed and thinly sliced
¼ cup chopped cilantro
2 tablespoons ginger, cut into very thin strips

* * *

1. Bring the water and salt to a boil in a large stockpot. Place the chicken breast side down in the pot. Return the water to a boil, then adjust the heat to a simmer, cover the pot, and cook until the meat near the thigh bone is no longer pink, 45 minutes to 1 hour. Test for doneness with the point of a small knife.

2. Lift the chicken from the broth by inserting a sturdy wooden or metal spoon into its cavity and supporting the chicken from underneath with a wire skimmer or large spatula. Hold the chicken over the pot for a few seconds, tilting the chicken away from you to drain out the hot broth. Set the chicken aside on a plate to cool.

3. Meanwhile, skim any excess fat from the broth. Reheat the broth to a boil, stir the rice into the broth, and adjust the heat to a simmer. Cover the pot and cook until the rice is soft and creamy, 1½ to 2 hours; stir occasionally to keep the rice from sticking to the bottom of the pot. If the *jook* becomes too thick before the rice is creamy and soft, add up to 2 cups more boiling water. The finished *jook* should have an oatmeal-like consistency.

4. While the rice is cooking, remove and discard the chicken skin. Strip the chicken meat from the bones and shred the meat, placing it in a bowl.

5. To serve, ladle the jook into individual soup bowls. Offer the shredded chicken, green onions, cilantro, and ginger in separate bowls as toppings.

MORE ABOUT JOOK: CHINESE COMFORT FOOD

Some call it *congee*, or *zhou*, or more likely, *jook*. By any name, jook is a thick, velvety porridge made from simmering rice slowly in up to twelve times the usual amount of cooking liquid (the preferred choice is a mixture of water and simple chicken broth). ✳ I think of jook as a blank canvas waiting to be turned into a masterpiece dish by adding ingredients, toppings, and condiments. The most basic jook is also called "white jook," plain and flavored simply with a little white pepper, soy sauce, sesame oil, and maybe a sprinkling of green onion or slivered ginger. More elaborate versions contain chicken, pork, seafood, or ground beef or pork meatballs. But what really makes jook the perfect breakfast treat is the addition of salted duck eggs, thousand-year-old eggs, and slivers of roast duck. That's my comfort food. ✳ Don't limit jook to just breakfast. In many Chinatowns, you will see people slurping it up for lunch or as a late-night snack. Nothing is more satisfying than a midnight bowl of jook. That's why you'll find tons of rice having a "breakdown" in boiling cauldrons all over Chinatowns. Joy to jook!

GOLDEN SHRIMP PUFFS | *Makes 8 puffs*

Chefs at the Tou Tou Koi restaurant in Macau uphold many culinary traditions of Canton, such as using pork fatback as a wrapper. I suggest siu mai wrappers. If you can find only square wonton wrappers, use a round cutter to cut them into circles. Serve this with Sweet-and-Sour Sauce (page 251) or Zesty Lemon Sauce (page 231).

FOR THE FILLING

2 dried wood ear mushrooms

1/4 pound uncooked shrimp, shelled, deveined, and minced

2 ounces ground pork (about 1/4 cup)

1 fresh shiitake, stem discarded and cap minced

1 teaspoon minced bamboo shoot

1 teaspoon shrimp paste (optional)

1/2 teaspoon sesame oil

1 teaspoon sugar

1/2 teaspoon salt

1/8 teaspoon ground white pepper

1 teaspoon cornstarch

FOR THE PUFFS

16 siu mai wrappers

1 egg white, lightly beaten

Vegetable oil for deep-frying

* * *

1. Pour enough warm water over the wood ears in a bowl to cover them completely. Let soak until softened, about 20 minutes. Drain the mushrooms well and mince them.

2. Make the filling: Stir the wood ears, shrimp, ground pork, shiitake, bamboo shoot, shrimp paste, if using, sesame oil, sugar, salt, pepper, and cornstarch together in a bowl until well mixed.

3. Prepare the puffs: Place a heaping teaspoon of filling in the center of one of the wrappers, keeping the remaining wrappers covered with a damp kitchen towel or plastic wrap to prevent them from drying out. Brush the edges of the circle with the egg white, place a second wrapper on top, and press the edges firmly to seal. Repeat with the remaining filling and wrappers, keeping the formed dumplings covered with a damp kitchen towel to prevent them from drying out.

4. Pour enough vegetable oil into a wok or 2-quart saucepan to come to a depth of 3 inches. Heat the oil over medium heat to 350°F. Slide a few of the puffs into the oil and cook, turning occasionally, until golden brown, about 3 minutes. Scoop the puffs from the oil with a slotted spoon or wire skimmer and drain on paper towels. Repeat with the remaining puffs. Serve warm, with a variety of dipping sauces.

SHRIMP AND TROPICAL FRUIT ROLLS

Makes 8 rolls

At the 24-hour Yum Cha Tim Sum Restaurant in Singapore's Chinatown this is the signature dish. The chefs prefer light, flaky wafer wrappers, which are not easy to find. I use spring roll wrappers instead. The burst of sweetness, the contrast between the crispy wrappers and the hot soft bananas, and the hint of toasted sesame are unique.

FOR THE FILLING
5 slices candied papaya or candied mango
¼ cup roasted peanuts
¼ cup roasted almonds or glazed walnuts
¼ cup sugar
1 egg white

FOR THE ROLLS
8 spring roll wrappers
**8 uncooked large shrimp, shelled, deveined,
    and cut lengthwise in half**
2 bananas, cut lengthwise into quarters

1 tablespoon flour, dissolved in 1 tablespoon water
1 tablespoon toasted white sesame seeds
1 tablespoon black sesame seeds
1 egg white

Vegetable oil for deep-frying

✳   ✳   ✳

1. Prepare the filling: Combine the candied papaya, peanuts, almonds, sugar, and egg white in a food processor. Process using quick on/off pulses until the ingredients are coarsely chopped.

2. Make the spring rolls: Place a spring roll wrapper shiny side down, with one of the corners pointing toward you, on a work surface. Place 2 shrimp halves end to end across the lower third of the wrapper. Spread 1 heaping tablespoon of the filling over the shrimp and top with a banana quarter. Fold the corner closest to you over the filling, then fold the right and left corners over that. Give the roll just enough of a turn to enclose the filling completely. Brush the exposed part of the wrapper with some of the flour paste and continue rolling it into a compact roll, pressing lightly to seal. Repeat with the remaining wrappers and filling ingredients, covering the formed spring rolls with a damp kitchen towel to keep them from drying out.

3. Spread the white and black sesame seeds on a plate. Brush the rolls with a light coating of egg white, then roll them in the sesame seeds to coat.

4. Pour enough oil into a wok or 2-quart saucepan to come to a depth of 3 inches. Heat over medium heat to 350°F. Slip a few of the shrimp rolls into the oil and fry, turning occasionally, until golden brown, 3 to 4 minutes. Remove with a slotted spoon and drain on paper towels. Repeat with the remaining rolls. Serve warm.

JADE SCALLOP DUMPLINGS

Makes about 30 dumplings

The classic steamed dumplings with emerald green Chinese chives showing through the translucent wrappers are frequently found on the carts of better dim sum restaurants. Since Chinese chives can be difficult to find, I decided to do a variation using a popular vegetable—spinach!

FOR THE DOUGH
1 ½ cups wheat starch
2 tablespoons tapioca starch
1 cup boiling water
1 tablespoon lard or vegetable shortening

FOR THE FILLING
½ pound bay or sea scallops, minced
½ cup minced cooked spinach
¼ cup chopped water chestnuts
¼ cup chopped Chinese celery or regular celery
1 egg white
1 tablespoon Chinese rice wine or dry sherry
1 tablespoon soy sauce
1 teaspoon cornstarch
½ teaspoon minced ginger
½ teaspoon grated lemon zest
¼ teaspoon salt
⅛ teaspoon ground white pepper

FOR THE DIPPING SAUCE
¼ cup soy sauce
1 tablespoon plus 1 teaspoon rice vinegar
1 tablespoon plus 1 teaspoon fresh lemon juice
3 teaspoons minced garlic
2 teaspoons sugar
6 quarter-sized slices ginger, cut into thin strips

* * *

1. Make the dough: Sift the wheat starch and tapioca starch into a bowl. Make a well in the center of the starches and pour the boiling water all at once into the well. Stir vigorously until the mixture forms a ball. (The boiling water will cook the starches, which will result in transparent wrappers; it is important that the water is still boiling hot when you add it to the starches.)

2. Make a dent in the dough, insert the lard into it, and knead the dough until the lard is incorporated. (Kneading by hand works best, even though the mixture is quite hot.) Divide the dough in two. Roll each half into a cylinder 1 inch in diameter. Cover with a damp kitchen towel and let rest for 15 minutes.

3. Cut the dough cylinders into ¾-inch lengths and roll each piece into a ball. Cover with a damp towel until ready to use, up to 30 minutes.

4. Meanwhile, make the filling: Stir the scallops, spinach, water chestnuts, celery, egg white, rice wine, soy sauce, cornstarch, ginger, lemon zest, salt, and pepper together in a medium bowl until well blended. Let stand for 10 to 15 minutes.

5. Make the sauce: Stir the soy sauce, rice vinegar, lemon juice, garlic, sugar, and ginger together in a bowl until the sugar is dissolved. Set aside.

6. Form the dumplings: Place one of the dough balls between two squares of plastic wrap. Using a tortilla press, flatten the dough into a thin circle. (If you don't have a tortilla press, roll the dough balls out using a rolling pin.) Place 1 heaping teaspoon of the filling into the center of the wrapper and bring the edges of the wrapper together around the filling, lining up the edges to form a half-circle, and pinch the edges to seal. Repeat with the remaining dough and filling, placing the dumplings, without touching one another, on two heatproof dishes or glass pie plates covered with a damp kitchen towel to keep them from drying out.

7. Prepare a wok for steaming according to the directions on page xxvi. Steam the dumplings, one plateful at a time, over high heat until the dough is translucent, 12 to 15 minutes. Serve with the dipping sauce.

THANKS FOR THE TEA: GIVING THE THREE-FINGERED SALUTE

Ever noticed diners in dim sum restaurants tapping three fingers against the table after someone refills their teacups? They're not giving secret hand signals, they're performing an age-old tea-drinking custom. ✳ Legend has it that a Qing dynasty emperor once traveled incognito outside his palace to inspect his kingdom. Dressed as a commoner, he figured that he'd get a less biased view of how life was for his subjects. When he and his court officials (who, of course, knew his true identity) had tea in a local teahouse, the emperor humbly poured a round so the other patrons wouldn't suspect anything. But dutiful officials had to *kowtow* somehow—the prostrate bow that was a show of respect in China—so tapped their fingers on the table instead. The center finger stood for a bowed head, while the two flanking fingers represented arms laid on the ground, kowtow-style. ✳ Even today, this finger-tapping expresses gratitude toward those who pour our tea—a show of thanks that's fit for an emperor. ✳ And another universal sign of tea-drinking is tilting the lid on your pot slightly open to let servers know to replenish the hot water, NO kowtows needed.

BEEF-FILLED RICE NOODLE PILLOWS

Makes 8 rolls

Rice noodle sheets filled with everything from barbecued pork to shrimp are popular on dim sum trolleys. The secret of this dish is the thin, smooth, almost translucent rice noodle wrappers.

FOR THE FILLING

4 dried black mushrooms
½ pound ground beef
¼ cup minced water chestnuts
¼ cup minced green onions
1 egg, lightly beaten
3 tablespoons Chicken Stock (page 69) or
    canned chicken broth
2 tablespoons cornstarch
1 tablespoon oyster-flavored sauce
1 teaspoon soy sauce
1 teaspoon Chinese rice wine or dry sherry
1 teaspoon chopped cilantro
½ teaspoon minced ginger
½ teaspoon sesame oil
½ teaspoon sugar

FOR THE SAUCE

¼ cup water
4 teaspoons soy sauce or light soy sauce
1 teaspoon Chinese rice wine or dry sherry
1 teaspoon sugar

2 sheets fresh rice noodles (page 18)

✳   ✳   ✳

1. Pour enough warm water over the dried mushrooms in a small bowl to cover completely. Let soak until softened, about 20 minutes. Drain the mushrooms, discard the stems, and mince the caps.

2. Make the filling: Mix the mushrooms, ground beef, water chestnuts, green onions, egg, chicken stock, cornstarch, oyster-flavored sauce, soy sauce, rice wine, cilantro, ginger, sesame oil, and sugar together in a bowl. Refrigerate until firm, about 1 hour.

3. Prepare the sauce: Stir the water, soy sauce, rice wine, and sugar together in a small saucepan.

4. Make the rolls: Cut each rice noodle sheet into four 5 × 8-inch rectangles. Lay one of the rice noodle rectangles on a work surface with one of the long edges toward you. Spread ¼ cup of the filling in a band along the bottom edge of the sheet. Roll up loosely to enclose the filling. Flatten the roll slightly with your hand and place it in a 9-inch glass pie plate. Repeat with the remaining noodles and filling, arranging the rolls in a single layer in the pie plate.

5. Prepare a wok for steaming according to the directions on page xxvi. Steam the rolls over high heat until the beef is cooked through, 5 to 7 minutes.

6. Meanwhile, heat the sauce to a simmer.

7. Pour the sauce over the steamed rolls and serve immediately.

PANFRIED TARO CAKES

Serves 6 to 8;
makes about 9 pieces

My dear friend June Kam Tong in Honolulu taught me her favorite childhood comfort food—taro root cake. Taro root is a staple in Hawaii and throughout Polynesia. These are also sold in Chinese bakeries. I like to eat my taro cakes with a bit of soy sauce mixed with sweet chili sauce.

4 dried black mushrooms
¼ cup dried shrimp

1 pound taro root, peeled and cut into ½-inch dice
1 tablespoon salt

2 tablespoons vegetable oil
½ cup chopped shallots
½ Chinese sausage (about 1 ounce), chopped
1 green onion, trimmed and chopped

1 cup rice flour
¾ cup room-temperature water
¾ cup boiling water
¼ cup potato starch
¼ teaspoon salt
1 tablespoon soy sauce
½ teaspoon sesame oil
1 teaspoon sugar
Pinch of ground white pepper

1 tablespoon vegetable oil
2 cilantro sprigs
Kecap manis
Sweet chili sauce

✳   ✳   ✳

1. Pour enough warm water over the mushrooms and the dried shrimp in separate small bowls to cover them completely. Soak until softened, about 20 minutes. Drain. Discard the mushroom stems and thinly slice the caps. Coarsely chop the shrimp.

2. Bring a medium saucepan of water to a boil. Add the taro and the salt. Adjust the heat so the water is simmering, cover the pot, and simmer until the taro is tender, 10 to 15 minutes. Drain. Mash the taro, leaving some lumps, and set aside.

3. Heat a wok over high heat until hot. Add the vegetable oil and swirl to coat the sides. Add the shallots, sausage, green onion, mushrooms, and dried shrimp and stir-fry until the shallots are soft and the sausage is cooked through, 2 to 3 minutes. Set aside.

4. Stir the rice flour and room-temperature water together in a large bowl until well blended. Add the boiling water, potato starch, and salt and stir until well blended, then stir in the mashed taro, shallot mixture, soy sauce, sesame oil, sugar, and pepper, mixing thoroughly. Spoon the batter into a greased 8-inch glass pie plate and smooth into an even layer.

5. Prepare a wok for steaming according to the directions on page xxvi. Set the pie dish in the steamer basket, cover, and steam over high heat until the cake is set and firm, about 30 minutes. Let cool slightly.

6. Unmold the taro cake onto a cutting board and cut into 2-inch pieces.

7. Heat a large skillet over high heat until hot. Add the vegetable oil and swirl to coat the bottom. Pan-fry the taro cake pieces, turning once, until golden brown, 1½ to 2 minutes per side. Transfer the cakes to a serving platter and garnish with the cilantro sprigs. Serve with kecap manis and sweet chili sauce.

TEA: THE BEVERAGE OF CHOICE

There are more than two hundred and fifty varieties of Chinese tea (*cha*), including some that are rare, precious, and expensive and sought after by connoisseurs throughout the world. Jasmine and oolong are the usual choices at dim sum teahouses, but try chrysanthemum flower tea or any of the antioxidant-laden green teas with your dim sum. ❈ Teas may be sampled in one of the many stores that sell tea in Chinatowns. Ask to smell the teas sold from large decorated canisters, especially the rare ones from Fujian and Taiwan. If you're interested in purchasing a particular tea, some shopkeepers will brew a tiny cup of tea for you to taste. ❈ In a traditional Chinese tea ceremony, a small unglazed clay teapot and small teacups that hold only a few sips of tea are used. The teapot and cups are first heated and cleaned with boiling water, the water then discarded. Loose tea leaves are placed in the pot, hot water is poured over them, and then it is drained, leaving the moistened and rinsed tea leaves in the pot. The teapot is refilled with hot water and left to brew for about 30 seconds. Then the tea is quickly poured into the warm teacups in one continuous motion and served. Any remaining tea is poured into another teapot or tea pitcher for immediate service. The brewing process can be repeated about three or four times with the same tea leaves, but with an added 10 to 15 seconds of steeping time each repetition, as the leaves weaken with each brew. To ensure that your tea leaves keep turning out flavorful pots of tea, store them in an airtight container in a cool, dry place away from spices or other strongly flavored items that could affect the tea's flavor. Kept this way, your tea should remain potent for up to a couple of years; some black varieties, when stored properly, stay fresh for quite a long time.

RICE NOODLES | *Makes 10 to 12 sheets*

If you don't have access to shops that sell these delicious noodles, be adventurous and try making them. Use the fruits of your labor in the Beef-Filled Rice Noodle Pillows (page 15) and the Fun Chicken (page 301).

2 cups rice flour
¾ cup wheat starch
½ teaspoon salt
5 cups room-temperature water

Vegetable oil cooking spray

❋   ❋   ❋

1. Stir the rice flour, wheat starch, and salt together in a large bowl. Pour in the water and stir until smooth.

2. Prepare a wok for steaming according to the directions on page xxvi. Coat an 8-inch square glass baking dish with cooking spray. Pour ¼ cup of the batter into the dish, then tilt the dish to cover the bottom with an even layer of the batter. Set the dish in the steamer and steam over high heat until the batter is set, 2 to 3 minutes.

3. Remove the dish from the steamer and, using a rubber spatula, carefully loosen the noodle sheet from the dish and slide it onto a platter. Cover with wax paper. Repeat with the remaining batter, spraying the dish with cooking spray before each addition. Stack the cooked noodles on the platter, separating them with wax paper. The rice noodles can be stored in the refrigerator for up to 3 days.

DRAGON BOAT FESTIVAL

Don't you love summer, when that irresistible urge to jump into a cool stream comes over you? In Imperial China, people knew that urge too. Revelers took to the water on the fifth day of the fifth lunar month to celebrate the Dragon Boat Festival. It was sort of a summer fair and sporting event, with spectators crowding local riverbanks and lake shores to watch elaborately decorated dragon boats race while musicians kept the rowing tempo. ☀ It is said that the races began as a way to pay respect to the dragon gods who provided crop-giving summer rains. But others trace the festival back to a beloved Chou Dynasty court poet. Not liking the practices of his noble employers, the poet took his final dive into the Mi Lo River. When loyal fans back at court learned of his suicide, they took to the river in boats, searching in vain for his body. ☀ Each tale has a tasty culinary symbol. According to the dragon-gods version, the celebrants offered the hungry gods rice dumplings wrapped in bamboo leaves. Alternatively, the bereaved fans of the poet supposedly threw rice into the river as nourishment for their muse's soul. Either way, you can still find the traditional treat today in the form of the bamboo-leaf–wrapped glutinous rice dumpling known as *jung* in Cantonese (*jungdz* in Mandarin). They're as common around Dragon Boat festivals as cotton candy at a summer carnival. ☀ I enjoy my Dragon Boat *jung* every summer in Oakland. In an estuary at the edge of the San Francisco Bay, a multicultural community celebration brings together dozens of dragon boat teams and hundreds of spectators to celebrate summer, sportsmanship, Chinese heritage, and food. Local schools, clubs, and community organizations launch entries, and groups from all over the world get in on the action too. It doesn't matter what shape you are in, how old you are, or how much experience you have, as long as you can work with the other nineteen paddlers to keep those oars moving in unison to the finish line. ☀ Personally, I'm glad to be on the sidelines so I can make my way over to where local Chinese restaurants set up carts selling a variety of *jung*. As a kid in China, I had only the fillings typical to the southern region where I grew up. But there are so many immigrants from all over China in the Bay Area that I now have my pick of sweet centers such as cherries, berries, peaches, and bean, lotus seed, and date pastes. The leaf-wrapped packets may also contain pork, chicken, Chinese sausage, dried shrimp, or mushrooms. It's like holding a little bit of summer itself, in the perfect edible package.

CHINESE SWEET RICE "TAMALES"

Makes 8 to 10 "tamales"

Called *jung,* Chinese tamales are traditionally made only during the Dragon Boat Festival. They're most abundant in markets at that time, but that doesn't limit the Chinese or yourself. Make them and find them in Chinatowns any time of the year. Bamboo leaves or large tea leaves are the traditional wrappers, but you can also use lotus leaves. Because they cook for such a long time, all the flavors blend together, making for an aromatic and texturally exciting package.

Note that the rice, mung beans, and chestnuts must be soaked overnight before using.

2 pounds glutinous rice
½ pound dried mung beans
20 dried chestnuts
1 tablespoon salt
⅛ teaspoon Chinese five-spice powder

10 dried black mushrooms
20 bamboo leaves
10 ounces pork belly or well-marbled boneless
    pork shoulder or butt, sliced
5 salted duck eggs, rinsed, cut in half, and yolks
    removed (discard the whites)

❋   ❋   ❋

1. Pour enough warm water over the glutinous rice, the mung beans, and the chestnuts in separate bowls to cover them completely. Soak overnight.

2. Drain the rice, mung beans, and chestnuts. Stir them together with the salt and five-spice powder in a large bowl.

3. Pour enough warm water over the mushrooms in a large bowl to cover them completely. Let soak until softened, about 20 minutes. Drain. Discard the stems and thinly slice the caps.

4. Meanwhile, pour enough water over the bamboo leaves in a large pot to cover them completely. Bring to a boil, then remove the pot from the heat, let cool slightly, and drain. Pat the leaves dry and set them aside.

5. Make the tamales: Place 2 bamboo leaves, one overlapping the other halfway, on a work surface. Place about ⅓ cup of the rice mixture in the center. Top with a slice of pork, half a duck egg yolk, and 3 or 4 mushroom slices. Cover with about 2 tablespoons of the rice mixture. Fold the leaves over the stuffing, bottom up, sides over, then top, to enclose it completely, then tie the package closed with kitchen string. Repeat with the remaining ingredients.

6. Place the tamales in a large pot, pour in enough water to cover them, and bring to a boil. Adjust the heat so the water is simmering and cook until the tamale filling feels tender when you squeeze it gently, 4 to 5 hours. Replenish the water in the pot as necessary to keep the tamales covered during cooking.

7. Drain the tamales and serve warm.

NORI-SESAME SHRIMP TOASTS | *Makes 12 toasts*

For those who like crunchy textures, this dish is a must try. Nori is the lightly toasted seaweed sheet that is used to wrap sushi, hand rolls, and rice balls in Japanese restaurants. It adds a nice dimension to the appearance and taste of this appetizer. For easy handling, use day-old bread, as it is drier and firmer.

FOR THE SHRIMP PASTE

**6 ounces uncooked shrimp, shelled and
     deveined**
1 egg white
2 tablespoons chopped green onion
2 teaspoons cornstarch
1 teaspoon Chinese rice wine or dry sherry
1 teaspoon minced ginger
1/2 teaspoon salt
1/8 teaspoon sesame oil
1/8 teaspoon ground white pepper

3 slices day-old white sandwich bread
1 egg, lightly beaten
3 sheets nori
1 tablespoon black sesame seeds

Vegetable oil for deep-frying

❊   ❊   ❊

1. Make the shrimp paste: Combine the shrimp, egg white, green onion, cornstarch, rice wine, ginger, salt, sesame oil, and pepper in a food processor. Process until the mixture is smooth, stopping once or twice to scrape down the sides.

2. Trim the crusts from the bread. Brush one side of one of the bread slices with the beaten egg and lightly press a nori sheet over it. Place the bread nori side down on a cutting board and trim any of the nori that extends past the edges of the bread. Spread about a third of the shrimp paste over the bare side of the bread, mounding it slightly in the center. Sprinkle one-third of the black sesame seeds over the shrimp paste. With a chef's knife, cut the slice into four triangles. Repeat with the remaining ingredients.

3. Pour enough oil into a wok or a high-sided frying pan to come to a depth of 2 inches and heat over medium heat to 350°F. Slide 3 or 4 toasts shrimp side down into the oil. Cook for about 1 minute, turn over, and continue cooking until the edges are golden brown, about 1 minute longer. Scoop the toasts from the oil with a slotted spoon and drain on paper towels. Repeat with remaining shrimp toasts. Serve warm.

STEAMED BUNS | *Makes 15 buns*

Once steamed, this dough becomes very white. It is often stuffed with char siu or vegetable fillings.

1⅓ cups warm (105° to 110°F) water
One ¼-ounce package active dry yeast
1 teaspoon sugar
2¼ cups all-purpose flour, plus more for
    kneading
1 cup cake flour

Vegetable oil for greasing
½ teaspoon water
2 teaspoons baking powder

Char Siu Filling (page 24), "Buddha Bun"
    Vegetable Filling (page 24),
    or Chicken-Mushroom Filling (page 27)

* * *

1. Stir the warm water, yeast, and sugar together in a large bowl. Let stand until the mixture begins to bubble, about 10 minutes.

2. Meanwhile, cut fifteen 3-inch squares of parchment paper and set them aside.

3. Gradually stir the all-purpose and cake flours into the yeast mixture, then beat the dough with a wooden spoon (or use a heavy-duty mixer) until it holds together.

4. Turn the dough out onto a lightly floured board and knead, adding more flour as necessary to prevent sticking, until smooth and elastic, 5 to 10 minutes. Lightly grease the inside of a 2-gallon resealable plastic bag with vegetable oil.

Slip the dough into the bag, add the ½ teaspoon water, and seal the bag. Let rise in a warm location until the dough doubles in size, 2 to 3 hours.

5. Remove the dough from the bag and place on a lightly floured surface. Sprinkle the baking powder over the dough and knead, adding flour as necessary to prevent sticking, until the dough is smooth, about 5 minutes.

6. Divide the dough into 15 equal pieces. Roll one piece into a round about 4 inches in diameter. Press the edges of the dough circle with your fingers to make them slightly thinner than the center. Place about 2 tablespoons of the filling in the center of the round. Gather the edges of the dough up over the filling, completely enclosing the filling, and twist them together to seal. Place the bun twisted side up on a parchment paper square and set on a baking sheet. Repeat with the remaining dough and filling.

7. Cover the buns with a kitchen towel and let rise in a warm location until puffy, about 30 minutes.

8. Prepare a wok for steaming according to the directions on page xxvi. Place half the buns in the steaming basket, cover the basket, and steam over high heat until the dough is cooked and the buns have slightly cracked on top, 15 to 20 minutes. Transfer to a serving plate. Repeat with the remaining buns. Serve warm.

"BUDDHA BUN" VEGETABLE FILLING

Pour enough warm water over 5 dried black mushrooms in a bowl to cover them and let soak until softened, about 20 minutes. Drain, discard the stems, and finely dice the caps; set aside. Dice 1 small carrot (about ¼ cup). Cook in boiling water for 1 minute, then remove with a slotted spoon. Place 2 tablespoons diced Sichuan preserved vegetable in the boiling water for 15 seconds to remove excess salt, then drain (this ingredient is optional). Heat a wok until hot, add 1 tablespoon vegetable oil, and swirl to coat the sides. Stir-fry the carrot, mushrooms, 1 cup chopped baby bok choy (about 3), ¼ cup chopped Chinese celery, ¼ cup regular celery plus 2 teaspoons cilantro, and the preserved vegetable, if using, for about 1 minute. Stir in 2 tablespoons oyster-flavored sauce, 1 tablespoon toasted white sesame seeds, 1 tablespoon soy sauce, ½ teaspoon sugar, and ⅛ teaspoon white pepper. Scoop the mixture out of the wok and let cool to room temperature before using. Makes enough filling for 15 buns.

CHAR SIU FILLING

Heat a wok until hot. Add ¼ cup vegetable oil and 2 tablespoons fried shallots (or raw shallots), and cook over high heat until the oil is smoking, about 1 minute. Remove the shallots with a slotted spoon. Add ¼ cup sugar, ¼ cup diced onion, 2 tablespoons soy sauce, 2 tablespoons oyster-flavored sauce, 2 tablespoons sesame oil, and 1 tablespoon dark soy sauce to the hot oil and cook until the onion is soft, about 2 minutes. Stir in ¾ cup Chicken Stock (page 69) or canned chicken broth and sprinkle 3 tablespoons all-purpose flour over the mixture. Reduce the heat to low and cook, stirring, until the flour has been absorbed and the mixture is slightly thickened. Remove the wok from the heat and stir in 1 pound diced Char Siu (page 259), about 2 cups. Scoop the mixture out of the wok and let cool before using. Makes enough filling for 15 buns.

GOLDEN BAKED BUNS | *Makes 15 buns*

In addition to loving steamed buns, the Chinese love the baked variation too. In Chinatowns around the world you'll see people munching on them as part of their meal or as an anytime snack.

¼ cup warm (105° to 110°F) water

1 tablespoon sugar

One ¼-ounce envelope active dry yeast

2 cups all-purpose flour

2 cups bread flour

1 cup plus 2 tablespoons milk, heated until warm (105°F)

½ cup warm (105°F) water

½ cup plus 1 tablespoon sugar

3 tablespoons unsalted butter, softened

1 egg yolk, beaten with 1 tablespoon water

All-purpose flour for rolling out the dough

Chicken-Mushroom Filling (page 27) or Shrimp-Scallop Filling (page 27)

2 eggs, well beaten

❋   ❋   ❋

1. Stir the ¼ cup warm water, 1 tablespoon sugar, and yeast together in a large bowl until the sugar is dissolved. Set aside until the mixture begins to bubble, about 10 minutes.

2. Stir the all-purpose flour and bread flour together in a medium bowl. Into the yeast mixture stir the warm milk, the ½ cup water, ½ cup plus 1 tablespoon sugar, butter, and yolk mixture until well blended. Stir the flour mixture into the yeast mixture, one-half at a time, and mix until you have a soft dough, 3 to 4 minutes. Cover the bowl with plastic wrap and place in a warm location. Let the dough rise until roughly doubled in size, about 2 hours.

3. Preheat the oven to 350°F.

4. Turn the dough out onto a floured cutting board. With a sharp knife, divide the dough into 15 roughly equal pieces. Roll a piece of dough out onto a floured work surface to a 4-inch circle. Place 1½ tablespoons of the filling in the center of the dough circle. Gather the edges of the dough up over the filling and twist them together to seal. Place the bun seam side down on a parchment paper–lined baking sheet. Repeat with the remaining dough and filling.

5. Brush all the exposed surfaces of the buns with the beaten eggs. Bake until golden brown, 15 to 18 minutes. Serve warm.

新合誠樂樓

SUN HOP SHING

DIM SUM

新
合
誠

SUN HOP SHING

TEA HOUSE

CHICKEN-MUSHROOM FILLING

Pour enough warm water over 10 dried black mushrooms in a bowl to cover them completely and let soak until softened, about 20 minutes. Drain, discard the stems, and chop the caps. Cook 2 baby bok choy or 1/2 pound mustard greens in a large pot of boiling water until tender. Drain, rinse under cold water, and drain again. Squeeze out the excess liquid and place in a large bowl. Add 2/3 pound minced boneless, skinless chicken meat, chopped mushrooms, 1 green onion trimmed and minced, 1 tablespoon sesame oil, 2 tablespoons soy sauce, 1 teaspoon Chinese rice wine or dry sherry, 1 teaspoon minced ginger, 1 teaspoon salt, and a pinch of white pepper. Mix until well blended. Use right away, or refrigerate for up to 1 day. Makes enough filling for 15 buns.

SHRIMP-SCALLOP FILLING

Feel free to add a variety of your favorite seafood in addition to the shrimp and scallops. In a large bowl, mix together 6 ounces uncooked shrimp, shelled, deveined, and chopped, 6 ounces bay scallops, chopped, 2 green onions, trimmed and chopped, 1/4 cup minced water chestnuts, 1/4 cup hoisin sauce, 1 teaspoon Chinese rice wine, and 1/2 teaspoon salt. Use the filling right away, or refrigerate for up to 1 day. Makes enough filling for 15 buns.

CHINESE TWISTED DOUGHNUTS

Makes 10 to 12 doughnuts

These aren't the doughnuts you're probably used to—no holes in the middle! And there's only a tablespoon of sugar in the dough. Because of carefully guarded family secrets and mistranslation, many traditional Chinese recipes are difficult to duplicate. Another challenge with Chinese pastry recipes is that some traditional ingredients just aren't available in this country. We spent hours getting this one as close as possible to the original. This dough can be frozen, then defrosted and fried at a later time. For ways to use these fascinating doughnuts, try Comfort-Food Fish Custard (page 139) or Shrimp and Scallops with Chinese Doughnuts (page 179). Or serve with jook as the Chinese do, or for a twist sprinkle with powdered sugar.

1½ cups water
1 tablespoon sugar
2½ teaspoons baking powder
1½ teaspoons baking soda
1½ teaspoons salt
1 teaspoon alum powder
4 cups all-purpose flour,
    plus more for kneading

1 tablespoon vegetable oil

Vegetable oil for deep-frying
Confectioners' sugar for dusting (optional)

* * *

1. Stir the water, sugar, baking powder, baking soda, salt, and alum together in a large bowl. Let stand until small bubbles form, about 5 minutes.

2. Stir in the flour and mix until a stiff, smooth dough forms. Turn the dough out onto a lightly floured work surface. Knead, adding more flour as necessary to prevent sticking, until the dough is smooth and elastic, about 5 minutes. Cover the dough with a damp kitchen cloth and let stand until slightly puffy, about 30 minutes.

3. Knead the dough again for 5 minutes. Recover and let stand for 30 minutes.

4. Knead the dough briefly to burst any air bubbles. Rub the 1 tablespoon oil over the surface of the dough, then place the dough in a 2-gallon resealable plastic bag. Seal the bag, then press the dough into a rectangle. Let the dough rise in a warm location until it puffs slightly, about 4 hours.

5. Place the dough on a lightly floured work surface. Flatten and stretch the dough to make a 12 × 8-inch rectangle about ¼ inch thick. Cut the dough crosswise into 12 strips, each about 1 inch wide, then cut the strips crosswise in half. To form each doughnut, stack two strips of dough, then press a thin chopstick lengthwise down the center of the top to seal the two pieces of dough together.

6. Pour enough oil into a wok to reach a depth of 3 inches and heat over medium heat to 350°F. Holding the ends of one of the doughnuts, stretch it out to about 6 inches, then carefully slip it into the hot oil. The doughnut will shrink in length, then puff. Add 1 or 2 more doughnuts and fry, turning continuously, until golden brown, 1½ to 2 minutes. Remove the doughnuts with a wire skimmer or slotted spoon and drain on paper towels. Fry the remaining doughnuts. Serve with jook (see page 9) or sprinkled with powdered sugar, if you like.

PINEAPPLE BUNS | *Makes 24 buns*

Visit any Chinese bakery and you'll see these in the glass cases. In Cantonese, they're called *baw law bao,* which translated literally means "pineapple bun," but don't expect them to taste like pineapple! The original versions had a topping that resembled the diamond-shaped pattern of a pineapple's skin. In my version, though, I've added a touch of pineapple to the bun topping. If you add the custard filling (see the variation), the candied pineapple gives a nice sweetness and a bit of texture.

FOR THE YEAST PASTE
One 1/4-ounce package active dry yeast
3/4 teaspoon sugar
1/2 cup warm (110°F) water
3/4 cup bread flour

FOR THE DOUGH
4 cups bread flour
3/4 cup plus 2 tablespoons sugar
3 eggs
1/2 cup warm (110°F) water
1/4 cup milk
2 tablespoons nonfat dry milk
1/4 cup lard or vegetable shortening, melted

FOR THE TOPPING DOUGH
1 1/4 cups all-purpose flour
1/4 cup nonfat dry milk
3/4 cup superfine sugar
1/4 cup chilled lard or vegetable shortening
1 tablespoon milk
1 tablespoon mashed pineapple
1/2 egg yolk (beat the yolk, then measure out half)
1/2 teaspoon baking soda
1/4 teaspoon baking powder

1/4 teaspoon vanilla extract
1 egg, lightly beaten

* * *

1. Make the yeast paste: Stir the yeast and sugar into the warm water in a bowl until dissolved. Let stand for 10 minutes. Add the bread flour and stir until the mixture forms a paste. Let stand until frothy, about 10 minutes.

2. Make the dough: Sift the bread flour into a mound on a work surface and make a well in the center of it. Add the sugar, eggs, warm water, milk, and dry milk to the well. Using a fork, beat the ingredients in the well until blended, then gradually draw the flour from the sides of the well into the mixture to make a soft dough.

3. Stir the melted lard into the yeast paste. Stir the yeast paste mixture into the soft dough until incorporated. Stretch and pound the dough against the counter several times until elastic. Place the dough in a greased mixing bowl, turn to coat all sides, and cover the bowl with a damp kitchen towel. Let rise in a warm place until the dough is doubled in bulk, about 1 1/2 hours.

4. Remove the dough from the bowl and shape into a long narrow cylinder about 18 inches long. Cut crosswise into 24 pieces. Knead each piece of dough into a ball. Arrange the dough balls on a greased baking sheet and cover them with a damp kitchen towel. Let rise in a warm place until doubled, about 1 hour.

5. Meanwhile, make the topping dough: Sift the flour and dry milk into a mound on the work surface. Make a well in the center of the mound and add the superfine sugar, chilled lard, milk, pineapple, egg yolk, baking soda, baking powder, and vanilla extract to the well. Using a fork, beat the ingredients in the well until well blended, then gradually draw the flour into the ingredients in the well and mix to form a soft dough.

6. Divide the topping into 24 equal portions. Roll each into a circle 1/4 inch thick; it should cover the top of the bun and extend partially down the sides. If the dough balls haven't finished rising by the time you've made the topping, cover the topping dough with a damp cloth to prevent it from drying out.

7. Preheat the oven to 350°F.

8. When the dough balls have doubled in size, top each with a round of the topping dough and brush the tops with the beaten egg. Bake the buns until golden brown, for 15 to 18 minutes. Serve hot, warm, or at room temperature.

VARIATION This dough can also be used to make custard-filled buns. After the dough has risen for the first time, divide it into 24 pieces as directed above. With the palms of your hands or a rolling pin, flatten each piece of dough into a 3-inch circle. Place 1 heaping tablespoon Pineapple Bun Custard Filling (page 33) and 1 teaspoon chopped candied pineapple (a total of 1/2 cup) in the center. Gather the sides of the dough together to enclose the filling and pinch to seal. Place the bun seam side down on greased parchment paper. Set in a warm place and let rise until doubled. Before baking, sprinkle 1 tablespoon white sesame seeds or flaked sweetened coconut (you'll need 1 1/2 cups in all) over the topping on each bun. Bake as directed above.

PINEAPPLE BUN CUSTARD FILLING

Makes about 1 1/2 cups, enough to fill 24 buns

6 tablespoons unsalted butter, at room temperature

¾ cup sugar

2 eggs

One 14-ounce can unsweetened coconut milk

¼ cup cornstarch

2½ tablespoons evaporated milk

½ tablespoon nonfat dry milk

1 teaspoon custard powder (available in most supermarkets)

*   *   *

1. Beat the butter and sugar with a wire whisk or hand-held electric mixer in a medium bowl until creamy. Add the eggs one at a time, beating until each is incorporated. Shake the can of coconut milk to combine the coconut milk with the coconut cream, which will have separated in the can. Measure out half the contents (½ cup plus 2 tablespoons) and add to the butter mixture. (Save the remaining coconut milk for another use.) Beat until the coconut milk is incorporated into the batter. Add the cornstarch, evaporated milk, dry milk, and custard powder and mix until smooth. Pour into a 9-inch glass pie dish.

2. Prepare a wok for steaming according to the directions on page xxvi. Set the pie dish in the steamer, cover, and steam over high heat, stirring the custard every 10 minutes, until firm, about 30 minutes. Remove and let cool before using. The custard is easier to work with if made a day before you plan to use it; it can be refrigerated for up to 1 week.

APPETIZERS

This is one of the most interesting appetizer sections in any of my books simply because I was given so many recipes from Chinatowns all over the globe. From crispy Bacalhau Macau to the inventive Char Siu Quesadillas, the variety of recipes and their uniqueness will give you a great resource for entertaining.

In China, except at formal banquets, appetizers are not usually served as a separate first course—they usually share the table with the main event. Serve a selection of these at your next cocktail party. Make the appetizers a day or two ahead, and make more than you think you'll need so you'll have more time to spend with your friends and family.

YIN-AND-YANG VEGETABLE BUNDLES

Serves 4 to 6 as part of a multicourse meal

Use a mandoline to get paper-thin slices of daikon. If you don't have one, just be extra careful with your knife when cutting these strips. If you can't find daikon, you can use slices of cucumber, carrot, or even winter melon. The yin and yang represent the two different cooking styles. To maintain true balance, you should not consume too much of one or the other. The Bayview Garden Restaurant in Toronto serves this culinary harmony to their customers as one beautiful presentation.

FOR THE DAIKON ROLLS
8 dried black mushrooms
8 paper-thin slices peeled daikon, each trimmed
    to a 4 × 1½–2-inch rectangle
8 ears baby corn
8 medium asparagus spears, trimmed to
    4 inches
8 thin 4-inch-long carrot sticks

FOR THE VEGETABLE SPRING ROLLS
6 dried black mushrooms
4 dried wood ear mushrooms
1 piece dried snow fungus
½ cup chopped button mushrooms
3 tablespoons oyster-flavored sauce
2 teaspoons sesame oil
1 teaspoon salt
¼ teaspoon ground white pepper

8 spring roll wrappers
1 tablespoon flour, mixed with 1 tablespoon
    water

FOR THE SAUCE
½ cup Chicken Stock (page 69) or canned
    chicken broth
¼ teaspoon salt

¼ teaspoon ground white pepper
1 teaspoon cornstarch, dissolved in 1 tablespoon
    water

Vegetable oil for deep-frying
Sweet chili sauce

❋ ❋ ❋

1. Prepare the daikon roll ingredients: Pour enough warm water over the mushrooms in a medium bowl to cover them completely. Soak until softened, about 20 minutes. Discard the stems and lightly squeeze the caps to remove excess liquid.

2. Meanwhile, bring a small saucepan of water to a boil. Add the daikon slices and cook until pliable, 20 to 30 seconds. Drain.

3. Prepare the spring roll ingredients: Pour enough warm water over the black mushrooms, wood ears, and snow fungus in a medium bowl to cover them completely. Soak until softened, about 20 minutes. Drain. Discard the black mushroom stems and coarsely chop the caps. Finely chop the wood ears. Slice off the yellow stem from the snow fungus and coarsely chop.

Combine the black mushrooms, wood ears, and snow fungus with the button mushrooms, oyster-flavored sauce, sesame oil, salt, and pepper in a bowl and stir until well blended.

4. Make the spring rolls: Place a wrapper shiny side down and with one of the corners pointing toward you on a work surface. Spoon ⅓ cup of the filling across the lower third of the wrapper. Fold the corner closest to you over the filling, then fold the right and left corners over that. Roll up firmly just enough to completely enclose the filling. Brush the exposed part of the wrapper with some of the flour paste, then continue rolling into a compact roll, pressing lightly to seal. Repeat with the remaining ingredients. Cover the filled spring rolls with a damp kitchen towel to prevent them from drying out.

5. Make the vegetable rolls: Place a rectangle of daikon on the work surface with one of the short ends closest to you. Lay one of each vegetable—mushroom, baby corn, asparagus, and carrot—across the strip. Gently roll the vegetables up in the daikon. (The ends of the vegetables will be sticking out of the sides of the rolls.) Place the roll in a heatproof dish and form the remaining rolls.

6. Prepare a wok for steaming according to the directions on page xxvi. Set the dish of vegetable rolls in the steamer basket and steam over high heat until the vegetables are tender crisp, about 10 minutes. Turn off the heat and keep the vegetable rolls warm in the steamer while you prepare the sauce and fry the spring rolls.

7. Make the sauce: Stir the chicken stock, salt, pepper, and dissolved cornstarch together in a small saucepan over medium heat until the sauce boils and thickens, about 1 minute. Pour over the steamed vegetable rolls.

8. Pour enough vegetable oil into a wok or 2-quart saucepan to come to a depth of 3 inches. Heat over medium heat to 350°F. Deep-fry the spring rolls in two batches until golden brown, 3 to 4 minutes, turning occasionally. Remove with a slotted spoon and drain on paper towels.

9. Place the spring rolls on one side of a platter and the vegetable rolls on the other, and serve with sweet chili sauce.

MANDARIN GREEN ONION PANCAKES

Makes 4 cakes

You will find this easy-to-make anytime snack in most Peking or northern Chinese restaurants. It's a wonderful make-ahead recipe. Make a double batch and freeze some to fry later (for easier handling, separate stacked cakes with wax paper or plastic wrap). For a nice variation, add some caramelized yellow and red onions to the cake.

½ cup boiling water

1½ cups all-purpose flour, plus more for
    kneading the dough

2 tablespoons plus 2 teaspoons cold water

1 teaspoon sesame oil

¼ cup plus 1 teaspoon vegetable oil

2 green onions, trimmed and thinly sliced on
    the bias

2 tablespoons chopped cilantro

1 teaspoon salt

Cornstarch for dusting

*   *   *

1. Pour the boiling water over the flour in a medium bowl and mix, using chopsticks or a fork, until combined. Add the cold water and stir until the dough is evenly moistened. Turn the dough out onto a lightly floured work surface and knead until it is smooth and satiny, about 5 minutes; reflour the work surface and your hands as necessary to prevent the dough from sticking. Return the dough to a clean bowl, cover with a damp kitchen towel, and let rest for 30 minutes.

2. Stir the sesame oil and 1 teaspoon of the vegetable oil together in a small bowl. Set aside.

3. Cut the dough into 4 equal portions. Roll one portion of the dough into a circle 5 to 6 inches in diameter and about ⅛ inch thick. Brush the dough circle with a thin film of the oil mixture. Sprinkle one-eighth of the green onions, cilantro, and salt over the dough and roll the dough up into a cylinder. Coil the dough cylinder into a round patty and tuck the end of the cylinder under the patty. Lightly dust your work surface with cornstarch and roll the patty out to a ¼-inch-thick circle, dusting with more cornstarch as necessary to prevent sticking. Repeat with the remaining dough and filling.

4. Heat a skillet wide enough to hold a cake comfortably over medium heat until hot. Add 1 tablespoon of the oil and swirl to coat the bottom. Slip a cake into the skillet and cook, turning once, until golden brown, about 2 minutes on each side. Repeat with the remaining cakes, adding more oil as needed. Slice each pancake into 6 wedges and serve hot.

TORONTO

What do you get when a quarter-million Chinese have come to one city in the last quarter-century? You don't just have one or two Chinatowns, but five! Many clusters of Chinese businesses can be found throughout the sprawling suburbs of this lovely Canadian city on Lake Ontario. ❊ The core Chinatown of today, along Dundas and Spadina—to which the Chinese moved in the 1950s—is quaint and the most multicultural, with plenty of street life, fragrant scents, and influence from even newer Asian immigrants, including Vietnamese, Thais, and Laotians. The other Chinatowns in the the suburbs are under a single climate-controlled roof with sprawling parking lots, where everything Chinese—from the latest Canto-pop CDs to calligraphy scrolls to herbal cough syrup—can be found. Toronto is pushing the boundaries of the twenty-first-century Chinatown. ❊ And chefs here, many from Hong Kong, are pushing the boundaries of Chinese cuisine. Toronto has become a kind of "United Nations" of eating, and the Chinese make their contribution with high style and cosmopolitan service. A demanding clientele of professionals—who have come to Canada for quality of education and environment—always expect the best. Believe me, in Toronto, they get it.

BAYVIEW GARDEN RESTAURANT
Colony Hotel
89 Chestnut Street
(416) 971-8811
What to order: *mixed seafood soup; baked chicken with herb salt*

BRIGHT PEARL SEAFOOD RESTAURANT
346–348 Spadina Avenue, 2nd and 3rd floors
(416) 979-3988
What to order: *braised e-fu noodles; birthday buns; steamed dried scallops with fuzzy melon*

CHAMPION HOUSE RESTAURANT
480 Dundas Street West
(416) 977-8282
What to order: *Peking duck*

KING'S NOODLE RESTAURANT
296 Spadina Avenue
(416) 598-1817
What to order: *steamed and braised stuffed tofu with shrimp; deep-fried tofu; seafood soup; eight-treasure tofu in clay pot; house special noodles*

MAPLE PEPPER GARDEN RESTAURANT
670 Highway 7, East, #8
Richmond Hill
What to order: *baked lobster with Chinese wine; steamed favorite fish with tangerine peel; pan-fried mushrooms with garlic and soy sauce; stir-fried chicken, shallots, and vegetables with black beans*

BACALHAU MACAU

Makes about 12 cakes; serves 4 as part of a multicourse meal

Fish is plentiful in Macau. Chefs at the Litoral Restaurant use Portuguese-style salt cod (*bacalhau*) to prepare these fish cakes. You'll need to soak the salt cod overnight in cold water, changing the water a few times. You can make ahead and refrigerate before frying.

½ pound salt cod fillet

¾ pound russet (Idaho) potatoes (about 2 small potatoes), peeled and cut into ½-inch dice

1½ tablespoons unsalted butter

¼ cup chopped green onions

¼ cup minced cilantro

¼ cup chopped Chinese olives or pitted oil-cured olives

1 egg white

2 teaspoons sesame oil

1½ teaspoons minced garlic

1 teaspoon grated ginger

1 teaspoon salt

¼ teaspoon ground white pepper

¼ teaspoon Chinese five-spice powder

½ cup heavy cream

FOR THE COATING

1 cup Japanese bread crumbs (panko) or very coarse dry bread crumbs

1 egg

Vegetable oil for shallow-frying

* * *

1. Place the cod in a bowl and cover with cold water. Soak overnight in the refrigerator, changing the water two or three times.

2. Drain the cod, rinse very well, and pat dry. Shred the fish with your fingers.

3. Pour 3 inches of water into a medium saucepan and bring to a boil. Add the diced potatoes and cook until tender, 10 to 12 minutes. Drain the potatoes and return them to the pan briefly so the heat from the pan will evaporate the excess moisture in the potatoes. Mash the potatoes until smooth, then beat in the butter. Transfer to a bowl.

4. Stir the cod into the mashed potatoes. Stir in the green onions, cilantro, olives, egg white, sesame oil, garlic, ginger, salt, pepper, and five-spice powder.

5. In a chilled bowl, whip the cream until it holds soft peaks. Gently fold the whipped cream into the cod-potato mixture with a rubber spatula.

6. Using two large soup spoons, form about 3 tablespoons of the cod-potato mixture into an oval fish cake. Set the cod cake on a baking sheet and repeat with the remaining cod-potato mixture.

7. Spread the bread crumbs on a plate. Beat the egg in a wide shallow bowl. Dip each cod cake

into the egg, turning it gently to coat all sides, then allow any excess egg to drip back into the bowl and roll the cake in bread crumbs to coat all sides. Set the coated cod cakes on a baking sheet.

8. Place a large skillet over medium heat and pour vegetable oil to come to a depth of ¼ inch. When the oil is hot—a corner of a cod cake will give off a lively sizzle when dipped in the oil—add as many of the cod cakes to the skillet as will fit without touching each other. (You will probably need to do this in two batches; add more oil if needed.) Cook, turning once, until golden brown, 5 to 7 minutes. Remove the cod cakes with a slotted spoon and drain them on paper towels. If necessary, repeat with the remaining cod cakes. Serve warm.

CRISPY SEAFOOD AND MANGO PACKETS

Makes 12 rolls

The Pan Pacific Hotel is home to one of Singapore's finest Chinese restaurants, the Hai Ten Lo Chinese Restaurant, where Chef Chan creates his elegant take on the familiar spring roll with a unique combination of salmon, halibut, mango, ginger, and cilantro.

FOR THE MARINADE

2 teaspoons Chinese rice wine or dry sherry

2 teaspoons cornstarch

1 teaspoon grated ginger

½ teaspoon salt

⅛ teaspoon ground white pepper

6 ounces skinless salmon fillet, cut into strips ½ inch wide by 1½ inches long

6 ounces skinless halibut fillet, cut into strips ½ inch wide by 1½ inches long

1 ripe mango

12 spring roll wrappers

24 cilantro leaves

2 quarter-sized slices ginger, cut into thin strips

1 tablespoon flour, dissolved in 1 tablespoon water

Vegetable oil for deep-frying

* * *

1. Marinate the fish: Stir the rice wine, cornstarch, ginger, salt, and pepper together in a medium bowl. Toss the salmon and halibut gently in the marinade until coated. Let stand for 10 minutes.

2. Peel the mango and slice off the fleshy portions from each side of the pit. Cut the flesh into 12 pieces more or less the same size as the fish.

3. Make the spring rolls: Place a wrapper shiny side down and with one of the corners pointing toward you on a work surface. Place a strip of salmon, a strip of halibut, a strip of mango, 2 cilantro leaves, and a few strips of ginger across the lower third of the wrapper. Fold the corner closest to you over the filling, then fold the right and left corners over that. Roll up firmly just enough to completely enclose the filling. Brush the exposed part of the wrapper with some of the flour paste, and continue rolling into a compact roll, pressing lightly to seal. Cover the spring roll with a damp kitchen towel to keep it from drying out while you prepare the remaining rolls.

4. Pour enough oil into a wok or 2-quart saucepan to come to a depth of 3 inches. Heat over medium heat to 350°F. Carefully slide a few spring rolls into the oil and fry, turning occasionally, until golden brown, 3 to 4 minutes. Remove with a slotted spoon and drain on paper towels. Repeat with the remaining rolls. Serve warm.

BEER-BATTERED AHI ROLLS

Serves 4 as part of a multicourse meal

You'll find three common types of rice in most supermarkets: long-, medium-, and short-grain. Japanese sushi calls for medium-grain, which tends to stick together better than long-grain. This recipe is a simplified version of one from Chef Glenn Chu of Indigo Restaurant in Honolulu. A master of fusion cuisine, Chef Chu uses ingredients from Chinatown to re-create a lot of the recipes he learned from his grandma.

FOR THE DIPPING SAUCE
1½ tablespoons light soy sauce
2 teaspoons wasabi powder
1 tablespoon plum sauce
1 teaspoon hoisin sauce

FOR THE CHIPOTLE AÏOLI
¼ cup mayonnaise
1 garlic clove, minced
1 teaspoon minced canned chipotle peppers in adobo

2 sheets nori
2 cups cooled cooked medium-grain rice
Wasabi paste
4 strips ahi tuna, ¼ inch thick and 4 inches long
¼ carrot, shredded
2 tablespoons pickled ginger, plus more for serving with the rolls
2 chives
½ teaspoon salt
½ teaspoon ground white pepper
1 teaspoon toasted white sesame seeds

FOR THE BATTER
¼ cup bread flour
¼ cup all-purpose flour
¼ cup almond meal, or finely ground almonds
¼ teaspoon baking powder
⅛ teaspoon kosher salt
Pinch of ground white pepper
6 tablespoons beer, or as needed

Vegetable oil for deep-frying
Cornstarch for dusting

✳   ✳   ✳

1. Make the dipping sauce: Stir the soy sauce and wasabi powder together in a small bowl until blended, then stir in the plum sauce and hoisin sauce.

2. Make the chipotle aïoli: Stir the mayonnaise, garlic, and chipotle peppers together in a small bowl until blended.

3. Make the rolls: Place a sheet of nori horizontally across a bamboo mat or a piece of plastic wrap. Spread 1 cup of the rice evenly over the nori, leaving a ½- to ¾-inch border along the top edge. Spread a thin film of wasabi paste over the rice. Place 2 thin strips of ahi end-to-end across the bottom third of the rice. Spread 2 teaspoons of chipotle aïoli down one side of the ahi. Sprinkle half the carrot and half the ginger over the ahi. Lay one of the chives alongside the ahi. Sprinkle ¼ teaspoon each salt and pepper and ½ teaspoon of the sesame seeds over the filling. Starting with the edge closest to you, and lifting the mat or plastic wrap to help you along, roll up the nori to form a compact cylinder. Wet the top edge of the nori and press to seal. Repeat to make the second roll.

4. Make the batter: Stir the bread flour, all-purpose flour, almond meal, baking powder, salt, and pepper together in a wide shallow bowl until blended. Stir in the beer. The batter should be just thick enough to coat a spoon. If it is too thick, add more beer 1 tablespoon at a time as necessary.

5. Pour enough vegetable oil into a deep wide skillet to come to a depth of 2 inches. Heat over medium heat to 350°F. Dredge the rolls in cornstarch to coat them lightly, and shake off the excess. Dip the rolls in the batter, rolling them to coat evenly on all sides. Let the excess batter drip back into the bowl, then immediately slide the rolls into the hot oil. Deep-fry, turning as necessary, until the batter is golden brown, about 1½ minutes. Remove with a slotted spoon and drain on paper towels.

6. Slice each roll diagonally into 3 or 4 pieces. Serve hot with the chipotle aïoli sauce and additional pickled ginger.

STEAMED SHRIMP BOUQUETS

Serves 4 as part of a multicourse meal

Julienne sticks of colorful vegetables are steamed inside these shrimp. Get the largest uncooked shrimp available for easy assembly. Serve at your next dinner party or pass it around during cocktail hour. It's bound to be a hit either way.

12 large shrimp (about 1 pound) peeled, leaving the tails intact, and deveined
6 fresh shiitake, stems discarded and caps cut into thin strips
¼ cup smoked ham, cut into thin strips
¼ cup thinly sliced bamboo shoots
¼ cup thin carrot strips, about 2 inches long
¼ cup snow peas, cut into thin strips
¼ cup green onion strips, about 2 inches long, or 12 Chinese chive flowers

FOR THE SAUCE
2 teaspoons vegetable oil
½ teaspoon minced ginger
⅓ cup Chicken Stock (page 69) or canned chicken broth
½ teaspoon sesame oil
¼ teaspoon salt
¼ teaspoon ground white pepper
1 teaspoon cornstarch, dissolved in 2 teaspoons water

1. Prepare the bundles: Butterfly the shrimp according to the directions on page 181. Cut a slit lengthwise down the back of the shrimp. Push the tail through the slit, then insert a couple of strips each of shiitake, ham, bamboo shoots, carrot, snow peas, and green onion into the same opening. Repeat with the remaining shrimp and strips, placing the shrimp bundles in a 9-inch glass pie dish as you work.

2. Prepare a wok for steaming according to the directions on page xxvi. Set the pie dish in the steamer basket, cover the wok, and steam over high heat until the shrimp are pink, 3 to 4 minutes.

3. Meanwhile, make the sauce: Heat a skillet over high heat until hot. Add the oil, swirling to coat the bottom. Add the ginger and cook, stirring, until fragrant, about 30 seconds. Add the chicken stock, sesame oil, salt, and pepper and bring to a boil. Pour in the dissolved cornstarch, bring to a boil, and cook until the sauce is lightly thickened, about 30 seconds.

4. Pour the sauce over the steamed shrimp bundles and serve.

VIETNAMESE RICE-PAPER ROLLS

Makes 12 rolls

More and more Vietnamese eateries are popping up in Chinatowns. On almost every menu, you will find these light, fresh rolls. I use a combination of both shrimp and chicken, or you can go the vegetarian route: omit them, and increase the vegetables. To add another layer of flavor, soften the rice paper rounds in warm beer instead of water. And if you want a bit more crunch to your rolls, add some chopped nuts.

2 ounces dried rice stick noodles (about ¼ package)

3 cups shredded cooked chicken
1 tablespoon fish sauce
1 teaspoon sesame oil
1 teaspoon chopped cilantro
Pinch of ground black pepper

Twelve 7-inch rice paper rounds
12 cooked medium shrimp, shelled, deveined, and split lengthwise in half horizontally
Soft tops of 12 red leaf lettuce leaves
3 green onions, trimmed and cut into thin 2-inch strips
12 cilantro sprigs

Mint leaves for garnish
Peanut Dipping Sauce (page 49)

1. Bring a saucepan of water to a boil, add the rice stick noodles, separating the strands, and cook for 1 minute. Drain, rinse in cold water, and drain again. Cut into 3-inch lengths.

2. Toss the chicken, fish sauce, sesame oil, chopped cilantro, and pepper in a medium bowl until the chicken is evenly coated. Set aside.

3. Make the rolls: Immerse a rice paper round in warm water just until it begins to soften, about 10 seconds, then lay it out on a work surface. Let stand until it becomes soft and pliable, about 1 minute. Place 2 shrimp halves, tail to head, in the center of the rice paper. Place a lettuce leaf on top of the shrimp. Place about ¼ cup of the chicken mixture over the lettuce and top with a small mound of the noodles, 3 to 4 strips green onions, and a cilantro sprig. Fold the right and left sides of the wrapper over the filling, then, starting at the bottom, roll the wrapper and filling into a neat, compact roll. Repeat with the remaining wrappers and filling.

4. Serve the bundles on a platter, garnished with the mint leaves. Offer the dipping sauce at the table.

PEANUT DIPPING SAUCE

This sauce is super with satay and savory in stir-fries, and, thinned out with coconut milk, makes a great salad dressing. A peanut sauce is only as good as the coconut milk and peanut butter used in it. It's a breeze to make. Simply combine ½ cup unsweetened coconut milk, ¼ cup chunky peanut butter, ¼ cup sa cha sauce, 2 tablespoons sugar, 1 tablespoon fresh lemon juice, 2 teaspoons soy sauce, 2 teaspoons chili garlic sauce, 1 teaspoon sesame oil, and ½ teaspoon curry powder in a bowl, stirring until incorporated. Serve chilled or at room temperature. Makes about 1 cup. Keeps for up to 3 days.

GUM-LO WONTONS WITH SEAFOOD SWEET-AND-SOUR SAUCE

Serves 4 as part of a multicourse meal

London's Fung Shing Restaurant deserves credit for keeping this timeless classic on its menu; you won't find this dish in too many Chinatown restaurants anymore. The crispy wontons are served with a special sweet-and-sour seafood sauce, unique and so much tastier than any bottled sweet-and-sour sauce. You can make the wontons a few weeks ahead and store them in an airtight container in the freezer.

FOR THE FILLING
1/4 pound uncooked shrimp, shelled, deveined, and finely chopped
1 egg white
1 1/2 tablespoons chopped cilantro
1/2 teaspoon toasted white sesame seeds
1/4 teaspoon salt
1/4 teaspoon ground white pepper

20 wonton wrappers

FOR THE SAUCE
1/3 cup sugar
1/3 cup rice vinegar
1/3 cup water
1/4 cup ketchup
1 teaspoon grated ginger
1/2 teaspoon chili sauce or Tabasco
1 teaspoon cornstarch, dissolved in 1 tablespoon water

1 tablespoon vegetable oil
6 bay scallops
6 slices Char Siu (page 259)

1/4 cup cleaned squid (see page 189), cut into 1/2-inch rings
1/4 cup diced onion

1/4 cup diced red bell pepper
1/4 cup diced green bell pepper
1/4 cup diced fresh or canned pineapple

Vegetable oil for deep-frying

* * *

1. Make the filling: Stir the shrimp, egg white, cilantro, sesame seeds, salt, and pepper together in a bowl until well blended.

2. Make the wontons: Place a heaping teaspoonful of the filling in the center of a wonton wrapper. (Keep the remaining wonton wrappers covered with a damp kitchen towel to prevent them from drying out.) Brush the edges of the wrapper with a fingertip dipped in water, then fold the wrapper in half to form a triangle. Pinch the edges firmly to seal. Pull the opposite corners of the base of the triangle together, moisten one of the corners with water, and press them together to seal. Repeat with the remaining wrappers and filling, covering the formed wontons with a damp kitchen towel to prevent them from drying out.

3. Prepare the sauce: Combine the sugar, vinegar, water, ketchup, ginger, and Tabasco together in a small saucepan and cook, stirring, over medium heat, until the sugar dissolves. Add the dissolved cornstarch and cook, stirring, until the sauce boils and thickens, about 30 seconds. Remove the pan from the heat and cover to keep warm.

4. Heat a wok over high heat until hot. Add the oil and swirl to coat the sides. Add the scallops, char siu, squid, and onion and stir-fry for 1 minute. Add the bell peppers, pineapple, and sauce. Bring to a boil, adjust the heat so the sauce is simmering, and simmer for 1 minute. Turn off the heat and cover the wok to keep the sauce warm until you cook the wontons.

5. Pour enough vegetable oil into a 2-quart saucepan to come to a depth of 3 inches. Heat over medium heat to 350°F. Slip a few of the wontons into the oil and fry, turning occasionally, until golden brown, 3 to 3½ minutes. Remove with a slotted spoon and drain on paper towels. Repeat with the remaining wontons.

6. To serve, place the wontons in a wide serving bowl. Spoon the hot sauce over the wontons, or serve it on the side.

TEMPURA SHRIMP AND TOFU ROLLS

Makes 16 rolls

Chef Wilson Ho of the Legend Seafood Restaurant in Honolulu fries Chinese ingredients in a Japanese-style tempura batter. What a treat to bite through the light crispy outer layer into a soft center filled with tofu and shrimp—two of my favorite ingredients.

FOR THE FILLING

½ package (7 ounces) soft tofu, drained
½ pound uncooked shrimp, shelled, deveined, and minced
¼ cup chopped cilantro
¼ cup grated carrot
2 teaspoons oyster-flavored sauce
2 tablespoons cornstarch
1 teaspoon salt
¼ teaspoon ground white pepper

8 sheets nori, cut in half

FOR THE BATTER

1¼ cups all-purpose flour
2 teaspoons baking powder
1 egg
1 cup water
1 tablespoon vegetable oil

Vegetable oil for deep-frying

Spicy Ginger Dipping Sauce (page 53)

1. Make the filling: Mash the tofu and place it in a clean kitchen towel. Gather the towel around the tofu and squeeze firmly to remove the excess liquid. Shake the tofu into a bowl. Stir in the shrimp, cilantro, carrot, oyster-flavored sauce, cornstarch, salt, and pepper until well blended. Let stand for 10 minutes.

2. Make the rolls: Place a half sheet of nori on a work surface with one of the long sides closest to you. Spoon 2 tablespoons of the tofu mixture in a band 1 inch from the edge closest to you, stopping 1 inch from each side. Fold the bottom edge of the nori over the filling, then fold the left and right sides over. Roll up jelly-roll style into a compact cylinder. Wet the top edge and press to seal. Place seam side down on a baking sheet and repeat with the remaining filling and nori.

3. Make the batter: Stir the flour and baking powder together in a medium bowl. Whisk the egg, water, and oil in a separate bowl just until blended. Stir the egg mixture into the dry ingredients until a slightly lumpy batter forms. The batter should be just thick enough to coat the nori rolls lightly; if not, add more flour or water. Let the batter rest for 10 minutes.

4. Pour enough oil into a 2-quart saucepan to come to a depth of 2 inches. Heat over medium heat to 350°F. One at a time, dip two rolls in the batter, letting the excess batter drip back into the bowl, then immediately slip them into the hot oil. Deep-fry until the batter is golden brown, about 1½ minutes. Remove with a slotted spoon and drain on paper towels. Repeat with the remaining rolls. Slice each roll diagonally in half and serve warm with the dipping sauce.

＊   ＊   ＊

SPICY GINGER DIPPING SAUCE

This versatile dipping sauce takes no time to put together. All of the ingredients can be found in your local supermarket's Asian food aisle. Whisk together ¼ cup rice vinegar, 2 tablespoons soy sauce, 1 tablespoon oyster-flavored sauce, 2 teaspoons chopped green onions, 1 teaspoon sesame oil, 1 teaspoon chili garlic sauce, and 1 teaspoon grated ginger in a bowl until thoroughly blended. Makes about ½ cup; refrigerate for up to 1 week, and bring to room temperature before serving.

MACAU-STYLE STUFFED PRAWNS

Serves 4 as part of a multicourse meal

Macau cooks are known for combining traditional Chinese ingredients in Western-style dishes such as these stuffed jumbo prawns with a flavorful butter and wine sauce.

8 uncooked head-on jumbo prawns in the shell
1¼ teaspoons salt

FOR THE STUFFING
¼ cup chopped onions
2 tablespoons minced garlic
¼ cup finely chopped button mushrooms
2 tablespoons finely chopped water chestnuts
2 tablespoons sweet chili sauce
1 tablespoon finely chopped green onion
1 tablespoon chopped mint
1 tablespoon chopped cilantro
1 tablespoon curry paste
1 teaspoon vegetable oil
1 tablespoon cornstarch
2 teaspoons all-purpose flour

Cornstarch for dusting

1 tablespoon unsalted butter
2 teaspoons vegetable oil
¼ cup dry white wine

Cilantro sprigs

1. With kitchen shears or scissors, cut the top shells of the prawns open down the back, starting at the tail end and scoring the tail meat about ½ inch deep as you go; leave the heads intact.

Remove the veins and rub the flesh with the salt. Let the seasoned prawns stand for 10 minutes.

2. Prepare the stuffing: Stir the onions, mushrooms, garlic, water chestnuts, sweet chili sauce, green onion, mint, cilantro, curry paste, cornstarch, and flour together in a bowl until well blended.

3. Place the wok over high heat until hot. Add 1 teaspoon oil, swirling to coat the sides. Cook the stuffing until the onion is tender, 1 to 2 minutes, remove from the wok, and set aside. Spoon about 2 heaping teaspoons of the stuffing along the opening of each prawn. Set any remaining stuffing mixture aside to cool. Dust the stuffed prawns with cornstarch.

4. Heat the butter and oil in a large skillet over medium heat until the butter is foaming. Lay the prawns in the pan stuffing side down and cook until they turn pink, 5 to 7 minutes. Transfer the prawns to a serving plate and cover with aluminum foil, shiny side down, to keep warm.

5. Scrape any remaining stuffing into the pan and stir-fry over medium heat until fragrant, about 1 minute. Pour in the wine and cook, stirring well until the flavors are blended, about 1 minute.

6. Spoon the sauce in the pan over the prawns, garnish with the cilantro sprigs, and serve.

STEAMED OYSTERS ON THE HALF-SHELL

Serves 2 as part of a multicourse meal

At Sydney Chinatown's Golden Century Seafood Restaurant, chefs prepare a Hong Kong classic—steamed oysters with a spicy sauce over bean thread noodles.

1 package (2 ounces) dried bean thread noodles

6 large oysters in the shell, scrubbed
4 lettuce leaves

FOR THE SAUCE
2 tablespoons XO sauce
1 tablespoon minced green onion
2 teaspoons soy sauce
1/2 teaspoon minced garlic
1/2 teaspoon sugar

✳   ✳   ✳

1. Pour enough warm water over the bean thread noodles in a large bowl to cover them completely. Soak until softened, about 10 minutes. Drain the noodles, lay them out on a cutting board, and cut them crosswise in half.

2. Using an oyster knife, shuck the oysters, removing the meat from the shells and setting them aside on a plate as you go. Discard the flat half of each shell. Line a Chinese steaming basket with the lettuce. Nestle the reserved cupped half-shells in the lettuce so they won't tip over during steaming.

3. Make the sauce: Stir the XO sauce, green onion, soy sauce, garlic, and sugar together in a small bowl until the sugar is dissolved.

4. Divide the noodles among the oyster shells. Top each bed of noodles with an oyster, then spoon about 2 teaspoons sauce over the oyster.

5. Prepare a wok for steaming according to the directions on page xxvi. Set the steaming basket in the wok, cover the wok, and steam over high heat until the oysters are just cooked through, 6 to 8 minutes. Serve the oysters hot, directly from the steamer basket.

DUCK-FILLED SWEET SESAME BALLS

Makes 20 dumplings

Take a walk down any Chinatown main street and you are bound to see trays of *gin doi*—golden fried rice flour balls with a sweet filling and a sesame seed coating—in most delis or bakeries. Chef Glenn Chu of Indigo in Honolulu creates this new version of an old classic.

FOR THE FILLING

1½ cups Roast Duck meat (page 239), coarsely chopped (about 1½ cups)

½ cup coarsely chopped dried apricots

¼ cup finely chopped green onions

2 tablespoons hoisin sauce

½ teaspoon salt

¼ teaspoon sesame oil

¼ teaspoon ground white pepper

FOR THE DOUGH

1 pound glutinous rice flour

¾ cup sugar

2½ teaspoons baking powder

1¼ cups water

¼ cup gin

1 cup raw white sesame seeds

Vegetable oil for deep-frying

* * *

1. Make the filling: Stir the duck, apricots, green onions, hoisin sauce, salt, sesame oil, and pepper together in a medium bowl until blended.

2. Make the dough: Stir the rice flour, sugar, and baking powder in a bowl. Make a well in the center and pour in the water and gin. Stir with chopsticks or a fork until smooth. Turn the dough out onto a work surface and knead until smooth, about 5 minutes.

3. Divide the dough into 20 pieces. With your fingers, flatten one piece into a 2-inch circle. Place about 1 tablespoon of the filling in the center of the circle. Gather up and pinch the edges of the circle together to seal in the filling, then roll between your palms into a ball. Repeat with the remaining dough and filling, keeping the filled rolls covered with a damp kitchen towel to prevent them from drying out.

4. Spread the sesame seeds on a plate. Roll the dough balls in the seeds, pressing lightly to help the seeds adhere to the dough.

5. Pour enough oil into a 2-quart saucepan or a wok to come to a depth of 3 inches. Heat over medium heat to 350°F. Slide a few of the dough balls into the oil and, using a Chinese strainer or flat skimmer, move the dumplings around so they brown evenly. When the dumplings rise to the top of the oil, use the strainer to keep them submerged until they are golden brown, 5 to 6 minutes. Remove with a slotted spoon and drain on paper towels. Repeat with the remaining dumplings. Serve warm.

ROAST DUCK NACHOS

Serves 4 to 6 as part of a multicourse meal

Chef Alan Wong of Alan Wong's Restaurant frequently shops in Honolulu's Chinatown markets. He's known for adding a special Asian twist to his fusion dishes, and there are many delicious surprises on his King Street restaurant menu. This is my version of his popular duck nachos. If you don't have time to make your own chips, substitute store-bought tortillas, taro root chips, or shrimp chips.

FOR THE ASIAN GUACAMOLE

2 ripe but firm avocados, peeled, pitted, and diced
1/2 cup diced onion
1/2 cup diced tomato
1/4 cup sliced green onions
2 tablespoons minced ginger
1 tablespoon chopped cilantro
3 tablespoons sake
2 tablespoons fresh lime juice
1 tablespoon vegetable oil
1 teaspoon chili garlic sauce
1/2 teaspoon salt

Vegetable oil for deep-frying
1 small taro root, peeled and very thinly sliced
2 small sweet potatoes, peeled and very thinly sliced

1/2 pound Roast Duck meat (page 239), thinly sliced (about 1 cup)
2 teaspoons hoisin sauce
2 green onions, trimmed and thinly sliced

✳   ✳   ✳

1. Make the guacamole: Mix the avocados, onion, tomato, green onions, ginger, cilantro, sake, lime juice, vegetable oil, chili garlic sauce, and salt together in a large bowl, being careful not to mash the avocado. Cover with plastic wrap pressed directly against the surface and refrigerate until ready to serve.

2. Pour enough vegetable oil into a wok or 2-quart saucepan to come to a depth of 3 inches. Heat to 375°F. Slip only as many taro slices into the oil at a time as will float freely and fry until crisp and golden, 3 to 4 minutes. Remove with a skimmer or slotted spoon and drain on paper towels. Repeat with the sweet potatoes.

3. To serve, mound 1 cup of the guacamole in the center of a serving plate. Insert a few of each type of chip into the dip. Use the remaining guacamole to top as many of the remaining chips as possible with 1 heaping teaspoonful each. Top each spoonful of guacamole with a slice of duck, a pea-sized dot of hoisin sauce, and a few green onion slices. Serve immediately.

WONTONS IN HOT-AND-SOUR CHILI SAUCE

Serves 4 as part of a multicourse meal

Wontons can be fried or boiled. These are boiled, then tossed in a spicy sauce. You can use these wontons in any of the other wonton recipes. Make a double batch of them at a time and freeze some for later: Line a baking sheet with wax paper, place the wontons on the sheet, and freeze them. Once they are frozen hard, store the wontons in plastic zipper bags, ready for a quick, anytime meal.

FOR THE SAUCE

1½ tablespoons soy sauce

1 tablespoon seasoned rice vinegar

1 tablespoon sweet chili sauce

1 tablespoon minced green onion

1 teaspoon hot chili oil

1 teaspoon minced cilantro

½ teaspoon minced garlic

¼ teaspoon minced ginger

FOR THE FILLING

¼ pound ground pork

2 ounces uncooked shrimp, shelled, deveined, and finely chopped

1 egg white

1 teaspoon minced cilantro

½ teaspoon minced ginger

½ teaspoon sugar

½ teaspoon salt

⅛ teaspoon sesame oil

Pinch of ground white pepper

16 wonton wrappers

1. Prepare the sauce: Stir the soy sauce, rice vinegar, chili sauce, greens onion, chili oil, cilantro, garlic, and ginger together in a small bowl until blended.

2. Make the filling: Combine the ground pork, shrimp, egg white, cilantro, ginger, sugar, salt, sesame oil, and pepper together in a medium bowl and stir rapidly with a fork in one direction until the mixture is stiff and spongy. Set aside.

3. Make the wontons: Place 1 heaping teaspoon of the filling in the center of a wrapper. (Keep the remaining wrappers covered with a damp kitchen towel or plastic wrap to prevent them from drying out.) Brush the edges of the wrapper with a fingertip dipped in water, then fold the wrapper in half to form a triangle. Pinch the edges firmly to seal. Pull the opposite corners of the base of the triangle together, moisten one of the corners with water, and press the two corners firmly together to seal. Repeat with the remaining wrappers and filling, keeping the filled wontons covered with a damp kitchen towel to prevent drying out.

4. Bring a large pot of water to a boil. Slip the wontons into the water and bring the water back to a boil, stirring occasionally, especially just after you've added the wontons, to prevent them from sticking to the bottom of the pot. Cook until the wontons rise to the top of the water, about 5 minutes.

5. Scoop the wontons into a colander with a wire skimmer or slotted spoon and drain well. Toss the wontons and sauce together gently in a serving bowl until the wontons are lightly coated. Serve hot.

SUITED FOR BIRTHDAYS

So who needs a birthday cake anyway, with all those candles turning into a big bonfire that makes over-40 somethings feel burned? While the Chinese have begun to adapt the Western method for marking each year's passage, they have long-practiced tastier ways to go from "Sweet Sixteen" to the great beyond. Longevity noodles, unraveling forever, are the preferred dish, along with steamed, peach-shaped buns symbolizing the human heart. ❋ While the Chinese don't always make a big deal of a single year's passing, preferring to chat, snack, and play mah-jongg, they do mark milestones such as sixty or seventy years with great banquets and gatherings of friends and family. All the generations gather to help in the preparations: the more courses the better, always including a lucky fish. And the fifteenth day after every Chinese New Year is considered a shared birthday for all, and a time to ponder time's passing. In a society that has always respected the wisdom and experience of age, a birthday is no cause for shame. To the Chinese, you're never over the hill—just climbing the hill. And you need food, plenty of it, to get to the top!

DOUBLE-HARMONY MEATBALLS IN SWEET-AND-SOUR SAUCE

Serves 4 to 5 as part of a multicourse meal

Yin-yang is a philosophy that many Chinese practice. Chinese cooks create dishes with contrast, yet all the ingredients and flavors are in harmony. Two meats, one yin and one yang, give you a contrast of texture and taste.

FOR THE YIN MEATBALLS
½ pound ground chicken or turkey
¼ cup finely chopped pimento
2 tablespoons cornstarch
1½ tablespoons minced green onion
2 teaspoons minced ginger
1 teaspoon minced garlic
½ egg (beat the egg, then measure out half; reserve the remainder for the pork meatballs)
¼ teaspoon sesame oil
¼ teaspoon salt
Pinch of ground white pepper

FOR THE YANG MEATBALLS
½ pound ground pork
¼ cup finely chopped pine nuts
2 tablespoons cornstarch
1½ tablespoons minced cilantro
2 teaspoons minced ginger
1 teaspoon minced garlic
½ beaten egg (reserved from above)
¼ teaspoon sesame oil
¼ teaspoon salt
Pinch of ground white pepper

½ cup raw white sesame seeds
Vegetable oil for deep-frying

½ cup sweet-and-sour sauce, homemade (page 251) or store-bought

* * *

1. Combine all the ingredients for the yin meatballs in a bowl and mix with your hands until the ingredients are evenly blended and the mixture is spongy. Repeat with the ingredients for the yang meatballs. Shape the two mixes into 1-inch balls (about the size of Ping-Pong balls) and coat the yin meatballs in sesame seeds.

2. Pour enough oil into a wok or 2-quart saucepan to come to a depth of 3 inches. Heat over medium heat to 350°F. Deep-fry the meatballs in three batches, turning occasionally, until golden brown and cooked through, 6 to 7 minutes. Remove with a slotted spoon and drain on paper towels.

3. Heat the sauce in a skillet large enough to hold all the meatballs over medium heat until hot, about 1 minute. Add the meatballs and toss until coated and heated through.

4. Mound the meatballs on a platter, spoon any sauce in the pan over them, and serve.

CHAR SIU QUESADILLAS

Serves 4 as part of a multicourse meal

Quesadillas in a Chinese cookbook? This is another ingenious creation from Honolulu's Chef Alan Wong, using common ingredients found in Chinese delis. I've altered it a bit for those of you who don't live near a Chinese deli. What makes this dish outstanding is the sweet, crunchy fresh water chestnuts, which are available only a few months of the year. For this recipe, canned water chestnuts are a poor substitute, but jicama is a fine option.

FOR THE SALSA

2 medium tomatoes, cored and coarsely
    chopped
6 fresh water chestnuts, peeled and cut into
    ¼-inch dice, or jicama
2½ tablespoons finely diced onion
2½ tablespoons thinly sliced green onions
1 tablespoon minced cilantro
Salt to taste

FOR THE FILLING

1 tablespoon vegetable oil
3 tablespoons minced onion
1½ teaspoons minced garlic
½ cup minced Char Siu (page 259) plus
    ½ cup diced (½-inch) Char Siu
½ cup chopped Roast Duck meat (page 239)
1 Chinese sausage (about 2 ounces), thinly
    sliced
3 tablespoons thinly sliced green onion
2 tablespoons hoisin sauce
2 tablespoons chili garlic sauce

Eight 8-inch flour tortillas

½ pound mozzarella cheese, cut into
    8 thin slices
32 cilantro leaves (optional)
2 green onions, trimmed and cut into thin strips
    about 2 inches long

＊   ＊   ＊

1. Make the salsa: Toss the tomatoes, water chestnuts, onion, green onions, cilantro, and salt together in a medium bowl until well mixed.

2. Make the filling: Heat a wok over high heat until hot. Add the oil and swirl to coat the sides. Add the onion and garlic and cook, stirring, until fragrant, about 30 seconds. Add the char siu, roast duck, Chinese sausage, and green onion and stir-fry until the sausage is cooked through, about 2 minutes. Remove from the heat and stir in the hoisin sauce and chili garlic sauce.

3. Heat a 9- or 10-inch nonstick pan over medium-high heat until hot. Place 1 tortilla in the pan and top with 1 slice cheese, 2 to 3 tablespoons of the filling, 8 cilantro leaves, if using, one-quarter of the green onions, and a second slice of cheese. Cover with another tortilla and cook, turning once, until the cheese is melted and the tortilla is browned on both sides, 1½ to 2 min-utes per side. Transfer to a plate. Repeat with the remaining ingredients to make 3 more quesadil-las. Cut the quesadillas in wedges and serve hot, with the salsa.

干齋菜
RICE CAKE
NET.WT.:6oz MADE IN CHINA
干齋菜
RICE CAKE
NET.WT.:6oz MADE IN CHINA

SOUPS

s there anything more comforting and nourishing for the body and mind than a bowl of savory soup? Lighter than their Western counterparts, Asian soups cleanse the palate, invigorate the taste buds, and quench the thirst. Soups of all kinds are so loved that many Chinese restaurants are devoted exclusively to them.

In my previous books, I included soups that are quick and simple to prepare, but this time around I also offer some I found in various Chinatowns that take a bit more effort. For instance, the Eight-Treasure Honeydew Melon Bowl Soup is unique and makes a great main course. The Shandong noodle soup, also a meal in itself, will take only 30 minutes to make, once you have the ingredients together. With today's hectic speed of life, soups slow us down and give us time to smell the jasmine.

EGG-FLOWER SOUP WITH LEMONGRASS AND MUSHROOMS

Serves 4 as part of a multicourse meal

My friend Kwan Lui of Café At-Sunrice in Singapore prepared a very different version of the classic egg-flower soup for me. She added lemongrass to flavor the broth and a bit of black moss. What a delicious combination. Black moss is hard to come by outside of Asian markets, but you can use nori, which has been popularized by sushi restaurants around the world.

4 cups Chicken Stock (page 69) or canned
    chicken broth
2 stalks fresh lemongrass, bottom 6 inches only,
    lightly crushed
3 fresh shiitake, stems discarded and caps thinly
    sliced
1 ounce enoki mushrooms
1/4 cup thinly sliced red bell pepper
1/4 cup frozen peas, thawed
1/4 cup thinly sliced bamboo shoots
1/4 package (2 ounces) black moss, soaked
    (about 1/4 cup after soaking), or 1/4 cup
    shredded nori
1 teaspoon salt
1/4 teaspoon ground white pepper
1/4 package (3 1/2 ounces) soft tofu, cut into 1/4- ×
    1/4- × 2-inch-long strips
1/3 cup chopped, peeled fresh or canned tomatoes
2 tablespoons cornstarch, dissolved in
    3 tablespoons water
1 egg, beaten
1 teaspoon sesame oil

1. Bring the chicken stock and lemongrass to a boil in a 3-quart saucepan. Reduce the heat to a simmer and cook for 10 minutes.

2. Stir in the shiitake and enoki mushrooms, bell pepper, peas, bamboo shoots, black moss, salt, and pepper and bring to a boil. Add the tofu and tomatoes, stirring gently so the tofu does not break apart. Pour in the dissolved cornstarch and cook, stirring gently, until the soup returns to the boil and is lightly thickened.

3. Slowly pour in the beaten egg, stirring slowly but constantly to create "egg flowers." Ladle the soup into a tureen or individual serving bowls. Drizzle the sesame oil over and serve immediately.

✳   ✳   ✳

CHICKEN STOCK

A good stock is indispensable when preparing authentic Asian dishes. It is literally the foundation of flavor for soups, sauces, stews, and, sometimes, dressings. This stock is cooked for less time than the French-style stock, and as a result has a lighter flavor. It can be reduced, fortified, clarified, or used just as it is.

In a large pot, cover about 3 pounds chicken parts (backs, necks, wings) with cold water. Bring to a boil and cook for 2 minutes; drain. Return the parts to the pot, add 4 quarts water, and bring to a boil. Lower the heat and simmer for 1½ hours. Add 3 green onions, trimmed, 6 slices ginger, and a pinch of white pepper and simmer for 20 minutes. Skim any foam from the stock, strain the stock, and discard the solids. Makes about 3½ quarts; refrigerate for up to 3 days or freeze for 3 months.

SINGAPORE'S FISH HEAD SOUP

Serves 4 as part of a multicourse meal

The chefs at Damenlou in Singapore simmer a fish head to produce a thick fish stock, then use it to prepare rice noodle soup dishes. The chef who invented this dish was known as Mr. Fish Head. Use a whole striped bass, fish fillets, or other bones in place of the fish head; it will still be delicious.

FOR THE FISH STOCK

Head (1 to 1½ pounds) of a large firm-fleshed white fish

Bones from firm-fleshed white fish (optional)

Cornstarch for dusting

3 tablespoons vegetable oil

4 green onions, trimmed and cut into 2-inch lengths

12 quarter-sized slices peeled ginger

8 cups water

FOR THE SEASONINGS

1 tablespoon Chinese rice wine or dry sherry

2 teaspoons soy sauce

1 teaspoon fish sauce

½ teaspoon sesame oil

¼ teaspoon salt

¼ teaspoon ground white pepper

8 ounces dried rice noodles (about ¼ inch wide)

¼ pound white fish fillets, thinly sliced

2 green onions, trimmed and thinly sliced
¼ cup cilantro leaves

❋   ❋   ❋

1. Rinse the fish head under cold running water; remove the gills. Pat dry, then dust the fish head and bones with cornstarch to coat them lightly.

2. Heat a stockpot over medium heat until hot. Add the oil and swirl to coat the bottom. Add the fish head and bones, green onions, and ginger and cook, turning once, until the fish head is lightly browned, about 2 minutes per side.

3. Pour the water into the pot and bring to a boil. Adjust the heat so the liquid is simmering and cook for 45 minutes.

4. Prepare the seasonings: Stir the rice wine, soy sauce, fish sauce, sesame oil, salt, and pepper together in a small bowl until the salt is dissolved.

5. Strain the stock and discard the solids. Return the stock to the pot.

6. Bring a large pot of water to a boil. Stir in the rice noodles and cook until tender but firm, 4½ to 5 minutes. Drain, rinse, and drain again. Lay the noodles on a cutting board and cut them crosswise in half.

7. Reheat the stock to a simmer. Add the seasonings and fish slices and simmer until the fish is cooked, 1½ to 2 minutes. Add the noodles and simmer until heated through, about 30 seconds. Ladle into serving bowls and garnish with green onions and cilantro.

GOOD FORTUNE FISH CHOWDER

Serves 4 as part of a multicourse meal

The chefs at Fortune Garden Restaurant in Vancouver make use of the local abundance of fresh fish to create this dish. Soft tofu will break into pieces if you don't handle it with care.

4 dried black mushrooms

FOR THE MARINADE
1 teaspoon cornstarch
¼ teaspoon salt

½ pound firm-fleshed white fish fillets, such as snapper, sea bass, or halibut, thinly sliced

4 cups Fish Stock (this page), Chicken Stock (page 69), or canned chicken broth
⅓ cup Chinese black or balsamic vinegar
3 quarter-sized slices peeled ginger, cut into thin strips
½ teaspoon sesame oil
½ teaspoon salt
¼ teaspoon ground white pepper
½ package (7 ounces) soft tofu, drained and cut into thin strips
2 tablespoons cornstarch, dissolved in 3 tablespoons water

1 tablespoon chopped cilantro

*   *   *

1. Pour warm water over the mushrooms in a medium bowl to cover them completely. Let soak until softened, about 20 minutes. Discard the stems and thinly slice the caps.

2. Marinate fish: Stir cornstarch and salt in a medium bowl. Toss the sliced fish fillets gently in the marinade until coated. Set aside for 10 minutes.

3. Heat the fish stock, vinegar, ginger, sesame oil, salt, pepper, and sliced mushrooms to a boil in a saucepan. Add the fish and stir gently to separate the slices. Adjust the heat so the liquid simmers; cook until the fish is opaque, about 2 minutes.

4. Slide the tofu into the pan and cook until heated through. Increase heat, stir in dissolved cornstarch, and cook, stirring, until soup boils and thickens, 1 minute. Ladle the soup into warm bowls and sprinkle with chopped cilantro.

*   *   *

FISH STOCK

Fish stock is simmered just long enough to extract the flavor and gelatin from the bones. In a large stockpot, combine 2 pounds white fish bones and heads, 8 cups water, 2 tablespoons dried shrimp, 3 celery stalks, sliced, 1 carrot, sliced, ¼ cup sliced ginger, 1 green onion, trimmed, 1 bay leaf, and 1 stalk lemongrass, crushed. Bring to a boil, reduce heat, and simmer for 30 minutes, occasionally skimming the foam. Strain. Makes about 1½ quarts; refrigerate for up to 3 days or freeze for 3 months.

VANCOUVER

Once upon a time, I came to this Chinatown to stay in the back of my uncle's used book shop. Things weren't so prosperous for the Yans back then, but we didn't mind. At the end of each day, I'd head out to pick up vegetables being sold off at bargain prices and prepare something special for my uncle's family. ✳ First known as Saltwater City, this Soy City, close to one of the most abundant harbors on the Pacific Rim, was first populated by the Chinese who laid track for the Canadian railroad. But the neighborhood's vitality belies being anywhere near the end of the line. Hard by honky-tonk Gastown, this is where China came out in coveralls and flannel shirts. Brawny and always busy, the place had a real Wild West feel. ✳ Vancouver Chinatown is a place to get downright crabby, as in the yummiest Dungeness. But one Chinese businessman got so angered at losing his lot that he constructed the Jack Chow Building, considered the world's narrowest at just six feet across. Pender Street bursts with festivals and the lunar shoot-'em-up of firecrackers. ✳ As in many of the cities I visited, the core Chinatown has been supplanted by outer Chinatowns more suited to the new millennium. All of Vancouver is Van Kong now, a polite city as Taiwanese and Cantonese as it is "may-I-help-you-please?" This is the major draw for migrants yearning to breathe free—especially when it's the clear air of British Columbia. Nearer the airport, the suburb of Richmond is a first stop for many new immigrants who feel no need to drive farther. It's an all-Canadian strip full of malls that are all Chinese, all the time. Every Chinese treat imaginable is under one roof, including the roasted squab from the Sun Sui Wah Seafood Restaurant.

FORTUNE GARDEN RESTAURANT

1475 West Broadway

(604) 736-6868

What to order: *hot-and-sour fish and tofu soup Hangzhou-style; five-favorite braised tofu appetizer; stir-fried Kung Pao lobster*

MING YUEN RESTAURANT

4030 Cambie Street

What to order: *steamed crab over rice with green onion, roasted duck, and dried scallops wrapped in lotus leaf; sautéed pork chop with strawberry sweet-and-sour sauce; wine-braised oysters with fried garlic*

SUN SUI WAH SEAFOOD RESTAURANT

102 Alderbridge Place, 4940 No. 3 Road

Richmond, B.C.

(905) 872-8822

What to order: *roasted squab; braised squab in soybean sauce; drunken squab; deep-fried squab; geoduck (sautéed with XO sauce, poached, or sashimi)*

VICTORIA CHINESE RESTAURANT

1088 Melville Street

(604) 669-8383

What to order:*steamed crab and egg custard with Shaoxing wine sauce; honeymoon fried rice; baked squab and fresh mushrooms with oyster-flavored sauce*

EIGHT-TREASURE HONEYDEW MELON BOWL SOUP

Serves 2 as part of a multicourse meal

One of the classic Cantonese banquet dishes is double-steamed winter melon soup. It is light and delicious. Chef Hui at Ping's Restaurant in New York City's Chinatown has gone even further. He created a light, sweet, refreshing, and delicious version of the soup with honeydew melon; it is easy to do at home.

1 large honeydew melon

½ boneless, skinless chicken breast, cut into ½-inch cubes

2 ounces boneless pork, cut into ½-inch cubes

2 to 3 sea scallops (about 2 ounces), cut horizontally in half

6 uncooked medium shrimp (about 2 ounces), shelled, tails left intact, and deveined

¼ cup canned straw mushrooms, drained

¼ cup thinly sliced carrot

2 tablespoons Smithfield ham or other smoked ham, cut into thin strips (optional)

2 tablespoons frozen peas, thawed

2 teaspoons minced ginger

½ teaspoon sesame oil

½ teaspoon salt

¼ teaspoon ground white pepper

2 cups Chicken Stock (page 69) or canned chicken broth, or as needed

❁　❁　❁

1. Cut off one-quarter of the honeydew melon at one of the ends; set aside. Scoop out the seeds and place the melon cut side up in a deep heatproof bowl large enough to hold it snugly.

2. Bring a small saucepan of water to a boil. Stir the chicken and pork into the water and cook until white, for 1 to 1½ minutes. Drain. Add the chicken and pork, scallops, shrimp, straw mushrooms, carrot, ham, peas, ginger, sesame oil, salt, and pepper to the melon. Pour in enough of the chicken stock to fill the melon to just below the top. Cover the top with the cut piece of melon.

3. Lower the bowl into a stockpot and pour in enough water to come halfway up the sides of the bowl. Bring the water to a boil, cover the pot, and steam over medium-high heat until the pork is cooked through, 25 to 30 minutes. Replenish the water in the pot as necessary.

4. Lift the bowl from the stockpot and serve the soup directly from the melon, including if you like, a little of the melon with every serving.

DRUNKEN SHRIMP SOUP

Serves 4 as part of a multicourse meal

Live shrimp are placed in a bowl of rice wine and left to swim around for a while, drinking up the savory nectar. You can make the dish without the live shrimp.

1 pound large shrimp (15 to 17)
    in the shell

3 tablespoons Chinese rice wine or
    dry sherry
1 tablespoon minced ginger
1 tablespoon minced garlic

1 teaspoon vegetable oil
½ medium onion, thinly sliced
2 quarter-sized slices peeled ginger
½ cup fen chiew (Chinese distilled spirits)
    or brandy

3 cups Chicken Stock (page 69) or canned
    chicken broth
¼ cup Chinese rice wine or dry sherry
2 green onions, trimmed and cut into
    2-inch lengths

Steamed Rice (page 285)

1. Using kitchen shears, cut through the shells down the back of each shrimp, working from the head to the tail. Remove the vein. Toss the shrimp in a bowl with the rice wine, ginger, and garlic. Let stand for 10 minutes.

2. Heat a 2-quart saucepan over medium-high heat until hot. Add the oil and swirl to coat the bottom. Add the onion and cook, stirring constantly, until softened and lightly browned, 2 to 3 minutes. Add the ginger and shrimp, along with the marinade, and remove the pan from the heat. Pour the distilled spirits into the pan, then return the pan to the heat and, standing back, ignite the wine with a long match. Let burn until the flames die down, 5 to 7 minutes. Add the chicken stock and rice wine, stir in the green onions, and bring to a boil. Cook until the shrimp are cooked through, for about 1 minute. Serve with steamed rice.

MACAU SHRIMP AND RICE NOODLE SOUP

Serves 4 as part of a multicourse meal

Macau is known for its sweet snacks and for dishes made with shrimp paste. If you can't find real shrimp paste in your local grocery store, go to the nearest Asian store. The strong taste of pungent shrimp paste may take a little getting used to, but it's well worth the effort because it adds an unmistakable flavor.

½ package (about 2 ounces) dried rice
    vermicelli noodles

FOR THE SEASONINGS
¼ cup Chinese rice wine or dry sherry
1 tablespoon fresh lime juice
2 teaspoons chili garlic sauce
2 teaspoons fish sauce
1 teaspoon shrimp paste
2 bay leaves

2 teaspoons vegetable oil
10 ounces uncooked medium shrimp,
    shelled, tails left intact, and deveined
½ onion, thinly sliced

3 cups Chicken Stock (page 69) or canned
    chicken broth
2 green onions, trimmed and cut into
    1-inch lengths

4 lime wedges

1. Pour enough warm water over the rice noodles in a medium bowl to cover completely. Soak until softened, about 15 minutes. Drain thoroughly.

2. Prepare the seasonings: Stir together the rice wine, lime juice, chili garlic sauce, fish sauce, shrimp paste, and bay leaves in a small bowl.

3. Heat a wok over high heat until hot. Pour in the oil and swirl to coat the sides. Add the shrimp and onion and stir-fry until the shrimp turn pink, about 2 minutes. Add the seasonings and stir-fry for 1 minute. Pour the chicken stock into the wok, add the green onions, and bring to a boil. Boil for 1 minute.

4. Stir in the rice noodles and cook until heated through, about 1 minute. Discard the bay leaves, and ladle the soup into individual serving bowls. Garnish with the lime wedges.

HONG KONG WONTON NOODLE BOWL

Serves 4 as part of a multicourse meal

A meal in a bowl, such as this tasty broth combined with Hong Kong–style egg noodles, wontons, and a bit of vegetables, is a popular lunchtime treat throughout Asia. If you don't have the time to make your own wontons, frozen ones are available in many supermarkets or Asian markets.

1 pound fresh thin Chinese egg noodles or dried angel hair pasta

3 cups Chicken Stock (page 69), Super Stock (this page), Fish Stock (page 71), Vegetable Stock (page 105), or canned chicken broth

½ teaspoon sesame oil

½ teaspoon salt

⅛ teaspoon ground white pepper

12 pre-made or store-bought wontons

¼ cup Chinese yellow or regular green chives, cut into 1-inch lengths (optional)

1 green onion, trimmed and coarsely chopped

1 sheet nori, cut in half, then cut crosswise into thin strips

1 tablespoon toasted white sesame seeds

* * *

1. Bring a large pot of water to a boil. Add the noodles and cook according to the package directions. Drain, rinse with cold water, and drain again. Divide the noodles among four soup bowls.

2. Bring the chicken stock, sesame oil, salt, and pepper to a boil in a medium saucepan over high heat. Add the wontons and cook until they float to the top, 3 to 4 minutes.

3. Divide the wontons and broth among the soup bowls. Scatter some of the chives, green onion, nori, and sesame seeds over each bowl. Serve hot.

* * *

SUPER STOCK

This flavorful fortified stock can be used in place of chicken stock, especially with wontons. Since the recipe calls for the salt-cured Smithfield ham, there's no need for additional salt.

Cover 1 pound chicken legs and thighs and ¼ pound lean pork with water in a large pot. Bring to a boil and cook for 2 minutes. Drain and return the chicken and pork to the pot. Add ¾ pound Smithfield ham, 4 dried black mushrooms, 3 dried longans, 5 quarter-sized slices ginger, and 5 quarts water. Bring to a boil, reduce the heat to low, and simmer for 4 hours, occasionally skimming the foam from the stock. Strain. Makes about 4 quarts; refrigerate for up to 5 days.

DUCK SOUP WITH NAPA CABBAGE

Serves 4 as part of a multicourse meal

After Thanksgiving or Christmas, I would often call up my relatives to collect their turkey or duck carcasses, to make a soup stock or jook. When a duck is roasted, it imparts a concentration of flavors into the bones, and the bits of meat remaining on the carcass will be especially tasty. So don't throw away that duck carcass. You don't need much else to make this soup, just some vegetables for a nice accompaniment to the rich broth, but if you have a bit of leftover duck meat, add a few slices. This soup is part of a typical Peking duck dinner—one duck, three dishes.

2 cups Chicken Stock (page 69), Vegetable
    Stock (page 105), or canned chicken broth
5 cups cool water
Carcass from a roast duck (page 239),
    cut into 8 pieces, plus the neck
1 stalk Chinese or regular celery with leaves,
    trimmed and coarsely chopped
1 carrot, peeled and coarsely chopped
½ medium onion
3 quarter-sized slices peeled ginger
5 black peppercorns
2 whole star anise

2 cups sliced napa cabbage
½ cup carrot, cut into thin strips
3 large fresh shiitake, stems discarded and
    caps thinly sliced

2 green onions, trimmed and cut into
    2-inch lengths
½ package (7 ounces) soft tofu, drained and
    cut into 8 pieces
Salt and freshly ground black pepper

1. Bring the chicken stock, water, duck carcass, celery, chopped carrot, onion, ginger, pepper, and star anise to a boil in a large pot. Adjust the heat so the liquid is simmering, cover the pot, and simmer for 3 hours. Strain the broth and discard the solids.

2. Pour the broth back into the pot and bring to a simmer. Add the cabbage, carrot strips, and shiitake and simmer until the vegetables are tender, 7 to 8 minutes.

3. Add the green onions and tofu and simmer gently until the tofu is heated through. Season to taste with salt and pepper and ladle into warm soup bowls.

SHANDONG STIR-FRY SOUP NOODLES

Serves 4 as part of a multicourse meal

In northern China, particularly in Shandong province, wheat, flour, and noodle-based dishes are the staple. Here is a uniquely Shandong dish—a stir-fry dish turned into a noodle soup, for a meal in a bowl.

2 dried wood ear mushrooms
8 dried lily buds
1 teaspoon dried shrimp

FOR THE MARINADE
1 tablespoon cornstarch
1 tablespoon soy sauce
2 teaspoons sesame oil

1/2 pound boneless pork, cut into thin strips

FOR THE SOUP BASE
3 cups Chicken Stock (page 69) or
    canned chicken broth
3 tablespoons soy sauce
1 tablespoon Chinese black vinegar or
    balsamic vinegar
2 teaspoons sesame oil
1/8 teaspoon ground white pepper

1 pound fresh wide Chinese egg noodles, or
    substitute fettuccine

1 tablespoon vegetable oil
1 tablespoon minced garlic

1 small napa cabbage, cored and cut crosswise
    into 1/2-inch strips
1/4 cup sliced bamboo shoots

4 oyster mushrooms, sliced in half
4 green onions, trimmed and cut into
    2-inch lengths

2 tablespoons cornstarch, dissolved in
    1/4 cup water
4 eggs

*　　*　　*

1. Put the wood ears, lily buds, and dried shrimp in separate small bowls and pour enough warm water over them to cover completely. Soak until softened, about 20 minutes. Drain. Cut the wood ears into thin strips. Trim the hard ends from the lily buds, and tie each bud into a knot.

2. Marinate the pork: Stir the cornstarch, soy sauce, and sesame oil together in a medium bowl. Add the pork and toss gently until coated. Let stand for 10 minutes.

3. Prepare the soup base: Stir the chicken stock, soy sauce, black vinegar, sesame oil, and pepper together in a medium bowl until blended.

4. Bring a large pot of water to a boil. Add the noodles and cook according to the package directions. Drain, rinse with cold water, and drain again. Divide the noodles among four large soup bowls.

5. Heat a wok over high heat until hot. Add the oil and swirl to coat the sides. Add the garlic and dried shrimp and cook, stirring, until fragrant, about 10 seconds. Add the pork and stir-fry until lightly browned, about 2 minutes. Add the wood ears, lily buds, cabbage, bamboo shoots, oyster mushrooms, and green onions. Stir-fry until the vegetables are softened, about 2 minutes.

6. Pour the soup base into the wok and bring to a boil. Stir the dissolved cornstarch into the wok and cook, stirring, until the soup is lightly thickened, about 30 seconds. Turn the heat to low. One at a time, carefully crack the eggs into the soup and cook until the whites are set but the yolks are still runny, about 2 minutes.

7. To serve, remove the eggs with a slotted spoon and set one atop each bowl of noodles. Ladle the broth into the bowls, dividing the ingredients evenly.

HOT-AND-SOUR EGG FLOWER SOUP

Serves 4 as part of a multicourse meal

Hot-and-sour soup can be found in Chinese restaurants everywhere. But you probably won't find one with my little twist—bean thread noodles. The soup is getting to be very popular in Cantonese and Taiwanese restaurants.

3 dried black mushrooms
1 dried wood ear mushroom
1 ounce dried bean thread noodles

4 cups Chicken Stock (page 69)
    or canned chicken broth
3 ounces boneless lean pork, cut into thin strips
1/4 cup carrot, cut into thin strips
1 tablespoon sliced preserved vegetables
    (optional)

1/2 package (8 ounces) soft tofu, drained and
    cut into 1/4-inch strips
3 tablespoons distilled white vinegar
3 tablespoons soy sauce or 2 tablespoons regular
    soy sauce and 1 tablespoon dark soy sauce
1 tablespoon chili garlic sauce
2 teaspoons sugar
1 teaspoon ground white pepper
2 tablespoons cornstarch, dissolved in
    3 tablespoons water
1 egg, lightly beaten

2 green onions, trimmed and cut diagonally
    into thin strips

1. Pour enough warm water over the black and wood ear mushrooms in a medium bowl to cover them completely. Soak until softened, about 20 minutes. Drain the mushrooms. Cut off and discard the black mushroom stems. Thinly slice the black mushroom caps and the wood ears.

2. Meanwhile, pour enough warm water over the noodles in a separate bowl to cover completely. Soak until softened, about 10 minutes. Drain thoroughly and cut the noodles into 4-inch lengths.

3. Bring the chicken stock to a boil in a large saucepan. Stir in the wood ears, black mushrooms, pork, carrot, and preserved vegetables, if using, and simmer for about 2 minutes.

4. Stir in the noodles, tofu, vinegar, soy sauce, chili garlic sauce, sugar, and pepper. Simmer until heated through, about 2 minutes. Pour in the dissolved cornstarch and cook, stirring, until the soup boils and thickens, about 30 seconds. Slowly pour in the egg, stirring the soup in a circular motion to create "egg flowers."

5. Ladle the soup into a tureen or individual serving bowls and scatter the green onions over the top.

BIG POT WOR WONTON SOUP

Serves 4 as part of a multicourse meal

This Chinatown classic is hard to find these days. For hungry diners who weren't satisfied with wontons and broth, chefs added substantial ingredients, like meat, seafood, chicken, and vegetables. *Wor* means "pot" or "bowl" in Cantonese.

FOR THE FILLING

1 piece (about 1½ inches square)
    dried tangerine peel
¼ pound (about ⅔ cup) Fish Mousse
    (page 152)
¼ pound uncooked medium shrimp, shelled,
    deveined, and finely chopped
2 stalks Chinese celery with leaves, minced,
    or 1 stalk regular celery, minced, plus
    ¼ cup chopped celery leaves
1 green onion, trimmed and minced
1 teaspoon grated ginger
1 egg white
¼ teaspoon sesame oil
¼ teaspoon salt
⅛ teaspoon ground white pepper

16 wonton wrappers

FOR THE MARINADE

2 teaspoons Chinese rice wine or dry sherry
¼ teaspoon sesame oil
⅛ teaspoon ground white pepper

12 uncooked medium shrimp,
    shelled and deveined
6 sea scallops, cut horizontally in half

6 cups Fish Stock (page 71)
    or canned chicken broth
16 snow peas, ends trimmed

12 thin slices Char Siu (page 259)
¼ teaspoon salt
Pinch of ground white pepper

❋   ❋   ❋

1. Pour enough warm water over the tangerine peel in a small bowl to cover. Soak until softened, about 20 minutes. Drain the peel and mince.

2. Make the filling: Stir the fish mousse, shrimp, celery, green onion, ginger, egg white, sesame oil, salt, pepper, and tangerine peel together in a small bowl until well mixed and spongy.

3. Make the wontons: Place 1 heaping teaspoonful of the filling in the center of a wrapper. (Keep the remaining wrappers covered with a damp kitchen towel or plastic wrap to prevent them from drying out.) Brush the edges of the wrapper with a fingertip dipped in water, then fold the wrapper in half to form a triangle. Pinch the edges firmly to seal. Pull the opposite corners of the base of the triangle together, moisten one of the corners with water, and press the corners together firmly to seal. Repeat with the remaining wrappers and filling, keeping the formed wontons covered with a damp kitchen towel to prevent them from drying out.

4. Marinate the seafood: Stir the rice wine, sesame oil, and pepper together in a small bowl until blended. Toss the shrimp and scallops gently in the marinade until coated. Set aside for 10 minutes.

5. Bring a large pot of water to a boil over high heat. Add the wontons and cook until they rise to the surface, about 5 minutes after the water returns to a boil. Drain well.

6. Meanwhile, bring the fish stock to a boil in a separate pot. Adjust the heat so the stock is simmering, then stir in the marinated shrimp and scallops and the snow peas. Simmer until the seafood is cooked through, about 3 minutes.

7. Slide the cooked wontons and char siu into the broth and season the broth with the salt and pepper. Ladle the soup into large warm bowls, dividing the wontons, shrimp, scallops, and snow peas evenly.

IN GOOD SPIRITS WITH CHINA'S RICE WINES

Chinese wine (called, along with all other Chinese alcoholic beverages, *chiew*) is fermented mainly from glutinous rice (sometimes mixed with other grains such as millet and sorghum) and water. China also produces distilled rice beverages in the same category as whiskey and vodka, with alcohol contents up to 130 proof! So those who toast with kan pei—or "bottoms up"—beware! ✳ Among the most world-renowned is the amber-yellow rice wine made in Shaoxing, near Shanghai. This smooth, nutty concoction resembles sherry and is also one of the most called-for flavoring ingredients in Chinese cuisine. The popular Shanghai dish, Drunken Chicken—or Drunken Shrimp or even Drunken Lobster—couldn't get soused without it. Originally aged for up to 100 years in glazed and decorated pottery jars that are themselves works of art, the wine now comes more conveniently, albeit less decoratively, in bottles. ✳ Like Japanese sake, it's good cold or hot. By sipping lightly, you, too, can get in touch with these "ancient spirits."

VEGETABLES
and SALADS

Stacks of squash, pyramids of peppers, mounds of eggplant, and piles of peas, boxes of cold fuzzy melons, and crates full of greens are a few of my favorite things. Vegetables have been an indispensable part of Chinese cooking for thousands of years. Nowhere is this more visible than in any Chinatown around the world. It's a farmers' market every day, with streets, markets, and alleys lined with tables full of fresh produce. When I first came to America, it was impossible to find Asian produce in supermarkets. Chinatowns were the only places where I could find the freshest. But now, with the growing popularity of produce from all Asian countries, finding lemongrass is becoming less of a treasure hunt.

DRY-FRIED GREEN BEANS

Serves 4 as part of a multicourse meal

Double-cooked green beans are popular in American Chinese restaurants, where chefs often put their own twists on this classic. Some add dried black mushrooms, others fresh mushrooms, or maybe fresh chili peppers to give it a kick. Cooking the green beans in oil removes the excess moisture, intensifies the flavor, and gives the beans a blistery appearance. Use green beans or long beans; the latter will be a bit firmer in texture.

FOR THE MARINADE

1 tablespoon soy sauce

1 teaspoon cornstarch

½ pound ground pork

FOR THE SAUCE

¼ cup Chicken Stock (page 69) or canned
    chicken broth

1 tablespoon soy sauce or dark soy sauce

1 tablespoon sugar

2 teaspoons minced garlic

2 teaspoons chili bean sauce or chili garlic sauce

¼ teaspoon sesame oil

2 cups vegetable oil

¾ pound green beans, ends trimmed and cut
    into 2-inch lengths

❉   ❉   ❉

1. Marinate the pork: Stir the soy sauce and cornstarch together in a medium bowl until the cornstarch is dissolved. Mix the pork gently in the marinade until incorporated. Let stand for 5 to 10 minutes.

2. Prepare the sauce: Stir the chicken stock, soy sauce, sugar, garlic, chili bean sauce, and sesame oil together in a small bowl until the sugar is dissolved.

3. Pour the oil into a 2-quart saucepan and heat to 350°F over medium-high heat. Carefully slip the green beans into the oil and cook, stirring continuously, until they are wrinkled, about 5 minutes. With a slotted spoon or wire skimmer, transfer the beans to paper towels to drain. Reserve the oil.

4. Heat a wok over high heat until hot. Pour in 2 teaspoons of the reserved oil and swirl to coat the sides. Slide the pork into the wok and stir-fry until the meat is crumbly and changes color, about 2 minutes. Add the green beans and sauce and stir until heated thorough, 1 to 2 minutes. Scoop the contents of the wok onto a serving plate and serve immediately.

MRS. OZORIO'S OKRA WITH SHRIMP PASTE

Serves 4 as part of a multicourse meal

My friend Mrs. Ozorio in Toronto taught me this Macanese-style dish with its East-meets-West combination of okra, tomato, and shrimp paste. Shrimp paste is ground fermented shrimp sold in jars. Step back, as a very strong odor will escape when you open a jar of it. If you can't find this pungent delicacy, substitute fish sauce (nuoc man or nam pla) instead.

½ pound fresh okra

FOR THE SAUCE
½ cup Vegetable Stock (page 105) or canned
    vegetable broth
2 teaspoons oyster-flavored sauce
1 teaspoon shrimp paste
1 teaspoon sugar

2 tablespoons vegetable oil
1 medium onion, diced

½ cup sugar snap peas, trimmed
1 medium tomato, cored and diced

2 teaspoons cornstarch, dissolved in
    1 tablespoon water
2 teaspoons sesame oil

1. Bring a medium saucepan of water to a boil. Trim the stems from the okra pods, being careful to avoid piercing the pods. Add the okra to the boiling water and cook for 3 minutes. Drain, rinse under cold water, and drain again.

2. Prepare the sauce: Stir the vegetable stock, oyster-flavored sauce, shrimp paste, and sugar together in a small bowl until the sugar is dissolved.

3. Heat a wok over high heat until hot. Add the oil and swirl to coat the sides. Add the onion and stir-fry until fragrant, about 1 minute. Add the okra and the sauce and bring to a boil. Adjust the heat so the sauce is simmering, cover the wok, and simmer for 5 minutes.

4. Stir in the sugar snap peas and tomato and cook until the sugar snap peas are tender-crisp, about 1 minute. Pour in the dissolved cornstarch and cook, stirring, until the sauce boils and thickens, about 30 seconds. Stir in the sesame oil, scoop onto a platter, and serve.

SPICY EGGPLANT

Serves 4 as part of a multicourse meal

Chef Neil Perry of Rockpool restaurant in Sydney whipped up this spicy eggplant dish after taking me on a tour of Chinatown. Hot-oil blanching removes some of the water from the eggplant, intensifying and concentrating the flavor of the vegetable while preserving the purple color. Chop up some char siu and toss it in if you like; the sweetness complements the spiciness of this dish.

FOR THE SAUCE

1/3 cup Chicken Stock (page 69) or
    canned chicken broth
1 tablespoon hoisin sauce
2 teaspoons soy sauce
2 teaspoons fresh lemon juice
1 teaspoon plum sauce

4 Chinese eggplants (about 1 pound),
    stems removed
Vegetable oil for deep-frying

2 teaspoons minced garlic
1 teaspoon minced ginger
1/2 red or green jalapeño chili,
    sliced into thin rings
Pinch of ground toasted Sichuan peppercorns

Basil leaves
Chopped cilantro or sliced green onions

*   *   *

1. Prepare the sauce: Stir the chicken stock, hoisin sauce, soy sauce, lemon juice, and plum sauce together in a small bowl until blended.

2. With a vegetable peeler, remove 1-inch lengthwise strips of the eggplant skin, leaving a 1-inch strip of skin in between each. Cut the eggplant lengthwise into quarters, then cut crosswise into 3-inch pieces.

3. Pour enough oil into a 2-quart saucepan to come to a depth of 3 inches. Heat over medium heat to 350°F. Deep-fry the eggplant in two batches until tender, 1 1/2 to 2 minutes. Remove with a slotted spoon and drain well on paper towels. Reserve the oil.

4. Heat a wok over high heat until hot. Add 1 tablespoon of the reserved oil and swirl to coat the sides. Add the garlic, ginger, chili, and Sichuan peppercorns and stir-fry until fragrant, about 20 seconds. Add the sauce and bring to a simmer.

5. Add the eggplant and stir to coat. Scoop onto a warm serving platter. Serve garnished with basil leaves and cilantro or green onions.

MARKET BASKET VEGETABLE STIR-FRY

Serves 4 as part of a multicourse meal

At Vegetarian Paradise 3 in New York City, a popular stir-fry combines fresh and dried vegetables to give a complexity of textures. Don't be limited by the ingredient list; substitute your favorite vegetables.

3 dried black mushrooms
4 dried wood ear mushrooms
1 piece dried snow fungus (optional)

FOR THE SEASONINGS
2 tablespoons oyster-flavored sauce
1 tablespoon soy sauce
2 teaspoons sesame oil

2 tablespoons vegetable oil
2 garlic cloves, minced
1 cup broccoli florets
1 cup cauliflower florets
$\frac{1}{2}$ cup diced (1-inch squares) purple cabbage
$\frac{1}{2}$ cup Vegetable Stock (page 105) or
    canned vegetable broth

$\frac{1}{2}$ cup snow peas, trimmed
$\frac{1}{2}$ cup bean sprouts

❋   ❋   ❋

1. Put the black mushrooms, wood ears, and snow fungus in separate small bowls and pour enough warm water over them to cover. Soak until softened, about 20 minutes. Drain. Discard the black mushroom stems and cut the caps in half. Thinly slice the wood ears. Discard the hard yellow portion of the snow fungus, then cut the remainder into bite-sized pieces.

2. Prepare the seasonings: Stir the oyster-flavored sauce, soy sauce, and sesame oil together in a small bowl.

3. Heat a wok over high heat until hot. Add the oil and swirl to coat the sides. Add the garlic and stir-fry until fragrant, about 20 seconds. Add the broccoli, cauliflower, cabbage, vegetable stock, black mushrooms, wood ears, and snow fungus, cover the wok, and cook until the cauliflower is tender-crisp, 2 to 2$\frac{1}{2}$ minutes.

4. Add the seasonings, snow peas, and sprouts and stir-fry until the snow peas are tender, about 1 minute. Scoop onto a serving platter and serve.

YOKOHAMA

J apanese culture has been strongly influenced by China. Buddhism and Taoism, paper, and tea are among the exports the Japanese learned to refine in their own ways. And when Japanese eaters want culinary inspiration, there's just one place in the country where they all head. In fact, eighteen million tourists a year pile into their Toyotas and tour buses to have a meal in Yokohama, on the outskirts of Tokyo. ✻ As one of Japan's most popular destinations, this Chinatown seems more like a theme park than a real community—and its main theme is restaurants. In typical Japanese style, the Chinatown eateries coexist harmoniously in a very limited space. There is not one, but ten Chinese-style gates at the myriad entrances to these places. And each narrow building houses numerous Chinese restaurants in vertical layers, like stacked steamers of Chinese buns. With so many establishments on a single block, competition breeds excellence. One Chinese chef here, Wah-Hai Tse, even beat Japanese masters on TV's popular cooking competition, *Iron Chef*. ✻ When in Yokohama, do as the Japanese do—eat Chinese, and be inspired!

CHINATOWN YOKOHAMA DAIHANTEN RESTAURANT

164 Yamashita-cho, Naka-ku

(81-45) 641-0001

What to order: *pan-fried duck fillet with lemon sauce; fried rice Fujian-style*

CHUNGKING CHINESE SZECHWAN RESTAURANT

5F Ryunichi Kanton Kaikan Building

118-2 Yamashita-cho, Naka-ku

(81-45) 622-1252

What to order: *stir-fried squid with Shanghai pickled mustard green vegetables; shrimp stir-fry in Szechwan spicy sauce; Kung Pao chicken*

HEICHINROU RESTAURANT

143 Shin-Yokohama Kohoku-ku

(81-45) 663-5126

What to order: *Japanese tilefish; sautéed beef fillet with black pepper; shark's fin with lobster bisque; deep-fried seafood with fruit salad; seasonal vegetables with XO sauce; yin-yang shrimp*

NEW PEARL RIVER RESTAURANT

160 Yamashita-cho, Naka-ku

(81-45) 681-2286

What to order: *Cantonese sweet-and-sour pork tenderloin with onions; stir-fried shrimp, clams, and asparagus*

YUEN'S BEIJING RESTAURANT

136 Yamashita-cho, Naka-ku

(81-45) 681-5513

What to order: *Point to the photographs—the menu is not in English.*

EVERYBODY LOVES CHINATOWN IN YOKOHAMA!

STIR-FRIED SOYBEAN SPROUTS WITH BEAN THREAD NOODLES

Serves 4 as part of a multicourse meal

Even though the Peking Duck House in New York City is best known for its namesake dish, this vegetable dish is a favorite of mine. I make it with soybean sprouts, which are a bit larger than mung bean sprouts. Soybean sprouts may be difficult to find; substitute any type of bean sprout that you can get your hands on.

2 dried wood ear mushrooms (optional)
1 package (about 2 ounces) dried bean thread noodles

FOR THE SEASONINGS
¼ cup Sichuan pickled vegetables, rinsed and chopped
3 tablespoons Chicken Stock (page 69) or canned chicken broth
2 tablespoons soy sauce
2 teaspoons sesame oil

2 tablespoons vegetable oil
2 teaspoons minced garlic
3 green onions, trimmed and cut into 2-inch lengths
1 cup bean sprouts
¼ cup carrot, cut into thin strips

1 tablespoon toasted white sesame seeds

* * *

1. If using the wood ear mushrooms, pour enough warm water over them in a small bowl to cover them completely. Soak until softened, about 20 minutes. Drain and cut into thin strips.

2. Meanwhile, pour enough warm water over the bean thread noodles in a medium bowl to cover them completely. Soak until softened, about 10 minutes. Drain. Lay the noodles out on a cutting board and cut into 4-inch lengths.

3. Prepare the seasonings: Stir the pickled vegetables, chicken stock, soy sauce, and sesame oil together in a small bowl.

4. Heat a wok over high heat until hot. Add the vegetable oil and swirl to coat the sides. Add the garlic and cook, stirring, until fragrant, about 10 seconds. Add the green onions, bean sprouts, wood ears, and carrot and stir-fry for 30 seconds. Add the seasonings and bring to boil. Stir in the noodles. Cook, stirring, until the carrot is tender-crisp, another minute or so. Scoop onto a serving plate and sprinkle with the sesame seeds.

MUSHROOMS AND BABY BOK CHOY WITH FRIED GARLIC

I can't get enough of mushrooms. With so many varieties and different textures and flavors I'm never bored. I use the common button mushroom, but once you taste this, you won't find those mushrooms so common.

The master chefs at Maple Pepper Garden Restaurant in Toronto taught me to blanch the mushrooms before pan-frying them; it speeds up the cooking process once they hit the wok. If you can't find fried garlic in your local grocery, cut garlic cloves into paper-thin slices, drop into a pan of hot oil, and fry until golden brown. Drain and store in an airtight container—don't throw away that garlicky oil, use it in your next stir-fry.

¾ **pound button mushrooms (each about**
    1½ inches in diameter), trimmed
4 baby bok choy, halved lengthwise

FOR THE SEASONINGS
2 tablespoons Chinese rice wine or dry sherry
1 teaspoon oyster-flavored sauce
1 teaspoon soy sauce
1 teaspoon dark soy sauce

2 tablespoons vegetable oil
1 tablespoon minced garlic
1 teaspoon sesame oil

3 tablespoons prepared fried garlic

*   *   *

1. Bring a large pot of water to a boil. Add the mushrooms and cook for 2 minutes. With a slotted spoon or wire skimmer, scoop them into a colander. Rinse under cold water and drain again.

2. Add the bok choy to the boiling water and cook until tender-crisp, 30 seconds to 1 minute. Drain, rinse under cold water, and drain again.

3. Prepare the seasonings: Stir the rice wine, oyster-flavored sauce, soy sauce, and dark soy sauce together in a small bowl until blended.

4. Heat a wok over high heat until hot. Add the mushrooms and cook, stirring, until their surface is dry. Remove the mushrooms from the wok.

5. Pour the vegetable oil into the wok and swirl to coat the sides. Add the garlic and stir-fry until fragrant, about 10 seconds. Return the mushrooms to the wok and pour in the seasonings. Stir-fry until the mushrooms are tender, 1½ to 2 minutes. Add the sesame oil and bok choy and toss until the bok choy is heated through, about 30 seconds. Scoop the mushrooms onto a serving platter, surround with the bok choy, and scatter the fried garlic over the top.

SYDNEY

t's not about history, it's about the harbor. While the Chinese have been living in this vast and vibrant gateway to Australia for a century and a half, today's Chinatown was relocated from its original location along the wharves of "The Rocks"—where Chinese laborers arrived in the days of the Opium Wars. Later, many became the gardeners and landscapers of the Australian outback. In the 1920s, Dixon Street became the center of Sydney's Chinese community and it was here, on another spit of oceanfront land, that a modern new Chinatown rose in the 1970s. ✳ This Chinatown's seaside pedestrian walks are breezy, the malls and adjoining side streets chockful of as many restaurants as there are sea views. Under one roof here, you'll find Mongolian beef and Cantonese-style tiger shrimp. In some of the windows, you'll see tanks full of some of the largest and most luscious creatures of the deep. Everything about Australia is brawny, brash, and over-sized—especially the giant Tasmanian crab that, once steamed by Chinese masters, can serve eight from just a single set of claws. ✳ Visitors may come to view the distinctive sail-like roofs of the beautiful Sydney Opera House, but my idea

THE BBQ RESTAURANT DOES MORE DUCKS IN A DAY THAN ANYWHERE ELSE IN THE WORLD!

of a landmark is the Sydney Seafood Market—
an incredible array of ultrafresh fish that's just a
rowboat ride from this nautical Chinatown. Look
at this Chinatown—and the thousands of miles of
coastline serving so small a populace—and I'm
sure you'll agree with the Aussies when they say
they live in "The Lucky Country."

BBQ KING RESTAURANT
18 Goulburn Street
(61-2) 267-2433
What to order: *BBQ pork; suckling pig; roasted
duck; roasted duck over rice noodle soup*

EAST OCEAN RESTAURANT
421-429 Sussex Street
(61-2) 9212-4198, 9212-1989
What to order: *dim sum*

FU LIN SEAFOOD RESTAURANT
Harbour Plaza
25-29 Dixon Street
(61-2) 9281-3151
What to order: *lichee flavored pork; "daisy-style"
fish in sweet and vinegar sauce; mushroom-
decorated prawn birds on net*

GOLDEN CENTURY SEAFOOD
RESTAURANT
G/F & 1/F, 393-399 Sussex Street
(61-2) 9212-3901
What to order: *salt-and-pepper king crab; stir-fry
butter garlic crab; soup with king crab; steamed
oysters with garlic and mung bean in XO sauce;
seafood hot pot; honey-glazed eel*

HAPPY CHEF SEAFOOD NOODLES HOUSE
Sussex Centre
Shop F3, 401 Sussex Street
(61-2) 9281-5832
What to order: *Chinese noodle soup with beef and
vegetables; Thai favorite noodle soup; noodle soup
with Korean kim chi; Singapore lasak noodles*

KAM FOOK SEAFOOD RESTAURANT
Level 3, Market City, 9 Hay Street
(61-2) 9211-8988
What to order: *stir-fried kangaroo with XO sauce*

MOTHER CHU'S TAIWANESE GOURMET
Shop No. 1—4
86—88 Dixon Street
(61-2) 9211-0288
What to order: *steamed chicken bun; steamed BBQ
pork bun*

ROCKPOOL
107 George Street
The Rocks
(61-2) 9252-2188
What to order: *clam, abalone, and winter melon
soup; Sichuan-style eggplant; steamed silken tofu with
black vinegar; red-braised pork hock with shiitake*

SUPER BOWL RESTAURANT
41 Dixon Street
Haymarket
(61-2) 9281-2462
What to order: *congee (chicken, beef, pork, or
seafood); house special noodle soup*

HAKKA SHRIMP-STUFFED PEPPERS AND EGGPLANT

Serves 4 as part of a multicourse meal

Within Cantonese cuisine, there's a subcategory known as Hakka-style food. Hakka people stuff everything from tofu to peppers with pork, poultry, or seafood. When pan-frying the peppers, cook them only on the side with the fish stuffing so as not to blemish the brilliant color of the skin.

* * *

FOR THE STUFFING

1 tablespoon dried shrimp

½ pound firm-fleshed white fish fillets, such as
    snapper or cod, diced

1 egg white

2 teaspoons cornstarch

1 teaspoon chopped cilantro

½ teaspoon sugar

¼ teaspoon salt

1 Asian eggplant

1 red bell pepper

2 Anaheim chilies

Cornstarch for dusting

2 tablespoons vegetable oil

⅓ cup water

1 tablespoon salted black beans, rinsed, drained,
    and chopped

2 teaspoons minced garlic

½ teaspoon dried red chili flakes

¼ cup Fish Stock (page 71), Chicken Stock
    (page 69), or canned chicken broth

1 tablespoon soy sauce

½ teaspoon sugar

1 teaspoon cornstarch, dissolved in
    1 tablespoon water

1. Pour enough warm water over the dried shrimp in a small bowl to cover them completely. Soak until softened, about 20 minutes. Drain and squeeze out the excess water with your hands.

2. Prepare the stuffing: Combine the dried shrimp, fish fillets, egg white, cornstarch, cilantro, sugar, and salt in a food processor and process to a smooth paste.

3. Trim off the eggplant stem. Cut the eggplant on the bias into 1-inch slices. Butterfly each slice by cutting horizontally almost all the way through it, starting at one of the long sides. Core and quarter the red bell pepper and remove the seeds. Trim the ends so the pieces lie flat. Cut the chili lengthwise in half and discard the stem, seeds, and white fleshy ribs.

4. Dust the vegetables lightly with cornstarch. Spread the fish stuffing in an even layer over the inside of the pepper and chili pieces. Fill the butterflied eggplant slices with the remaining stuffing, dividing it evenly. Dust the vegetables with additional cornstarch to coat them lightly.

5. Heat a 9- or 10-inch nonstick skillet over medium-high heat until hot. Add 1 tablespoon of the oil and swirl to coat the bottom. Fry the peppers, stuffing side down, and eggplant, flesh side down, turning once, until lightly browned, 3 to 4 minutes. Add the water, cover the skillet, and cook until the stuffing is cooked through, about 3 minutes. Transfer the vegetables to a warm serving platter.

6. Pour off the water from the skillet and dry it throughly. Pour in the remaining 1 tablespoon oil and heat over medium heat until hot. Add the black beans, garlic, and chili flakes, and cook, stirring, until fragrant, about 10 seconds. Add the fish stock, soy sauce, and sugar and bring to a boil. Add the dissolved cornstarch and cook, stirring, until the sauce thickens slightly, about 30 seconds. Spoon the sauce over the peppers and eggplant and serve hot.

BROCCOLI FRITTERS IN SICHUAN PEPPER-SALT

Serves 4 as part of a multicourse meal

Typically this spice combination is used on chicken wings, rarely on vegetables—until Chef Christina Yau of YMing's Restaurant in London came up with this idea. Serve the fried broccoli with fresh steamed broccoli for an interesting combination of textures.

FOR THE BATTER
¾ cup all-purpose flour
½ cup water
1 egg
½ teaspoon baking powder
¼ teaspoon salt

2 cups bite-sized broccoli florets
¼ cup cornstarch

FOR THE SEASONINGS
1 tablespoon dried red chili flakes, finely chopped
½ teaspoon salt
¼ teaspoon ground white pepper
¼ teaspoon ground toasted Sichuan peppercorns
¼ teaspoon Chinese five-spice powder

Vegetable oil for deep-frying

1 tablespoon minced garlic
1 tablespoon chopped green onion

❅   ❅   ❅

1. Make the batter: Whisk the flour, water, egg, baking powder, and salt together in a mixing bowl until smooth. Let the batter rest for 10 minutes.

2. Shake the broccoli and cornstarch together in a paper bag until the broccoli is evenly coated.

3. Prepare the seasonings: Stir the chili flakes, salt, white pepper, ground Sichuan peppercorns, and five-spice powder together in a small bowl.

4. Pour enough vegetable oil into a 2-quart wok or saucepan to come to a depth of 3 inches. Heat over medium heat to 350°F. Dip the dusted broccoli into the batter, a few pieces at a time, letting the excess batter drip back into the bowl, then carefully slide the battered broccoli into the hot oil and fry until the batter is golden brown and the broccoli is tender-crisp, about 1½ minutes. Remove with a slotted spoon and drain on paper towels. Reserve the oil.

5. Heat a wok over high heat until hot. Add 1 tablespoon of the reserved oil and swirl to coat the sides. Add the garlic, green onion, and seasonings and stir-fry until fragrant and pungent, about 30 seconds. Toss the fried broccoli with the seasonings until coated. Scoop onto a serving platter and serve immediately.

BUDDHA'S FEAST

Serves 4 as part of a multicourse meal

Known as *jia*, which means "vegetarian," this dish is served on the first day of the Chinese New Year and during the Ching Ming Festival (see page 107). Fermented bean curd adds a flavorful dimension to the dish; it is found in jars in Asian groceries. If you can't locate it, just omit it.

2 dried bean curd sticks

6 dried black mushrooms

2 dried wood ear mushrooms

¼ cup dried lily buds

1 bundle (about 2 ounces) dried bean thread
    noodles

FOR THE SAUCE

2½ cups Vegetable Stock (page 105) or canned
    vegetable broth

¼ cup oyster-flavored sauce

1 tablespoon soy sauce

1 teaspoon sugar

2 tablespoons vegetable oil

1 tablespoon fermented red bean curd

1 cup button mushrooms, trimmed and
    quartered

1 cup napa cabbage, cut into 1-inch pieces

6 tofu puffs

½ cup canned water chestnuts, drained

½ cup green beans, trimmed and cut into
    2-inch lengths

½ cup cut baby corn, cut in halves

¼ cup canned gingko nuts, drained

2 teaspoons sesame oil

¼ cup walnut halves

1. Pour enough warm water over the dried bean curd sticks in a medium bowl to cover them completely. Soak until soft enough to cut, about 1 hour. Drain the bean curd and cut into bite-sized pieces.

2. Meanwhile, pour enough warm water over the black mushrooms, wood ears, and lily buds in a large bowl to cover them completely. Soak until softened, about 20 minutes. Drain. Discard the black mushroom stems and leave the caps whole. Cut the wood ear mushrooms into thin strips. Cut off the hard tips of the lily buds, then tie each bud into a knot.

3. Pour enough warm water over the bean thread noodles in a medium bowl to cover them completely. Soak until softened, about 10 minutes. Drain the noodles, lay them out on a cutting board, and cut them crosswise in half.

4. Prepare the sauce: Stir the vegetable stock, oyster-flavored sauce, soy sauce, and sugar together in a medium bowl until the sugar is dissolved.

5. Heat a wok over high heat until hot. Add the oil and swirl to coat the sides. Add the soaked bean curd and cook, stirring, for 1 minute. Add

the fermented red bean curd, black mushrooms, wood ears, lily buds, noodles, button mushrooms, cabbage, tofu puffs, water chestnuts, green beans, baby corn, gingko nuts, and the sauce. Stir once or twice to mix well and bring to a boil. Adjust the heat so the liquid is simmering, cover the wok, and simmer until the bean curd sticks are tender, 8 to 10 minutes.

6. Stir in the sesame oil and walnuts, scoop onto a serving platter, and serve.

VEGETABLE STOCK

Unlike most vegetarian stocks, this one is rich and full flavored. I often freeze the leftover mushroom pulp to use as dumpling filling. Soak 14 dried black mushrooms in warm water to cover until soft, about 20 minutes. Drain, discard the stems, and coarsely chop. Wash and coarsely chop 2 pounds button mushrooms. Combine the mushrooms, 3 stalks Chinese celery (or ¾ cup celery leaves), three ¼-inch-thick slices ginger, and 3 quarts water in a large saucepan. Bring to a boil, reduce the heat, and simmer for 2½ hours. Strain the stock, squeezing the excess liquid from the mushroom mixture. Makes about 2½ quarts; refrigerate for up to 5 days or freeze for 3 months.

SEAFOOD-STUFFED FUZZY MELON

Serves 4 as part of a multicourse meal

At the Bright Pearl Seafood Restaurant in Toronto the chefs stuff the fuzzy melon with the expensive and elusive dried scallop, a delicacy traditionally found at the finest of Chinese banquets. If you can locate this little bit of heaven and are willing to pay the price, use dried scallop sparingly to add a sweet richness. This recipe uses shrimp and pork instead. A large zucchini or cucumber can be used in place of the fuzzy melon.

FOR THE STUFFING

¼ cup Chicken Stock (page 69), Fish Stock (page 71), or canned chicken broth
¼ pound ground pork
¼ pound uncooked medium shrimp, shelled, deveined, and minced
¼ teaspoon salt
⅛ teaspoon ground white pepper

1 medium fuzzy melon (about ½ pound; see headnote), peeled and cut into 1-inch slices
Cornstarch for dusting

FOR THE SAUCE

½ cup Chicken Stock (page 69), Fish Stock (page 71), or canned chicken broth
2 tablespoons Chinese rice wine or dry sherry
2 teaspoons oyster-flavored sauce
¼ teaspoon dried red chili flakes
1 teaspoon cornstarch, dissolved in 1 tablespoon water
Tobiko caviar (optional)

✳   ✳   ✳

1. Prepare the stuffing: Stir the chicken stock, ground pork, minced shrimp, salt, and pepper together in a small bowl until well blended. Let stand for 10 minutes.

2. Using a 1-inch round cutter, cut a hole in the center of each melon slice. Dust the sides of each hole with cornstarch to coat, then fill with the stuffing, mounding it slightly. Place the slices in a glass pie dish.

3. Prepare a wok for steaming according to the directions on page xxvi. Set the pie dish in the steamer basket, cover, and steam over high heat until the filling is cooked through, about 10 minutes.

4. Meanwhile, make the sauce: Stir the chicken stock, rice wine, oyster-flavored sauce, and chili flakes together in a small saucepan over medium heat. Bring to a simmer. Stir in the dissolved cornstarch and cook, stirring, until the sauce boils and thickens slightly, about 30 seconds.

5. Spoon the sauce over the stuffed melon slices, garnish with tobiko caviar, and serve directly from the pie plate.

CHING MING

PAYING MY RESPECTS AT MY FATHER'S GRAVE

Ching Ming means "pure and bright." The Festival of Pure Brightness falls on the 106th day after the winter solstice, in the middle of spring. It's a touching coincidence, don't you think, that we pay tribute to our departed ancestors when the world is full of the renewal of life? ✳ According to many Chinese, the practice of sharing the earth with those who came before is as much a fact of life as of death. We consider ghosts as blessings, not as hauntings. We welcome their invisible guidance on our own earthly journeys. The least we can do is pay them back in grand Chinese style with plenty of good food. ✳ Ching Ming also unites the generations. Families gather to pay their respects and appreciate their shared heritage. My family and I recently had that rare opportunity when I traveled to my ancestral village, Toi San, in China to celebrate Ching Ming. For me, a true observance of Ching Ming required that I go back to where my forefathers were buried. I visited aunts, uncles, and cousins in the village where my people had lived for centuries. Surprisingly, not much has changed since I lived there as a child. Not much has changed about the way people celebrate Ching Ming either. We made our way by foot to the rural gravesite on the grassy outskirts of the village, cleaned off the graves, laid out fresh flowers, and lit incense candles. There's nothing like some spring blooms and the soothing smells of incense to make a departed ancestor feel appreciated. ✳ But the most important part of Ching Ming is the offering of food to the departed. I could practically hear my ancestors crying from beyond, "All right, all right. Enough cleaning and flowers. Where's the food?" When a ghost is hungry, you needn't fuss too much over the menu. A humble bowl of steamed rice or a whole roast pig is equally appreciated. ✳ I had prepared some barbecued pork and stir-fried pea shoots picked that morning from my cousin's garden. My mother brought along my dad's favorite—her famous clams in black bean sauce. Younger family members left apples and oranges and egg custard tarts from the village bakery. ✳ Our departed relatives never seem to have the appetite to finish off everything. So, after offering the food and saying the requisite prayers, it is customary for the living to enjoy the food. At the gravesite, we had a Ching Ming picnic that I like to think left everyone satisfied. And we made sure to leave a few oranges and pears at the graves, just in case our ancestors needed a midnight snack.

NOODLE SALAD WITH BLACK BEAN AND MINT DRESSING

Serves 4 as part of a multicourse meal

Oodles of noodles of all kinds are almost as popular as rice in Chinatown restaurants. There are noodle restaurants in Chinatown that serve only *fun* (rice noodles) and *mein* (wheat flour noodles). Many of these are small crowded eateries where you can eat well for just a few dollars. If you don't have Chinese egg noodles, substitute soba (buckwheat) or spaghetti. Pea sprouts are available in some specialty stores and Asian markets. But feel free to use any type of sprout, mung or soybean, to add the crunch.

8 ounces fresh Chinese egg noodles

FOR THE NOODLE DRESSING
¼ cup chopped mint
1 tablespoon black bean garlic sauce
1 tablespoon soy sauce
1½ teaspoons chili garlic sauce
1½ teaspoons minced garlic
1 teaspoon sesame oil
1 teaspoon sugar

FOR THE SALAD DRESSING
2 tablespoons rice vinegar
2 tablespoons honey

1 cup pea sprouts or bean sprouts
3 cups shredded napa cabbage

1. Cook the noodles in a large pot of boiling water according to the package directions. Drain the noodles, rinse them with cold water, and drain again.

2. Make the noodle dressing: Stir the mint, black bean garlic sauce, soy sauce, chili garlic sauce, garlic, sesame oil, and sugar together in a large bowl until blended.

3. Make the salad dressing: Stir the rice vinegar and honey together in a large bowl until the honey is dissolved.

4. Toss the noodles and pea sprouts in the noodle dressing until the noodles are coated with dressing. Toss the cabbage with the salad dressing until coated, then mound the cabbage on a serving plate. Spoon the noodle mixture over the cabbage and serve.

OKEY DOKE POKE | *Serves 4 as part of a multicourse meal*

In Hawaiian, *poke* is pronounced "pokey," and it means "cut piece" or "small piece." This is a down-home version of the more elegant sashimi. When preparing sashimi, cut the tuna into perfect even slices; with poke, a little raggedness does not matter. This is one of the most popular dishes at Sam Choy's restaurant in Honolulu.

FOR THE SEASONINGS

2 tablespoons soy sauce

1 tablespoon seasoned rice vinegar

1 teaspoon mirin (Japanese sweet cooking wine)

1 teaspoon sesame oil

1 teaspoon chili garlic sauce

1 teaspoon chopped cilantro

1 pound sushi-grade ahi tuna, cut into 1/2-inch cubes

1 medium tomato, cored and diced

1/2 cup chopped onion

1/4 cup shredded nori

1. Prepare the seasonings: Stir the soy sauce, rice vinegar, mirin, sesame oil, chili garlic sauce, and cilantro together in a large bowl until blended.

2. Add the tuna, tomato, onion, and nori to the bowl and toss until coated. Marinate for 5 to 10 minutes, then serve.

SWEET AND TANGY LOTUS ROOT SALAD

Serves 4 as part of a multicourse meal

The unusual lotus root has a crisp texture like jicama or raw potato, but with dressing, cucumber, and radish, it makes a nice side dish or accompaniment to any stir-fry. My herbalist in San Francisco reminded me that the lotus root is considered a fresh herb. When boiled in a soup with pork and peanuts, it is believed to be good for your lungs.

FOR THE DRESSING

6 tablespoons sugar

¼ cup rice vinegar

2 tablespoons minced cilantro

1 tablespoon fresh lime juice

1 tablespoon minced ginger

1 red or green jalapeño chili, minced

1 tablespoon rice vinegar

¾ pound fresh lotus root, peeled and cut into
    ⅛-inch-thick slices

1 English cucumber, cut into ¼-inch slices

1 bunch red radishes,
    trimmed and cut into ¼-inch slices

4 cilantro sprigs

1. Prepare the dressing: Stir the sugar, rice vinegar, cilantro, lime juice, ginger, and jalapeño together in a small saucepan. Set aside.

2. Add the rice vinegar to a medium pot of boiling water. Add the lotus root and cook until tender-crisp, 2 to 3 minutes. Remove from the heat, drain, and place in a large serving bowl, along with the cucumber and radishes.

3. Heat the dressing over medium heat, stirring until the sugar is dissolved. Pour the dressing over the vegetables, toss well to coat, and let marinate for 10 minutes.

4. Serve the salad at room temperature, or refrigerate until chilled. Garnish with the cilantro sprigs.

YEAR OF GOOD FORTUNE FISH SALAD

Serves 4 as part of a multicourse meal

During Chinese New Year, most Chinese restaurants offer this dish. At Bow Hon Restaurant in San Francisco, order it a day ahead to make sure they have the fish on hand. The chefs will pluck a freshwater fish right from their own tanks. The Cantonese word for raw fish, *yu,* sounds like the word for prosperity. Present this dish to your guests and bring them good fortune. Ginger juice is easy to make: Grate some ginger, place into cheesecloth, and squeeze to remove the juice. Or if you need to make more, place ½ cup water in a blender with ½ cup chopped ginger, blend, and strain to remove the fibrous ginger that remains.

FOR THE DRESSING

¼ cup rice vinegar

3 tablespoons sugar

1 teaspoon ginger juice

1 teaspoon salt

½ teaspoon ground white pepper

Vegetable oil for deep-frying

6 wonton wrappers, cut into ¼-inch-wide strips

¼ pound sushi-grade ahi tuna, sliced ⅛ inch thick into ¼-inch-wide strips

¼ head iceberg lettuce, cored and shredded (about 1½ cups)

½ cup Sichuan pickled vegetables, rinsed and chopped

¼ cup pickled ginger

¼ cup shredded unsweetened coconut, toasted

¼ cup lightly packed cilantro leaves

2 green onions, trimmed and cut into thin strips about 2 inches long

½ red jalapeño chili, cut into thin strips

½ green jalapeño chili, cut into thin strips

1 tablespoon grated lemon zest

½ teaspoon mustard seeds (optional)

1 tablespoon chopped roasted peanuts

1 tablespoon toasted white sesame seeds

4 cilantro sprigs (optional)

    ❋   ❋   ❋

1. Make the dressing: Stir the rice vinegar, sugar, ginger juice, salt, and pepper together in a small bowl until the sugar is dissolved.

2. Pour enough oil into a 2-quart saucepan to come to a depth of 3 inches. Heat over medium-high heat to 350°F. Deep-fry the wonton strips in 2 batches, stirring to separate the strips, until golden brown, 15 to 20 seconds. Remove with a slotted spoon and drain on paper towels.

3. Gently toss the tuna, lettuce, pickled vegetables, pickled ginger, toasted coconut, cilantro leaves, green onions, chili peppers, lemon zest, and mustard seeds together with the dressing in a large bowl. Scoop onto a serving platter and scatter the wonton strips, peanuts, sesame seeds, and cilantro sprigs over the salad. Serve immediately.

THAI RICE SALAD WITH SHRIMP

Serves 4 as part of a multicourse meal

Often these days you will stumble across a Thai restaurant while walking the streets of a China-town. This salad is quite tasty and great for a party. Make the rice ahead so it will cool to room temperature, but don't put it in the refrigerator or it will become hard.

FOR THE SAUCE

3 stalks lemongrass, bottom 6 inches only
8 quarter-sized slices peeled ginger
2 tablespoons grated lime zest
1 cup fish sauce
2¾ cups water
1 cup palm sugar or packed light brown sugar

FOR THE SALAD

1 grapefruit
1 cup shredded unsweetened coconut, toasted
1 cup thinly sliced green beans
1 cup thinly sliced English cucumber
1 cup bean sprouts
1 small green apple, cored and cut into small cubes
2 tablespoons dried red chili flakes
1 stalk lemongrass, bottom 6 inches only, minced
2 tablespoons grated lime zest

4 cups Steamed Rice (page 285)
½ pound cooked large shrimp, shelled, tails left intact, and deveined

❋   ❋   ❋

1. Make the sauce: Bring the lemongrass, ginger, lime zest, fish sauce, water, and palm sugar to a boil in a 2-quart saucepan over high heat. Adjust the heat so the sauce is simmering and simmer, uncovered, until the sauce is dark and reduced by half to a thick syrup, about 20 minutes.

2. Strain the sauce into a sauce bowl. Discard the solids, cover the bowl, and set it aside.

3. Peel the grapefruit with a sharp knife, removing all the bitter white pith. Slice between the membranes to release the segments. Cut the segments into small dice.

4. Arrange small piles of the grapefruit, toasted coconut, green beans, cucumber, bean sprouts, apple, chili flakes, lemongrass, and lime zest on a large serving platter. Place 1 cup rice on each guest's plate and divide the cooked shrimp evenly among the plates. Let the guests add the accompaniments they prefer to their plates. Pass the sauce for guests to drizzle a little (1 to 2 table-spoons) over their plates, then toss the ingredients together.

TRICOLOR MELON SALAD WITH COCONUT PRAWNS

Serves 4 as part of a multicourse meal

In the late '60s and early '70s, talented young Hong Kong chefs went global. They made use of the new ingredients they found in Western-style supermarkets to prepare dishes that please the local palates as well as the millions of tourists who visit this Pearl of the Orient. This recipe is similar to the favorite American fruit salad. Use unsweetened coconut for the shrimp crust so it won't caramelize too fast when the shrimp is cooked. Macadamia nuts also add a nice crunch to the salad. You can pan-fry the scallops for a sweet caramelized flavor.

¼ pound large sea scallops
2 teaspoons cornstarch

FOR THE DRESSING
½ cup mayonnaise
2 tablespoons rice vinegar
1 tablespoon honey
1 teaspoon wasabi paste
½ teaspoon sesame oil
¼ teaspoon salt

1 cup diced (1-inch) honeydew
1 cup diced (1-inch) cantaloupe
½ cup diced (1-inch) watermelon

½ cup Japanese bread crumbs (panko)
½ cup shredded unsweetened coconut
1 tablespoon white sesame seeds
2 egg whites

Vegetable oil for deep-frying
Cornstarch for dusting
8 to 10 uncooked large shrimp, shelled, tails left intact, and deveined
¼ teaspoon salt
⅓ cup chopped macadamia nuts

* * *

1. Place the scallops in a small bowl, sprinkle with the cornstarch, and stir until the scallops are evenly coated. Set aside.

2. Make the dressing: Stir the mayonnaise, rice vinegar, honey, wasabi, sesame oil, and salt together in a small bowl until well blended. Refrigerate.

3. Bring a small pan of water to a boil. Slip the scallops into the water and simmer until opaque, about 2 minutes. Drain and chill until ready to assemble the salad.

4. Toss the melon cubes together in a bowl. Cover and refrigerate until ready to serve.

5. Stir the bread crumbs, coconut, and sesame seeds together in a wide shallow bowl. Whisk the egg whites in a separate bowl until frothy.

6. Pour enough oil into a 2-quart saucepan to come to a depth of 3 inches. Heat over medium heat to 350°F. While the oil is heating, coat the shrimp: Dip a shrimp in the cornstarch to coat it lightly, and tap off the excess. Holding the shrimp by the tail, dip it in the egg white so it covers the meat but not the tail, then let the excess egg white drip back into the bowl. Coat the shrimp on both sides with the crumb mixture, patting lightly to help the crumbs adhere. Repeat with the remaining shrimp and coating. Set on a plate.

7. Deep-fry the shrimp in two batches until the coating is golden brown, 2 to 3 minutes. Remove with a slotted spoon and drain on paper towels. Sprinkle evenly with the salt.

8. To serve, pour the dressing over the melon and toss to coat. Mound the fruit on a serving plate and surround with the scallops and shrimp and sprinkle with macadamia nuts.

SPICY-COOL SHRIMP AND SQUID SALAD

Serves 4 as part of a multicourse meal

Macau, a Portuguese colony for four hundred years, until 1999, has a unique culture and an equally unique cuisine. Many dishes combine Chinese and Portuguese ingredients. At Litoral, a Macanese restaurant, ingredients unfamiliar in Chinese cooking, like mint and raw onions, are used. Don't overcook the squid, or you will be chewing on rubber!

FOR THE DRESSING
1 tablespoon fresh lemon juice
2 teaspoons fish sauce
1 teaspoon vegetable oil
1 teaspoon minced mint
1 teaspoon minced garlic
1 teaspoon chili oil or Tabasco
½ teaspoon minced cilantro
½ teaspoon minced red or green jalapeño chili
¼ teaspoon sesame oil

¼ pound uncooked medium shrimp, shelled,
    tails left intact, and deveined
¼ pound cleaned squid (see page 189),
    cut into ½-inch rings

¼ cup sliced pitted black olives
¼ cup diced yellow onion
¼ cup diced English cucumber

1 cup shredded iceberg lettuce
Thin half-moon slices cucumber
Cilantro sprigs

1. Make the dressing: Stir the lemon juice, fish sauce, vegetable oil, mint, garlic, chili oil, cilantro, jalapeño, and sesame oil together in a medium bowl until blended.

2. Bring a large saucepan of water to a boil. Add the shrimp and cook until pink and opaque in the center, about 2 minutes. With a slotted spoon, transfer the shrimp to a bowl. Set aside. Return the water to a boil, add the squid rings, and cook just until opaque, about 1 minute. Drain and set aside in another bowl.

3. Divide the dressing, olives, onion, and cucumber equally between both seafood bowls. Toss well.

4. Spread the lettuce out in an even layer on a serving platter. Top one side with the squid mixture and the other side with the shrimp mixture. Garnish with the cucumber slices and cilantro sprigs.

NEW CLASSIC CHINESE CHICKEN SALAD

Serves 4 as part of a multicourse meal

A Chinese-American classic served in different versions in Chinese restaurants around the world. Here's one with an appealing salad dressing. Extra crunch comes from the fried wonton strips and bean thread noodles.

2 skinless, boneless chicken breast halves
    (about ½ pound)
½ teaspoon salt
¼ teaspoon Chinese five-spice powder

FOR THE DRESSING
¼ cup rice vinegar
2½ tablespoons honey or sugar
2 tablespoons plum sauce
1 tablespoon sesame oil
1 tablespoon Dijon mustard
2 teaspoons soy sauce
1 teaspoon chili garlic sauce or chili sauce
½ teaspoon grated ginger
½ cup vegetable oil

½ head iceberg lettuce, thinly shredded
½ cup loosely packed cilantro leaves,
    roughly chopped
2 green onions, trimmed and thinly sliced
    on the bias

Vegetable oil for deep-frying
10 wonton wrappers, cut into ¼-inch-wide
    strips
1 ounce dried bean thread noodles

¼ cup chopped roasted peanuts
1 tablespoon toasted white sesame seeds

* * *

1. Preheat the oven to 350°F.

2. Rub the chicken breasts with the salt and five-spice powder. Lay the chicken on a baking sheet and bake until cooked through, about 20 minutes. Cool the chicken on a rack until cool enough to touch, then shred the meat, cover with plastic wrap, and refrigerate.

3. Make the dressing: Combine the rice vinegar, honey, plum sauce, sesame oil, mustard, soy sauce, chili sauce, and ginger in a blender and blend on medium speed until well blended. With the motor running, pour in the vegetable oil in a slow, steady stream and blend until the dressing is smooth and emulsified. Refrigerate until needed.

4. Toss the lettuce, cilantro, and green onions together in a large salad bowl. Cover and refrigerate.

5. Pour enough oil into a wok to come to a depth of 3 inches. Heat over medium-high heat to 350°F. Carefully slip a few of the wonton strips into the oil and fry until light golden brown, 15 to 20 seconds. Remove with a slotted spoon and drain on paper towels. Repeat with the remaining wonton strips.

6. Increase the heat under the wok slightly and heat until the oil reaches 375°F. Deep-fry the bean thread noodles, stirring them gently to separate the strands, until they puff and expand, 5 to 10 seconds. Remove and drain on paper towels.

7. Scatter the chicken over the lettuce mixture, pour the dressing over the salad, and toss together. Scatter the wonton strips, chopped peanuts, and sesame seeds over the top, then scatter the fried bean thread noodles over all.

LUCKY DUCK MELON SALAD

Serves 4 as part of a multicourse meal

Most Chinese restaurants have only chicken salad on the menu. Here's a nice addition to your salad selection. Savory roast duck, fresh fruit, and a simple dressing give you an amazing combination.

Vegetable oil for deep-frying
20 wonton wrappers, cut into ¼-inch-wide
    strips

FOR THE DRESSING
2 tablespoons rice vinegar
2 tablespoons chunky peanut butter
1 tablespoon soy sauce
2 teaspoons sesame oil
2 teaspoons sugar

1 cup Roast Duck meat (page 239),
    cut into ¼-inch strips, with skin
3 green onions, trimmed and cut into thin strips
1 small jicama (about ¾ pound), peeled
    and cut into ¼-inch-thick strips
    about 2 inches long
½ English cucumber, cut into
    ¼-inch-thick strips about 2 inches long
½ honeydew melon, rind and
    seeds removed, cut into ¼-inch-thick
    strips about 2 inches long
½ cantaloupe, seeded, rind removed, and cut
    into ¼-inch-thick strips about 2 inches long

1 lime, cut into wedges
½ cup Glazed Walnuts (page 177)
¼ cup chopped cilantro

*   *   *

1. Pour enough oil into a wok to come to a depth of 2 inches. Heat to 300°F over medium-high heat. Fry the wonton strips, in small batches, until golden brown, 20 to 30 seconds. Scoop the wonton strips from the oil with a slotted spoon or wire skimmer and drain on paper towels.

2. Make the dressing: Stir the rice vinegar, peanut butter, soy sauce, sesame oil, and sugar together in a small bowl until smooth.

3. Mound the duck in the center of a large platter and surround it with the vegetables and melons. Squeeze the lime wedges over the salad and drizzle the dressing over all the ingredients. Scatter the wonton strips, glazed walnuts, and cilantro over the salad and bring to the table. Toss the salad and serve.

TOFU AND EGGS

Tofu is always available, so versatile and healthy that it is used in all courses, and it can be paired with an endless variety of ingredients. The recipes here feature tofu that has been steamed, deep-fried, stir-fried, stuffed, used as a filling, pureed, and braised.

And to think it all starts with a bean, or rather many beans. Soybeans are pureed with water, then strained through a fine-mesh strainer. The resulting liquid is then coagulated with either a mined mineral called gypsum, which gives the tofu a slight smoky flavor, or nigari, an ocean derivative, which yields a slightly sweeter tofu. The amount of coagulant used determines the tofu's final consistency, soft, medium, firm, or extra-firm. The tofu curd is then racked and pressed to remove excess water. The Chinese get hungrier looking at a field of soybeans than a meadow full of cattle grazing.

In China, eggs from chickens, ducks, geese, and quail are prepared in countless ways. The Chinese could give classic French chefs a run for their chickens with their claim of 101 ways to cook an egg. Eggs are steamed in custards, preserved, marbleized, stir-fried, and hard-boiled so long they turn soft again. They are used in batters, coatings, and a mind-boggling array of baked and steamed goods. Discarded shells provide calcium to Chinese gardens. In fact, a good Chinese waiter will remind you if your meal is missing an egg dish for balance.

SA CHA TOFU WITH BROCCOLI AND CAULIFLOWER

Serves 4 as part of a multicourse meal

Sa cha sauce is another regional Chinese gem that doesn't get much publicity outside China. A blend of brill fish, shrimp, and spices, sa cha adds pungent complexity to a variety of dishes, such as hot pots and noodle salads. It is sold in jars along with the other condiments in Asian grocery stores. Just one tablespoon of the sauce gives this dish quite a kick . . . a little goes a long way!

2 tablespoons dried shrimp (optional)

FOR THE SAUCE
1 tablespoon sa cha sauce
1 tablespoon soy sauce
1 teaspoon Chinese rice wine or dry sherry
1 teaspoon sugar
$\frac{1}{2}$ teaspoon salt

1 cup broccoli florets
1 cup cauliflower florets
1 teaspoon minced garlic
$\frac{1}{3}$ cup water
One 14-ounce package firm or regular tofu, drained and cut into $\frac{1}{2}$-inch cubes

1. If using the shrimp, pour enough warm water over them in a small bowl to cover completely. Soak until soft, about 20 minutes. Drain the shrimp and coarsely chop them.

2. Prepare the sauce: Stir the sa cha sauce, soy sauce, rice wine, sugar, and salt together in a medium bowl until the sugar is dissolved.

3. Heat a wok over high heat until hot. Add the broccoli, cauliflower, garlic, and water, cover the wok, and steam until the vegetables are tender, 2 to 3 minutes. Add the sauce, tofu, and chopped shrimp, if using. Cook until the tofu is heated through, about 1 minute. Scoop onto a serving platter and serve immediately.

SOFT TOFU WITH MUSHROOMS AND BLACK VINEGAR SAUCE

Serves 4 as part of a multicourse meal

Another interesting dish from Chef Neil Perry of Rockpool restaurant in Sydney. You won't find this dish on many restaurant menus in the world, so if you can't eat it in the land down under, make it in your own kitchen. Use any combination of mushrooms, but I like the texture and flavors of the shiitake and oyster mushrooms together with the tangy sauce. Serve with steamed rice to capture all the great sauce.

FOR THE SAUCE

2 tablespoons Chinese black vinegar or
    balsamic vinegar

2 tablespoons soy sauce

1 tablespoon sugar

1/2 teaspoon dried red chili flakes

2 teaspoons vegetable oil

1 teaspoon minced garlic

5 fresh shiitake, stems discarded and
    caps thinly sliced

5 oyster mushrooms, tough ends trimmed

3/4 cup Chicken Stock (page 69) or canned
    chicken broth

One 14-ounce package soft tofu, drained and
    cut into 1/2-inch cubes

2 teaspoons cornstarch, dissolved in
    1 tablespoon water

1 green onion, trimmed and minced

1. Prepare the sauce: Stir the black vinegar, soy sauce, sugar, and chili flakes together in a small bowl until well blended.

2. Heat a wok over high heat until hot. Add the oil and swirl to coat the sides. Add the garlic and stir-fry until fragrant, about 10 seconds. Add the mushrooms, stirring constantly, and cook for about 30 seconds. Pour in the chicken stock, cover the wok, and cook until the mushrooms are tender, about 2 minutes.

3. Slide the tofu gently into the wok, cover, and cook until the tofu is heated through, about 2 minutes. Pour in the sauce and bring to a boil, then stir in the dissolved cornstarch. Stir gently until the sauce boils and thickens, about 1 minute. Scoop onto a warm serving platter, sprinkle with the green onion, and serve hot.

TOFU PUFFS WITH LONG BEANS AND MUSHROOMS

Serves 4 as part of a multicourse meal

Sam Choy of Honolulu, Hawaii, made me this simple, intensely flavored stir-fry. What a great balance of tastes and textures! He used tofu puffs (a.k.a. fried tofu). But, if you can't find them in Asian markets, simply cut firm tofu into ¾-inch cubes, dust them with cornstarch, and deep-fry until crispy and light golden brown. To keep it all in the soy family, use soybean sprouts for bean sprouts; they have a great firm texture and nutty flavor.

FOR THE SAUCE

½ cup Vegetable Stock (page 105) or
    canned vegetable broth

1 tablespoon soy sauce

2 teaspoons Chinese black vinegar or
    balsamic vinegar

2 teaspoons oyster-flavored sauce

1 teaspoon sugar

⅛ teaspoon ground white pepper

2 tablespoons vegetable oil

1 teaspoon minced ginger

2 ounces Chinese long beans, cut into
    2-inch lengths

4 fresh shiitake, stems discarded and caps
    quartered

2 tablespoons bamboo shoots cut into thin strips

2 cups tofu puffs, cut in half

2 cups bean sprouts

½ teaspoon sesame oil

2 teaspoons mashed and crumbled fermented
    bean curd (optional)

1. Prepare the sauce: Stir the vegetable stock, soy sauce, black vinegar, oyster-flavored sauce, sugar, and pepper together in a small bowl until the sugar is dissolved.

2. Heat a wok over high heat until hot. Add the vegetable oil and swirl to coat the sides. Add the ginger and cook, stirring, until fragrant, about 20 seconds. Add the beans, shiitake, and bamboo shoots and stir-fry for 1 minute. Pour in the sauce, then stir in the tofu puffs. Adjust the heat so the sauce is simmering, cover the wok, and simmer until the beans are tender, 5 to 6 minutes.

3. Stir in the bean sprouts and cook, uncovered, for 1 minute. Stir in the sesame oil, then scoop onto a warm serving platter. Serve with the fermented bean curd sprinkled over the top, if you like.

EIGHT-FLAVOR BEAN CURD

Serves 4 as part of a multicourse meal

Chinese consider the number eight to be lucky because it sounds like the word for prosperity. Here, eight refers to the number of vegetables, or treasures, combined with bean curd. You can find pressed tofu that has been flavored or is just plain. Try using the teriyaki-flavored version if available. If you can't find either, use the always available firm or extra-firm tofu.

FOR THE SAUCE

2 tablespoons hoisin sauce

1 tablespoon soy sauce

1 tablespoon hot bean paste

2 teaspoons sesame oil

2 teaspoons Chinese black vinegar or
   balsamic vinegar

2 teaspoons vegetable oil

½ cup ½-inch length green beans

¼ cup water chestnuts, quartered

¼ cup diced zucchini or Chinese okra

¼ cup diced carrot

3 button mushrooms, stems trimmed and
   quartered

¼ cup diced bamboo shoots

4 cakes pressed tofu (about 8 ounces), cut into
   ¼-inch cubes

1 teaspoon cornstarch, dissolved in
   2 teaspoons water

¼ cup roasted peanuts

1. Prepare the sauce: Stir the hoisin sauce, soy sauce, hot bean paste, sesame oil, and black vinegar together in a small bowl.

2. Heat a wok over high heat until hot. Pour in the oil and swirl to coat the sides. Add the green beans, water chestnuts, zucchini, carrot, mushrooms, and bamboo shoots. Stir-fry until the carrots are tender-crisp, 2 to 3 minutes.

3. Add the pressed tofu and sauce and cook until heated through, about 2 minutes. Pour in the dissolved cornstarch and cook, stirring, until the sauce boils and thickens, about 30 seconds. Transfer to a serving platter, sprinkle with the peanuts, and serve immediately.

TRIPLE-DECKER EGG FU YOUNG

Serves 4 as part of a multicourse meal

Egg fu young was made by some of the first Chinese immigrants to San Francisco's Chinatown. Using local ingredients, like onions and mushrooms, it became a popular dish, but through the years, most versions served in restaurants have become mediocre at best. Ideally, the eggs should be moist and fluffy.

FOR THE SAUCE

½ cup water
1½ tablespoons oyster-flavored sauce
1 tablespoon soy sauce
1 teaspoon honey
1 teaspoon Chinese rice wine or dry sherry
1 teaspoon cornstarch

8 eggs, lightly beaten
¼ cup water
⅛ teaspoon Chinese five-spice powder
4 green onions, trimmed and thinly sliced
¾ cup bean sprouts
1 teaspoon minced garlic

1 tablespoon vegetable oil

¼ pound Char Siu (page 259), chopped
    (generous ¾ cup)

❋   ❋   ❋

1. Prepare the sauce: Stir the water, oyster-flavored sauce, soy sauce, honey, rice wine, and cornstarch together in a small saucepan. Set aside.

2. In a large bowl, beat the eggs, water, and five-spice powder until well blended. Set aside a small amount of the green onions for topping the omelet, then stir the remaining green onions, bean sprouts, and garlic into the eggs.

3. Heat an 8- or 9-inch nonstick frying pan over medium heat until hot. Pour in 1 teaspoon of the oil and swirl to coat the bottom. When it is hot, add one-third of the egg mixture (about ⅔ cup) to the pan. Cook, without stirring, until the edges begin to set, about 1½ minutes. Carefully turn and cook the other side until lightly browned. Slide the omelet onto a warm plate and cover with foil, shiny side down, to keep warm. Repeat with the remaining egg mixture, adding more oil to the pan as needed, to make a total of 3 omelets.

4. Heat the sauce, stirring, over medium-high heat, until it boils and thickens.

5. Place one omelet on a serving platter. Set aside about 3 tablespoons of the chopped char siu and scatter half of the remaining char siu over the omelet. Top with another omelet and the second half of the char siu. Top with the third omelet. Drizzle the warm sauce over the omelets and sprinkle the reserved char siu and green onions over the top. Cut into wedges. Serve immediately.

HIDDEN-TREASURE OMELET

Serves 4 as part of a multicourse meal

All the hidden treasures enclosed in this thin Chinese-style omelet will please your family. Omelets are popular in Chinese cuisine, especially for lunch and dinner. Use a variety of mushrooms—take a trip to a specialty grocery and check out all the different varieties: lobster, shiitake, enoki, and oyster, to name just a few.

FOR THE SAUCE

2 tablespoons soy sauce

2 tablespoons oyster-flavored sauce

1 tablespoon water

1 teaspoon chili garlic sauce

3 medium portobello mushrooms

6 eggs, lightly beaten

¼ cup water

2 teaspoons vegetable oil, plus more as needed

3 green onions, trimmed and cut into
    2-inch lengths

2 teaspoons minced ginger

1 teaspoon minced garlic

5 oyster mushrooms

5 fresh shiitake, stems removed and
    caps thinly sliced

6 button mushrooms, trimmed and thinly sliced

¾ cup bean sprouts

5 snow peas, trimmed and thinly sliced

¼ cup pine nuts

1 tablespoon soy sauce

1 tablespoon oyster-flavored sauce

1. Prepare the sauce: Stir the soy sauce, oyster-flavored sauce, water, and chili garlic sauce together in a saucepan. Set aside.

2. Remove and discard the stems from the portobello mushrooms. Scrape the dark gills from the underside of the caps with a teaspoon. Thinly slice the caps.

3. Whisk the eggs and water together in a bowl.

4. Heat a 7- or 8-inch nonstick skillet over medium-high heat until hot. Add 1 teaspoon of the oil and swirl to coat the bottom of the pan. Pour about ⅓ cup of the egg mixture into the pan, tilting the pan so the egg coats the bottom, and cook until the bottom of the omelet is set, about 1 minute. Turn the omelet and cook until the second side is lightly browned, about 1 minute. Slide the omelet onto a warm plate and cover with aluminum foil, shiny side down, to keep warm. Repeat with the remaining egg mixture, adding oil to the skillet as needed, to make 4 omelets.

5. Heat the sauce over medium heat until hot, about 3 minutes. Set aside, covered, to keep warm.

6. Heat a wok over high heat until hot. Add the remaining 1 teaspoon oil and swirl to coat the sides. Add the green onions, ginger, garlic, and all the mushrooms and stir-fry until the mushrooms are tender, about 2½ minutes. Add the bean sprouts, snow peas, pine nuts, soy sauce, and oyster-flavored sauce and cook until the snow peas are tender, 1 to 1½ minutes.

7. To serve, spoon one-quarter of the mushroom mixture onto the upper right quarter of one of the omelets. Fold the bottom of the omelet over the top then fold the left side over the right side to make a triangle that encloses the filling. Repeat with the remaining omelets and filling. Arrange the stuffed omelets on a serving platter and spoon the sauce over them. Serve immediately.

HONOLULU

MARTIN AND SAM CHOY

WEDDING CAKES ARE STAMPED WITH THE CHINESE CHARACTERS FOR "DOUBLE HAPPINESS."

Some Chinatowns have to import their atmosphere, with boxcar loads of paper lanterns. Not Nu'uanu, as the locals call Honolulu's Chinatown. Tropical fruits and flowers front tiny groceries in narrow alleys, and the old-time lunch counters seem to be straight out of the movie *Pearl Harbor*. Far from the beaches of Waikiki, this place is about as "inner city" as Hawaii gets. And even more historic. The first ship carrying Chinese workers for Hawaiian plantations arrived in 1789—the year George Washington became president! And this enclave began soon after—looking after the needs of many from the Jung San region of South China, where Sun Yat-sen also came from. I was amazed to hear the Jung San dialect even today. ❋ But something new is brewing in this oldest Pacific melting pot. It's not just the trendy art galleries and clubs that now take best advantage of the old architecture. With Japanese, Filipino, Vietnamese, Thai, Korean, and native islanders working together in the sunshine, it was only a matter of time before true fusion food was born. And three of my dear friends—Sam Choy, Alan Wong, and Glenn Chu—were among the pioneers of so-called pan-Asian cooking. They've applied their Chinese love of food and family to Hawaii's amazing mix of ingredients. ❋ Just like the pineapple, the sweet fruit of so many generations has grown into a totally new kind of cuisine, full of startling, happy combinations for the world to try. So put on your lei, pick up your chopsticks, and join the con-"fusion."

ALAN WONG'S RESTAURANT

1857 South King Street, Third Floor

(808) 949-2526

What to order: *braised Chinatown duck risotto; ginger-crusted onaga; Manapua-style quesadilla; duck nachos*

HONG KONG NOODLE HOUSE

100 North Beretania Street, #172

(808) 536-5409

What to order: *Hong Kong—style wonton noodles; tossed noodles with roast duck; tossed noodles with beef*

INDIGO RESTAURANT

1121 Nu'uanu Avenue

(808) 521-2900

What to order: *Chinese gin doi; tempura ahi roll; goat cheese wontons with four-fruit sauce*

LEGEND SEAFOOD RESTAURANT

100 North Beretania Street, #108

(808) 532-1868

What to order: *spinach and scallop dumplings; tofu and shrimp seaweed rolls; egg white custard*

SAM CHOY'S DIAMOND HEAD RESTAURANT

580 North Nimitz Highway

(808) 732-8645

What to order: *beef or pork lu'au stew; tofu puffs stir-fried with mushrooms and bean spouts; steamed whole fish over sweet-and-sour fruit sauce*

SHUNG CHONG YUEIN CHINESE CAKE SHOP

1027 Maunakea Street

(808) 531-1983

What to order: *wedding cake; chicken mushroom buns; macadamia nut candy*

WO FAT SEAFOOD RESTAURANT

115 North Hotel Street

(808) 521-5055

What to order: *braised oysters with ginger and scallions; deep-fried shrimp balls; stuffed taro with scallops*

IT TAKES TEAMWORK TO MAKE FRESH RICE NOODLES, SPREAD THIN TO SET.

AT THE SHUNG CHONG YUEIN CHINESE CAKE SHOP

MA PO BEAN CURD

Serves 4 as part of a multicourse meal

Walk into a Chinese restaurant, and this popular Sichuanese dish will be on the menu. As the legend goes, a peasant woman, only able to afford tofu and vegetables, created the deep-fried tofu dish and sold it on the street. It was later dubbed "Ma Po," which literally means "pockmarked grandmother." A favorite among native Chinese, it has traveled the world with Chinese immigrants. Many like the contrast of textures in the silky creaminess of the tofu and the slight crunchiness of the water chestnuts. If you can't find Sichuan peppercorns, add a pinch of Chinese five-spice powder in its place. Handle soft tofu gently; it is very delicate and will break easily. If you cannot locate hot bean paste, substitute chili garlic sauce.

3 dried black mushrooms

FOR THE MARINADE
6 ounces ground pork
1 teaspoon soy sauce
2 teaspoons cornstarch

FOR THE SAUCE
1 cup water
2 tablespoons soy sauce
$\frac{1}{2}$ teaspoon sesame oil

1 tablespoon vegetable oil
1 teaspoon minced garlic
1 teaspoon hot bean paste or chili garlic sauce
$\frac{1}{4}$ teaspoon toasted Sichuan peppercorns, ground

$\frac{1}{4}$ cup chopped water chestnuts
2 green onions, trimmed and cut into $\frac{1}{2}$-inch pieces
One 14-ounce package soft tofu, drained and cut into $\frac{1}{2}$-inch cubes
2 teaspoons cornstarch, dissolved in 1 tablespoon water

1. Pour enough warm water over the mushrooms in a small bowl to cover them completely. Soak until softened, about 20 minutes. Drain. Discard the stems and coarsely chop the caps.

2. Marinate the pork: Stir the ground pork, soy sauce, and cornstarch together until evenly mixed. Let stand 10 minutes.

3. Prepare the sauce: Stir the water, soy sauce, and sesame oil together in a small bowl.

4. Heat a wok over high heat until hot. Add the oil and swirl to coat the sides. Add the garlic and stir-fry until fragrant, about 20 seconds. Add the pork, hot bean paste, and Sichuan peppercorns and stir-fry until the pork is crumbly, 2 to 3 minutes.

5. Pour the sauce into the wok, then stir in the water chestnuts and green onions. Slide the tofu into the wok and stir gently (or simply swirl the wok) to coat the tofu with the sauce and heat through, about 2 minutes.

6. Pour in the dissolved cornstarch and cook gently, stirring, until the sauce boils and thickens, about 1 minute. Spoon the tofu and sauce onto a serving platter and serve hot.

TRIPLE-EGG CUSTARD WITH MINCED PORK

Serves 4 as part of a multicourse meal

Meat or seafood is often added to egg custards. At the New Loon Fung Chinese Restaurant in London, three types of eggs are used. Salted duck eggs are found in Asian markets. Remove them from the bag, rinse them free of salt, and remove the yolk to use it.

4 ounces boneless pork, minced

One 1,000-year-old egg, coarsely chopped

1 salted duck egg, yolk only (discard the white), smashed with a cleaver

3 large eggs

1½ cups water

¼ teaspoon salt

⅛ teaspoon ground white pepper

2 tablespoons soy sauce

2 tablespoons finely chopped green onions

1 teaspoon sesame oil

1. Scatter the pork, 1,000-year egg, and duck egg yolk over the bottom of a glass pie dish.

2. Beat the eggs lightly in a medium bowl. Add the water, salt, and pepper and stir just to blend (the custard should not be foamy). Pour the custard over the ingredients in the pie dish.

3. Prepare a wok for steaming according to the directions on page xxvi. Set the pie dish in the steamer basket, cover the wok, and steam over low heat until a knife inserted into the center of the custard comes out clean, 10 to 15 minutes.

4. Stir the soy sauce, green onions, and sesame oil together in a small bowl. Spoon the dressing over the custard and serve directly from the dish.

VEGETARIAN "FAUX" FISH

Serves 4 as part of a multicourse meal

Vegetarian Paradise 3 in New York City has some dishes that could fool you into thinking that you're eating meat. "Vegetarian fish" can be found already made in some health food stores or specialty stores, but that takes the fun out of the kitchen. Most of the ingredients are easily found in your local supermarket; you'll find the bean curd sheets in Asian markets.

FOR THE FILLING
One 14-ounce package firm or medium tofu, drained
1 tablespoon vegetable oil
1 tablespoon minced garlic
4 water chestnuts, finely diced
1/3 cup chopped walnuts
2 tablespoons cornstarch
2 teaspoons vegetarian oyster-flavored sauce
1 teaspoon sesame oil
1 teaspoon toasted white sesame seeds
1/4 teaspoon salt

FOR THE SEASONINGS
1/3 cup water
2 tablespoons soy sauce
1 tablespoon dark soy sauce
1 tablespoon Chinese black vinegar or balsamic vinegar
1 tablespoon vegetarian oyster-flavored sauce
2 teaspoons sugar

2 large round bean curd sheets
2 sheets nori
1 tablespoon flour, dissolved in 1 tablespoon water
1/4 teaspoon salt

1 tablespoon vegetable oil
4 to 6 fresh shiitake, stems discarded and caps thinly sliced
1/4 cup thin carrot strips
1/4 cup thinly sliced snow peas
1/3 cup thinly sliced bamboo shoots
1 green onion, trimmed and cut into 2-inch lengths
2 teaspoons cornstarch, dissolved in 1 tablespoon water

✳   ✳   ✳

1. Make the filling: Mash the tofu and place it in a clean kitchen towel. Gather the towel around the tofu and squeeze firmly to remove the excess liquid from the tofu.

2. Heat a wok over high heat until hot. Add the vegetable oil and swirl to coat the sides. Add the garlic and cook, stirring, until fragrant, about 10 seconds. Add the tofu, water chestnuts, walnuts, cornstarch, oyster-flavored sauce, sesame oil, sesame seeds, and salt and cook, stirring, until the flavors are blended and the mixture is lightly thickened, about 2 minutes. Remove and let cool to room temperature.

3. Prepare the seasonings: Stir the water, soy sauces, black vinegar, oyster-flavored sauce, and sugar together in a small bowl until the sugar is dissolved.

4. Rinse the bean curd sheets under cold water; drain. Cover with a damp kitchen towel to prevent them from drying out. Cut two approximately 12-inch squares from each bean curd sheet. Center one nori sheet over each square of bean curd sheet; the bean curd sheet will extend about 2 inches beyond each side of the nori. Divide the filling between the two sheets, molding each batch of filling into a fish shape about as wide as the nori sheet. Starting at the bottom, roll the filling up in the bean curd and nori sheets, maintaining the shape of the fish as you do. Moisten the top edge of the bean curd sheet with some of the flour paste and press lightly to seal. Tuck the part of the bean curd sheet that extends from the head of the fish underneath the fish. Make a tail at the other end of the fish by scoring the bean curd with a knife. Repeat with the remaining sheets and filling. Sprinkle the "fish" with the salt.

5. Heat a medium skillet over high heat until hot. Add the vegetable oil and swirl to coat the bottom. Slip the bean curd fish into the pan and pan-fry, turning once, until golden brown, about 2 minutes per side. Repeat with the remaining fish.

6. Transfer the fish to a cutting board. Add the shiitake and carrot to the skillet and cook, stirring, for 2 minutes. Add the snow peas, bamboo shoots, and green onion. Cook, stirring, for 1 minute. Pour the seasonings into the skillet and bring to a boil. Pour in the dissolved cornstarch and cook until the sauce boils and thickens, 30 seconds to 1 minute. Pour the sauce onto a serving plate.

7. Cut the tofu fish into 1-inch slices with a sharp knife and carefully reassemble them on the sauce, so they retain their shape.

COMFORT-FOOD FISH CUSTARD

Serves 4 as part of a multicourse meal

This dish is a wonderful quick meal in many Asian homes. It's true comfort food. The Supper Inn Café in Melbourne adds Chinese twisted doughnuts to this popular late-night dish. I like to slice the doughnuts into ½-inch slices and fry until golden brown, then sprinkle on top once the custard is steamed. Quite a combination of textures.

5 large eggs

1¼ cups Chicken Stock (page 69) or canned chicken broth

2 teaspoons minced ginger

½ teaspoon salt

⅛ teaspoon ground white pepper

¼ pound firm-fleshed white fish fillets, such as sea bass, halibut, or catfish, thinly sliced

Vegetable oil for deep-frying

½ cup thinly sliced Chinese Twisted Doughnuts (page 28; optional)

1 tablespoon soy sauce

½ teaspoon sesame oil

1 green onion, trimmed and thinly sliced

* * *

1. Beat the eggs, chicken stock, ginger, salt, and pepper together lightly in a large bowl until combined. Fold in the sliced fish fillets. Pour the mixture into a 9-inch glass pie dish.

2. Pour enough oil into a 2-quart saucepan to a depth of 3 inches and heat it to 350°F. Fry the doughnut slices until crisp and golden brown, 2½ to 3 minutes. Remove the doughnuts with a slotted spoon and drain on paper towels.

3. Prepare a wok for steaming according to the directions on page xxvi. Set the pie plate in the wok, cover, and steam over medium heat until the custard jiggles only slightly in the center when the dish is shaken gently, 12 to 15 minutes.

4. Stir the soy sauce and sesame oil together in a small bowl and drizzle over the steamed custard. Scatter the green onion and doughnut slices over the custard and serve directly from the dish.

HAKKA-STYLE STUFFED TOFU

Serves 4 as part of a multicourse meal

Hakka cuisine, a kind of Cantonese cuisine, is known for its many stuffed dishes. Pieces of tofu are filled with minced pork and shrimp, lightly dusted with cornstarch, and then fried.

2 dried black mushrooms

FOR THE SAUCE
**1 cup Chicken Stock (page 69) or
     canned chicken broth
2 tablespoons oyster-flavored sauce
1 tablespoon soy sauce
1 teaspoon chili garlic sauce**

FOR THE STUFFING
**2 ounces ground pork
2 ounces uncooked medium shrimp, shelled,
     deveined, and minced
2 tablespoons minced water chestnuts
1 egg white
1 teaspoon minced cilantro
1 teaspoon sesame oil
1/2 teaspoon salt
1/8 teaspoon ground white pepper**

**One 14-ounce package firm or regular tofu,
     drained
Cornstarch for dusting**

Vegetable oil for deep-frying

**1/4 cup thinly sliced bamboo shoots
1/4 cup thinly sliced green onions
1/4 cup thinly sliced carrot**

*   *   *

1. Pour enough warm water over the mushrooms in a small bowl to cover them completely. Soak until softened, about 20 minutes. Drain. Discard the stems and cut the caps into thin strips.

2. Prepare the sauce: Stir the chicken stock, oyster-flavored sauce, soy sauce, and chili garlic sauce together in a small bowl until well blended.

3. Make the stuffing: Stir the ground pork, shrimp, water chestnuts, egg white, cilantro, sesame oil, salt, and pepper together in a medium bowl until well blended.

4. Cut the tofu horizontally in half to make 2 pieces each about 3/4 inch thick. Cut each piece into quarters. Using a spoon, hollow out the center of each tofu rectangle to make a little box. Pat the tofu boxes dry and dust them with cornstarch to coat them lightly. Fill each with about 1 tablespoon of the stuffing, mounding it slightly. Dust each piece of stuffed tofu with additional cornstarch to coat them lightly.

5. Pour enough oil into a 2-quart saucepan to come to a depth of 3 inches. Heat the oil over medium-high heat to 350°F. Deep-fry the stuffed tofu, a few pieces at a time, until the tofu is golden brown and the filling is cooked through, 5 to 6 minutes. Remove with a slotted spoon and drain on paper towels. Reserve the oil.

6. Heat a wok over high heat until hot. Add 1 tablespoon of the reserved oil and swirl to coat the sides. Add the black mushrooms, bamboo shoots, green onions, and carrot and stir-fry until the carrot is tender-crisp, about 2 minutes. Add the sauce and bring to a simmer. Slip the fried tofu into the sauce and stir gently to coat. Transfer the tofu to a serving platter, stuffing side up, with the sauce, and serve hot.

HAKKA CUISINE: FOOD THAT TRAVELS

The Hakka make simple, hearty food that travels well or can be easily cooked while traveling, like stuffed tofu and vegetables. Descendants of Han Chinese (the majority ethnic group in China), Hakka are one of the most researched and documented ethnic groups in China's 5,000-year written history. The Hakka migrated south in waves, beginning in the third century A.D., from the central plains of China to the provinces of Fujian and Guangdong, and became known as a very migrant group. They were dubbed "Hakka" by Cantonese already living in Guangdong—"ha" means guest and "ka" means group of people. And, the first time "Hakka" appeared in print was in 1808, when author Xu Xuzeng referred to himself and his people as Hakka. ✳ In the late 1600s some Hakka were forced to move for political reasons by the Qing (Manchu) government, from their coastal lands in Fujian, 500 miles to the southwest. After a few more moves, in search of resources and fertile land, and a couple of civil wars later, many Hakka ended up in Mei Xian village in eastern Guangdong, while others moved to Hong Kong and Taiwan. Despite all their wanderings and having no centralized homeland, the Hakka have maintained nearly the same language, cultural practices, and solidarity as they had in the time of the Han dynasty (c. 206 B.C. to A.D. 220). ✳ From wheat noodles and cakes, millet, and grazing animals in the central plains to rice noodles, root cakes, and soybean products in the south, Hakka cuisine has evolved to incorporate the foods of wherever they live. Whatever the history of the Hakka people, and regardless of their origins, the Hakka are an irreplaceable part of the culinary, ethnic, and cultural fabric of Chinatowns throughout the world. With all the traveling I do, I could almost call myself a Hakka.

CLAY POT BEAN CURD

Serves 4 as part of a multicourse meal

Clay pot cooking is centuries old. Clay pots are porous and efficient at conducting and holding heat. These properties not only aid in the development of flavors but also impart a taste that can be achieved only with clay pots. If you want to save time, use packaged tofu puffs, or fried tofu. And, so I don't have to sacrifice flavor for quickness, I use both the hot and fast wok and the low and slow clay pot. (If you don't have a clay pot, just keep the ingredients in the wok; cover and braise until the vegetables are tender.)

4 dried black mushrooms

FOR THE SAUCE
½ cup Vegetable Stock (page 105) or canned vegetable broth
2 tablespoons oyster-flavored sauce
1 teaspoon sugar
¼ teaspoon ground white pepper

Vegetable oil for deep-frying
One 14-ounce package firm or regular tofu, drained and cut into 1-inch cubes

5 quarter-sized slices peeled ginger
2 shallots, quartered
1 leek, white part only, halved lengthwise, rinsed well, and cut into 2-inch lengths
1 carrot, thinly sliced on the bias

*   *   *

1. Pour enough warm water over the mushrooms in a small bowl to cover them completely. Soak until softened, about 20 minutes. Drain. Discard the mushroom stems and cut the caps into quarters.

2. Prepare the sauce: Stir the vegetable stock, oyster-flavored sauce, sugar, and pepper together in a small bowl until the sugar is dissolved.

3. Pour enough oil into a 2-quart saucepan to come to a depth of 3 inches. Heat to 350°F over medium-high heat. Slip about one-third of the tofu into the oil and deep-fry until golden brown, 3 to 4 minutes. Remove the tofu with a slotted spoon and drain on paper towels. Repeat with the remaining tofu. Reserve the oil.

4. Heat a wok over high heat until hot. Add 1 tablespoon of the reserved oil and swirl to coat the sides. Add the ginger and shallots and cook, stirring, until fragrant, about 20 seconds. Add the mushrooms, leek, and carrot. Stir-fry for 1 minute.

5. Transfer the contents of the wok to a clay pot. (If you do not have a clay pot, leave the ingredients in the wok.) Pour in the sauce and stir in the tofu. Bring to a boil over medium heat, then adjust the heat so the sauce is simmering. Cover the pot and simmer until the vegetables are tender, about 8 minutes. Serve hot from the pot (or ladle the contents of the wok into a warm serving bowl).

SEAFOOD

This is the largest section of the book. Chinatowns really shine in their preparation of seafood, largely because many have sprung up in the port cities. On a daily basis, fishermen bring into port the best and freshest selections of seafood available. Chinese have such a love of freshness that in Chinatown you will see fish markets that resemble aquariums, with dozens of different fish still swimming. You pick the one you want and then it is cleaned while you wait. Now that is fresh! So many chefs shared their seafood dishes with me during my trips to various Chinatowns that I thought my lungs would turn into gills.

FAMILY-STYLE FISH
WITH BEAN SPROUTS

*Serves 4 as part of a
multicourse meal*

For my taste, simple everyday family dishes are every bit as good as banquet dishes—better in fact, since they are easier and less expensive to prepare. While I was dining at Soup Restaurant in Singapore (see page 147), I enjoyed this simple soup.

FOR THE MARINADE

2 teaspoons cornstarch

$^1\!/_2$ teaspoon salt

$^3\!/_4$ pound firm-fleshed white fish fillets, such as
    sea bass or halibut, cut into 1 × 2-inch slices
    about $^1\!/_4$ inch thick

FOR THE SAUCE

1 tablespoon fresh lemon juice

2 teaspoons oyster-flavored sauce

$^1\!/_8$ teaspoon ground white pepper

1 tablespoon vegetable oil

2 tablespoons finely shredded ginger

2 green onions, trimmed and cut into
    2-inch lengths

2 cups mung bean sprouts, root ends removed

$^1\!/_4$ cup thin strips red bell pepper

$^1\!/_4$ cup thinly sliced button mushrooms

Cilantro leaves

*　　*　　*

1. Marinate the fish: Stir the cornstarch and salt together in a medium bowl. Add the fish slices and toss gently to coat them evenly with the marinade. Let stand for 10 minutes.

2. Prepare the sauce: Stir the lemon juice, oyster-flavored sauce, and pepper together in a small bowl.

3. Heat a wok over medium heat until hot. Pour in the oil and swirl to coat the sides. Add the marinated fish and stir-fry gently until the fish is cooked through, 2 to 3 minutes. Scoop the fish out onto a plate and set aside.

4. Add the ginger, green onions, bean sprouts, bell pepper, and mushrooms to the wok and stir-fry until the bell peppers are tender-crisp, about 2 minutes. Pour the sauce into the wok and slide in the cooked fish. Continue cooking until the fish is heated through, about 1 minute.

5. Scoop the contents of the wok onto a serving platter and scatter the cilantro leaves over the top.

SINGAPORE'S RED-HATTED SAM SUI WOMEN

During the 1800s, a time when Chinese immigrants in Singapore were predominantly male, a small group of women from Sam Sui village near Guangzhou in southern China emigrated to Singapore. Sam Sui, whose name means "three-water," is located near the junction of three rivers. Characteristically independent, Sam Sui women often chose not to marry. In Sam Sui, these hard-working women farmed the land, while the men stayed home. In Singapore, where they were well respected, these small-framed Chinese women, recognizable by their red hats, worked as laborers, helped build the city, and played a pivotal role in the construction of Chinatown. ✳ In more recent years, after years of hard labor, four Sam Sui women decided to open a small restaurant in Chinatown. When they passed away, the Sam Sui community followed tradition and burned their belongings—including their recipes—so they could take them to the afterlife. As a result of this tradition of burning, little information about these women is available. However, about six years ago, one of the Sam Sui women's nephews decided to reconstruct the restaurant and develop the menu based on his memories in tribute to these amazing women. Soup Restaurant in Singapore's Chinatown carries on the Sam Sui culinary heritage.

DOUBLE-GINGER FISH

A stir-fry full of ginger flavors! I use fresh ginger, pickled ginger (Japanese-style), and, if you can find it, preserved red ginger. Different from pickled ginger, red ginger is cooked several different times in a dark red sugar syrup until all the syrup is absorbed by the ginger. Chef Kwan Lui developed this recipe at Singapore's Café At-Sunrice. One tip for you, make sure the lemongrass for this dish is chopped very, very fine or it will be too fibrous to enjoy.

FOR THE MARINADE

2 teaspoons cornstarch

½ teaspoon salt

¾ pound firm-fleshed white fish fillets, such as sea bass, halibut, or cod, cut into 1 × 2½-inch slices

FOR THE SAUCE

2 tablespoons Chinese rice wine or dry sherry

1 teaspoon fish sauce

1 tablespoon vegetable oil

1 teaspoon minced ginger

2 stalks lemongrass, bottom 6 inches only, minced

3 green onions, trimmed and cut into ½-inch lengths

1 tablespoon pickled ginger, chopped

1 tablespoon chopped preserved red ginger (optional)

1 small hot chili, such as jalapeño, seeded and minced

Cilantro sprigs (optional)

1. Marinate the fish: Stir the cornstarch and salt together in a bowl. Add the fish slices and toss gently to coat. Let stand for 10 minutes.

2. Prepare the sauce: Stir the rice wine and fish sauce together in a small bowl.

3. Heat a wok over high heat until hot. Add the oil and swirl to coat the sides. Add the minced ginger and lemongrass and stir-fry until fragrant, 30 seconds to 1 minute. Add the fish and gently stir-fry for 30 seconds. Add the green onions, pickled ginger, red ginger (if using), chili, and the sauce. Cook until the onions are tender and the fish is cooked through, 1 to 2 minutes.

4. Scoop the contents of the wok onto a serving platter and garnish with cilantro, if you like.

SHANGHAINESE WOK-SEARED FISH IN WINE SAUCE

Serves 4 as part of a multicourse meal

Shanghai is located close to the heart of Shaoxing, the rice wine–producing center of China. Naturally, many Shanghainese dishes use rice wine. The chefs at San Francisco's Old Shanghai Restaurant add a bit of fermented rice to enhance the flavor. Fermented rice is found in Asian grocery stores. Replace fermented rice with 2 teaspoons Chinese black vinegar or balsamic vinegar.

1 dried wood ear mushroom

FOR THE MARINADE
1 teaspoon Chinese rice wine or dry sherry
2 teaspoons cornstarch
¼ teaspoon salt
⅛ teaspoon ground white pepper

¾ pound firm-fleshed white fish fillets, such as halibut, sea bass, or grouper

FOR THE SEASONINGS
¼ cup Fish Stock (page 71) or dissolved seafood bouillon
¼ cup Chinese rice wine or dry sherry
1 tablespoon fermented rice
2 teaspoons sugar

Vegetable oil for shallow-frying

¼ cup carrots, thinly sliced on the bias
¼ cup sliced bamboo shoots
3 fresh shiitake, stems discarded and caps halved (optional)
4 thin slices peeled ginger
1 green onion, trimmed and cut into 1½-inch lengths

1. Pour enough water over the wood ear mushroom in a small bowl to cover. Soak until softened, about 20 minutes. Drain and cut into thin strips.

2. Marinate the fish: Stir the rice wine, cornstarch, salt, and pepper together in a medium bowl. Toss the fish gently in the marinade until coated. Let stand for 10 minutes.

3. Prepare the seasonings: Stir the fish stock, rice wine, fermented rice, and sugar together in a small bowl until the sugar is dissolved.

4. Heat a wok over high heat until hot. Pour in enough oil to come to a depth of ½ inch. When the oil is very hot, add the marinated fish and cook, turning once, just until the fish begins to flake, about 2 minutes per side. Remove the fish with a slotted spoon and drain on paper towels. Spoon off all but 1 tablespoon of the oil from the pan.

5. Return the wok to high heat and swirl oil to coat the sides. Add the wood ear mushroom, carrots, bamboo shoots, shiitake, ginger, and green onion and stir-fry until the carrots are tender-crisp, 2 to 2½ minutes. Pour in the seasonings and bring to a boil. Return the fish to the pan and cook, stirring so the fish does not break up, until heated through, 1 minute. Scoop onto a platter and serve.

TROUT STUFFED WITH FISH MOUSSE

Serves 4 to 6 as part of a multicourse meal

Classic grandiose, labor-intensive banquet dishes like this are rare in today's high-volume China-town restaurants. But if you're in San Francisco's Chinatown, you will find this at Bow Hon Restaurant on Grant Avenue. The chef carefully removes most of the flesh from the fish, leaving a thin layer next to the skin. The flesh is seasoned and ground into a paste, then the fish is stuffed with the paste and slowly pan-fried. It's quite a task, but definitely a treat for the eyes and tongue. This is a rendition that a weekend cook, with time and patience, can prepare with a measure of confidence.

1 dried black mushroom

FOR THE SAUCE
½ cup Chicken Stock (page 69) or
    canned chicken broth
1 tablespoon Chinese rice wine or dry sherry
2 teaspoons oyster-flavored sauce
1 teaspoon brown bean sauce
1 teaspoon sesame oil

FOR THE FILLING
1 cup Fish Mousse (page 152)
4 cilantro sprigs, minced
1 green onion, trimmed and minced

One 1¼- to 1½-pound trout, boned
    (head left on; gills removed)
Cornstarch for dusting

4 uncooked medium shrimp, shelled,
    butterflied, and deveined
¼ pound salmon fillet, cut into thick strips
2 eggs, lightly beaten

3 tablespoons vegetable oil
3 tablespoons minced onion

1. Pour enough warm water over the mushroom in a small bowl to cover it completely. Soak until softened, about 20 minutes. Drain. Discard the stem and mince the cap.

2. Prepare the sauce: Stir the chicken stock, rice wine, oyster-flavored sauce, brown bean sauce, and sesame oil together in a small bowl.

3. Make the filling: Stir the minced black mushroom, fish mousse, cilantro, and green onion together in a small bowl until blended.

4. Pat the inside of the fish dry with paper towels and dust the inside with cornstarch to coat it lightly. Spread the filling in an even layer over the inside, then top the filling with an even layer of overlapping shrimp and salmon strips. Make sure the filling is enclosed, then wrap the fish in plastic wrap. Refrigerate for at least 30 minutes or up to 1 hour.

5. Preheat the oven to 350°F.

6. Dust the fish with cornstarch to coat it lightly; shake off the excess. Dip the fish in egg and then again in cornstarch. Heat a flameproof baking pan or ovenproof nonstick skillet over high heat until hot. Add the oil and swirl to coat the bottom. Lay the fish in the pan and pan-fry, turning once, until golden brown, about 3 minutes per side. Transfer the pan to the oven and bake until the filling is cooked through, about 20 minutes.

7. With a large heavy-duty spatula, transfer the fish to a serving platter. Drain any excess oil from the pan and set the pan over medium-high heat. Add the onion and stir until wilted, about 2 minutes. Pour in the sauce and cook, scraping up any browned bits on the bottom of the pan, until the sauce is hot, 30 seconds to 1 minute. Slice the fish into 1½-inch pieces, spoon the sauce over the fish, and serve.

FISH MOUSSE | *Makes about 2 cups*

Afilling of fish mousse is used in Trout Stuffed with Fish Mousse (page 150). It's quite simple to prepare.

2 tablespoons dried shrimp

2 tablespoons dried black moss (optional)

1 pound skinless cod fillet,
    cut into small pieces

2 tablespoons minced Chinese bacon or
    smoked bacon

1 teaspoon sesame oil

1 teaspoon sugar

½ teaspoon salt

¼ teaspoon ground white pepper

¼ cup water

* * *

1. Pour enough warm water over the dried shrimp and black moss (if using) in separate small bowls to cover them completely. Soak until softened, about 20 minutes. Drain. Squeeze the excess liquid from the moss with your hands.

2. Combine the cod, dried shrimp, bacon, sesame oil, sugar, salt, and pepper in a food processor. Process to a fairly smooth paste. Add the water and process until the paste is very smooth.

3. Scrape the fish mixture into a bowl and stir in the optional black moss. The mousse can be stored in the refrigerator for up to 3 days.

SWEET AND TANGY CATFISH FILLETS

Serves 4 as part of a multicourse meal

Catfish is ideal for soups, casseroles, or deep-fried dishes. Chef Tse of Yokohama Chinatown's Heichinrou seasons this catfish preparation with a combination of soy sauce, sugar, and black vinegar.

FOR THE SAUCE

¼ cup Chicken Stock (page 69) or
   canned chicken broth
1 tablespoon soy sauce
2 teaspoons sugar
2 teaspoons chili sauce
1 teaspoon rice vinegar
1 teaspoon minced garlic
1 teaspoon minced ginger
1 teaspoon salt
⅛ teaspoon ground white pepper

¾ pound catfish fillets or other firm-fleshed
   white fish fillets, such as sea bass

1 egg
½ cup cornstarch

Vegetable oil for shallow-frying
3 quarter-sized slices peeled ginger

1 teaspoon cornstarch, dissolved in
   2 teaspoons water

2 cilantro sprigs
1 leek, white part only, cut into thin strips

＊　＊　＊

1. Prepare the sauce: Stir the chicken stock, soy sauce, sugar, chili sauce, rice vinegar, garlic, ginger, salt, and pepper together in a medium bowl until the sugar and salt are dissolved.

2. Remove any bones or skin from the catfish fillets and cut into roughly 4 equal pieces. Pat them dry.

3. Beat the egg lightly in a wide shallow bowl. Spread the cornstarch out on a plate. Dust each piece of the fish with the cornstarch, then dip in the beaten egg to coat it evenly; allow any excess egg to drip back into the bowl, and return the fish to the cornstarch, turning to coat all sides evenly. Set on a rack or a plate.

4. Place a wide deep skillet over medium heat and pour in oil to a depth of ¼ inch. When the oil shimmers, add the ginger slices and cook until fragrant, about 30 seconds. Slide the fish into the hot oil and fry, turning once, until golden brown, about 3 minutes per side. Remove with a slotted spoon and drain on paper towels.

5. Remove all but 1 tablespoon of the oil from the pan. Place the pan over medium-high heat. When the oil is hot, pour in the sauce and bring to a boil. Stir in the dissolved cornstarch and cook, stirring, until the sauce boils and thickens, 30 seconds to 1 minute.

6. Spoon the sauce over the fish on a serving platter; scatter the cilantro and leek over it and serve.

CHINESE NEW YEAR

Ever since my kids were old enough to open a red envelope (*lai see*), I've taken them to the Chinese New Year celebration in San Francisco's Chinatown. For them, it's like Christmas, Halloween, Fourth of July, and their birthdays all rolled into one. For me, it's living, breathing—and eating—proof that the Chinese community is alive and well. ✳ Chinese New Year is a celebration of rebirth. It officially begins on the first day of the first moon of the Chinese lunar calendar, around the end of January or beginning of February. In agricultural southern China, farmers began gearing up for spring, and the New Year coincided with the first spring planting. The farmers' hopes for their harvest and their families made the New Year a time for optimism. ✳ Today, the parades through Chinatown attract tourists and corporate sponsors, but

there's always a foundation of respect for the past. Scholarship contests and health fairs may have supplanted the traditional planting rituals, but local kung fu troupes still perform lion dances in full costume, and the sounds of firecrackers and drums echo throughout the streets. The New Year celebration remains a way for Chinese communities all over the world to appreciate their heritage. ✳ The celebrations I enjoyed as a kid are still vivid in my memory. Preparations kept us busy for days in advance. Like most Chinese families, we made an extra effort to begin everything anew. This meant new clothes and shoes for my brother and me. Any outstanding debts—the tab I kept with the snack vendor or the arm-wrestling bet I still hadn't settled—had better be paid off. We'd work overtime to wrap up any projects, and in keeping with the idea of a fresh, clean slate, we'd busy ourselves cleaning the house from floor to ceiling. ✳ In the kitchen, my mother mobilized various relatives and neighbors to get things ready for the feast. They stuffed savory Chinese sausages and hung them to dry near the windows. The counters and tables were stacked with mandarin oranges and other seasonal bounty. Their golden colors symbolized the prosperity we hoped the year would bring. I can still see my mom mixing dumpling fillings by hand, the whisper of a smile betraying her own well-controlled excitement. If I paid enough attention as she stuffed the dumplings, I might spot which one held the gold coin put there for good luck. (It was only good luck, though, if you didn't swallow it or chip a tooth on it.) ✳ Mom spent an entire day steaming the sweet glutinous rice puddings and New Year cakes, sweetened with brown sugar and red dates. My brother and I helped her set out octagonal lacquered boxes of New Year candies, lotus seeds, crystallized ginger, and other sweets for guests to enjoy before the real feasting began. Mom told me that the eight sides of the boxes would bring good luck, as eight is a particularly propitious number. ✳ Then the banqueting began. Every year, we'd celebrate somewhere different, the only prerequisite being that the location had to be big enough to hold an entire village. And there had to be enough food to feed everyone. As a kid, I didn't give much thought to the symbolism of the New Year banquet; but I could feel in the air—and taste on the tips of my chopsticks—that this was a special time. ✳ So, what did we eat? Whatever was on the table represented our good fortune in a tangible, as well as a symbolic, sense. Each course added another layer of meaning. The spring rolls were like edible gold bars, the coin-filled dumplings were the target of every kid's pair of chopsticks, and the lacy cross sections of lotus roots were filled with holes through

which we hoped good luck would flow. My brother, cousins, and I traded and hoarded our candy coins like budding bankers. No Chinese New Year banquet was complete without a whole fish to usher in good fortune. The Chinese word for fish sounds so much like the word for abundance that, in the minds of Chinese diners, the two are inextricably linked. We always left the table dreaming of fish and abundance.

CHRYSANTHEMUM FISH IN SWEET VINEGAR SAUCE

Serves 4 as part of a multicourse meal

This is Chef Ma's specialty at Sydney's Fu Lin Seafood Restaurant. His knife skills ensure the fish fillet is cut properly so that it opens and curls when deep-fried, resembling a flower. When paired with the sweet-and-sour-style sauce, the moist and crispy petals of fish blossom into a real bouquet of flavor.

1 pound firm-fleshed white fish fillets, such as catfish or grouper

1 teaspoon salt
¼ teaspoon ground white pepper

FOR THE SEASONINGS
¼ cup ketchup
¼ cup rice vinegar
3 tablespoons Chicken Stock (page 69) or canned chicken broth
2 tablespoons plum sauce
2 tablespoons packed light brown sugar
1 tablespoon Chinese pickled cucumber or ginger

1 tablespoon vegetable oil
¼ cup finely chopped celery
¼ cup finely chopped carrot
¼ cup finely chopped onion
¼ cup finely chopped green bell pepper

Vegetable oil for deep-frying
Cornstarch for dusting

* * *

1. Lay one of the fillets on a cutting board with the tail (tapered) end facing you. Working with a thin-bladed knife and holding the blade parallel to the cutting board, cut through the center of the fillet, starting at one of the long sides—do not cut all the way through the fillet: the idea is to "butterfly" it, so it opens up like a book. Close the fillet back up and cut it crosswise—from the uncut side—into ½-inch-wide strips. Repeat with the remaining fillets. Sprinkle the fish with the salt and pepper. Let stand for 10 minutes.

2. Prepare the seasonings: Stir the ketchup, rice vinegar, chicken stock, plum sauce, brown sugar, and pickled cucumber together in a small bowl until well blended.

3. Heat a 2-quart saucepan over high heat until hot. Add the oil and swirl to coat the bottom. Add the celery, carrot, onion, and bell pepper and stir-fry until the carrots are tender-crisp, 2 to 3 minutes. Pour in the seasonings and bring the sauce to a boil, then reduce the heat to low to keep the sauce warm.

4. Pour enough vegetable oil into a wok to come to a depth of 3 inches. Heat over high heat to

375°F. Dust the fish strips with the cornstarch to coat them lightly and shake gently to remove any excess. Hold one of the fish strips by the uncut end and slowly lower the cut end into the oil. Move the fish constantly as you lower it so the cut ends begin to curl. Once the ends begin to curl, release the fish into the oil. Repeat with as many of the remaining fish strips as will fit into the oil without crowding. Cook until golden brown, 2 to 3 minutes. Remove the fish with a slotted spoon and drain on paper towels. Repeat with the remaining fish strips.

5. Arrange the fish strips on a warm platter with the curled ends facing up or toward the sides. Spoon the sauce over the fish and serve immediately.

SAM CHOY'S WHOLE FISH WITH FRUIT SALSA

Serves 4 as part of a multicourse meal

Chef Sam Choy is a true giant of Hawaii's new cuisine. In this dish he achieves what all chefs aspire to, yin-yang balance. The tropical fruits, dressed only with vinegar and sugar, the crisp deep-fried whole fish, and the moist, flaky meat result in balance and harmony.

2 small fish (about 1 pound each),
    such as red snapper, cleaned

FOR THE MARINADE
1 tablespoon soy sauce
1 teaspoon salt
½ teaspoon ground white pepper

Vegetable oil for deep-frying
Cornstarch for dusting

FOR THE SAUCE
⅓ cup rice vinegar
⅓ cup water
¼ cup diced (½-inch) mango
¼ cup diced (½-inch) pineapple
¼ cup diced (½-inch) red bell pepper
2 tablespoons sugar

1 teaspoon cornstarch, dissolved in
    1 tablespoon water
1 tablespoon chopped cilantro

❋　　❋　　❋

1. Prepare the fish for frying: Cut 3 diagonal slashes about ¾ inch deep into both sides of each fish. With the tip of a knife, make two ½-inch-deep cuts that run the length of the fish along either side of the backbone.

2. Marinate the fish: Stir the soy sauce, salt, and pepper together in a small bowl until blended. Rub the marinade onto both sides of the fish. Let stand for 30 minutes.

3. Pour enough oil into a wok to come to a depth of 3 inches. Heat over medium heat to 350°F. Dust the entire fish with cornstarch, including the exposed flesh. Carefully slip one of the fish into the oil and deep-fry turning once until the meat along the backbone is opaque, about 3 minutes per side. Carefully lift the fish from the oil using a large wire skimmer or two slotted spoons and drain on paper towels. Repeat with the other fish, then transfer both fish to a serving platter.

4. Make the sauce: Heat the rice vinegar, water, mango, pineapple, bell pepper, and sugar together in a small saucepan over medium heat, stirring, until the sugar is dissolved. Stir in the dissolved cornstarch and cook, stirring, until the sauce boils and is slightly thickened, about 30 seconds.

5. Pour the sauce over the fish. Top with the cilantro and serve.

CRISPY HALIBUT WITH MISO VINAIGRETTE

Serves 4 as part of a multicourse meal

Alan Wong, Hawaii's native prince of Asian fusion cuisine, is a creative chef who combines traditional Chinese, Japanese, and classical French influences in his cooking. He created this inventive dish, which combines the flavors of crispy halibut with a bold vinaigrette, a flavored oil, and a bed of sautéed sweet corn and Japanese mushrooms.

FOR THE SEASONED OIL

2 tablespoons minced green onion

1 tablespoon minced ginger

$\frac{1}{2}$ cup vegetable oil

FOR THE VINAIGRETTE

$\frac{1}{2}$ cup vegetable oil

$\frac{1}{4}$ cup Chinese rice vinegar

2 tablespoons Chicken Stock (page 69) or canned chicken broth

2 tablespoons mayonnaise

1 tablespoon ground bean sauce or white miso

$1\frac{1}{2}$ tablespoons sugar

1 tablespoon finely chopped peanuts

1 teaspoon Chinese mustard powder

1 teaspoon sesame oil

$\frac{1}{4}$ cup water, or as needed

Two 7-ounce halibut fillets

Salt and dash of ground white pepper

$\frac{1}{2}$ cup Japanese bread crumbs (panko) or coarse dry bread crumbs

$\frac{1}{4}$ cup vegetable oil

2 teaspoons unsalted butter

$\frac{1}{2}$ cup sliced fresh shiitake caps

$\frac{1}{2}$ cup enoki mushrooms

1 cup corn kernels (from about 2 ears)

Salt and ground black pepper

2 green onions, trimmed and cut into thin strips about 2 inches long

2 teaspoons black sesame seeds

❊ ❊ ❊

1. Make the seasoned oil: Stir the green onion and ginger together in a heatproof bowl. Heat a small skillet over high heat until hot. Add the vegetable oil and heat just until it begins to smoke. Carefully pour the oil into the bowl. Let cool.

2. Make the vinaigrette: Combine the vegetable oil, rice vinegar, chicken stock, mayonnaise, ground bean sauce, sugar, peanuts, mustard powder, and sesame oil in a blender or food processor and blend until smooth. With the motor running, pour in enough water to attain a consistency like that of heavy syrup.

3. Season the halibut fillets with the salt and pepper. Drizzle just enough of the seasoned oil onto the fillets to coat both sides completely. Pat the bread crumbs onto both sides of the halibut.

4. Heat a sauté pan over medium-high heat until hot. Heat the ¼ cup vegetable oil and place the halibut fillets in the pan, dropping them away from you to avoid splashing yourself with the oil. Cook, turning once, making sure the bread crumbs do not burn, until both sides are golden brown and the halibut is cooked through, about 3 minutes per side. Remove and place on paper towels to drain. Pour the oil out of the pan.

5. Add the butter to the pan and melt over high heat. Add the shiitake and all but a few of the enoki mushrooms and sauté until tender, about 2 minutes. Add the corn kernels and sauté for another 1 to 1½ minutes. Season the vegetables with the salt and pepper to taste.

6. Spoon 2 tablespoons of the vinaigrette onto each of two plates. Make a well in the center of the vinaigrette. Spoon half the mushroom and corn mixture into the well on each plate. Set the halibut fillets on top. Scatter the green onion strips, black sesame seeds, and the reserved enoki over the fillets. Drizzle a small amount of the seasoned oil over the fillets and serve.

NORI-DUSTED FLOUNDER BUNDLES

Serves 4 as part of a multicourse meal

I discovered this unique dish by accident in New York City's Chinatown. The rolled-up fish fillets are dredged in crushed nori and other spices, fried, and then served over a crispy fried flounder frame. Your local fishmonger will be the best place to find a whole flounder. Ask the fishmonger to fillet the fish for you. Just make sure to bring the fish bones home.

One 2- to 3-pound flounder or sole, cleaned, or 1 pound skinless flounder or sole fillets

FOR THE SEASONINGS
5 sheets nori
½ teaspoon Chinese five-spice powder
½ teaspoon salt
¼ teaspoon ground white pepper

2 tablespoons flour, mixed with 1 tablespoon water

Vegetable oil for deep-frying
Cornstarch for dusting

✻　　✻　　✻

1. If using a whole fish, remove the fillets. Reserve the fish frame. Skin each fillet.

2. Rinse the fillets under cold water and pat them dry with paper towels. Cut each fillet crosswise into 2 or 3 equal pieces. If any of the pieces are more than ¼ inch thick, cut them horizontally in half to make slices of more or less equal thickness.

3. Prepare the seasonings: Crumble the nori, place it in an electric spice grinder, and grind to a powder. Turn the powder out onto a plate and stir together with the five-spice powder, salt, and pepper, mixing well.

4. Place the fillet pieces skinned side up on a work surface. Roll each piece up into a compact roll, sealing the end of the roll with a little of the flour paste. Dredge the rolls in the seasonings to coat them lightly.

5. Pour enough oil into a wok to come to a depth of 3 inches. Heat over medium heat to 350°F. Dust the fish frame with cornstarch to coat it lightly. Add the frame to the wok and, using a large slotted spoon or wire basket, press the frame against the curved bottom of the wok to make a bowl shape. Deep-fry until golden brown, about 8 minutes; adjust the heat as necessary to keep the temperature of the oil constant. Carefully remove with a slotted spoon, so the frame retains its bowl shape, and drain on paper towels.

6. Deep-fry the fish bundles, a few at a time, turning them until the flesh is opaque and the edges are golden brown, 3 minutes; make sure the temperature of the oil remains at 350°F. Remove with a slotted spoon and drain on paper towels.

7. Mound the fish bundles in the fish "bowl" and serve with Spicy Ginger Dipping Sauce (page 53) or hot mustard.

STEAMED FISH WITH MUSHROOMS AND BABY BOK CHOY

Serves 4 as part of a multicourse meal

To serve fish is to serve a Chinese symbol of prosperity. Chefs Wing and Jerry Lao, the father-and-son team at the Maple Pepper Garden Restaurant in Toronto, created this special dish. The fish fillets are steamed with ham, mushrooms, and tangerine peel, and then garnished with blanched baby bok choy or other Asian greens such as Chinese mustard green or *gai lan*.

1 piece (about 1½ inches square) dried
    tangerine peel
4 dried black mushrooms

FOR THE MARINADE
1 teaspoon sesame oil
½ teaspoon salt
¼ teaspoon ground white pepper

¾ pound firm-fleshed white fish fillets, such as
    grouper, halibut, or sea bass, cut into pieces
    about 2 inches long, 1½ inches wide, and
    ½ inch thick

12 thin slices (about ⅓ pound) Smithfield ham
    or other salt-cured ham
2 heads baby bok choy, quartered lengthwise,
    or other Asian greens such as *gai lan* or
    Chinese mustard greens

FOR THE SAUCE
½ cup Chicken Stock (page 69) or
    canned chicken broth
1 tablespoon Chinese rice wine or dry sherry
2 teaspoons oyster-flavored sauce

2½ teaspoons cornstarch, dissolved in
    1 tablespoon water

＊   ＊   ＊

1. Pour enough warm water over the tangerine peel and mushrooms in separate small bowls to cover them completely. Soak until softened, about 20 minutes. Drain. Mince the tangerine peel. Discard the mushroom stems and slice each cap into three pieces.

2. Marinate the fish: Stir the sesame oil, salt, pepper, and tangerine peel together until the salt is dissolved. Toss the fish slices gently in the marinade until coated. Let stand for 10 minutes.

3. Bring a pot of water to a boil. Meanwhile, arrange the fish, mushrooms, and ham in an alternating overlapping pattern in the bottom of an 8- or 9-inch glass pie plate. Prepare a wok for steaming according to the directions on page xxvi. Set the dish in the steamer, cover, and steam over high heat until the fish is opaque, 4 to 5 minutes.

4. While the fish is steaming, cook the bok choy in the boiling water until tender, 2 to 3 minutes. Drain.

5. Make the sauce: Stir the chicken stock, rice wine, oyster-flavored sauce, and dissolved cornstarch together in a small saucepan. Cook over medium-high heat, stirring, until the sauce boils and thickens slightly.

6. Arrange the bok choy around the fish on the pie dish, drizzle the sauce over the fish and vegetables, and serve.

CHINESE FOOD AND WINE?

Toasting with fine Western wine in a Chinese restaurant? In recent years, many Chinese restaurants have added large wine lists. And pairing the best of the grape with the best of the wok can be an exciting endeavor. But it doesn't have to be all trial-and-error. Of course, the simple rules don't quite apply, when so many Chinese dishes offer a combination of proteins and flavors on a single plate. It isn't just a matter of white with fish and red with meat. For instance, some hearty reds stand up very well to anything with soy sauce; Pinot Noir brings out sea cucumber. Still, a Chardonnay is an obvious choice with subtle steamed fish. And roast duck can work with a Syrah. ☀ Rieslings often cleanse the greasiness from deep-fried foods such as spring rolls. Sparkling wines also scour away oiliness. And spicy foods can sometimes get cooled down with honeyed sweet wines. More tannic wines can tame a clay pot casserole — but don't let the Chinese food get too tame. A contrasting wine can sometimes bring out the sweetness or smokiness or strong garlic influence. With so much variety in a Chinese banquet, this can only mean that it's the perfect opportunity to work your way through a number of far different varietals. Chinese food is nothing to wine about!

STEAMED WHOLE FISH WITH GINGER AND GREEN ONIONS

Serves 4 as part of a multicourse meal

George Young, a prominent Honolulu Chinatown community supporter, invited me to his home, and shared many stories about Honolulu's Chinese communities. Here's a classic dish that made its way from China to Hawaii, and one of my all-time favorite dishes—fresh fish simply steamed with ginger and green onions, then dressed with a bit of soy sauce.

One 1½- to 2-pound whole fish, such as sea bass or snapper, cleaned

FOR THE STUFFING
¼ cup thinly sliced ginger
2 green onions, trimmed and cut into thin strips about 1 inch long
3 tablespoons Sichuan preserved vegetables, rinsed, drained, and cut into thin strips
1 teaspoon minced garlic

1 teaspoon salt
¼ teaspoon ground white pepper

¼ cup soy sauce
2 teaspoons sugar
¼ cup vegetable oil
1 teaspoon sesame oil
1 tablespoon chopped green onion

Steamed Rice (page 285)

❋ ❋ ❋

1. Prepare the fish for steaming: Cut 3 diagonal slashes about ¾ inch deep into both sides of the fish. With the tip of a knife, make two ½-inch-deep cuts that run the length of the fish along either side of the backbone. Place the fish on an 8- or 9-inch pie plate.

2. Stuff the fish: Stir the ginger, green onions, preserved vegetables, and garlic together in a bowl until blended. Rub half of the stuffing mixture into the cuts on the sides of the fish. Stuff the remaining stuffing into the cavity. Sprinkle the fish inside and out with the salt and pepper.

3. Prepare a wok for steaming according to the directions on page xxvi. Set the plate in the steamer basket, cover the wok, and steam the fish over high heat until the flesh turns opaque along the backbone, 8 to 10 minutes. Remove.

4. Stir the soy sauce and sugar together in a small bowl until the sugar is dissolved. Pour over the steamed fish.

5. Heat the vegetable and sesame oils in a small skillet or saucepan over high heat just until they begin to smoke. Pour the hot oil over the fish, stand back, and watch it sizzle. Sprinkle with the green onions. Serve with steamed rice.

RED-COOKED FISH TAIL

Serves 4 as part of a multicourse meal

Shanghainese love red-cooking—braising meat or fish in a rich flavored sauce that is reduced until it becomes a caramelized brown glaze coating the meat or fish. Traditionally chefs use the tail section of a large freshwater fish, but any fish fillet will do.

1½ pounds fish steaks or tail sections from firm-fleshed white fish, such as grouper or snapper

3 tablespoons cornstarch

Vegetable oil for deep-frying

FOR THE SEASONINGS

2½ tablespoons Chinese black vinegar or balsamic vinegar

2 tablespoons Chicken Stock (page 69) or canned chicken broth

1 tablespoon Chinese rice wine or dry sherry

1 tablespoon dark soy sauce

1 tablespoon soy sauce

1 teaspoon sugar

½ teaspoon salt

¼ teaspoon ground white pepper

3 green onions, trimmed and chopped

2 quarter-sized slices ginger, cut into thin strips

＊　＊　＊

1. If using fish tails, butterfly them: One at a time, lay the tails flat on a cutting board. With a thin knife, make a cut from one side of the fish through to the backbone, resting the knife on the top of the bones as you work. Lift up the flap of fish you just cut to get a better view, and continue the cut along the top of the bones and through to the other side. Repeat on the other side of the tail. Cut out and discard the tail bone or reserve it for making fish stock.

2. Dust the fish lightly with the cornstarch. Pour oil into a wok to a depth of 3 inches. Heat over medium heat to 350°F. Carefully lower the fish into the hot oil. Cook until the fish is golden brown, 2 to 3 minutes. Remove with a slotted spoon and drain on paper towels. Turn off the heat and ladle all but 2 tablespoons of the oil into a heatproof container. Set the wok aside.

3. Prepare the seasonings: Stir the black vinegar, chicken stock, rice wine, soy sauces, sugar, salt, and pepper together in a small bowl.

4. Heat the oil remaining in the wok over high heat until hot. Add two-thirds of the green onions and all of the ginger and cook until fragrant, about 20 seconds. Add the fried fish and pour in the seasonings. Bring to a boil, then adjust the heat to a simmer. Cook, turning the fish once, until the fish is cooked through and the sauce is reduced to a glaze, 5 to 6 minutes.

5. Transfer the fish to a platter, spoon the sauce over it, and scatter the remaining green onions over the sauce. Serve with steamed rice.

BRAISED FISH FILLETS WITH TOFU PUFFS

Serves 4 as part of a multicourse meal

Putting the right ingredients together is an art as much as it is food science. Yet the Sam Sui women (see page 147) have been doing this for centuries, first in China, then in Singapore. Fish fillets and tofu puffs go together perfectly to make a simple, down-home dish. The tofu puffs absorb the flavors from the seasoning sauce, then release them into your mouth at first bite. If you can't find ready-made tofu puffs, simply cut firm tofu into ¾-inch cubes and deep-fry them until golden brown.

FOR THE MARINADE

1 teaspoon cornstarch

½ teaspoon salt

⅛ teaspoon ground white pepper

¾ pound firm-fleshed white fish fillets, such as sea bass, grouper, or halibut, cut into 1-inch cubes

FOR THE BROTH

1 cup Chicken Stock (page 69), Fish Stock (page 71), or bottled clam juice

2 tablespoons Chinese rice wine or dry sherry

2 teaspoons oyster-flavored sauce

2 teaspoons fish sauce

1 teaspoon sugar

2 teaspoons vegetable oil

4 quarter-sized slices peeled ginger

1 leek, white part only, thinly sliced

3 button mushrooms, trimmed and cut in half

3 fresh shiitake, stems removed and caps cut into quarters

½ cup well-drained canned straw mushrooms

½ cup thinly sliced carrots

4 ears baby corn, cut in half on the bias

2 shallots, peeled and halved

½ package tofu puffs, about 8, halved

＊　＊　＊

1. Marinate the fish: Stir the cornstarch, salt, and pepper together in a medium bowl. Add the fish and toss gently to coat. Let stand for 10 minutes.

2. Prepare the broth: Stir the chicken stock, rice wine, oyster-flavored sauce, fish sauce, and sugar together in a bowl until the sugar is dissolved.

3. Heat a wok over high heat until hot. Pour in the oil and swirl to coat the sides. Add the ginger and cook, stirring, until fragrant, about 20 seconds. Add the fish and gently stir-fry until the fish is partially cooked, about 2 minutes. Scoop the fish out onto a plate and set aside. Add the leek, all the mushrooms, carrots, baby corn, and shallots and stir-fry for 2 minutes.

4. Pour the broth into the wok and bring to a boil. Slide the fish into the broth and stir in the tofu. Reduce the heat to medium, cover the wok, and simmer until the shallots are tender, about 7 minutes. Serve immediately, ladled into warm bowls.

SHANGHAI LACQUERED BASS

Serves 4 as part of a multicourse meal

Here's another popular Shanghai red-cooked dish with a rich, shiny brown sauce and lots of green onions, ginger, and garlic. Use a whole striped bass or meaty fish steaks.

FOR THE SEASONINGS

⅓ cup Fish Stock (page 71), Chicken Stock (page 69), or canned chicken broth

3 tablespoons Chinese rice wine or dry sherry

2 tablespoons dark soy sauce

1 tablespoon sesame oil

2 teaspoons brown bean sauce

2 teaspoons sugar

1 teaspoon hot bean sauce or chili garlic sauce

½ teaspoon salt

One 2-pound striped bass, cleaned, or 1½ pounds firm-fleshed fish steaks such as sea bass or halibut

3 tablespoons vegetable oil

1 cup sliced bamboo shoots

½ cup fresh wood ear mushrooms, cut into thin strips, or 4 fresh shiitake, stems discarded and caps cut into thin strips

4 green onions, trimmed and cut into 2-inch lengths

6 quarter-sized slices peeled ginger, cut into thin strips

3 garlic cloves, thinly sliced

1 teaspoon cornstarch, dissolved in 1 tablespoon water

1. Prepare the seasonings: Stir the fish stock, rice wine, soy sauce, sesame oil, brown bean sauce, sugar, and hot bean sauce together in a small bowl until the sugar is dissolved.

2. Sprinkle the salt over the fish, inside and out if using a whole fish, and let stand for 10 minutes.

3. Heat a wok over high heat until hot. Add 2 tablespoons of the oil and swirl to coat the sides. Slide the fish into the wok and pan-fry, turning once, until golden brown, about 2 minutes per side. Once the skin is firm and no longer sticks to the wok, transfer the fish to a plate using two spatulas.

4. Return the wok to high heat and add the remaining 1 tablespoon oil. Add the bamboo shoots, mushrooms, green onions, ginger, and garlic and cook, stirring, until fragrant, about 30 seconds. Add the seasonings and bring to a boil.

5. Return the fish to the wok and bring to a boil. Adjust the heat so the liquid is simmering, cover the wok, and simmer until the meat along the backbone is cooked through, about 10 minutes; turn the fish once during cooking. Remove the fish from the wok and place on a platter.

6. Stir the dissolved cornstarch into the sauce and cook, stirring 30 seconds to 1 minute. Spoon the sauce over the fish and serve.

OVEN-BAKED SALMON IN SPICY CHILI-BEAN SAUCE

Serves 4 as part of a multicourse meal

Salmon is one of the most popular fish in the Northern Hemisphere. So when I visited Sun Sui Wah Seafood Restaurant in Vancouver's Chinatown, I asked for their popular baked salmon. The salmon is marinated in a thick vegetable-based sauce for hours, then baked and served simply.

FOR THE MARINADE

3 tablespoons soy sauce

2 tablespoons hoisin sauce

2 tablespoons Chinese rice wine or dry sherry

2 tablespoons sugar

2 tablespoons minced onion

2 tablespoons minced carrot

2 tablespoons minced shallot

2 tablespoons minced cilantro

1 tablespoon chili bean sauce

1 teaspoon minced garlic

1 pound center-cut salmon fillets, cut into 8 pieces

4 green onions, trimmed and cut in half

½ cup Chicken Stock (page 69) or canned chicken broth

1 teaspoon cornstarch dissolved in 1 teaspoon water

    ❋   ❋   ❋

1. Make the sauce: Combine the soy sauce, hoisin sauce, rice wine, sugar, onion, carrot, shallot, cilantro, chili bean sauce, and garlic in a blender and blend at low speed until smooth.

2. Pour the sauce over the salmon in a medium bowl and stir gently to coat the fish completely. Cover with plastic wrap and refrigerate for 1 hour.

3. Preheat the oven to 325°F.

4. Arrange the green onions in a row down the center of a rimmed baking sheet. (They will act as a rack for cooking the salmon on.) Lift the salmon from the sauce, letting the excess sauce drain back into the bowl, and place atop the onions, leaving a little space between each; reserve the marinade. Bake the salmon to the desired doneness, about 10 minutes for medium or up to 15 minutes for well-done.

5. Meanwhile, pour the remaining marinade into a small saucepan. Add the chicken stock and heat over medium heat until hot, 3 to 4 minutes. Use the dissolved cornstarch to thicken if desired.

6. Transfer the salmon and green onions to a warm platter, drizzle a little sauce over the fish, and serve the remaining sauce separately.

HAKKASAN SALMON AND SEA BASS IN CHAMPAGNE SAUCE

Serves 4 as part of a multicourse meal

In Mandarin Chinese, *Xiangpin* means "Champagne." It is written this way at Hakkasan in London; the restaurant has received rave reviews as one of the most innovative Chinese restaurants anywhere. Chef Tong Chee-Hwee first marinates the fish in Champagne and spices, then bakes it to perfection. The excess marinade is added to the sauce, boiled, and drizzled on top of the baked fillets.

FOR THE MARINADE

3 tablespoons mirin
    (Japanese sweet cooking wine)
2 tablespoons Champagne or
    other sparkling wine
1 tablespoon fresh lime juice
½ teaspoon dark soy sauce
2 teaspoons sugar

½ pound skinless salmon fillet, cut into 4 pieces
½ pound skinless sea bass fillet, cut into 4 pieces

FOR THE SAUCE

¼ cup Champagne or other sparkling wine
2 tablespoons Chicken Stock (page 69) or
    canned chicken broth
1 tablespoon fresh lime juice
¼ teaspoon sugar
¼ teaspoon salt

2 green onions, trimmed and cut crosswise in half
2 tablespoons unsalted butter

❋   ❋   ❋

1. Marinate the seafood: Stir the mirin, Champagne, lime juice, dark soy sauce, and sugar together in a medium bowl until the sugar is dissolved. Toss the fish pieces gently in the marinade until coated. Let stand for 10 minutes.

2. Prepare the sauce: Stir the Champagne, chicken stock, lime juice, sugar, and salt together in small bowl until the sugar is dissolved.

3. Preheat the oven to 350°F.

4. Arrange the green onions in a row down the center of a foil-lined baking sheet. Lift the fish from the marinade, allowing the excess to drip back into the bowl, and set the fish over the green onions; reserve the marinade. Bake the fish until cooked through, 8 to 10 minutes.

5. While the fish is baking, melt the butter in a small saucepan over medium-high heat. Add the sauce and the reserved marinade. Bring to a boil, stirring occasionally. Remove the pan from the heat and cover to keep warm.

6. Transfer the fish and green onions to a platter, spoon the sauce over the fish, and serve immediately.

SIZZLING SINGAPORE CHILI SHRIMP

Serves 4 as part of a multicourse meal

When visiting Singapore's Chinatown, there are two world-renowned dishes you don't want to miss—black pepper crabs and chili crabs. Chef Zhi of Soup Restaurant adapted the recipe for large shrimp.

¾ pound uncooked large shrimp (about 16), shelled, tails left intact, and deveined

FOR THE MARINADE
1½ teaspoons cornstarch
½ teaspoon salt
⅛ teaspoon white pepper

FOR THE SAUCE
¼ cup Chicken Stock (page 69) or canned chicken broth
¼ cup ketchup
2 tablespoons soy sauce
2 tablespoons rice vinegar
2 tablespoons chili garlic sauce

1 teaspoon vegetable oil
1 tablespoon minced garlic
1 teaspoon minced ginger
1 tablespoon minced shallots
1 red or green jalapeño chili, seeded and minced

1 egg, lightly beaten

1. Marinate the shrimp: Place the shrimp in a bowl, sprinkle with the cornstarch, salt, and pepper. Stir until the shrimp are evenly coated. Let stand for 10 minutes.

2. Prepare the sauce: Stir the chicken stock, ketchup, soy sauce, rice vinegar, and chili garlic sauce together in a small bowl.

3. Heat a wok over high heat until hot. Add the oil and swirl to coat the sides. Add the garlic, ginger, shallots, and chili and stir-fry until fragrant, about 20 seconds. Add the shrimp and stir-fry until they turn pink and curl slightly, 1 to 2 minutes.

4. Pour the sauce into the wok and stir-fry for 1 minute. While stirring in a circular motion, slowly pour in the beaten egg, to create "egg flowers."

5. Turn off the heat, scoop the contents of the wok onto a platter, and serve immediately.

SWEET-AND-SPICY GARLIC SHRIMP

Serves 4 as part of a multicourse meal

Chances are that this dish is on the menu of your favorite Sichuan or Peking-style restaurant. The combination of onion, sweetened chili sauce, and fragrant dried chili pepper with shrimp is one of my favorites.

¾ pound uncooked large shrimp, shelled, tails left intact, and deveined

FOR THE MARINADE
1½ teaspoons cornstarch
½ teaspoon salt

FOR THE SAUCE
1½ tablespoons soy sauce
1 tablespoon ketchup
1 tablespoon honey
2 teaspoons chili garlic sauce

2 tablespoons vegetable oil
¼ cup finely diced yellow onion
1 tablespoon minced garlic
6 dried red chilies (see page 207)

1. Marinate the shrimp: Place the shrimp in a medium bowl and sprinkle with the cornstarch and salt. Toss the shrimp gently in the marinade until coated. Let stand for 10 minutes.

2. Prepare the sauce: Stir the soy sauce, ketchup, honey, and chili garlic sauce together in a small bowl.

3. Heat a wok over high heat until hot. Add the oil and swirl to coat the sides. Add the shrimp and stir-fry until pink, about 2 minutes. Add the onion, garlic, and chilies and stir-fry until fragrant, about 30 seconds. Add the sauce and cook, stirring, until heated through, about 30 seconds. Scoop onto a platter and serve.

CREAMY WALNUT SHRIMP

Serves 4 as part of a multicourse meal

During the '70s, young Hong Kong chefs began experimenting with ingredients unfamiliar to them—Worcestershire sauce, mayonnaise, olive oil, cheeses, white wine, ketchup, etc. Among the results is one of the most successful creations on today's Chinese menus. The lightly tangy-sweet, smooth sauce gives the shrimp a creamy texture.

FOR THE MARINADE

1 egg, lightly beaten

2 tablespoons cornstarch

1 teaspoon minced shallot

1 teaspoon minced garlic

1 teaspoon toasted white sesame seeds

¾ pound uncooked medium shrimp, shelled and deveined

FOR THE SAUCE

½ cup mayonnaise

2 teaspoons honey

2 teaspoons soy sauce

1 teaspoon fresh lime juice

1 teaspoon sesame oil

¼ teaspoon mustard powder

Vegetable oil for deep-frying

¼ cup Glazed Walnuts (page 177)

Sesame seeds (optional)

Grated lime zest (optional)

1. Marinate the shrimp: Stir the egg, cornstarch, shallot, garlic, and sesame seeds together in a bowl until blended. Toss the shrimp gently in the marinade until coated. Let stand for 10 minutes.

2. Make the sauce: Stir the mayonnaise, honey, soy sauce, lime juice, sesame oil, and mustard powder together in a medium bowl until smooth.

3. Pour enough vegetable oil into a wok to come to a depth of 3 inches. Heat over high heat to 375°F. Carefully slip the shrimp into the hot oil, using a spoon to keep them from sticking together, and deep-fry until opaque in the center, 2 to 3 minutes. Lift the shrimp out with a slotted spoon and drain on paper towels.

4. Transfer the shrimp to a large bowl and drizzle the sauce over them. Using two spoons, toss the shrimp to coat them evenly with the sauce.

5. Scoop the shrimp onto a serving plate and scatter the glazed walnuts over them. Garnish with sesame seeds and lime zest, if desired.

GLAZED WALNUTS

If you can't find these nuts in the grocery store, they are easy to make. You can use them in the Creamy Walnut Shrimp or the Lucky Duck Melon Salad (page 121), or enjoy them by the handful.

Blanch 1 pound walnut halves in a pan of boiling water for 2 minutes; drain. Combine 1 cup sugar and 1/2 cup water in a 3-quart saucepan and cook over medium heat until the sugar has dissolved. Add the nuts and cook, stirring continuously, until the sugar caramelizes and turns golden brown, about 5 minutes. Pour into a colander to drain the excess syrup. Pour enough vegetable oil to come to a depth of 3 inches into a wok and heat over medium heat to 300°F. Add the walnuts and deep-fry, stirring often, for 5 minutes. Gradually increase the heat to 350°F and cook until the walnuts turn deep brown and glossy and float to the surface. Using a slotted spoon, remove the walnuts, draining them well, and place in a shallow pan to cool. Shake the pan often to prevent the nuts from sticking. When cool, pack in an airtight container. Makes about 2 1/2 cups; refrigerate for 2 months or freeze for up to 6 months.

A PRAWN IN THE GAME OF SHRIMP

Visiting a new country can be disorienting, especially if you don't speak the language. I found this out firsthand when I went to Great Britain. That's right, Great Britain. Living in the United States, I'd always thought that we spoke the same language as our friends in the United Kingdom. But after a few meals in London, I learned that while the British have English down pat, what I speak back in San Francisco is something altogether different: American, and the Californian dialect, at that. ✳ Although it took me no time to pick up the basics, like "biscuit" instead of cookie, or "chips" instead of fries, the whole matter of shrimp versus prawn remains socked in a linguistic fog. But, with a little explanation from a guide called *Catalogue of Shrimps and Prawns of the World,* put out by the United Nations Food and Agriculture Organization, I think I've finally figured it out. According to the FAO, in Great Britain, all prawns are shrimp, but all shrimp are not prawns. While "shrimp" is the more general name given to all the ten-footed crustaceans that turn pinkish when cooked and taste so irresistible dipped in Sichuan spicy salt, a "prawn" refers more specifically to the larger species of shrimp. At least, that's the way it goes in the British Isles. Across the pond in North America, however, the FAO says "prawn" has become almost meaningless as a specific designation. We're more likely to use "shrimp" to mean any type of the creature, from popcorn-sized to jumbo. ✳ But what's in a name, anyway? After all, wasn't it Shakespeare, that master of the English tongue, who said, "A shrimp by any other name would taste as sweet?"

SHRIMP AND SCALLOPS WITH CHINESE TWISTED DOUGHNUTS

Serves 4 as part of a multicourse meal

In Melbourne's Chinatown, many restaurants do not get busy until 11:00 P.M. and they stay open until 5:00 A.M.! Chef Lau at the Super Inn Café uses a Chinatown favorite, Chinese twisted doughnuts. If you walk though Chinatown and see these being made, wait in line to get yourself a few; they are best when hot. Tossing a few thin slices of deep-fried doughnuts into a stir-fry as Chef Lau does in this dish adds a nice crispy texture contrast.

¼ pound uncooked medium shrimp, shelled and deveined

¼ pound sea scallops

1 teaspoon cornstarch

½ teaspoon salt

⅛ teaspoon ground white pepper

1 tablespoon vegetable oil

1 tablespoon minced ginger

1 teaspoon thin strips seeded red or green jalapeño chili

1 cup snow peas, trimmed

⅓ cup Chicken Stock (page 69) or canned chicken broth

¼ cup sliced water chestnuts

1 tablespoon Chinese rice wine or dry sherry

1 teaspoon salt

1½ cups thinly sliced Chinese Twisted Doughnuts (page 28), freshly made or store-bought

⅓ cup chopped macadamia nuts

1. Toss the shrimp and scallops together with the cornstarch, salt, and pepper in a medium bowl until the seafood is coated. Let stand for 10 minutes.

2. Heat a wok over high heat until hot. Add the oil and swirl to coat the sides. Add the ginger and chili and stir-fry until fragrant, about 30 seconds. Add the shrimp and scallops and stir constantly until the shrimp turn pink, 2 to 3 minutes. Add the snow peas, chicken stock, water chestnuts, rice wine, and salt and cook until the snow peas begin to soften, about 2 minutes.

3. Toss in the Chinese twisted doughnuts and cook until they are heated through, about 1 minute. Scoop the contents of the wok onto a serving platter, sprinkle with the macadamia nuts, and serve immediately.

STEAMED KING PRAWNS WITH CHINESE PESTO

Serves 4 as part of a multicourse meal

You might think pesto sounds a bit odd in Chinese cooking. But today's Chinatowns are full of surprises and a diverse Asian mix; Vietnamese cuisine often combines the best of French and Chinese. Here cilantro and Thai basil lend a scent of fresh herbs. The dish is more visually appealing with prawns or jumbo shrimp.

FOR THE PESTO

1/4 **cup pine nuts**

2 **tablespoons vegetable oil**

2 **garlic cloves, coarsely chopped**

1/2 **teaspoon minced ginger**

1 **cup coarsely chopped cilantro leaves**
   and stems

1/2 **cup Thai or regular basil leaves**

1/2 **teaspoon sesame oil**

1/4 **teaspoon salt**

1/4 **teaspoon sugar**

8 **large head-on uncooked prawns in the shells**
   or jumbo shrimp

* * *

1. Prepare the pesto: Combine the pine nuts, oil, garlic, and ginger in a food processor and process to a coarse paste. Add the cilantro, basil, sesame oil, salt, and sugar and process to a smooth puree.

2. Clip the legs off the prawns with kitchen shears. Cut the top shell of the prawns open down the back, starting at the tail end and scoring the tail meat about 1/2 inch deep as you go; leave the heads intact. Arrange the prawns in a glass pie dish large enough to hold them comfortably, with the butterflied openings facing up. Rub the tail meat of each prawn with a teaspoon of the pesto. Dot the prawns with the remaining pesto.

3. Prepare a wok for steaming according to the directions on page xxvi. Set the pie dish into the steamer basket, cover, and steam over high heat until the shells are bright pink and the meat is opaque, 6 to 8 minutes.

4. Remove the pie plate from the steamer and serve directly from it.

PEPPER-SEARED SCALLOPS

Serves 4 as part of a multicourse meal

Lobster, crab, and scallops are among the most popular seafoods served in Chinatown restaurants. At Chinese fish markets, frozen scallops as well as live ones still in their shells are sold. Scallops have a tender, juicy texture and a mild flavor, which goes particularly well with black pepper. Chinatown chefs love XO sauce too, a special seafood chili sauce available in most Asian markets.

1 teaspoon black peppercorns, coarsely cracked

1 teaspoon white peppercorns, coarsely cracked

1 teaspoon Sichuan peppercorns, toasted and coarsely cracked

1 teaspoon salt

1 teaspoon cornstarch

1 pound large sea scallops (about 12)

⅓ cup Fish Stock (page 71), Vegetable Stock (page 105), or seafood bouillon, prepared according to package instructions

1 tablespoon oyster-flavored sauce

1 teaspoon XO sauce

2 tablespoons vegetable oil

½ teaspoon minced garlic

1 pound asparagus, trimmed and cut into ½-inch lengths

½ red bell pepper, cut into ½-inch squares

1 teaspoon cornstarch, dissolved in 1 tablespoon water

1 tablespoon toasted sliced almonds

     ✳   ✳   ✳

1. Spread the black, white, and Sichuan peppercorns, salt, and cornstarch out on a plate. Dredge the scallops in the seasonings until lightly coated.

2. Prepare the sauce: Stir the fish stock, oyster-flavored sauce, and XO sauce together in a small bowl.

3. Heat a wok over high heat until hot. Add the oil and swirl to coat the sides. Add half the scallops and cook until lightly caramelized, 1 to 2 minutes on each side. Transfer the scallops to a plate as they brown and replace with the remaining scallops, until all are cooked. Set the scallops aside.

4. Pour off the excess oil from the wok, then return the wok to high heat. Add the garlic and cook, stirring, until fragrant, about 10 seconds. Add the asparagus and bell pepper and stir-fry for 1 minute. Add the sauce and simmer until the vegetables are tender-crisp, 1½ to 2 minutes.

5. Pour the dissolved cornstarch into the wok and cook, stirring, until the sauce boils and thickens, about 30 seconds. Scoop the contents of the wok onto a plate and arrange the scallops over the vegetables. Sprinkle with the almonds and serve immediately.

WHITE CLOUD WOK-SEARED SCALLOPS

Serves 4 as part of a multicourse meal

Seared large sea scallops over a light fluffy cloud of egg whites were served to me by Chef Hei Chan at Hai Ten Lo Chinese Restaurant in Singapore's Pan Pacific Hotel. One bite, and I thought I was in heaven! Take care not to overcook the egg whites; you want them soft, moist, and fluffy.

FOR THE MARINADE
1 teaspoon cornstarch
¼ teaspoon salt
⅛ teaspoon ground white pepper

¾ pound large sea scallops (about 10),
    cut horizontally in half

FOR THE CLOUD
4 egg whites
¼ cup half-and-half
1 teaspoon cornstarch

FOR THE SEASONINGS
1 tablespoon soy sauce
1 teaspoon sesame oil
½ teaspoon sugar
¼ teaspoon salt

3 tablespoons vegetable oil

1 teaspoon minced ginger
1 tablespoon diced red bell pepper
1 tablespoon diced green bell pepper

* * *

1. Marinate the scallops: Stir the cornstarch, salt, and pepper together in a medium bowl. Toss the scallops gently in the marinade until coated evenly. Let stand for 10 minutes.

2. Make the cloud: Whisk the egg whites, half-and-half, and cornstarch together in a small bowl until well blended.

3. Prepare the seasonings: Stir the soy sauce, sesame oil, sugar, and salt together in a small bowl until the sugar is dissolved.

4. Heat a wok over high heat until hot. Add the oil and swirl to coat the sides. Pan-fry the scallops, turning once, until golden brown on both sides and just opaque in the center, about 1 minute per side. Remove the scallops from the wok and pour off all but 1 tablespoon of the oil from the wok.

5. Return the wok to medium-high heat. When the oil is hot, add the ginger and cook, stirring, until fragrant, about 30 seconds. Pour in the cloud and cook, stirring, until the mixture is softly scrambled. Pour in the seasonings and stir in the bell peppers. Cook for 1 minute. Scoop the cloud onto a serving platter.

6. Return the scallops to the wok and cook until heated through, about 1 minute. Spoon the scallops over the cloud and serve.

SPICY CLAMS WITH PORK SAUSAGE

Serves 4 as part of a multicourse meal

One of the best-known Portuguese dishes is clams with sausage. The chefs at Miss Macau Restaurant taught me this Macanese-style version that combines clams, Portuguese sausage, and tomato paste.

1¼ pounds mussels or medium Manila or
    littleneck hard-shell clams

FOR THE SAUCE
1 cup Chicken Stock (page 69) or
    canned chicken broth
2 tablespoons Chinese rice wine or
    dry sherry
1 tablespoon fresh lime juice
1 tablespoon chopped cilantro
2 teaspoons chili garlic sauce
½ teaspoon sugar
¼ teaspoon salt

1 teaspoon olive oil
1 teaspoon minced garlic
1 teaspoon minced ginger
1 Portuguese sausage or 2 Chinese sausages
    (about 2 ounces each), thinly sliced
2 tablespoons tomato paste

Cilantro sprigs

*   *   *

1. Scrub the mussels or clams under cold running water. Discard any with open shells that don't close when tapped.

2. Prepare the sauce: Stir the chicken stock, rice wine, lime juice, cilantro, chili garlic sauce, sugar, and salt together in a bowl until the sugar is dissolved.

3. Pour 2 cups water into a medium saucepan and bring to a boil. Add the mussels or clams to the water, cover the pot, and cook until they have opened, 2 to 3 minutes for mussels, slightly longer for clams. Discard any unopened mussels or clams.

4. With a slotted spoon, transfer the mussels or clams to a serving bowl. Cover with aluminum foil, shiny side down, to keep warm. Discard the cooking liquid.

5. Heat a wok over high heat until hot. Add the oil to the wok and swirl to coat the sides. Add the garlic, ginger, and sausage. Cook, stirring, until the sausage is cooked through, about 5 minutes.

6. Add the tomato paste and sauce. Bring to a boil, adjust the heat to a simmer, and simmer for 1 minute. Ladle the sauce over the shellfish, garnish with the cilantro sprigs, and serve immediately.

GINGER-CHILI CLAMS WITH BROTHY GLASS NOODLES

1 pound medium hard-shell clams, such as
    Manila or littleneck

FOR THE BROTH
¾ cup Chicken Stock (page 69) or
    canned chicken broth
2 tablespoons Chinese rice wine or dry sherry
1 tablespoon oyster-flavored sauce
1 teaspoon fish sauce
½ teaspoon sugar

1 tablespoon vegetable oil
4 quarter-sized slices peeled ginger, cut into
    thin strips
1 teaspoon minced garlic
1 red or green jalapeño chili, seeded and
    cut into thin strips
1 tablespoon Sichuan preserved vegetables
    (optional)
2 ounces dried bean thread noodles

2 green onions, trimmed and cut into
    thin 2-inch strips
¼ red bell pepper, cut into thin strips
1 cilantro sprig (optional)

*　　*　　*

1. Scrub the clams under cold running water. Discard open shells that don't close when tapped.

2. Prepare broth: Stir the chicken stock, rice wine, oyster-flavored sauce, fish sauce, and sugar together in a medium bowl until the sugar dissolves.

3. Pour 2 cups water into a medium saucepan and bring to a boil. Add the clams, cover, and cook until they open, 2 to 3 minutes. Scoop the clams into a bowl with a slotted spoon, discarding any unopened clams. Set the clams aside and discard the broth.

4. Heat a wok over high heat until hot. Add the oil and swirl to coat the sides. Add the ginger, garlic, chili, and preserved vegetables, if using. Stir-fry until fragrant, about 30 seconds. Pour in the broth and bring to a boil. Adjust the heat so the broth is simmering, add the bean thread noodles, and cover the wok. Simmer, stirring occasionally to separate the noodles, until the noodles are soft, 2 to 3 minutes. Stir the clams into the broth and continue stirring until the clams are heated through.

5. Scoop the broth, noodles, and clams into a large serving bowl. Scatter the green onions and bell pepper over the noodles, top with the cilantro sprig, if using, and serve.

BLACK BEAN SAUCE CLAMS WITH BASIL

Serves 4 as part of a multicourse meal

For many Cantonese diners, this is one of the old standbys when eating out. Steam or parboil fresh clams until their shells pop open, then toss them in the sauce just to coat. If you can't find whole salted black beans, substitute a few teaspoons of black bean sauce or black bean garlic sauce.

1½ pounds medium Manila or littleneck
    hard-shell clams

FOR THE SEASONINGS
2 tablespoons salted black beans,
    rinsed and lightly mashed
2 teaspoons chili sauce
1 teaspoon minced ginger
1 teaspoon minced garlic

FOR THE BROTH
½ cup Chicken Stock (page 69) or
    canned chicken broth
1 tablespoon soy sauce or light soy sauce
1 tablespoon Chinese rice wine or dry sherry

1 tablespoon vegetable oil
¼ cup lightly packed basil leaves, shredded
2 green onions, trimmed and cut into thin strips
1 tablespoon cornstarch, dissolved in
    2 tablespoons water

1. Scrub the clams under cold running water. Discard any with open shells that don't close when tapped.

2. Prepare the seasonings: Stir the salted black beans, chili sauce, ginger, and garlic together in a small bowl.

3. Prepare the broth: Stir the chicken stock, soy sauce, and rice wine together in a small bowl.

4. Pour 2 cups water into a large saucepan and bring to a boil. Add the clams, cover, and cook until they open, 5 to 6 minutes.

5. Drain the clams, discarding any unopened ones, and set aside.

6. Heat a wok over high heat until hot. Add the oil and swirl to coat the sides. Add the seasonings and stir-fry until fragrant, about 1 minute. Add the broth and bring to a boil. Adjust the heat to medium and add the clams, basil, and green onions. Stir gently to coat the clams with the sauce. Add the dissolved cornstarch and cook, stirring, until the sauce boils and thickens, about 30 seconds.

7. Scoop the clams and sauce onto a warm serving platter and serve immediately.

VELVET OYSTERS WITH GINGER–GREEN ONION SAUCE

Serves 4 as part of a multicourse meal

When you travel to Hawaii, visit Wo Fat, Honolulu Chinatown's oldest restaurant, and order this dish. The original recipe involves shucking fresh oysters, which may be difficult for the home chef. Buy freshly shucked oysters in a jar, in the seafood section of your market. You can also substitute 1½ pounds clams or mussels in the shell.

FOR THE SAUCE
2 tablespoons oyster-flavored sauce
2 teaspoons Chinese rice wine or dry sherry
1 teaspoon fish sauce
1 teaspoon sugar

2 teaspoons cornstarch
½ teaspoon salt

Two 10-ounce jars shucked oysters

1 tablespoon vegetable oil
½ medium onion, thinly sliced
½ red bell pepper, cut into ¾-inch dice
4 green onions, trimmed and cut into
    2-inch lengths
4 thin slices peeled ginger,
    cut into very thin strips
3 garlic cloves, thinly sliced

1. Prepare the sauce: Stir the oyster-flavored sauce, rice wine, fish sauce, and sugar together in a small bowl until the sugar is dissolved.

2. Bring a small pot of water to a simmer. Spread the cornstarch and salt out on a plate. Drain the oysters well, dredge them in the cornstarch mixture to coat them lightly, and shake off any excess. Slip the oysters into the simmering water and blanch for 1 minute. Drain well.

3. Heat a wok over high heat until hot. Add the oil and swirl to coat the sides. Add the onion, bell pepper, green onions, ginger, and garlic and cook, stirring, until the vegetables are tender, about 2 minutes. Add the oysters and cook, stirring gently for 2 minutes.

4. Pour in the sauce and heat through, about 30 seconds. Scoop the contents of the wok onto a serving platter and serve immediately.

CLEANING SQUID

Squid, which sounds more appetizing when called by its Italian name, *calamari*, is one of the most abundant seafoods. They're plentiful, inexpensive, tasty, and easy to clean once you know how. ✳ Many grocery and seafood stores sell squid already cleaned and prepared. But if you get a craving for squid once the last batch has been sold, and all that is left is "squid in the rough," here's how to clean and prepare them.

1. Using your fingers, rub off the dark mottled skin while holding the squid under running water to help wash it away.

2. Feel around within the tube-shaped head sac for the transparent cartilaginous "quill," grasp it at the tip, and pull it out. It should slip out easily and in one piece.

3. Using your fingers, search for the hard "beak" in the center of the tentacles and snip this and the eyes away with kitchen shears.

4. Hold the head sac in one hand and use the other to grasp the tentacles and pull them out, along with the squid's innards (which should come away with them).

5. Included with those innards is the squid's ink sac; be careful not to break it when pulling it out. Discard the sac.

6. Wash the head sac and tentacles thoroughly under cold running water and cut according to recipe instructions.

PEPPER-SALT SQUID IN LETTUCE CUPS

Serves 4 as part of a multicourse meal

Ready for a quick and easy dish that packs a punch? The chili peppers release their fragrant, pungent aroma as they cook in the wok. Substitute regular basil for the Thai basil if it is unavailable in your market. It will change the flavor in a subtle way.

1 pound squid, cleaned (see page 189)

FOR THE MARINADE
1 teaspoon cornstarch
1 teaspoon Chinese rice wine or dry sherry
¼ teaspoon salt

FOR THE SEASONINGS
1 tablespoon sugar
1 tablespoon sesame oil
1 red or green jalapeño chili, cut into rings
¼ teaspoon salt
¼ teaspoon garlic salt
¼ teaspoon Chinese five-spice powder

2 tablespoons vegetable oil
1 tablespoon minced garlic
½ cup Thai basil leaves or regular basil leaves

4 to 6 iceberg lettuce leaves

1. Separate the squid tentacles from the bodies. Leave the tentacles whole. Cut the bodies open down one side so they lie flat and lightly score the inner side with a small crisscross pattern. Cut the scored bodies into 1½ × 2-inch pieces.

2. Marinate the squid: Stir the cornstarch, rice wine, and salt together in a medium bowl until blended. Toss the squid gently in the marinade until coated. Let stand for 10 minutes.

3. Prepare the seasonings: Stir the sugar, sesame oil, chili, salt, garlic salt, and five-spice powder together in a small bowl until blended.

4. Heat a wok over high heat until hot. Add the oil and swirl to coat the sides. Add the garlic and cook, stirring, until fragrant, about 30 seconds. Add the squid and seasonings and cook, stirring, until the squid begins to curl, 1 to 1½ minutes. Add the basil and toss until fragrant, about 30 seconds.

5. Scoop the squid onto a serving platter and serve with the lettuce leaves formed into cups alongside, allowing guests to make their own lettuce cups.

WOK-FRIED GARLIC CRAB IN BUTTER-WINE SAUCE

Serves 4 as part of a multicourse meal

I admit I might have requested too many crab dishes from the chefs I met while traveling to Chinatowns around the world, but so many restaurants specialize in these tasty crustaceans. At the Golden Century Seafood Restaurant in Sydney, they have dozens of large fish and crab tanks. To prepare fresh crabs, all you need is high heat and lots of garlic and rice wine.

1 live Dungeness crab or 4 live blue crabs
1/4 teaspoon salt
1/4 teaspoon freshly cracked black pepper
1 cup cornstarch

Vegetable oil for deep-frying

4 ounces dried bean thread noodles

FOR THE SAUCE
1 cup Chicken Stock (page 69) or
   canned chicken broth
1/4 cup Chinese rice wine or dry sherry
2 tablespoons fish sauce

4 tablespoons unsalted butter
8 garlic cloves, thinly sliced

* * *

1. Clean the crab and cut into pieces according to the instructions on page 195. Sprinkle the crab pieces with the salt and pepper. Toss the crab pieces with the cornstarch in a large bowl to coat them evenly.

2. Pour enough oil into a wok to come to a depth of 3 inches. Heat over medium heat to 350°F. Slide the coated crab pieces into the hot oil and deep-fry until cooked through, 5 to 7 minutes. Scoop the crab from the oil with a wire skimmer or slotted spoon and drain on paper towels. Set the wok aside.

3. Meanwhile, pour enough warm water over the bean thread noodles in a large bowl to cover them completely. Soak until softened, about 10 minutes.

4. Drain the noodles, lay them out on a cutting board, and cut them crosswise in half. Drop the noodles into a pan of boiling water and cook until translucent, about 1 minute. Drain, rinse under cold water, and drain again. Place in a serving bowl.

5. Make the sauce: Stir the chicken stock, rice wine, and fish sauce together in a bowl.

6. Carefully ladle all but 1 tablespoon of the frying oil out of the wok into a heatproof container. Add the butter to the wok and heat until the butter is frothy and beginning to brown lightly. Add the garlic and cook until fragrant, about 30 seconds. Add the sauce and bring to a boil, stirring. Add the crab and toss to coat with the sauce. Continue cooking to allow the flavors to blend, 1 minute.

7. Spoon the crab and sauce over the bean thread noodles and serve immediately.

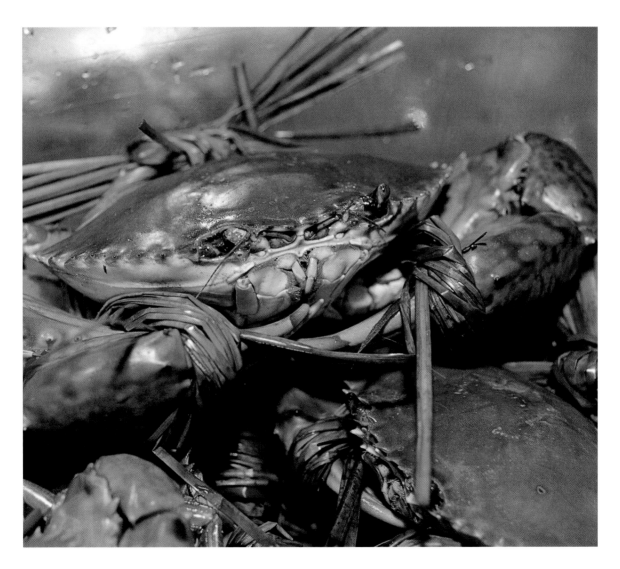

DUNGENESS CRAB WITH BASIL SAN FRANCISCO–STYLE

Serves 4 as part of a multicourse meal

One of my favorite restaurants is the Harbor Village Restaurant, just a stone's throw from San Francisco's Chinatown. Executive Chef Andy Wai originally trained as a French chef, and he is famous for giving classic Chinese dishes a new twist. Chef Wai uses butter and Western dried spices uncommon in Chinatown restaurants.

FOR THE SEASONINGS
1 tablespoon minced garlic
1 teaspoon garlic-herb seasoning (such as McCormick)
½ teaspoon garlic salt
½ teaspoon ground black pepper
½ teaspoon sugar

1 live Dungeness crab or 4 live blue crabs
Cornstarch for dusting
Vegetable oil for deep-frying

2 tablespoons unsalted butter
1 tablespoon olive oil

½ cup Chicken Stock (page 69) or canned chicken broth
8 basil leaves

*   *   *

1. Prepare the seasonings: Stir the garlic, garlic-herb seasoning, garlic salt, pepper, and sugar together in a small bowl until blended.

2. Bring a large pot of water to a boil. Slip the crab(s) into the water and cook for 2 minutes. Drain the crab(s), rinse under cold water, and drain again. If you like, pull off the top shell from the crab(s) in one piece and reserve for garnish (invert the top shell to scrape out the organs and excess water). Remove and discard the lungs attached to the shell above the legs and the spongy parts under the shell. Twist off the claws and legs, and crack them with a cleaver or mallet. Cut the body into 4 pieces, or in half, if using blue crabs, with a heavy chef's knife. Place the crab pieces in a colander to drain excess liquid, then dust with cornstarch to coat them lightly.

3. Pour enough oil into a wok to come to a depth of 3 inches. Heat over medium heat to 365°F. Deep-fry the crab, in batches if necessary to avoid crowding, until the shells change color, 2 to 3 minutes. Lift out the crab with a slotted spoon and drain on paper towels.

4. Spoon all the oil from the wok into a heatproof container and return the wok to high heat. Add the butter and olive oil and swirl to coat the sides. Add the seasonings and cook, stirring, until fragrant, about 20 seconds. Add the crab and stir to coat.

5. Pour in the chicken stock and bring to a boil. Adjust the heat so the sauce is simmering, cover the wok, and simmer until the crab is cooked through, 4 to 5 minutes.

6. Stir in the basil and transfer the crab to a serving platter. Spoon the sauce over the crab and serve hot.

CRACKING CRABS

Preparing a dish like whole steamed crabs with black bean sauce at home can be intimidating. For one thing, whole fresh crabs can be hard to find; fall and winter usher in the high season for Pacific Dungeness crabs, whereas those on the Atlantic seaboard wait for summer and fall for their blue crabs. And when you do nab crabs, you often pay dearly. What's more, a lot of people shy away from preparing fresh crab because they're not sure how to get inside that shell. ✳ Cracking a whole crab is easy; the only tool you need is a pair of crab or shellfish crackers. If you don't have a pair of those, a nutcracker, clean pliers, or even a good old-fashioned hammer will do.

1. Bring a large pot of water to a boil. Slide the crab into the water and cook for 2 minutes. Remove and rinse under cold water.

2. Hold the crab upside down in your non-writing hand and, with your other hand, grab the underside of the shell right where it joins the upper half of the shell, either at the head or tail end of the crab and pull the lower portion of the shell firmly away from the upper.

3. Remove the grayish, feathery gills and the intestines and discard them. Keep the remaining soft, yellowish-brown meat—that's the good stuff.

4. Grasping a crab leg firmly, pull it away from the body at its base; repeat with the remaining legs and claws.

5. Using a shellfish cracker or other sturdy tool, crack the claw shells to expose the tender white meat within.

6. With your hand or with the shellfish cracker, split the legs in two, freeing the leg meat for removal.

FLOWER DRUM CRAB BAKED IN THE SHELL

Serves 4 as part of a multicourse meal

This makes use of the abundance of crab from the Australian waters. In Melbourne Chinatown's Flower Drum Restaurant, they often serve up to three hundred orders of their baked crab per night. It is New Asian cuisine at its best. Serve it at your next dinner party. If you can't get blue crab shells, simply put the crab stuffing in small ramekins.

FOR THE STUFFING

2 tablespoons unsalted butter

½ cup finely diced onions

⅓ cup unsweetened coconut milk

1 teaspoon Chinese rice wine or dry sherry

½ pound crabmeat, flaked and picked over for shells and cartilage

½ teaspoon sesame oil

⅛ teaspoon ground white pepper

Salt to taste

Cornstarch for dusting (if using crab shells)

4 blue crab shells or broilerproof 4-ounce ramekins

1 egg, beaten with 2 teaspoons water

½ cup Japanese bread crumbs (panko)

* * *

1. Make the stuffing: Melt the butter in a 2-quart saucepan over medium-high heat. Add the onions and cook, stirring once or twice, until soft, about 3 minutes. Pour in the coconut milk and rice wine and heat to a simmer. Reduce the heat, add the crabmeat, sesame oil, and pepper and mix lightly. Cook just until the crab is heated through. Taste and add salt if necessary. Remove from the heat, about 1 minute.

2. Meanwhile, preheat the broiler, with the rack 4 to 6 inches from the heat.

3. Dust the crab shells, if using, with cornstarch to coat the insides lightly. Spoon the hot crab mixture into the shells or ramekins. Brush the tops with the beaten egg. Sprinkle 2 tablespoons of the bread crumbs over the filling in each shell. Broil until golden brown, about 2 minutes. Serve hot.

CRACKED CRAB IN GINGER-WINE SAUCE

Serves 4 as part of a multicourse meal

Lots of ginger and lots of wine make this dish a big hit. The natural juices of the fresh crab simmered with ginger and wine yield an intensely flavored sauce. When preparing the crab the Chinese way, lightly crack the shells to allow the sauce to seep into and flavor the meat.

1 live Dungeness crab or 4 live blue crabs
All-purpose flour for dusting

FOR THE SAUCE
½ cup Chicken Stock (page 69) or
canned chicken broth
¼ cup Chinese rice wine or dry sherry
6 green onions, trimmed and cut diagonally
into 1-inch lengths
¼ cup chopped basil
2 teaspoons Chinese black vinegar or
balsamic vinegar
2 teaspoons soy sauce or light soy sauce

1 tablespoon vegetable oil

½ cup minced ginger
1 tablespoon cornstarch, dissolved in
2 tablespoons water

✳   ✳   ✳

1. Bring a large pot of water to a boil. Slip crab(s) into the water and cook for 2 minutes. Drain the crab(s), rinse in cold water, and drain.

2. To clean the crab(s), pull off the top shell(s). Remove and discard the feathery off-white lungs and spongy parts under the shell(s). Break off the legs and claws and crack them with a cleaver or mallet. If using a Dungeness crab, cut the body into 4 pieces; if using blue crabs, cut the bodies in half. Dust the crab pieces with flour to coat lightly.

3. Prepare the sauce: Stir the chicken stock, rice wine, green onions, basil, black vinegar, and soy sauce together in a bowl.

4. Heat a wok over high heat until hot. Add the oil and swirl to coat the sides. Add the coated crab pieces and stir-fry for 1 minute. Add the ginger and stir-fry for 2 minutes. Pour in the sauce and bring to a boil. Reduce the heat to a simmer, cover the wok, and cook, stirring once, until the crab is cooked through, 3 to 4 minutes.

5. Stir in the dissolved cornstarch and cook, stirring, until the sauce boils and thickens, about 30 seconds.

6. Scoop the contents of the wok onto a serving platter and serve immediately.

STEAMED WHOLE LOBSTER WITH DRIED TANGERINE PEEL

Serves 4 as part of a multicourse meal

One of the least-known Chinese seasonings is the humble dried tangerine peel—which can cost up to $75 per pound. For Chinese master chefs, dried tangerine peel is a secret weapon. Its unique fragrance imparts a light flavor to many dishes. In London's Chinatown at Fung Shing Restaurant, lobster is steamed with a mixture of salted black beans and chopped tangerine peel, then served over a bed of rice or bean thread noodles.

1 bundle (about 2 ounces) dried bean thread
    noodles
2 pieces (each about 1½ inches square)
    dried tangerine peel or 1 tablespoon grated
    lemon zest

FOR THE SEASONINGS
⅓ cup Chicken Stock (page 69) or
    canned chicken broth
3 tablespoons chopped cilantro
2 tablespoons minced garlic
2 tablespoons vegetable oil
1 teaspoon oyster-flavored sauce
1 teaspoon salted black beans, rinsed, drained,
    and coarsely chopped
½ teaspoon salt
½ teaspoon sugar

1 live lobster (about 2 pounds) or 2 lobster tails
    (each about 8 ounces)

1. Pour enough warm water over the bean thread noodles and tangerine peel in separate bowls to cover them completely. Soak until softened, about 10 minutes. Drain the noodles, lay them out on a cutting board and cut them in half crosswise. Spread the noodles out on a large pie dish. Drain the tangerine peel and mince.

2. Prepare the seasonings: Stir the chicken stock, cilantro, garlic, oil, oyster-flavored sauce, black beans, salt, sugar, and tangerine peel together in a medium bowl until the sugar dissolves.

3. If using a live lobster, kill quickly by inserting a sharp heavy knife where the head meets the body or plunge the lobster head first into a pot of rapidly boiling water, cook for 1½ to 2 minutes, remove and plunge in an ice bath to stop the cooking process. Cut off the claws and legs with kitchen scissors or a knife. Give each claw a swift whack with the back of a heavy cleaver to crack the shell. (Be careful not to damage the shape of the claw; just crack the shell so the meat will be easy to remove after steaming.) Pull the tail off the body with a sharp downward quarter turn. Butterfly the tail: Place the tail, shell side up, on a cutting board. Using a large, sturdy knife and starting from the thick end of the tail, cut through the top shell and into the meat. Don't cut all the way through to the bottom, thinner shell. (If using the lobster tails in place of the whole lobster, follow the instructions for butterflying the tail.)

4. Reassemble the lobster parts over the noodles and spread the seasonings over the tail meat and claws. (If using the lobster tails, arrange them side by side over the noodles.)

5. Prepare a wok for steaming according to the directions on page xxvi. Set the plate into the steamer basket, cover the wok, and steam until the lobster is cooked through, about 8 minutes. Serve directly from the steaming plate.

FIERY KUNG PAO LOBSTER TAILS

Serves 4 as part of a multicourse meal

We can thank General Kung Pao for this spicy favorite. Every Kung Pao dish should always have dried red chilies, some vegetables, and a choice of meat, seafood, or tofu. If you can't find a Kung Pao dish on a Chinatown menu, something is wrong. Kung Pao shrimp and Kung Pao chicken are staples in most Chinatown restaurants. But you'll rarely see Kung Pao lobster, unless you visit the Fortune Garden in Vancouver's Chinatown. If you can't find hot bean paste, substitute chili garlic sauce.

2 lobster tails (each about 8 ounces)
1 tablespoon cornstarch

FOR THE SEASONINGS
¼ cup Fish Stock (page 71) or
     canned chicken broth
2 tablespoons Chinese rice wine or dry sherry
1 tablespoon hot bean paste
2 teaspoons soy sauce
2 teaspoons sesame oil
2 teaspoons sugar

2 tablespoons vegetable oil
2 tablespoons minced garlic
6 small dried red chilies (see page 207)
6 medium asparagus spears, trimmed and cut
     diagonally into 1½-inch pieces (about 1 cup)
¼ cup thinly sliced carrot

¾ cup canned straw mushrooms, drained and
     halved
1 green onion, trimmed and cut into
     1-inch lengths
⅓ cup roasted peanuts

1. Cut each lobster shell open along the underside with a pair of kitchen shears or a paring knife. Work the lobster meat from the shells and discard the shells. Cut the meat into 1-inch slices and pat dry with paper towels. Toss the lobster in a bowl with the cornstarch until coated.

2. Prepare the seasonings: Stir the fish stock, rice wine, hot bean paste, soy sauce, sesame oil, and sugar together in a bowl until the sugar is dissolved.

3. Heat a wok over high heat until hot. Add 1½ tablespoons of the oil and swirl to coat the sides. Add the lobster and stir-fry until it begins to turn opaque, 3 to 4 minutes. Scoop the lobster onto a plate.

4. Add the remaining ½ tablespoon oil to the wok and swirl to coat the sides. Add the garlic and chilies and cook, stirring, until fragrant, about 10 seconds. Add the asparagus and carrot and stir-fry until the vegetables are tender-crisp, about 1½ minutes. Add the seasonings and bring to a simmer.

5. Return the lobster to the wok and add the mushrooms, green onion, and peanuts. Cook until the mushrooms are tender, 1½ to 2 minutes. Scoop the lobster and vegetables onto a platter and serve.

WOK-BRAISED LOBSTER TAILS IN CREAMY RUM SAUCE

Serves 4 as part of a multicourse meal

I'd bet that you've never seen a Chinese dish where the chef uses rum as a flavoring agent. Chef Lai at Toronto Chinatown's Maple Pepper Garden Restaurant does. At first I couldn't imagine putting oyster-flavored sauce, fish sauce, rum, and evaporated milk together in one wok, but it works.

2 lobster tails (each about 8 ounces)

3 tablespoons unsalted butter
¾ cup finely diced onions
½ teaspoon cracked black pepper
1 cup Fish Stock (page 71), Chicken Stock
    (page 69), or canned chicken broth
½ cup evaporated milk
2 tablespoons oyster-flavored sauce
2 teaspoons fish sauce

¼ cup light rum

2 tablespoons cilantro leaves, plus
    1 sprig for garnish
¼ cup basil leaves

*   *   *

1. Butterfly the lobster tails: Clip off the fins along the outer edges of each shell. Bend the tail backwards—against its natural curve—cracking several joints in the shell. (This will prevent the tails from curling during cooking.) Place each tail right side up on a cutting board. Using a large sturdy knife, starting from the thick end of the tail, cut through the top shell and into the meat, without cutting all the way through to the bottom, thinner shell. Open up the lobster shells to expose the meat.

2. Heat the butter in a wok over high heat until bubbling. Add the onions and pepper and cook, stirring, until the onions are soft but not browned, about 1 minute. Pour the fish stock, evaporated milk, oyster-flavored sauce, and fish sauce into the wok and bring to a boil. Adjust the heat so the liquid is simmering and place the lobster tails, split side down, in the onion broth. Cover and simmer until the lobster meat is opaque, 6 to 8 minutes. Transfer the lobster to a plate and set aside.

3. Pour the rum into the wok and increase the heat to high. Bring to a boil, and cook until the sauce is reduced by half, about 1 minute, or until the sauce is as thick and rich as you like.

4. Add the cilantro leaves and all but a few of the basil leaves to the sauce. Turn the lobster tails in the sauce to coat, then transfer them to a serving platter and spoon the sauce over them. Garnish with the cilantro sprig and the remaining basil leaves.

POULTRY

nnovative Chinese chefs seem to migrate to the Chinatowns in large cities. Perhaps it's that so many techniques and ingredients are available to them they can invent creative ways of fusing traditional Chinese cooking with local flavors. Chefs are particularly inventive with game birds such as duck, game hen, quail, and squab. In New York and London, restaurants that feature duck are going strong. The chefs in these Peking-style restaurants make three or four different dishes from one duck. Chinese chefs in Vancouver's fine dining restaurants are turning squab into a work of art with parchment paper (page 242) and a master sauce (page 244).

KUNG PAO CHICKEN

Serves 4 as part of a multicourse meal

Is there a Chinese restaurant that doesn't have a Kung Pao dish on its menu? If you can't find unsalted peanuts, rinse salted ones and pat them dry. Don't use an excessive amount of cornstarch; dust the chicken lightly with it and then tap off the excess. Balsamic vinegar may be substituted for the black vinegar.

FOR THE MARINADE

1 tablespoon soy sauce or light soy sauce

1 teaspoon dried red chili flakes

1 teaspoon cornstarch

¾ pound boneless, skinless chicken breasts or thighs, cut into ¾-inch cubes

FOR THE SAUCE

¼ cup Chicken Stock (page 69) or canned chicken broth

2 tablespoons soy sauce

1 tablespoon Chinese black vinegar or balsamic vinegar

1 tablespoon sugar

2 teaspoons chili bean sauce or chili garlic sauce

1 teaspoon hoisin sauce

Vegetable oil for deep-frying

½ package (7 ounces) medium or firm tofu, drained and cut into ½-inch cubes (about 1 cup)

¼ cup cornstarch

½ red bell pepper, cut into 1-inch squares

½ green bell pepper, cut into 1-inch squares

1 teaspoon cornstarch, dissolved in 2 teaspoons water

¼ cup roasted unsalted peanuts

❋   ❋   ❋

1. Marinate the chicken: Stir the soy sauce, chili flakes, and cornstarch together in a medium bowl until the cornstarch is dissolved. Add the chicken and toss gently to coat. Let stand for 10 minutes.

2. Prepare the sauce: Stir the chicken stock, soy sauce, black vinegar, sugar, chili bean sauce, and hoisin sauce together in a bowl.

3. Pour enough oil into a 2-quart saucepan to come to a depth of 2 inches. Heat over medium-high heat to 300°F. Pat the tofu cubes dry, dust them with the cornstarch to coat lightly, and shake off the excess cornstarch. Slip the tofu cubes a few at a time into the hot oil and fry until golden brown, about 2 minutes. Gently remove the tofu cubes with a slotted spoon or wire skimmer and drain them on paper towels. Reserve the oil.

4. Heat a wok over high heat until hot. Add 1 tablespoon of the reserved oil and swirl to coat the sides. Add the chicken and stir-fry until opaque, 1 to 2 minutes. Add the bell peppers and stir-fry until tender-crisp, 1 to 2 minutes. Add the sauce and tofu and cook until heated through, about 1 minute. Add the dissolved cornstarch and cook, stirring gently, until the sauce boils and thickens, about 30 seconds. Stir in the peanuts.

5. Scoop the contents of the wok onto a serving platter and serve immediately.

DRIED RED CHILIES

Whole dried red chilies look like shriveled-up versions of the fresh kind. But make no mistake, these wrinkled red hots are fiery hot. Use them whole, as in some versions of Kung Pao chicken, or crumble them into smaller pieces. You can also purchase dried red chili peppers crushed into flakes, including the membranes and seeds. Since the hot pepper's oils are concentrated in the membranes and seeds, crushed chili peppers tend to be hotter than the whole ones, with their still-intact seeds and membranes. Either way, handle dried peppers with the same care as you would fresh: Their oils cling to your hands, so use gloves, and don't touch your eyes.

SANG CHOY BAO CHICKEN WRAPS

Serves 4 as part of a multicourse meal

Minced chicken cooked with many flavors and served in lettuce cups is a traditional Chinese New Year dish. In Cantonese, the lettuce cup is called *sang choy bao,* which sounds like "life, prosperity, wrapped together." For an extra "crunch," add some chopped water chestnuts to the dish.

FOR THE MARINADE
1 teaspoon cornstarch
1 teaspoon soy sauce

½ pound boneless, skinless chicken breasts or
    thighs, minced

1 tablespoon vegetable oil
⅓ cup finely diced onion
1 Chinese sausage (about 2 ounces),
    cut into ¼-inch dice
2 tablespoons minced shallots
2 tablespoons minced garlic

1 teaspoon sugar
¼ teaspoon salt
1 egg, lightly beaten

¼ cup chopped Chinese yellow chives,
    Chinese green chives, or regular chives
1 tablespoon chopped cilantro
1 tablespoon chopped red pickled ginger or
    regular pickled ginger

Hoisin sauce
4 iceberg lettuce cups

1. Marinate the chicken: Stir the cornstarch and soy sauce together in a medium bowl until the cornstarch is dissolved. Stir in the minced chicken and mix well. Let stand for 10 minutes.

2. Heat a wok over high heat until hot. Add the oil and swirl to coat the sides. Add the onion, Chinese sausage, shallots, and garlic and cook, stirring, until fragrant, about 30 seconds. Add the marinated chicken and stir-fry until the chicken is no longer pink but is still moist, 2 to 3 minutes.

3. Add the sugar and salt, then drizzle the egg over the chicken and cook, stirring, until the egg and chicken are cooked through, 2 to 3 minutes.

4. Stir in the chives, cilantro, and pickled ginger. Scoop onto a serving plate. To eat, spread some hoisin onto a lettuce cup, then spoon in some of the chicken. Roll the lettuce around the chicken and eat out of hand.

EMERALD CHICKEN WITH GRAPES AND KIWI

Serves 4 as part of a multicourse meal

While researching this cookbook and the TV series, I interviewed an elderly man from San Francisco's Chinatown who once operated a restaurant there. One of his most popular dishes was chicken with grapes. I decided to add another fruit—kiwi. Many Asians enjoy a bit of sweetness in their meat dishes to balance the spiciness of others in a multicourse meal. Serve with rice and a spicy vegetable dish.

FOR THE MARINADE

2 teaspoons soy sauce or light soy sauce
2 teaspoons minced ginger
1 teaspoon Chinese rice wine or dry sherry
1 teaspoon cornstarch
¼ teaspoon salt
⅛ teaspoon ground white pepper

¾ pound boneless, skinless chicken breasts or thighs, cut into ¾-inch cubes

FOR THE SAUCE

2 tablespoons honey
1 tablespoon fresh lemon juice
1 tablespoon soy sauce
2 teaspoons cornstarch
1 teaspoon hoisin sauce
¼ teaspoon salt

1 tablespoon vegetable oil

½ red bell pepper, cut into 1-inch squares
3 green onions, trimmed and cut into 2-inch lengths
½ cup green and red seedless grapes, cut in half
1 kiwi, peeled and cut into ½-inch cubes

1. Marinate the chicken: Stir the soy sauce, ginger, rice wine, cornstarch, salt, and pepper together in a bowl until combined. Add the chicken and stir to coat. Let stand for 10 minutes.

2. Prepare the sauce: Stir the honey, lemon juice, soy sauce, cornstarch, hoisin sauce, and salt together in a small bowl until combined.

3. Heat a wok over high heat until hot. Pour in the oil and swirl to coat the sides. Add the chicken and stir-fry until no longer pink, 2½ to 3 minutes. Add the bell pepper and green onions and stir-fry until the onions are tender, about 1½ minutes.

4. Pour the sauce into the wok and cook, stirring, until the sauce boils and thickens. Add the grapes and kiwi. Cook for 1 minute to heat through, then scoop the contents of the wok onto a serving platter. Serve immediately.

WALNUT CHICKEN

Serves 4 as part of a multicourse meal

Chinese chefs use a variety of nuts in their cooking, especially walnuts, since most Chinese believe that walnuts have many medicinal benefits. They are thought to invigorate the lungs and kidneys and to help lubricate the large intestine. I like walnuts for their great taste as well as their health benefits.

FOR THE MARINADE

1 tablespoon soy sauce

2 teaspoons cornstarch

¾ pound boneless, skinless chicken breasts or thighs, cut into bite-sized pieces

FOR THE SAUCE

¼ cup Chicken Stock (page 69) or canned chicken broth

1 tablespoon hoisin sauce

2 teaspoons Chinese rice wine or dry sherry

1 teaspoon sesame oil

¼ teaspoon salt

⅛ teaspoon Chinese five-spice powder

2 tablespoons vegetable oil

1 stalk celery, thinly sliced on the bias

½ medium onion, cut into ½-inch dice

½ red bell pepper, cut into ½-inch squares

1 small zucchini, cut into ½-inch dice

2 green onions, trimmed and cut into 2-inch lengths

½ teaspoon cornstarch, dissolved in 1 teaspoon water

½ cup Glazed Walnuts (page 177)

1. Marinate the chicken: Stir the soy sauce and cornstarch together in a bowl until the cornstarch is dissolved. Add the chicken and stir until evenly coated. Let stand for 10 minutes.

2. Prepare the sauce: Stir the chicken stock, hoisin sauce, rice wine, sesame oil, salt, and five-spice powder together in a small bowl until blended.

3. Heat a wok over high heat until hot. Add 1½ tablespoons of the oil and swirl to coat the sides. Add the chicken and stir-fry until it begins to brown, about 2 minutes. Scoop the chicken out of the wok and set aside.

4. Add the remaining ½ tablespoon of oil to the wok and swirl to coat the sides. Add the celery, onion, bell pepper, zucchini, and green onions and stir-fry until the vegetables are tender-crisp, 1½ to 2 minutes.

5. Return the chicken to the wok and stir-fry for 1 minute. Pour the sauce into the wok and bring to a boil. Pour in the dissolved cornstarch and cook, stirring, until the sauce boils and thickens, 30 seconds to 1 minute. Add the walnuts and stir to coat.

6. Scoop onto a serving platter and serve immediately.

BLACK BEAN– GARLIC CHICKEN

Serves 4 as part of a multicourse meal

This is one of my favorite Cantonese dishes—fragrant salted black beans with chicken. Dishes cooked in this style, with black beans, ginger, and garlic, are referred to as "fish-cooked" because traditionally these ingredients were used in fish dishes. You can even "fish-cook" beef or pork spareribs.

FOR THE MARINADE
1 tablespoon soy sauce
1 teaspoon cornstarch

¾ pound boneless, skinless chicken breasts
    or thighs, cut into bite-sized pieces

FOR THE SAUCE
¼ cup Chicken Stock (page 69) or
    canned chicken broth
2 tablespoons Chinese rice wine or dry sherry
2 teaspoons soy sauce
1 teaspoon sugar

1 tablespoon vegetable oil

1 tablespoon salted black beans,
    rinsed, drained, and mashed
½ cup diced (½-inch) yellow onions
1 green onion, trimmed and cut into
    1-inch lengths
2 teaspoons minced ginger
1 teaspoon minced garlic
1 teaspoon dried red chili flakes
1 teaspoon cornstarch, dissolved in
    2 teaspoons water

1. Prepare the marinade: Stir the soy sauce and cornstarch together in a bowl until the cornstarch is dissolved. Add the chicken and toss gently to coat. Let stand for 10 minutes.

2. Prepare the sauce: Stir the chicken stock, rice wine, soy sauce, and sugar together in a small bowl until the sugar is dissolved.

3. Heat a wok over high heat until hot. Pour in the oil and swirl to coat the sides. Add the chicken and stir-fry until it is no longer pink, 2½ to 3 minutes.

4. Add the black beans, yellow onions, green onion, ginger, garlic, and chili flakes. Stir-fry until the onion is softened, 1 to 2 minutes. Pour in the sauce and the dissolved cornstarch and cook, stirring, until the sauce boils and thickens, about 30 seconds.

5. Scoop the chicken and sauce onto a serving plate and serve immediately.

NEW YORK

MAH-JONGG IS A POPULAR GAME AMONG MANY CHINESE ELDERS.

CHEF HONG FROM SHANGHAI CUISINE BAR AND RESTAURANT TEACHES ME TO MAKE SHANGHAI SIU MAI.

Sirens screech, manholes smoke, chimneys belch, subways tremble. In the city that never sleeps, Chinatown always seems wide awake. Gritty and grimy, it's a place full of buildings of stacked floors of garment sewing shops and at least six hundred small-time factories. Where thousands work their way out of debt and into American society, one washed dish at a time, the Chinese seem to agree that if you make it here you can make it anywhere. An estimated 350,000 Chinese in Manhattan, with the same number in the other boroughs, have made the Big Apple a magnet of Chinese in the Americas. ❋ Why not call it the Big Kumquat? Instead of melting pot, how about "hot pot"? Restaurants line Mott and Mulberry Streets, every one of them, it seems, with Broadway-style rave reviews plastered on their windows. Steam rises from basement walk-downs, and some of the best eats are either underground or eight stories up. Laundry drapes fire escapes, elders play Go! in leafy pocket parks, and the lucky red of Chinese temples matches the trucks and fire stations of New York's Bravest. ❋ On Canal Street, you can buy snow fungus and lychees from pushcarts. Chef Yuen-Yan Wu at the Peking Duck House has been putting out some of the best Peking ducks east of the Mississippi for forty-two years. At Mott Street's Vegetarian Paradise 3, there's even a nutritional expert on staff. Where the mystical East meets the Lower East Side, you may run out of time, but you'll never run out of tastes, sights, or sensations.

JING FONG RESTAURANT

20 Elizabeth Street

(212) 964 5256

What to order: *anything from the dim sum carts*

MAY MAY GOURMET CHINESE BAKERY

35 Pell Street

(212) 267-0733

What to order: *BBQ buns; pineapple buns; jung (Chinese tamales)*

PEKING DUCK HOUSE

28 Mott Street

(212) 227-1810

What to order: *roasted Peking duck; minced duck in lettuce cups; hot-and-sour duck soup; stir-fry duck with bean sprouts*

PING'S RESTAURANT

22 Mott Street

(212) 602-9988

What to order: *steamed short ribs with black pepper sauce over soft tofu and Chinese mustard greens; eight-treasure melon soup; deep-fried prawns with shredded coconut*

SHANGHAI CUISINE BAR AND RESTAURANT

89-91 Bayard Street

(212) 732-8988

What to order: *steamed Shanghai siu mai; braised freshwater sea bass with green onion and ginger Shanghai-style; steamed unmolded shredded chicken, eggs, and ham in broth*

VEGETARIAN PARADISE 3

33 Mott Street

(212) 406-6988

What to order: *stir-fried mixed vegetables; vegetarian fish; vegetarian black pepper beef*

WO HOP RESTAURANT

17 Mott Street

(212) 267-2536

What to order: *wou wonton soup; egg flower soup with crispy wontons*

AT THE PEKING DUCK HOUSE

A STREET FORTUNE-TELLER PREDICTS WHAT THE FUTURE HOLDS.

SIZZLING CHICKEN WITH SHALLOTS

Serves 4 as part of a multicourse meal

The Hong Kong chefs who emigrated to Toronto and Vancouver brought with them Southeast Asian fusion dishes. Here classic Chinese black bean chicken is combined with shallots, a culinary inspiration from Malaysia and Thailand. If you have a sizzling metal platter available, use it to make a sizzling presentation!

FOR THE MARINADE
1 tablespoon soy sauce
2 teaspoons cornstarch
1 teaspoon sugar
½ teaspoon sesame oil

¾ pound boneless, skinless chicken breasts
    or thighs, cut into ½-inch dice

2 tablespoons vegetable oil
1 tablespoon salted black beans,
    rinsed, drained, and coarsely chopped
2 teaspoons minced garlic
4 green onions, trimmed and cut
    into 2-inch lengths

⅓ cup Chicken Stock (page 69) or
    canned chicken broth
1 tablespoon Chinese rice wine or dry sherry
6 walnut-sized shallots, halved
½ yellow bell pepper, cut into ½-inch squares
½ green bell pepper, cut into ½-inch squares

1. Marinate the chicken: Stir the soy sauce, cornstarch, sugar, and sesame oil together in a medium bowl until the cornstarch is dissolved. Toss the chicken gently in the marinade until coated. Let stand for 10 minutes.

2. Heat a wok over high heat until hot. Add the oil and swirl to coat the sides. Add the black beans and garlic and cook, stirring, until fragrant, about 10 seconds. Add the chicken and green onions and stir-fry until the chicken is no longer pink, 2 to 3 minutes.

3. Stir in the chicken stock, rice wine, shallots, and bell peppers. Cover and cook over medium-high heat until the shallots are tender, about 5 minutes. Meanwhile, heat a cast-iron platter over high heat until nearly smoking.

4. Spoon the chicken onto the platter and serve while still sizzling.

FIVE-FLAVOR CHICKEN AND EGGPLANT

Serves 4 as part of a multicourse meal

This dish has five immortal flavors; salty, sweet, sour, spicy, and fragrant. Like a sponge, the eggplant absorbs them all. I can never understand why eggplant is not more popular on the American table. It can be steamed, boiled, baked, or grilled. It can also be oil-blanched, to lock in the color and intensify the flavor, and used in recipes like this. Eggplant goes great with seafood and a whole range of seasonings. Substitute pork, shrimp, or lamb for the chicken.

FOR THE MARINADE
1 teaspoon cornstarch
1 teaspoon Chinese rice wine or dry sherry

½ pound boneless, skinless chicken breasts or
    thighs, minced

FOR THE SAUCE
1½ tablespoons soy sauce
1½ teaspoons Chinese black vinegar
    or balsamic vinegar
1½ teaspoons sugar
1 teaspoon Chinese rice wine or dry sherry
1 teaspoon sesame oil
1 teaspoon ketchup
1 teaspoon chili garlic sauce

Vegetable oil for deep-frying
¾ pound Asian eggplants, stems removed,
    cut crosswise into 2-inch lengths, and
    quartered lengthwise

1 tablespoon minced garlic
2 teaspoons minced ginger

¼ cup Thai or regular basil leaves

1. Marinate the chicken: Stir the cornstarch and rice wine together in a small bowl until the cornstarch is dissolved. Add the chicken and stir to coat. Let stand for 10 minutes.

2. Prepare the sauce: Stir the soy sauce, black vinegar, sugar, rice wine, sesame oil, ketchup, and chili garlic sauce together in a small bowl until blended.

3. Pour enough oil into a 2-quart saucepan to come to a depth of 3 inches. Heat over high heat to 375°F. Deep-fry the eggplant, in batches, until the skin is bright purple, about 2 minutes. Remove with a slotted spoon and drain on paper towels. Reserve the oil.

4. Heat a wok over high heat until hot. Add 1 tablespoon of the reserved oil and swirl to coat the sides. Add the garlic and ginger and cook, stirring, until fragrant, about 30 seconds. Add the chicken and stir-fry until crumbly, about 2 minutes. Pour in the sauce and bring to a boil.

5. Scoop the chicken and sauce onto a warm serving platter, scatter the basil leaves over the top, and serve hot.

HUNAN CHICKEN WITH NUTS

Serves 4 as part of a multicourse meal

Hunan and Sichuan cuisines get their flavors from a combination of dried red chilies and Sichuan peppercorns. Dried chilies provide heat; peppercorns deliver the spice and numbing sensation on the tongue.

FOR THE MARINADE

1 egg

¼ cup cornstarch

½ pound boneless, skinless chicken breasts or thighs, cut into ½-inch cubes

FOR THE SAUCE

¼ cup Chicken Stock (page 69) or canned chicken broth

1 tablespoon chili garlic sauce

1 tablespoon tomato paste

2 teaspoons soy sauce

1 teaspoon sugar

1 teaspoon salted black beans, rinsed, drained, and coarsely chopped

Pinch of ground toasted Sichuan peppercorns

Vegetable oil for deep-frying

3 dried red chilies

4 stalks asparagus, trimmed and cut on the bias into ½-inch pieces

1 small zucchini or Chinese okra, cut in half lengthwise, then cut on the bias into ¼-inch slices

⅓ cup toasted walnut halves

1. Marinate the chicken: Stir the egg and cornstarch together in a medium bowl until smooth. Add the chicken and stir to coat. Let stand for 10 minutes.

2. Prepare the sauce: Stir the chicken stock, chili garlic sauce, tomato paste, soy sauce, sugar, black beans, and ground Sichuan peppercorns together in a bowl until the sugar is dissolved.

3. Pour enough vegetable oil into a 2-quart saucepan to come to a depth of 3 inches. Heat over medium heat to 350°F. Deep-fry the chicken, a few cubes at a time, turning occasionally, until golden brown, 3 to 4 minutes. Remove with a slotted spoon and drain on paper towels. Reserve the oil.

4. Heat a wok over high heat until hot. Add 1 tablespoon of the reserved oil and swirl to coat the sides. Add the dried chilies, asparagus, and zucchini and stir-fry until tender-crisp, 1½ to 2 minutes. Pour in the sauce and bring to a boil. Stir in the chicken and simmer until heated through, about 1 minute. Stir in the walnuts until coated.

5. Scoop the chicken onto a warm serving platter and serve immediately.

SALT-BAKED EIGHT-FLAVOR CHICKEN

Serves 4 as part of a multicourse meal

At first glance, this dish seems cumbersome to prepare. But if you ever have the chance to taste it at Toronto's Bayview Garden Restaurant, you will desperately want to know how to make it. Although it takes a bit of effort, once you pop it in the oven, you can sit back and relax. Let it cook in its own juice and moisture. You can use any size chicken, as long as you have a roasting pan large and deep enough to cover the fowl with salt.

1 teaspoon soy sauce
1 teaspoon dark soy sauce

One 2½- to 3-pound chicken or 2 Cornish
    game hens, rinsed

FOR THE SEASONINGS
3 tablespoons Chinese rice wine or dry sherry
2 teaspoons hoisin sauce
2 teaspoons sugar
1 teaspoon sesame oil
¾ teaspoon Chinese five-spice powder
¾ teaspoon salt
½ teaspoon grated ginger
2 whole star anise

1 tablespoon vegetable oil
⅓ cup chopped shallots
3 tablespoons chopped ginger
3 tablespoons chopped green onion

2 cups rock salt, or as needed

1. Stir the soy sauces together in a small bowl. Rub into the skin of the chicken (or game hens). Let stand for 10 minutes.

2. Prepare the seasonings: Stir the rice wine, hoisin sauce, sugar, sesame oil, five-spice powder, salt, ginger, and star anise together in a small bowl until the sugar is dissolved.

3. Heat a wok over high heat until hot. Add the oil and swirl to coat the sides. Add the shallots, ginger, and green onion and cook, stirring, until fragrant, about 30 seconds. Add the seasonings and stir to combine. Scoop into a small bowl and let cool briefly.

4. Preheat the oven to 375°F.

5. Spoon the seasoning mixture into the cavity of the chicken (or divide between the game hens). Wrap the chickens (or game hens) in parchment, tucking any overhanging paper underneath the bird(s). Place half the rock salt in the bottom of a 2-quart clay pot or covered casserole into which the bird(s) fits snugly. Set the parchment-wrapped bird(s) on the salt. Pour enough additional rock salt into the pot to cover the bird(s) completely.

6. Cover the pot and bake until the bird(s) is no longer pink in the leg, for about 1 hour and 15 minutes. Remove the bird(s) from the salt, unwrap, and serve.

VARIATION To make a crispy-skinned version of this recipe is dangerous and is not for a beginner.

Let the cooked bird(s) stand after removing from the parchment while you heat 2 cups vegetable oil in a wok over medium-high heat to 350°F. Place a hook under the wing joint of the chicken (or each game hen) and hold it over the hot oil while, using a Chinese ladle, you spoon hot oil repeatedly from the wok over the bird, letting it drip back into the wok, until the skin is deliciously crisp and caramelized, 5 to 6 minutes.

LIGHT AND TENDER MUSHROOM-STEAMED CHICKEN

Serves 4 as part of a multicourse meal

The woodsy aroma and unique texture of mushrooms are prized in thousands of Chinese dishes. Mushrooms are also a great meat substitute for vegetarians. Serve this dish with a side of rice and vegetables.

4 dried wood ear or cloud ear mushrooms
4 dried black mushrooms
10 dried lily buds
2 teaspoons wolfberries

FOR THE SAUCE
1 tablespoon Chinese rice wine
    or dry sherry
1 tablespoon oyster-flavored sauce
2 teaspoons cornstarch
1½ teaspoons soy sauce
1 teaspoon grated ginger
¼ teaspoon sesame oil

¾ pound boneless, skinless chicken breasts
    or thighs, cut into bite-sized pieces

*   *   *

1. Pour enough warm water over the black mushrooms, wood ear mushrooms, lily buds, and wolfberries in separate small bowls to cover them completely. Soak until softened, about 20 minutes. Drain the mushrooms, lily buds, and wolfberries. Discard the black mushroom stems. Thinly slice the black mushroom caps and the wood ears. Cut the hard ends off the lily buds and tie each bud into a knot in its center.

2. Prepare the sauce: Stir the rice wine, oyster-flavored sauce, cornstarch, soy sauce, ginger, and sesame oil together in a small bowl until the cornstarch is dissolved.

3. Spread the chicken out in an even layer in a glass pie dish. Pour the sauce over the chicken and scatter the black mushrooms, wood ears, lily buds, and wolfberries over it.

4. Prepare a wok for steaming according to the directions on page xxvi. Place the plate of chicken in the wok, cover, and steam in the steaming basket until the chicken is no longer pink in the center, about 20 minutes. Serve immediately, directly from the plate.

CURE-ALL STEAMED CHICKEN WITH CHINESE HERBS

Serves 4 as part of a multicourse meal

This traditional Chinese tonic soup is meant as a form of preventive medicine. It naturally balances yin and yang within the body while building immunity. It is a great alternative for cold and flu season instead of the usual ho-hum chicken soup. It also energizes the body and mind.

1 pound chicken legs and thighs

4 slices quarter-sized peeled ginger, lightly crushed

3 fresh shiitake, stems discarded and caps halved

1 dried ginseng root (about ½ ounce)

1 tablespoon wolfberries

8 walnut halves

4 dried longans

4 red dates

3 cups water

½ cup Chinese rice wine or dry sherry

1 teaspoon salt

❋　　❋　　❋

1. Remove the skin and excess fat from the chicken pieces. Bring a pot of water to a boil. Add the chicken and return to a boil. Cook for 1 minute; drain.

2. Place the chicken pieces in a 2-quart casserole. Scatter the ginger, shiitake, ginseng, wolfberries, walnuts, longans, and dates over the chicken. Pour in the water and rice wine and add the salt.

3. Prepare a wok for steaming according to the directions on page xxvi. Cover the casserole and set it on the steaming rack. Cover the wok and steam over medium-high heat until the chicken is tender, about 2 hours. Replenish the water in the wok as needed during steaming.

4. Skim the fat from the broth in the casserole and discard the ginseng. Ladle the soup and chicken pieces into individual bowls and serve.

LOTUS BLOSSOM OMELET IN BROTH

Serves 4 as part of a multicourse meal

This Shanghai dish is a popular one in New York. Often served at banquets, it can be assembled a day in advance for the home. Simply steam the whole thing just before serving.

4 to 6 dried black mushrooms

2 large eggs
Pinch of salt
1 teaspoon vegetable oil

½ cup shredded cooked chicken breast
Two 4-ounce pieces pressed tofu,
    cut into thin strips
½ cup smoked ham, cut into thin strips
½ cup thinly sliced carrots

1 cup spinach leaves

FOR THE SEASONED BROTH
1 cup Chicken Stock (page 69) or
    canned chicken broth
2 tablespoons Chinese rice wine or dry sherry
1 teaspoon sesame oil
¼ teaspoon salt
¼ teaspoon ground white pepper

*   *   *

1. Pour warm water over the mushrooms in a small bowl to cover them completely. Let soak until softened, about 20 minutes. Drain. Discard the stems and cut the caps into thin strips.

2. Beat the eggs together with the salt in a small bowl. Heat a wide nonstick frying pan over medium heat until hot. Add the oil. Pour in the eggs and tilt the pan to coat the bottom evenly.

Cook until the eggs are lightly browned on the bottom and set on top, about 1 minute. Carefully turn the egg sheet over and cook for 5 seconds. Slide the omelet onto a plate.

3. Fit the omelet into a 1-quart heatproof bowl—6 inches in diameter and 4 inches deep—letting it hang over the edges. Use the mushroom, chicken, tofu, ham, and carrots to cover each quarter of the bottom of the omelet-lined bowl with a different ingredient. Fill in any empty spaces with any remaining tofu. Bring the edges of the omelet over the filling and press firmly to compact.

4. Prepare a wok for steaming according to the directions on page xxvi. Set the bowl into the steamer, cover, and steam until the omelet is heated through, about 10 minutes.

5. Invert the bowl into a large shallow serving bowl. Lift off the bowl carefully. With a paring knife, cut the top of the omelet in a cross and peel back the points to reveal the filling. Arrange the spinach around the filled omelet.

6. Make the broth while steaming the omelet: Bring the chicken stock, rice wine, sesame oil, salt, and pepper to a boil in a small saucepan.

7. Ladle the broth around the filled omelet and over the spinach, so it wilts the spinach. Serve hot.

SUCCULENT STEAMED CHICKEN WITH GINGER-SOY DIPPING SAUCE

Serves 4 as part of a multicourse meal

The Soup Restaurant in Singapore continues to prepare this simple dish as the Sam Sui women (see page 147) once did, but they serve it in a lettuce cup. Steaming, rather than roasting, the chicken helps it remain moist and tender. Tip: When a chicken is cut in half, it cooks much faster.

One 3- to 4-pound frying chicken, cut in half
1 tablespoon soy sauce or dark soy sauce

FOR THE DIPPING SAUCE
¼ cup grated ginger
3 green onions, trimmed and minced
1 tablespoon sesame oil
2 teaspoons soy sauce
1 teaspoon minced garlic
½ teaspoon ground ginger
¼ teaspoon salt
⅛ teaspoon ground white pepper
2 tablespoons vegetable oil

12 iceberg lettuce cups

❋　❋　❋

1. Arrange the chicken halves skin side up and side by side in a glass pie plate.

2. Rub the skin with the soy sauce. Let stand for 15 minutes.

3. Prepare a wok for steaming according to the directions on page xxvi. Place the pie plate in the steaming basket, cover, and steam over high heat until the chicken is no longer pink near the bone, about 30 minutes.

4. Meanwhile, make the dipping sauce: Stir the grated ginger, green onions, sesame oil, soy sauce, garlic, ground ginger, salt, and pepper together in a small heatproof bowl. Heat the vegetable oil in a small skillet just until it begins to smoke. Carefully pour the hot oil into the ginger-soy mixture (the mixture may sizzle). Stir well and let stand until cool.

5. Remove the plate of chicken from the steamer and let cool slightly.

6. Strip the meat from the bones and cut the meat into bite-sized pieces. Place on a serving platter with the lettuce cups alongside. Pass the platter and dipping sauce, allowing guests to make their own lettuce cups.

SPICY GRILLED CHICKEN THIGHS À LA MACAU

Serves 4 as part of a multicourse meal

Macanese cuisine has an African influence, since the Portuguese traveled to the east by way of Africa, where they learned about African spices and cooking techniques. The dill pickle garnish is a Western influence. Marinate the chicken in a plastic zipper bag.

FOR THE MARINADE

¼ cup dry white wine

¼ cup Chicken Stock (page 69) or canned chicken broth

¼ cup chopped shallots

3 garlic cloves, minced

2 bay leaves

3 teaspoons mild paprika

2 teaspoons bottled satay sauce

1 teaspoon dried red chili flakes

1 teaspoon sesame oil

1 teaspoon salt

1 teaspoon sugar

1 teaspoon curry powder

4 small chicken thighs (about 1 pound)

½ cup Chicken Stock (page 69) or canned chicken broth

1 dill pickle, thinly sliced lengthwise

Tomato wedges

❋   ❋   ❋

1. Marinate the chicken: Stir the white wine, shallots, garlic, bay leaves, paprika, satay sauce, chili flakes, sesame oil, salt, sugar, and curry powder together in a medium bowl. Add the chicken and turn to coat. Cover the bowl and refrigerate for 1 hour.

2. Prepare a charcoal fire or preheat a gas grill to medium high.

3. When the grill is ready, remove the chicken from the marinade; set the chicken aside. In a small saucepan bring the reserved marinade and additional stock to a boil and cook until the sauce is reduced by one-third. Remove from the heat, remove the bay leaves, and cover the sauce to keep warm.

4. Grill the chicken until the internal temperature at the thickest part of the thigh reaches 160°F, 6 to 8 minutes per side. Transfer the chicken to a serving plate.

5. Spoon the sauce over the chicken, garnish with the pickle and tomato wedges, and serve.

THREE-PEPPER GAME HEN

Serves 4 as part of a multicourse meal

Most home cooks stir-fry chicken, pork, or beef in their woks, but chefs often experiment with duck, squab, or game hen. Chef Chee-Hwee Tong, at the Hakkasan Restaurant near London's Chinatown, bones a game hen and seasons it with three peppers: Sichuan, black, and fresh chili pepper. For those who like their Chinese food hot and spicy, this is ideal.

FOR THE MARINADE
1/4 teaspoon salt
1/4 teaspoon sugar
1/4 teaspoon cornstarch

1 Cornish game hen (about 2 pounds), skinned and boned, or 1 pound boneless, skinless chicken breasts, cut into bite-sized pieces

FOR THE PEPPER SAUCE
1/4 cup Chicken Stock (page 69) or canned chicken broth
1 tablespoon ground bean paste or brown miso
2 teaspoons soy sauce
1 teaspoon sugar
1 teaspoon cracked black peppercorns

2 teaspoons vegetable oil
1 tablespoon unsalted butter
3 garlic cloves, sliced
1 teaspoon salted black beans, rinsed, drained, and mashed
1/8 teaspoon toasted ground Sichuan peppercorns

1 cup sugar snap peas, trimmed
1/2 cup sliced red bell pepper
1 green or red jalapeño chili, seeded and thinly sliced

* * *

1. Marinate the game hen: Stir the salt, sugar, and cornstarch together in a bowl until combined. Add the game hen pieces (or chicken pieces) and toss well to coat. Let stand for 10 minutes.

2. Prepare the pepper sauce: Stir the chicken stock, ground bean paste, soy sauce, sugar, and black peppercorns together in a small bowl until the sugar is dissolved.

3. Heat a wok over high heat until hot. Add the oil and swirl to coat the sides. Add the butter, garlic, black beans, and Sichuan peppercorns and cook, stirring, until fragrant, about 20 seconds. Add the game hen and stir-fry until no longer pink, 2 to 2 1/2 minutes. Scoop the hen from the wok and set aside.

4. Return the wok to the heat and add the snap peas, bell pepper, and jalapeño chili pepper. Cook, stirring, until the vegetables are tender-crisp, 1 to 1 1/2 minutes. Return the game hen to the wok and pour in the pepper sauce. Cook until heated through, 1 to 1 1/2 minutes.

5. Scoop onto a serving platter and serve immediately.

DOUBLE-DUTY DUCK WITH BEAN SPROUTS

Serves 4 as part of a multicourse meal

Like all good cooks, Chinese chefs waste nothing. At the Peking Duck House in New York City, the leftover meat from a Peking duck banquet is used in many ways, including this simple preparation. If you can't find yellow chives, use regular chives or green onions.

FOR THE SAUCE

3 tablespoons soy sauce

3 tablespoons Chicken Stock (page 69) or canned chicken broth

2 tablespoons hoisin sauce

1 teaspoon cornstarch

¼ teaspoon ground white pepper

1 tablespoon vegetable oil

½ red bell pepper, cut into thin strips

3 green onions, trimmed and cut into 2-inch lengths

1 teaspoon minced ginger

1 cup shredded Roast Duck meat (page 239)

2 cups bean sprouts

½ cup thinly sliced bamboo shoots

¼ cup chopped Chinese yellow or green chives, cut into 2-inch lengths (optional, see headnote)

1. Prepare the sauce: Stir the soy sauce, chicken stock, hoisin sauce, cornstarch, and pepper together in a small bowl until the cornstarch is dissolved.

2. Heat a wok over high heat until hot. Add the oil and swirl to coat the sides. Add the bell pepper, green onions, and ginger and stir-fry until the green onions are slightly wilted, about 1 minute. Add the duck, bean sprouts, bamboo shoots, and chives, if using, and stir-fry until the bean sprouts are tender, 1½ to 2 minutes.

3. Pour the sauce into the wok and cook, stirring, until the sauce boils and thickens, about 30 seconds. Scoop onto a serving platter and serve.

MU SHU DUCK WRAPS

Serves 4 as part of a multicourse meal

Here is another example of how Chinese chefs create many dishes from one or two roast ducks. If you can't find mu shu wrappers, substitute flour tortillas.

FOR THE SEASONINGS
1/4 cup Chicken Stock (page 69) or
　　canned chicken broth
1 teaspoon sesame oil
1/4 teaspoon salt
1/8 teaspoon ground white pepper

1 tablespoon vegetable oil
2 garlic cloves, minced
1 cup chopped Roast Duck meat
　　(page 239)
1/2 cup finely chopped carrots
3 fresh shiitake, stems discarded and
　　caps finely chopped
1/2 cup finely chopped celery
1/4 cup chopped green onions
　　(white parts only)
1/4 cup finely chopped water chestnuts

1 teaspoon cornstarch, dissolved in
　　2 teaspoons water

8 mu shu wrappers or small flour tortillas,
　　heated
Hoisin sauce for serving

1. Prepare the seasonings: Stir the chicken stock, sesame oil, salt, and pepper together in a small bowl until blended.

2. Heat a wok over high heat until hot. Add the oil and swirl to coat the sides. Add the garlic and stir-fry until fragrant, about 20 seconds. Add the duck, carrots, shiitake, celery, green onions, and water chestnuts and stir-fry until the carrots are tender-crisp, 1 1/2 to 2 minutes. Pour in the seasonings and cook for 1 minute, then add the dissolved cornstarch and cook, stirring, until the sauce boils and thickens, about 30 seconds.

3. Scoop onto a serving platter. Place the mu shu wrappers and a small bowl of hoisin sauce alongside. To eat, spread a small amount of the hoisin sauce and about 3 tablespoons of the duck mixture on a wrapper, roll up like a burrito, and eat out of hand.

ZESTY LEMON DUCK

Serves 4 as part of a multicourse meal

In Yokohama's Chinatown, this Cantonese dish, a variation on the popular lemon chicken, is a Japanese favorite. Boneless chicken thighs can be used in place of the duck.

2 boneless duck breast halves, skin on
1 teaspoon salt
1/8 teaspoon ground white pepper
Cornstarch for dusting

FOR THE SAUCE
Zesty Lemon Sauce (this page)
1/4 cup pineapple chunks
2 tablespoons Chicken Stock (page 69) or
    canned chicken broth
1 tablespoon crystallized ginger, cut into
    thin strips

2 teaspoons vegetable oil

1 teaspoon cornstarch, dissolved in
    2 teaspoons water (optional)

❋ ❋ ❋

1. Lay the duck breast halves skin side down on a work surface and trim any fat that extends beyond the breast meat. Turn the breasts over and, with the tip of a knife, lightly score the skin in a cross-hatch pattern to keep the skin from shrinking as it cooks. Sprinkle both sides of the duck breasts with the salt and pepper. Dust with the cornstarch to coat lightly, tapping off any excess.

2. Prepare the sauce: Stir the lemon sauce, pineapple chunks, chicken stock, and ginger together in a bowl.

3. Heat a wide skillet over medium-high heat until hot. Add the oil, swirling to coat the bottom of the pan. Add the duck breasts skin side down and cook until the skin is crisp and brown, 4 to 5 minutes. Flip the breasts and cook until the meat is cooked to medium, about 6 minutes.

4. Transfer the duck to a plate. Spoon off all but 1 tablespoon of the drippings from the pan. Return the pan to medium-high heat, pour in the sauce, and bring to a boil. For a thicker sauce, stir in the dissolved cornstarch and cook until the sauce boils and thickens, about 1 minute. Remove from the heat.

5. To serve, slice each duck breast on the bias into 6 slices. Fan the slices out on a plate and spoon the sauce over them.

❋ ❋ ❋

ZESTY LEMON SAUCE

Honey provides the sweet, and the lemon zest, pulp, and juice the sour. In a small bowl, whisk 6 to 8 tablespoons mild honey, 5 tablespoons fresh lemon juice, 2 tablespoons grated lemon zest, and 2 teaspoons minced lemon pulp. Stir in 2 tablespoons plum sauce and blend well. Serve at room temperature. Makes about 1 cup; the sauce can be stored for up to 2 weeks in the refrigerator, but the color may darken slightly.

EIGHT-TREASURE LUCKY DUCK

Serves 4 as part of a multicourse meal

Dishes such as this are usually served during festivals as a symbol of prosperity and good luck. Chinese chefs often bone the duck before stuffing it, making it easier to slice. Since not everyone has the knife skills of a Chinese chef, I reinvented this recipe using a whole duck.

FOR THE STUFFING

2 tablespoons barley

2 tablespoons dried shrimp

8 dried lily buds

2 tablespoons dark soy sauce

One 4- to 5-pound duck, rinsed, wing tips removed

2 teaspoons vegetable oil

½ cup canned lotus seeds, drained

2 to 3 medium fresh shiitake, stems discarded and caps chopped

1 salted duck egg, yolk only (discard the white)

1 Chinese sausage (about 2 ounces), sliced on the bias

2 tablespoons oyster-flavored sauce

1 teaspoon salt

1 teaspoon sugar

⅛ teaspoon ground white pepper

¼ cup vegetable oil

8 whole star anise

FOR THE SAUCE

½ cup Chicken Stock (page 69) or canned chicken broth

2 tablespoons oyster-flavored sauce

½ teaspoon salt

1. Pour warm water over the barley in a small bowl to cover completely. Soak for 2 hours; drain.

2. Pour warm water over the dried shrimp and lily buds in separate small bowls to cover. Soak until softened, about 20 minutes. Drain. Cut off the hard tips of the lily buds, then tie each bud into a knot.

3. Rub the dark soy sauce evenly over the skin of the duck. Let stand for 10 minutes.

4. Place a wok over high heat until hot. Pour in 2 teaspoons oil, swirling to coat the sides.

5. Cook the barley, dried shrimp, lily buds, lotus seeds, shiitake, egg yolk, sausage, oyster-flavored sauce, salt, sugar, and pepper for about 5 minutes. Spoon this stuffing into the duck body cavity. Stretch the flap of neck skin over the neck opening and fasten it in place with small metal or bamboo skewers. Overlap the flaps of skin on either side of the body cavity and fasten them securely with skewers. Let stand for 30 minutes.

6. Heat a wide skillet over high heat until hot. Add the ¼ cup oil. Place the duck breast side down in the pan and cook, turning once, until lightly browned, 4 to 5 minutes on each side.

7. Lift the duck from the pan and place the duck in a heatproof dish. Prepare a wok for steaming

(page xxvi), adding the star anise to the steaming liquid. Place the duck (in the dish) in the steamer basket; steam over medium-high heat until the meat is no longer pink and the barley is tender, about an hour. Occasionally check the steamer water level to ensure that it has not run dry.

8. Lift the duck from the heatproof dish and place on cutting board. Skim any visible fat from the top of the liquid, and pour the liquid into a small saucepan. Add the chicken stock, oyster-flavored sauce, and salt. Heat over medium heat until hot. Using a meat cleaver, cut off the legs at the thigh joints and cut off the wings; set aside. Cut the breast into 6 pieces. Transfer to a platter and place the pieces along the sides. Pour the sauce over the duck and serve immediately.

1,000-YEAR-OLD EGGS AND SALTED DUCK EGGS

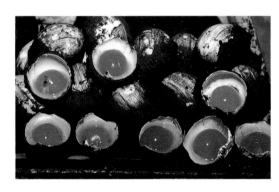

Also called 100-year-old eggs, they were developed as China's refrigeration-free way of preserving eggs. To make them, fresh duck eggs are mixed with preservatives that penetrate the shells, changing the eggs' texture within. Some are coated in nonacidic mud and buried in ash, rice hulls, or tea leaves for 100 days, which softens their shells and leaves them pungently flavored with gray, jelly-like whites. Salted duck eggs are soaked in a brine spiked with saltpeter or ground charcoal, which thins the whites and hardens the yolks, giving the latter a mild saltiness and bright orange color. Unlike the mud-buried variety, the brine-soaked duck eggs, used in fillings for moon cakes, need to be cooked before eating. When purchasing 1,000-year-old eggs or salted duck eggs, look for unblemished, dense-feeling ones sold in clear plastic egg containers in the refrigerated section of Asian markets.

WOK-BRAISED DUCK BREAST WITH CHILI-BEER SAUCE

Serves 4 as part of a multicourse meal

Beer in Chinese cooking? Even though many people like to drink beer with Chinese food, cooking with beer is not common in China. But the chefs at Post-Deng Café in Melbourne's Chinatown are not a common bunch of professionals. They like to experiment.

2 boneless duck breast halves with skin
    (4 to 6 ounces each)
1 teaspoon vegetable oil

FOR THE COOKING SAUCE
⅓ cup flat light or dark beer or ale
2 tablespoons Chicken Stock
    (page 69) or canned chicken broth
1 tablespoon Chinese rice wine or
    dry sherry
2 teaspoons hoisin sauce
2 teaspoons soy sauce
¼ teaspoon salt
¼ teaspoon ground toasted Sichuan
    peppercorns

2 green onions, trimmed and cut into
    2-inch lengths
4 quarter-sized slices peeled ginger,
    cut into thin strips
1 tablespoon chili bean sauce or
    chili garlic sauce

½ cup sliced button mushrooms
½ cup red bell pepper, cut into
    thin 2-inch lengths

*   *   *

1. Score the skin of the duck breasts with diagonal slashes 1 inch apart (the slashes should go almost all the way through the skin without reaching the meat). Repeat in the opposite direction to create a crosshatch.

2. Heat a wok over medium heat until hot. Add the oil and swirl to coat the sides. Place the breast halves skin side down in the wok and cook until the skin is crispy and brown, about 4 minutes. Turn the breast halves and cook until the meat is lightly browned, about 5 minutes. Transfer the duck to a plate and allow to rest. Turn off the heat and spoon off all but one 1 tablespoon of the drippings from the wok.

3. While the duck is resting, prepare the cooking sauce: Stir the beer, chicken stock, rice wine, hoisin sauce, soy sauce, salt, and Sichuan peppercorns together in a medium bowl until the salt is dissolved.

4. Cut the cooled duck breasts on the bias into ½-inch slices. Heat the drippings in the wok over high heat until hot. Add the green onions, ginger, and chili bean sauce and cook, stirring, until fragrant, about 30 seconds. Add the duck, cooking sauce, mushrooms, and bell pepper. Bring to a boil. Adjust the heat so the sauce is simmering, cover the wok, and simmer until the duck is just slightly pink in the center (cooked medium), 5 to 7 minutes. Scoop onto a warm serving platter and serve immediately.

TOASTING

Ingredients like sesame seeds and Sichuan peppercorns intensify in flavor and color with a light toasting in a small, dry pan. Just place the seeds or peppercorns in a pan with a heavy bottom, place the pan over low heat, and lightly shake until the ingredients start releasing their fragrance and darkening a bit, being careful not to burn them. ✳ If you want to toast a small amount of nuts, the stovetop method works, but for larger quantities spread in one layer on a baking sheet or pie pan and place in a 325° to 350°F oven until golden.

AROMATIC DUCK | *Serves 4 as part of a multicourse meal*

Crispy aromatic duck is as well-known in London and throughout England as Peking duck is in North America. While this dish takes some effort to prepare, it is well worth it for a special occasion. Like many tourists, every time I visit London's Chinatown, this is the first dish I order. This recipe is for a more advanced chef as the ladling of hot oil onto the duck is dangerous.

FOR THE SPICES

1 cup thinly sliced peeled ginger

8 whole star anise

2 pieces dried tangerine peel

2 cinnamon sticks

2 teaspoons toasted Sichuan peppercorns

3 cardamom pods, lightly crushed

1½ cups soy sauce

One 4- to 6-pound duck, rinsed and wing tips
    removed

¾ cup dark soy sauce

¾ cup soy sauce

¾ cup sugar

2 cups vegetable oil

⅓ English cucumber, cut into thin
    2-inch-long strips

5 green onions, trimmed and cut into thin
    2-inch strips

Hoisin sauce for serving

Mandarin pancakes or thin flour tortillas

    ❋   ❋   ❋

1. Prepare a spice bag: Place the ginger, star anise, tangerine peel, cinnamon, Sichuan peppercorns, and cardamom in the center of an 8-inch square of cheesecloth. Bring the corners of the square together and tie them with a string to form a bag.

2. Place the duck in a 5-quart pot and pour in enough cold water to cover. Add the spice bag and bring the water to a boil over high heat. Adjust the heat so the water is simmering, cover the pot, and simmer until the duck thigh is tender when pricked with a fork, 1½ to 2 hours.

3. Lift the duck from the water with a large wire skimmer or by inserting a sturdy wooden spoon into the body cavity and hold the duck over the pot to allow the water to drain back into the pot, then transfer the duck to a colander and drain completely. Cool to room temperature.

4. Stir the soy sauces and sugar together in a small saucepan over medium heat until the sugar is dissolved. Let cool.

5. Pat the duck dry on all sides with paper towels. Brush the duck 3 or 4 times with the soy syrup to coat it well.

6. Heat the oil in a wok over medium heat to 350°F. Holding the syrup-coated duck by a hook inserted under its wing joint or with a sturdy pair of tongs, suspend the duck over the hot oil and using a Chinese ladle, spoon the hot oil repeatedly over the duck until the skin is caramelized and crispy, 5 to 6 minutes. Let the duck cool briefly.

7. Remove the skin from the duck and cut the skin into thin strips. With your hands, using rubber gloves for protection if you find the duck too hot, remove the meat from the bones, tossing it into a bowl as you work. Shred the meat with two forks.

8. Place the duck meat and skin on a serving plate. Place separate bowls of the cucumber, green onions, and hoisin sauce and a plate of the pancakes alongside. To eat, spread a small amount of hoisin sauce over a pancake, top with some of the duck meat and skin, cucumber, and green onion, and roll the pancake around the filling like a burrito.

A GLUTTONOUS GOD

t says a lot about a culture's passion for food when it has a deity who lives over the stove. All across rural China, in the South especially, the image of the Kitchen God (Zao Shen in Chinese) is pasted up. Forget centerfolds; he's the country's most ubiquitous pin-up. And his job is to protect family harmony by watching over the place where families had better find their happiness if they're going to find it at all, and that's around the dining table. ✳ Once a year, on the 23rd day of the last lunar month to be exact, Zao Shen is supposed to report to the Jade Emperor, supreme ruler of heaven, on just how good or bad the family has behaved (and cooked). Like the best modern-day politician, he's quite open to gifts that might influence his report. So the family sets up an altar and lavishes on their heavenly watchman his favorite sweet treats, from mandarin oranges to candies and cakes. Big bowls of fresh rice studded with candied fruits and nuts are offered along with rice wine to soften his mood. ✳ Honey or molasses is smeared on the god's mouth to make his words sweeter, or, if that fails, to help glue his lips shut. It's all good practice for learning how to cook while learning the ways of the world—a little buttering-up of the authorities never hurts, even without butter. The image of Zao Shen is then set afire so he can rise, well-smoked, to complete his mission. But every Chinese family knows the Kitchen God will soon be back at his post: supervising next year's menus.

LONDON

Stroll down from Piccadilly or up from Leicester Square, turn onto Gerrard Street, and there you'll find London's Chinatown. In the late 1950s, Chinese moved here from the World War II bombed-out Limehouse dockside area, where they had first settled in London. ✳ Since growling lions are the symbol of both China and Great Britain, it took some time for these two nations to learn to get along. The first Chinese immigrants were seamen brought to England by the British East India Company. After the Opium Wars, more Chinese trickled in, but the big wave came as a result of Britain's possession of Hong Kong, allowing many Chinese to immigrate to London. ✳ From fewer than fifty Chinese in the British Isles at the turn of the nineteenth century, there are now at least 350,000 BBCs—

"British-born Chinese." The mix of British pubs with traditional red facades and trendy noodle shops with high-tech facades lends unusual character to the area's long pedestrian mall, which is alive with an international crowd of diners and "punters"—that's drinkers—at all hours and scented with this Chinatown's specialty, crispy aromatic duck.

FUNG SHING RESTAURANT

15 Lisle Street
(44-2) 7437-1539
What to order: *crispy lamb in lettuce cups; steamed lobster over rice noodles; deep-fried wontons with sweet-and-sour sauce*

HAKKASAN RESTAURANT

8 Hanway Place
(44-2) 7907-0700
What to order: *salmon and codfish with Xiangpin; black pepper squab; sweet four-treasure tea*

KOWLOON CHINESE CAKE SHOP

21–22 Gerrard Street
(44-2) 7437-0148
What to order: *crispy smiling cookies; Chinese doughnuts; Chinese steamed sponge cake; "Wife's Delight"; chestnut cake*

NEW LOON FUNG CHINESE RESTAURANT

42–44 Gerrard Street
(44-2) 7437-6232
What to order: *crispy aromatic duck with pancake; steamed triple egg custard with shredded pork*

YMING'S RESTAURANT

35–36 Greek Street
(44-2) 7813-1810
What to order: *ta t'sai mi; dragon broccoli; mint fried rice*

CHINATOWN DELI ROAST DUCK

Serves 4 to 6 as part of a multicourse meal

This is a classic recipe for roast duck, much like the roast ducks you see hanging from hooks in Chinatown windows. Although it is difficult to get professional results in your home kitchen, this version will get you pretty close. The most important step is to dry the skin of the duck to ensure a crispy skin. If there are any leftovers, use the meat in Lucky Duck Melon Salad (page 121) or Mu Shu Duck Wraps (page 229). Use the bones to make Duck Soup with Napa Cabbage (page 79).

One 4- to 5-pound duck

FOR THE MARINADE

¼ cup sugar

1 tablespoon hoisin sauce

1½ teaspoons salt

1 teaspoon toasted Sichuan peppercorns

½ teaspoon Chinese five-spice powder

3 whole star anise

2 to 3 thin slices peeled ginger

2 green onions, trimmed and cut into 2-inch lengths

2 medium garlic cloves, crushed

FOR THE GLAZE

1½ cups water

¼ cup distilled white vinegar

¼ cup maltose syrup or honey

⅛ teaspoon red food color (optional)

❋ ❋ ❋

1. Prepare the duck: Rinse the duck inside and out under cold water. Pat all surfaces dry. Clip off the wing tips with kitchen shears. If the head is not attached to the duck, pull the neck skin over the neck opening and secure the skin with a metal skewer.

2. Marinate the duck: Stir the sugar, hoisin sauce, salt, Sichuan peppercorns, five-spice powder, star anise, ginger, green onions, and garlic together in a small bowl until well blended. Pour the marinade into the cavity of the duck. Overlap the flaps of the skin on either side of the cavity and sew them shut with a trussing needle and thread—the opening must be sewn securely shut to keep the marinade from leaking out as the duck hangs.

3. Make the glaze: Stir the water, white vinegar, honey, and food color, if using, together in a small bowl until blended.

4. Tie a string securely around the duck's neck or under its wings to serve as a hanger. Leave about a foot of string attached.

5. Bring an 8- to 12-quart stockpot of water to a boil. Holding the duck by the string, slowly

lower it into the boiling water until it is completely submerged. Let steep for 2 minutes, then lift the duck from the water, letting the excess water drip back into the pot. Hold the duck over a large bowl and carefully pour the glaze over the duck, taking care to coat the entire duck with the glaze. Repeat the glazing process two to three times to ensure the duck is evenly coated.

6. Hang the duck in a cool place until the skin is taut and dry, at least 4 hours, or overnight. You can reduce the time to 2 hours by using an electric fan: Aim a fan, set on high, directly at the hanging duck. Move the fan, or the duck, as necessary to dry all the sides evenly.

7. Preheat the oven to 400°F.

8. Place the duck breast side up on a rack in a foil-lined roasting pan. Remove the string. Roast the duck until the skin is brown and crispy, 40 to 50 minutes. Remove from the oven and let stand for 10 minutes before carving. The duck can be served warm with bowls of steamed rice (page 285) or used as an ingredient in numerous dishes.

PARCHMENT-BAKED SQUAB WITH MUSHROOMS

Serves 4 as part of a multicourse meal

Fuel is a precious commodity in China, so oven-baking is rarely done, but this squab dish combines Chinese ingredients with Western technology.

FOR THE MARINADE

¼ cup Chinese rice wine or dry sherry

2 tablespoons soy sauce

2 tablespoons dark soy sauce

1 tablespoon oyster-flavored sauce

1 teaspoon sugar

2 squab (about 1 pound each), split in half, with backbones removed

1 Chinese sausage (about 2 ounces), sliced on the bias into 8 pieces

8 button mushrooms, trimmed and cut in half

4 fresh shiitake, stems discarded and caps cut in half

One 3- to 4-ounce package enoki mushrooms, bottom ends removed, divided into 4 sections

2 green onions, trimmed and cut into 2-inch lengths

4 cilantro sprigs

✳ ✳ ✳

1. Marinate the squab: Stir the rice wine, soy sauces, oyster-flavored sauce, and sugar together in a large bowl until the sugar is dissolved. Turn the squab pieces in the marinade until coated. Let stand for 10 minutes.

2. Preheat the oven to 350°F.

3. Cut four 12 × 18-inch rectangles of parchment paper or heavy-duty aluminum foil. Lay them out on a work surface and divide the sausage, all the mushrooms, and the green onions evenly among them, mounding them slightly in the center of the parchment. Place a half-squab skin side up on each pile. Bring the long sides of each parchment rectangle together over the squab and roll them as one to hold them together. Seal the ends of each packet with a series of small folds. Place the packets on a baking sheet large enough to hold them comfortably.

4. Bake the squab for 25 to 30 minutes, or until desired doneness (open one packet to test the squab for doneness before serving). Transfer each packet to a warm plate and garnish each with a cilantro sprig. Have your guests tear or cut open their own packets, being careful of the fragrant steam.

FAMILY MATTERS

Great food is the common Chinatown denominator. And one other thing—family and community support. The Chinese have always been a communal people, long before the People's Republic forced them into village "communes." Group interest came over the individual, the good of clan and society over the troubles of a single man. In a new country, the newcomers always found those who had just come before them ready to lend a hand, or at least offer a meal of their favorite dishes from home. Chinatowns became infamous for the "tongs," large family associations such as the Wongs, Lees, or Chans, which gave many a sense of security and belonging. But for the Chinese themselves, the real fame belongs to the "fongs." That's the name for smaller associations of clans, which would always offer comradeship, wisdom, and support to anyone who shared their family name. And with only twelve main names in China, a lot of people were helped on their way. ❋ I have fond memories of family associations. I remember when I first arrived on American soil, I was wandering around San Francisco's Chinatown and spotted a sign for the Yan family association. Being curious, I walked in and met four elderly Yans from the same village as my father. Once they found out I was a newcomer, they asked me if I needed a place to stay. Most of these associations provided room and board to newcomers or single people. Even today, I visit the Yan association when I can and chat with every elderly Yan I can find. I call all of them my uncles. Look carefully—beside the buzzers and mail drops, doorways to the walk-up offices above the shops and restaurants of every Chinatown—and you'll notice the plaques for the village associations. Fellow townsmen from Swatow or Foochow could always link up as though they were all still in the same village square. Many a job was landed in these places, many an enterprise undertaken, and many a bowl of egg drop soup offered.

More important, new arrivals could be understood here—literally. Inside the associations, people could speak their own dialects, sometimes languages distinct from those just a few miles away. Before the advent of cars and jets, or even roads in hilly China, people had long evolved separate tongues—and separate ways of cooking. I was born a Toisanese, so I originally learned to speak Toisanese, the dialect that most early Chinese immigrants spoke. Since my childhood years were spent in Guangzhou (Canton), I learned to speak Cantonese. Through the years, on my travels, I've also learned a few more dialects. But China has produced so many of these dialects, many of which sound like a completely foreign language to me. To this day, I cannot understand a word of the Chiu Chow or Shanghai dialects (which always remind me of a special kind of Japanese)! There was never one monolithic Chinatown.

MASTER SAUCE SQUAB

Serves 2 as part of a multicourse meal

In the kitchen of every fine Chinese restaurant, a pot with a special master sauce is kept simmering on a burner. Additional seasonings and liquid are added to the pot as necessary. The chefs at Sun Sui Wah in Vancouver must have had theirs cooking for twenty-five years. Chef Kim shared his secret master sauce recipe. Master sauce is never thrown away. Simply cool the leftover sauce and refrigerate or freeze for 6 months.

FOR THE MASTER SAUCE

1 tablespoon vegetable oil

2 green onions, trimmed and chopped

2 garlic cloves, peeled and crushed

2½ cups Chicken Stock (page 69) or
    canned chicken broth

1 cup soy sauce

⅓ cup dark soy sauce

2 medium lumps rock sugar or
    ½ cup packed light brown sugar

1 tablespoon rice vinegar

4 bay leaves

3 cardamom pods, cracked

3 cinnamon sticks

3 whole star anise

1 stalk lemongrass, bottom 6 inches only,
    lightly crushed

1 teaspoon whole cloves

2 squab (about 1 pound each) or
    1 Cornish game hen (about 2 pounds)

Steamed Rice (page 285)

1. Make the sauce: Heat a saucepan large enough to hold the squab (or game hen) comfortably over high heat until hot. Add the oil and swirl to coat the bottom. Add the green onions and garlic and cook, stirring, until fragrant, about 30 seconds. Add the chicken stock, soy sauces, rock sugar, rice vinegar, bay leaves, cardamom pods, cinnamon sticks, star anise, lemongrass, and cloves. Bring to a boil, then adjust the heat so the sauce is simmering and simmer for 10 minutes, stirring occasionally to dissolve the sugar.

2. Meanwhile, remove the neck and giblets from the bird(s) and reserve them for another use, if you like. Bring a pot of water large enough to hold the squab (or game hen) comfortably to a boil. Carefully lower the bird(s) into the water and blanch for 3 minutes after the water returns to the boil. Drain.

3. Rest the squab (or game hen) on a large wire skimmer or in a mesh strainer and lower into the pan of simmering master sauce until completely submerged. Hold in the liquid for about 20 seconds, then remove. Repeat this step four times to allow the skin to take on the dark color of the sauce. Then release the squab (or hen) into the liquid, cover the pan, and simmer until the flesh is no longer pink, 25 to 30 minutes (or 40 minutes for the game hen).

4. Lift the bird(s) from the sauce, allowing the excess sauce to drip back into the pan. (Cut the game hen in half before serving.) Serve warm with the steamed rice.

VARIATION You can substitute a 3- to 4-pound chicken, cut in half and backbone removed, for the squab. Increase the cooking time to 40 to 45 minutes.

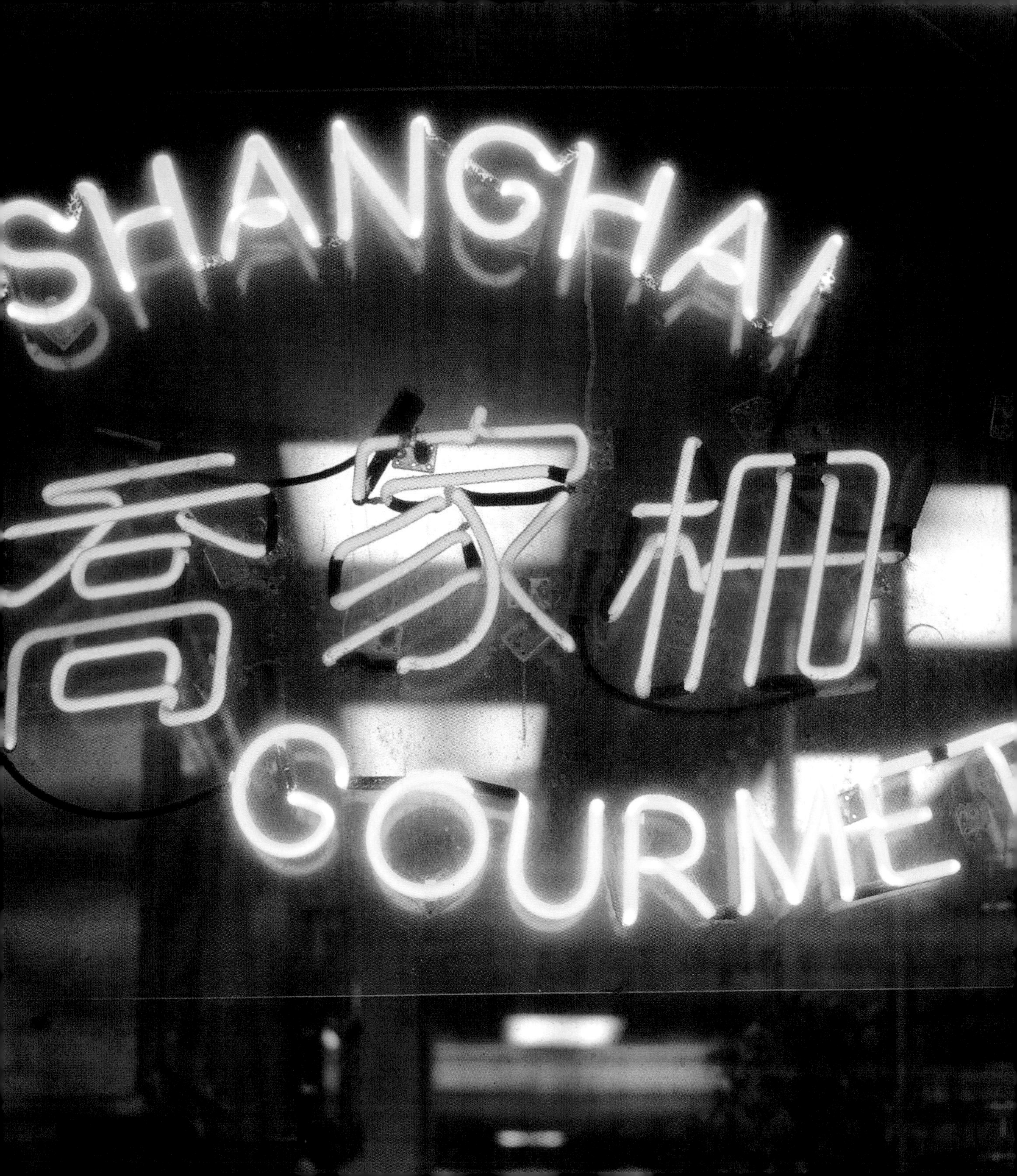
SHANGHAI
GOURMET

MEAT

Meat is used more as a flavoring agent in Chinese cooking than as the centerpiece of a meal. Well, there are always exceptions to a rule. Some of these Chinatown recipes use nothing but meat. Several dishes incorporate lamb, which is also a departure from the norm. Chefs everywhere use all that is edible and available at certain times of year in particular places, cooking ingredients using familiar techniques. The chefs of Chinatowns are no different. In China, they certainly didn't have an abundance of meat, but once they arrived in Toronto or Sydney it was plentiful.

MU SHU PORK

Serves 4 as part of a multicourse meal

Mu shu means "shredded." Pork and vegetables are shredded for this Chinatown favorite. Flour tortillas make excellent wrappers; just heat them briefly on a griddle until softened. To make this a vegetarian dish, omit the pork and add more mushrooms, such as fresh shiitake or portobellos.

8 dried wood ear mushrooms or
    dried black mushrooms

FOR THE MARINADE
2 teaspoons soy sauce or dark soy sauce
2 teaspoons cornstarch

½ pound boneless pork,
    cut into ¼ × 2-inch strips

FOR THE SEASONINGS
2 teaspoons soy sauce or dark soy sauce
1 tablespoon hoisin sauce
2 teaspoons sesame oil
⅛ teaspoon ground white pepper

2 tablespoons vegetable oil
2 eggs, beaten
½ medium green cabbage, cut into thin strips
    (about 2 cups)
6 green onions, trimmed and
    cut into thin strips
2 small carrots, peeled and
    cut into thin strips

8 mu shu wrappers or thin flour tortillas
Hoisin sauce for serving

1. Pour enough warm water over the mushrooms in a medium bowl to cover completely. Soak until softened, about 20 minutes. Drain the mushrooms, discard the stems, and cut the caps into thin strips.

2. Marinate the pork: Stir the soy sauce and cornstarch together in a medium bowl until the cornstarch is dissolved. Toss the pork in the marinade to coat. Let stand for 20 minutes.

3. Prepare the seasonings: Stir the soy sauce, hoisin sauce, sesame oil, and pepper together in a small bowl.

4. Heat a wok over high heat until hot. Pour in 1 tablespoon of the oil and swirl to coat the sides. Add the pork and stir-fry until cooked through, 2 to 3 minutes. Scoop the pork out onto a plate and set aside.

5. Pour the remaining 1 tablespoon oil into the wok. Add the eggs and cook, stirring, until scrambled. Add the mushrooms, cabbage, green onions, and carrots and stir-fry until the vegetables begin to wilt, about 1 minute. Slide the pork into the wok, pour in the seasonings, and stir until the carrots are tender-crisp, about 2 minutes.

6. Scoop the contents of the wok onto a warm serving plate. Serve with the mu shu wrappers and a small dish of hoisin sauce.

ONE-WOK-WONDER PORK AND POTATOES

Serves 4 as part of a multicourse meal

Northern China is meat-and-potatoes country. When Chinese students from there went to Australia for school, they took along this favorite, simple dish. They decided to stay, and so did this dish!

FOR THE SEASONINGS

⅓ cup Chicken Stock (page 69) or
    canned chicken broth
1 tablespoon soy sauce
1 teaspoon distilled white vinegar
½ teaspoon sugar

½ pound ground pork
1 teaspoon cornstarch

2 tablespoons vegetable oil
2 tablespoons minced garlic
2 dried hot chilies (see page 207), crushed, or
    1 teaspoon dried red chili flakes
1 russet (Idaho) potato, peeled and
    cut into ¼ × ¼ × 2-inch strips
1 medium carrot, peeled and
    cut into thin strips
2 green onions, trimmed and
    cut into 2-inch lengths

1. Prepare the seasonings: Stir the chicken stock, soy sauce, white vinegar, and sugar together in a small bowl until the sugar is dissolved.

2. Stir the cornstarch into the pork in a small bowl until well blended.

3. Heat a wok over high heat until hot. Add the oil and swirl to coat the sides. Add the garlic and chilies and cook, stirring, until fragrant, about 20 seconds. Add the pork and cook until the pork begins to crumble, about 2 minutes.

4. Add the potato, carrot, green onions, and seasonings. Reduce the heat to medium, cover the wok, and simmer until the potatoes are tender, 4 to 5 minutes. Scoop onto a warm serving platter and serve immediately.

MACAU'S MINCHEE MINCED PORK

Serves 4 as part of a multicourse meal

This is a signature Macanese dish, known as *minchee* in Portuguese. The Chinese love to stir-fry minced pork too, so it has become a Chinese favorite. It makes a great weeknight meal with sides of rice and vegetables. You can also use ground chicken or, for a vegetarian alternative, chopped mushrooms.

FOR THE SAUCE

1 tablespoon soy sauce or dark soy sauce

1 tablespoon Chinese black vinegar or
    balsamic vinegar

1 tablespoon fish sauce

2 teaspoons Chinese rice wine or dry sherry

2 teaspoons Worcestershire sauce

1/4 teaspoon ground black pepper

Vegetable oil for deep-frying

1 russet (Idaho) potato, peeled and
    cut into 1/4-inch dice

3/4 pound ground pork

1/2 cup diced onions

2 bay leaves

1 tablespoon minced garlic

1 tablespoon chopped mint

1/2 cup quartered water chestnuts

1. Prepare the sauce: Stir the soy sauce, black vinegar, fish sauce, rice wine, Worcestershire sauce, and black pepper together in a small bowl.

2. Pour enough vegetable oil into a medium saucepan to come to a depth of 2 inches. Heat the oil over medium-high to 350°F. Add the potato and cook until golden brown and tender, 3 to 4 minutes. Remove with a slotted spoon and drain on paper towels. Reserve the oil.

3. Heat a wok over high heat until hot. Add 1 tablespoon of the reserved oil and swirl to coat the sides. Crumble the ground pork into the wok, then add the onions, bay leaves, garlic, and mint. Stir-fry until the pork is browned and crumbly, 3 to 4 minutes. Add the water chestnuts, pour in the sauce, and cook until the water chestnuts are heated through, about 1 minute.

4. Stir in the potatoes and heat through. Pick out the bay leaves and transfer the contents of the wok to a serving platter.

SWEET-AND-SOUR PORK

Serves 4 as part of a multicourse meal

A classic. Need I say anything else?

FOR THE MARINADE

½ cup cornstarch

1 egg, lightly beaten

¾ pound boneless pork shoulder or butt,
    cut into 1-inch cubes

Vegetable oil for deep-frying

½ teaspoon minced garlic

½ teaspoon minced ginger

½ green bell pepper, cut into 1-inch dice

½ red bell pepper, cut into 1-inch dice

½ yellow onion, cut into 1-inch dice

½ cup Sweet-and-Sour Sauce (this page)
    or a store-bought version

1 cup fresh or canned pineapple chunks

*   *   *

1. Marinate the pork: Stir the cornstarch and egg together in a bowl until blended. Toss the pork gently in the marinade until coated. Let stand for 10 minutes.

2. Pour enough oil into a deep skillet to come to a depth of 2 inches. Heat over medium-high to 360°F. Deep-fry the pork, a few pieces at a time, turning occasionally, until golden brown, 3 to 4 minutes. Scoop the pork from the oil with a slotted spoon and drain on paper towels. Reserve the oil.

3. Heat a wok over high heat until hot. Add 1 tablespoon of the reserved oil and swirl to coat the sides. Add the garlic and ginger and stir-fry until fragrant, 20 seconds. Add the bell peppers and onion and stir-fry until tender-crisp, 2 to 3 minutes. Pour the sweet-and-sour sauce into the wok and stir to coat the vegetables.

4. Slide the pork into the wok, add the pineapple, and toss until heated through and evenly coated. Scoop the contents of the wok onto a warm platter and serve immediately.

*   *   *

SWEET-AND-SOUR SAUCE

Ketchup and Worcestershire sauce are regularly used in Asian cooking. Although this sauce is available in supermarkets everywhere, nothing beats the homemade version.

Whisk ¾ cup ketchup, 6 tablespoons sugar, 3 tablespoons rice vinegar, 2 tablespoons fresh lime juice, 1 tablespoon soy sauce, and 1 tablespoon Worcestershire sauce in a bowl until the sugar is dissolved. Makes about 1 cup; the sauce will keep refrigerated for 2 weeks. Bring it to room temperature or warm it in a microwave oven before serving.

SPICY SICHUANESE TWICE-COOKED PORK

Serves 4 as part of multicourse meal

A number of the Chinese who reside in Australia came from the southwestern regions of China, such as Sichuan, and Sichuan dishes are plentiful among the mates down under. Double-cooking—first simmering the pork in water, then stir-frying it with other ingredients—is the secret to this dish's texture. There is no substitute for pork belly—ask for it at any butcher; it is simply uncured bacon.

2 cups water
¾ pound pork belly, in one piece

FOR THE SAUCE
½ cup Chicken Stock (page 69) or
    canned chicken broth
¼ cup Chinese rice wine or dry sherry
2 tablespoons sweet bean paste or hoisin sauce
1 tablespoon soy sauce
½ tablespoon hot bean paste or
    chili garlic sauce
2 teaspoons sugar

2 tablespoons vegetable oil
2 green onions, trimmed and cut into
    2-inch lengths
2 quarter-sized slices peeled ginger,
    cut into thin strips
2 teaspoons minced garlic
1 red or green jalapeño chili, seeded and
    cut into thin rings
½ medium head napa cabbage, cut into 1-inch
    strips (about 3 cups)
1 tablespoon cornstarch, dissolved in
    3 tablespoons water

1. Pour the water over the pork belly in a medium saucepan and bring to a boil. Adjust the heat so the water is simmering, cover the pan, and simmer until the pork is no longer pink in the center, 10 to 15 minutes. Drain.

2. Starting at one of the short sides, cut the pork into ¼-inch slices; each slice should contain some meat and some fat.

3. Prepare the sauce: Stir the chicken stock, rice wine, sweet bean paste, soy sauce, hot bean paste, and sugar together in a medium bowl until the sugar is dissolved.

4. Heat a wok over high heat until hot. Add the oil and swirl to coat the sides. Add the green onions, ginger, garlic, and jalapeño and cook, stirring, until fragrant, about 30 seconds. Add the sliced pork and cabbage and stir-fry until the cabbage begins to brown, about 1 minute. Pour in the sauce, cover the wok, and simmer until the cabbage is soft and the flavors have blended, about 5 minutes.

5. Stir in the dissolved cornstarch and cook, stirring, until the sauce boils and thickens, about 1 minute. Spoon into warm shallow bowls.

TEA-SMOKED PORK AND TENDER CABBAGE STIR-FRY

Serves 4 as part of a multicourse meal

The wok has many uses. Since Chinese homes don't have ovens, cooks learned to use the wok and its lid as an oven and a smoker. The Hunan Chinese especially took to this method; their cuisine is known for its inclusion of smoked meats such as duck and pork. The smoking mixture of sugar and tea leaves provides the smoky flavor, while the rice provides the fuel for the smoke. Once smoked, the pork is stir-fried with cabbage in a mild spicy sauce.

½ pound boneless pork butt

4 cups water

3 quarter-sized slices peeled ginger

2 green onions, trimmed

2 teaspoons sugar

¼ teaspoon salt

FOR THE SMOKING MIXTURE

¼ cup black or oolong tea leaves

¼ cup uncooked rice

¼ cup packed light brown sugar

3 star anise

2 tablespoons vegetable oil

1 tablespoon minced garlic

2 teaspoons minced ginger

2 teaspoons minced red or green jalapeño chili

1½ to 2 cups sliced (1-inch) napa cabbage

⅓ cup thinly sliced carrot

⅓ cup sliced bamboo shoots

¼ cup Chicken Stock (page 69), Vegetable Stock (page 105), or canned chicken broth

2 tablespoons soy sauce

1½ teaspoons chili garlic sauce

2 teaspoons cornstarch, dissolved in 1 tablespoon water

¼ teaspoon sesame oil

*　　*　　*

1. Place the pork in a 2-quart saucepan, add the water, ginger, green onions, sugar, and salt, and bring to a boil. Adjust the heat so the liquid is simmering, cover the pot, and simmer until the pork is almost cooked through, about 8 minutes. Drain the pork and set aside.

2. Line the inside of a wok and the inside of its lid with aluminum foil. Make the smoking mixture: Stir the tea leaves, rice, sugar, and star anise together in the lined wok, then spread evenly over the bottom. Set a round rack over the smoking mixture, about 3 inches above the mixture, and set the pork on the center of the rack.

3. Place the wok, uncovered, over high heat. When the rice mixture begins to smoke, cover the wok, reduce the heat to medium, and smoke until the pork turns a rich, deep brown, about 25

minutes. Turn off the heat and let stand for 5 minutes before removing the lid.

4. Let the pork cool briefly, then cut into ⅛-inch-thick slices. (Discard the smoking mixture and foil.)

5. Clean the wok and heat it over high heat until hot. Add the oil and swirl to coat the sides. Add the garlic, ginger, and chili and cook, stirring, until fragrant, about 30 seconds. Add the pork, cabbage, carrot, and bamboo shoots and stir-fry until the cabbage is wilted, about 1 minute.

6. Add the chicken stock, soy sauce, and chili garlic sauce and bring to a boil. Adjust the heat so the sauce is simmering, cover the wok, and simmer until the carrot is tender, about 3 minutes.

7. Pour in the dissolved cornstarch and cook, stirring, until the sauce thickens slightly, about 30 seconds. Stir in the sesame oil, scoop onto a warm serving platter, and serve hot.

SWEET AND TANGY GLAZED PORK CHOPS

Serves 4 as part of a multicourse meal

Because of the influx of Cantonese immigrants to nearby Japan, you'll find this traditional Cantonese dish there. If you can't find the moke stick, substitute a 0.44-ounce package of haw flakes. What is haw? It is kind of a cross between a cherry and a cranberry. The haw is dried, ground, and mixed with sugar.

FOR THE MARINADE

1 egg, lightly beaten
1 tablespoon soy sauce or light soy sauce
1 teaspoon cornstarch
1 teaspoon Chinese rice wine or dry sherry

4 pork loin or shoulder chops, each about
    ½ inch thick, cut in half

FOR THE SAUCE

¼ cup warm water
2 pieces moke stick
2 tablespoons plum sauce
1 tablespoon packed light brown sugar
2 teaspoons soy sauce or light soy sauce
3 tablespoons Chinese black vinegar or
    balsamic vinegar
1 tablespoon Chinese rice wine or dry sherry
1 medium piece rock sugar, about ½ ounce, or
    1 tablespoon sugar

1 cup vegetable oil

½ yellow onion, thinly sliced
3 green onions, trimmed and cut into
    2-inch lengths

❋   ❋   ❋

1. Marinate the pork: Stir the egg, soy sauce, cornstarch, and rice wine in a bowl until blended. Pour into a plastic bag. Add the pork chops and turn to coat. Set aside for 10 to 15 minutes.

2. Prepare the sauce: Combine the water, moke stick, plum sauce, brown sugar, and soy sauce in a medium bowl and mash to a thick paste. Add the black vinegar, rice wine, and sugar and stir until the sugar is dissolved.

3. Pour the oil into a nonreactive skillet large enough to hold the pork in a single layer, and heat over medium heat until hot. Lift the chops from the marinade, shake off the excess liquid, and lay them in the oil. Pan-fry, turning once, until cooked through, about 2 minutes on each side. Remove the pan from the heat and drain the chops on paper towels.

4. Spoon off all but 1 tablespoon of the oil from the pan. Return the pan to high heat. When the oil is hot, add both onions and stir-fry until tender, about 2 minutes. Add the sauce and bring to a boil. Reduce the heat to medium and cook until the liquid is reduced by one-third. Slip the chops into the sauce and cook until heated through, about 1 minute. Serve immediately, spooning some of the sauce over each chop.

TAMARIND-BRAISED PORK

Serves 4 as part of a multicourse meal

Using salty dried shrimp is characteristic of Macanese cuisine. Because Macau was once a small fishing community, it produced a variety of seafood products like dried shrimp. When the Portuguese arrived, they incorporated local ingredients into their own style of cooking. Look for dried shrimp that are hard, plump, and bright pink-orange, not brown or gray. Even preserved ingredients lose quality after about six months. Keep in a tightly sealed jar in the refrigerator. If you can't find tamarind paste, use lime juice with a little brown sugar. The slow braising gives the pork wonderfully rich flavors and a moist texture.

¼ cup vegetable oil
1 tablespoon dried shrimp

1½ tablespoons unsalted butter
¼ cup sliced onion
2 tablespoons sliced shallots
2 tablespoons sliced garlic
1 pound boneless pork shoulder or butt,
    cut into 1½-inch pieces

2 cups Chicken Stock (page 69) or
    canned chicken broth
½ cup packed light brown sugar
2 tablespoons tamarind paste
2 teaspoons soy sauce
1 teaspoon fish sauce (optional)
1 teaspoon shrimp paste

3 red or green jalapeño chilies, thinly sliced
Lemon slices

1. Heat the vegetable oil in a wok over medium heat to 325°F. Add the dried shrimp and fry until golden brown, about 1 minute. Scoop the shrimp out with a slotted spoon and drain on paper towels. Let the shrimp stand until cool enough to handle, then finely chop.

2. Heat the butter in a large frying pan over medium-high heat until foaming. Add the onion, shallots, and garlic and cook, stirring, until softened. Add the pork and cook, turning as necessary, until browned on all sides, about 5 minutes.

3. Add the chicken stock, brown sugar, tamarind paste, soy sauce, fish sauce, and shrimp paste and bring to a boil. Adjust the heat to a simmer, cover, and simmer until tender, 35 to 40 minutes.

4. Transfer the contents of the wok to a serving bowl. Garnish with the fried shrimp, chilies, and lemon slices.

SEVEN-FLAVOR SLOW-COOKED PORK

Serves 6 to 8 as part of a multicourse meal

The Ozorio family in Toronto showed me that with just a few ingredients you can prepare a dish full of stunning flavors. With only seven ingredients in the marinade, this is very easy to put together. Once marinated, the pork is browned on all sides and then braised. The pork will taste best if allowed to marinate overnight.

One 2- to 3-pound boneless pork loin or pork butt, trimmed of all but a thin layer of fat

FOR THE MARINADE
1 cup chopped yellow onions
⅓ cup Chinese rice wine or dry sherry
2 tablespoons soy sauce
2 teaspoons dark soy sauce
4 to 6 bay leaves
1½ teaspoons turmeric powder
½ teaspoon ground white pepper
½ teaspoon Chinese five-spice powder

3 tablespoons vegetable oil
3 cups water

¼ cup Chinese rice wine or dry sherry
1 tablespoon cornstarch, dissolved in 2 tablespoons water

❋　❋　❋

1. Marinate the pork: Stir the onions, rice wine, soy sauces, bay leaves, turmeric, pepper, and five-spice powder together in a bowl until well blended. Put the pork into a heavy resealable plastic bag, then pour in the marinade. Squeeze the air out of the bag and seal. Shake the bag gently until the pork is evenly coated. Marinate the pork in the refrigerator overnight, turning once.

2. Remove the pork from the marinade; reserve the marinade. Pat the pork dry with paper towels. Heat a wok over high heat until hot. Add the oil and swirl to the coat the sides. Place the meat fat side down in the wok and cook, turning as necessary, until brown on all sides, about 2 minutes per side.

3. Discard the pan drippings and add the reserved marinade and the water to the wok. Bring to a boil, then adjust the heat so the liquid is simmering. Cover the wok and simmer until the meat is very tender, about 2 hours.

4. Lift the pork onto a carving board and let it rest for 5 to 10 minutes. Cut into slices about ¼ inch thick and arrange on a serving plate.

5. Add the rice wine and dissolved cornstarch to the cooking liquid and cook over high heat, stirring, until the sauce boils and thickens, about 1 minute. Serve the sauce alongside the pork.

CHINATOWN DELI CHAR SIU (BBQ PORK)

Makes about 2 pounds

Hanging among the roast ducks and spareribs, this is the barbecued pork seen in Chinatown deli windows. Char siu can be sliced and eaten as a snack, added to soups as a garnish, and used in many other ways. Five-spice powder and sesame paste or fermented bean curd give char siu its distinctive flavors. You can buy it from the delis or give it a try and make your own.

FOR THE MARINADE

⅓ cup sugar

¼ cup soy sauce

¼ cup hoisin sauce

¼ cup honey

2 tablespoons Chinese rice wine or dry sherry

1 tablespoon sesame paste or mashed white fermented bean curd

2 teaspoons minced garlic

1 teaspoon minced ginger

1 teaspoon sesame oil

1 teaspoon salt

1 teaspoon black pepper

1 teaspoon Chinese five-spice powder

1 to 5 drops red food color (optional)

2 to 2½ pounds boneless pork shoulder or butt, trimmed of excess fat and cut into pieces roughly 1 inch thick, 3 inches wide, and 8 inches long

❋   ❋   ❋

1. Marinate the pork: Stir the sugar, soy sauce, hoisin sauce, honey, rice wine, sesame paste, garlic, ginger, sesame oil, salt, black pepper, five-spice powder, and red food color, if using, together in a bowl. Place the pork in a large resealable plastic bag, pour the marinade into the bag, and seal the bag. Turn the bag to coat the pork. Refrigerate for at least 4 hours, or overnight, turning the bag occasionally.

2. Preheat the oven to 350°F.

3. Remove the pork from the marinade; reserve the marinade. Place the pork on a rack set in a foil-lined baking pan. Bake uncovered, brushing occasionally with the reserved marinade, for 30 minutes more.

4. Turn the pieces of pork over and bake, brushing occasionally with the reserved marinade, until cooked through and tender, about 45 minutes more.

5. Let the pork rest for 10 minutes before cutting into thin slices. Serve hot or cold.

BROCCOLI BEEF | *Serves 4 as part of a multicourse meal*

In China, this dish was traditionally made with Chinese broccoli, or *gai lan*, which wasn't available to the Chinese immigrants here. They adapted, using readily available common broccoli. More recently, Chinese broccoli can be found in many stores and farmers' markets. If using broccoli, blanch it first in water for more even cooking.

FOR THE MARINADE

1 teaspoon Chinese rice wine or dry sherry

1 teaspoon soy sauce

1 teaspoon cornstarch

1 teaspoon minced ginger

¾ pound beef tri-tip or flank steak,
   thinly sliced across the grain

FOR THE SAUCE

¼ cup Chicken Stock (page 69) or
   canned broth

2 tablespoons oyster-flavored sauce

1 tablespoon Chinese rice wine or dry sherry

1 tablespoon dark soy sauce

2 cups broccoli florets (about ½ pound) or
   ½ pound *gai lan*

2 tablespoons vegetable oil

1 teaspoon cornstarch, dissolved in
   1 tablespoon water

* * *

1. Marinate the beef: Stir the rice wine, soy sauce, cornstarch, and ginger together in a medium bowl until the cornstarch is dissolved. Stir the beef gently in the marinade until coated. Let stand for 10 minutes.

2. Prepare the sauce: Stir the chicken stock, oyster-flavored sauce, rice wine, and soy sauce together in a bowl.

3. Cook the broccoli in a small pot of boiling water until tender-crisp, about 2 minutes. Drain thoroughly.

4. Heat a wok over high heat until hot. Add the oil and swirl to coat the sides. Add the beef and stir-fry until no longer pink, 1½ to 2 minutes. Add the sauce and broccoli and bring to a boil. Pour in the dissolved cornstarch and cook, stirring, until the sauce boils and thickens, 30 seconds to 1 minute. Scoop the contents of the wok onto a serving platter and serve immediately.

MONGOLIAN BEEF

Serves 4 as part of a multicourse meal

Mongolian beef is a fixture on many Chinese restaurant menus. This dish is so simple and richly flavored that your family will ask for it again and again. You can make it also with chicken.

FOR THE MARINADE

2 tablespoons water

1 tablespoon soy sauce

1 tablespoon vegetable oil

1 teaspoon minced ginger

2 teaspoons cornstarch

¾ pound flank or tri-tip steak, sliced across the
    grain into ¼-inch slices

FOR THE SAUCE

2 tablespoons soy sauce

2 tablespoons sugar

2 teaspoons Chinese rice wine or dry sherry

1½ teaspoons Chinese black vinegar or
    balsamic vinegar

1 teaspoon hoisin sauce

1 teaspoon chili bean sauce or chili garlic sauce

Vegetable oil for deep-frying

2 ounces dried bean thread noodles

1 leek, white part only, halved lengthwise, and
    cut into 2-inch lengths

5 green onions, trimmed and cut into
    2-inch lengths

✳   ✳   ✳

1. Marinate the beef: Stir the water, soy sauce, oil, ginger, and cornstarch together in a medium bowl until the cornstarch is dissolved. Cut the slices of beef crosswise into 2-inch pieces and toss them in the marinade to coat. Let stand for 20 minutes.

2. Prepare the sauce: Stir the soy sauce, sugar, rice wine, black vinegar, hoisin sauce, and chili bean sauce together in a bowl.

3. Pour enough oil into a wide deep skillet to come to a depth of 3 inches. Heat over medium-high heat to 375°F degrees. Pull the bean thread noodles gently apart to loosen the strands (if too dense, those at the center will not cook). Slip the noodles into the oil and fry just until they puff and expand, about 5 seconds; turn the noodles in the oil if necessary, so they all puff evenly. Scoop the noodles from the oil with a slotted spoon and drain on paper towels, then arrange the noodles on a serving platter and set aside. Reserve the oil.

4. Heat a wok over high heat until hot. Add 1 tablespoon of the reserved oil and swirl to coat the sides. Scatter the steak slices into the wok and stir-fry just until barely pink in the center, 1 to 2 minutes. Scoop the beef onto a plate and set aside.

5. Add the green onions and leek to the wok and stir-fry until wilted, about 30 seconds. Pour in the sauce and return the beef to the wok. Cook until the beef is heated through and coated evenly with sauce, 1 to 2 minutes. Spoon the beef and sauce over the noodles and serve.

STIR-FRIED BEEF WITH BITTER MELON

Serves 4 as part of a multicourse meal

For centuries, bitter melon has been used all over the world for dozens of medicinal purposes. I could bore you with a discussion of all its active compounds and uses, but we are talking food here. Bitter melon is an acquired taste, but it is great in this dish. If you find it too bitter, you can salt it for two hours and rinse it before blanching.

FOR THE MARINADE

2 teaspoons Chinese rice wine or dry sherry

2 teaspoons soy sauce

2 teaspoons cornstarch

¾ pound beef tri-tip or flank steak, thinly sliced across the grain

FOR THE SAUCE

¼ cup Chicken Stock (page 69) or canned chicken broth

2 teaspoons soy sauce

1 teaspoon sesame oil

1 teaspoon sugar

¾ teaspoon dried red chili flakes

½ teaspoon salt

½ pound bitter melon or zucchini

2 tablespoons vegetable oil

½ cup sliced onion

1 tablespoon salted black beans, rinsed, drained, and coarsely chopped

1 teaspoon minced garlic

1 teaspoon cornstarch, dissolved in 1 tablespoon water

* * *

1. Marinate the beef: Stir the rice wine, soy sauce, and cornstarch together in a bowl until the cornstarch is dissolved. Toss the beef gently in the marinade to coat. Let stand for 10 minutes.

2. Prepare the sauce: Stir the chicken stock, soy sauce, sesame oil, sugar, chili flakes, and salt together in a small bowl until the sugar is dissolved.

3. Cut the bitter melon lengthwise into quarters. Discard the seeds and cut the flesh into slices on the bias. Or if using zucchini, roll-cut them according to the directions on page xxxi. Blanch the melon in a pot of boiling water until tender-crisp, about 2 minutes. Drain thoroughly.

4. Heat a wok over high heat until hot. Add 1½ tablespoons of the oil and swirl to coat the sides. Add the beef and stir-fry until no longer pink, 1½ to 2 minutes. Scoop the beef onto a plate.

5. Add the remaining ½ tablespoon oil to the wok and swirl to coat the sides. Add the onion,

black beans, and garlic and stir-fry until fragrant, about 30 seconds. Add the melon and sauce and bring to a boil.

6. Return the beef to the wok, pour in the dissolved cornstarch, and cook, stirring, until the sauce boils and thickens, about 1 minute. Scoop the contents of the wok onto a serving platter and serve immediately.

TOMATO BEEF

Serves 4 as part of a multicourse meal

Tomatoes were introduced to China in the late 1500s. Here's a popular tomato dish often served in homes and restaurants. Tri-tip and flank steaks are very flavorful cuts of beef, but it's important to cut them into very thin slices across the grain to make them tender. For easy slicing, freeze the meat for 20 minutes.

FOR THE MARINADE

1 tablespoon cornstarch

1 tablespoon oyster-flavored sauce

1 tablespoon soy sauce

2 teaspoons whiskey

1 teaspoon minced garlic

¾ pound flank or tri-tip steak, thinly sliced
    across the grain

FOR THE SAUCE

¼ cup ketchup

1½ teaspoons Chinese rice wine or dry sherry

1 teaspoon soy sauce

½ teaspoon Worcestershire sauce

1 teaspoon sugar

2 tablespoons vegetable oil

½ yellow onion, thinly sliced

1 stalk celery, trimmed and thinly sliced

½ green bell pepper, cut into ½-inch squares

½ cup quartered button mushrooms

1 tomato, cut into 8 wedges

Steamed Rice (page 285) or noodles

1. Marinate the beef: Stir the cornstarch, oyster-flavored sauce, soy sauce, whiskey, and garlic together in a medium bowl until the cornstarch is dissolved. Add the flank steak and toss gently to coat. Let stand for 10 minutes.

2. Prepare the sauce: Stir the ketchup, rice wine, soy sauce, Worcestershire sauce, and sugar together in a bowl until the sugar is dissolved.

3. Heat a wok over high heat until hot. Add 1 tablespoon of the oil and swirl to coat the sides. Add the beef and stir-fry until no longer pink, 1½ to 2 minutes. Scoop the beef from the wok and set aside.

4. Add the remaining 1 tablespoon oil to the wok and swirl to coat the sides. Add the onion, celery, bell pepper, and mushrooms and stir-fry until the vegetables are tender-crisp, about 2 minutes.

5. Add the sauce and tomato. Bring to a boil, return the beef to the wok, and cook until the meat is coated with the sauce and heated through, 1 to 1½ minutes. Serve with rice or noodles.

FOUR-MUSHROOM BEEF

Serves 4 as part of a multicourse meal

The original Cantonese version of this dish uses only one or two varieties of mushrooms, but with mushrooms so readily available, I like to add more. Since mushrooms have many of the savory flavor components of beef, for a vegetarian dish, omit the beef and increase the amount of mushrooms.

5 dried black mushrooms
1 large portobello mushroom

FOR THE MARINADE
2 tablespoons oyster-flavored sauce
1 teaspoon cornstarch

10 ounces beef flank or tri-tip steak, thinly sliced across the grain

1½ tablespoons vegetable oil
6 to 8 oyster mushrooms (about ¼ pound), rinsed, cut in half if large
½ cup drained canned straw mushrooms
2 tablespoons water
1 tablespoon soy sauce or dark soy sauce

❋   ❋   ❋

1. Pour enough warm water over the black mushrooms in a medium bowl to cover completely. Soak until softened, about 20 minutes. Drain the mushrooms. Discard the stems and thinly slice the caps.

2. Discard the portobello stem, and scrape off the gills from the underside of the cap with a spoon. Slice the cap ¼ inch thick.

3. Marinate the beef: Stir the oyster-flavored sauce and cornstarch together in a bowl until blended. Toss the beef slices gently in the marinade until coated. Let stand for 10 minutes.

4. Heat a wok over high heat until hot. Add 1 tablespoon of the oil and swirl to coat the sides. Add the beef and stir-fry until it is no longer pink, 1½ to 2 minutes. Transfer the meat to a plate.

5. Add the remaining ½ tablespoon oil to the wok, along with all the mushrooms, water, and soy sauce. Stir-fry until the mushrooms are tender, about 2 minutes.

6. Slide the beef back into the wok and cook, stirring, until heated through, about 1 minute. Scoop the beef and mushrooms onto a serving plate and serve immediately.

NANJING "SURF AND TURF" STIR-FRY

Serves 4 as part of a multicourse meal

Chinese cooks rarely put seafood and meat together in a dish, so this is very unusual. Sweet potato adds sweetness, a hallmark of Nanjing-style cooking. Sweet potatoes came from the New World, yams from Asia. Yams are less sweet. In this recipe they can be used interchangeably. Oil-blanching the potatoes concentrates their flavor and maintains their crisp texture.

FOR THE SAUCE

⅓ cup canned beef broth

2 tablespoons hoisin sauce

1 tablespoon sesame paste or smooth peanut butter

1 tablespoon dark soy sauce

1 tablespoon sugar

Vegetable oil for shallow-frying

1 small sweet potato, peeled and thinly sliced (about 1 cup)

1 tablespoon minced garlic

4 small dried red chilies (see page 207)

1 tablespoon chili garlic sauce

½ pound flank steak or beef tri-tip, thinly sliced across the grain

¼ pound raw medium shrimp, shelled, tails left intact, and deveined

½ cup snow peas, trimmed

⅓ cup sliced button mushrooms

1 teaspoon sesame oil

1. Prepare the sauce: Stir the beef broth, hoisin sauce, sesame paste, soy sauce, and sugar together in a small bowl until the sugar is dissolved.

2. Heat a wok over medium heat until hot. Pour in enough oil to come to a depth of 1 inch. When the oil is hot (you will notice that the surface will shimmer), add the sweet potato, stirring to separate the slices. Shallow-fry until the sweet potato is tender, 2 to 3 minutes. Remove the sweet potato with a slotted spoon and drain on paper towels. Reserve the oil.

3. Return the wok to high heat. When hot, add 2 tablespoons of the reserved oil, swirling to coat the sides. Add the garlic, dried chilies, and chili garlic sauce and cook, stirring, until fragrant, about 10 seconds. Add the beef and stir-fry until barely pink, 1 minute. Add the shrimp and stir-fry for 1 minute.

4. Add the snow peas, mushrooms, fried sweet potatoes, and sauce. Bring to a boil, then adjust the heat so the sauce is simmering and simmer until the vegetables are tender, about 1½ minutes.

5. Stir in the sesame oil, scoop onto a serving platter, and serve immediately.

BEEF STIR-FRY OVER GOLDEN PANCAKE

Serves 4 as part of a multicourse meal

In Cantonese, this crispy noodle dish is referred to as *lerng mein wong,* which means "both sides golden." Say this, and you'll impress the staff at a restaurant. Or impress your family and friends when you bring this classic to the table. For successful results, cut the flank steak across the grain.

FOR THE MARINADE

1 tablespoon Chinese rice wine or dry sherry

1 tablespoon soy sauce or dark soy sauce

2 teaspoons cornstarch

1 teaspoon minced garlic

1 teaspoon minced ginger

1/4 pound flank steak, thinly sliced across the grain

FOR THE SAUCE

1/4 cup Chicken Stock (page 69) or canned chicken broth

2 tablespoons oyster-flavored sauce or sa cha sauce

2 teaspoons chili garlic sauce

2 teaspoons cornstarch

1/8 teaspoon ground white pepper

1/8 teaspoon sesame oil

8 ounces fresh thin Chinese egg noodles

3 tablespoons vegetable oil

1/2 yellow onion, thinly sliced

1/2 pound asparagus, trimmed and cut into 1-inch pieces (about 1 cup)

1. Marinate the beef: Stir the rice wine, soy sauce, cornstarch, garlic, and ginger together in a bowl until the cornstarch is dissolved. Toss the beef slices gently in the marinade to coat. Let stand for 10 minutes.

2. Prepare the sauce: Stir the chicken stock, oyster-flavored sauce, chili garlic sauce, cornstarch, pepper, and sesame oil together in a bowl until the cornstarch is dissolved. Set aside.

3. Cook the noodles in a large pot of boiling salted water according to the package directions. Drain well, rinse under cool water, and drain again.

4. Heat a 10- or 12-inch nonstick frying pan over medium-high heat until hot. Add 1 tablespoon of the oil and swirl to coat the bottom. Spread the noodles in an even layer in the pan and cook, pressing lightly from time to time to make a firm cake, until the bottom is golden brown, about 5 minutes. Turn the cake over. Drizzle 1 tablespoon of the remaining oil around the edges of the pan and cook until the second side of the noodle cake is golden brown, 3 to 4 minutes. Transfer the noodles to a warmed serving plate.

5. Heat a wok over high heat until hot. Add the remaining 1 tablespoon oil, swirling to coat the sides. Add the meat and stir-fry until no longer pink, 1½ to 2 minutes. Remove from the pan.

6. Add the onion to the wok and stir-fry until almost tender, about 1 minute. Add the asparagus and cook, stirring, until tender-crisp, about 2 minutes. Return the meat to the wok, pour in the sauce, and bring to a boil. Cook until slightly thickened, about 30 seconds.

7. Spoon the stir-fry over the crispy noodle cake and serve immediately.

BEAUTY QUEEN BEEF

Serves 4 as part of a multicourse meal

Before Miss Macau 1993 won her crown, she worked at her father's restaurant, where this was her favorite beef dish. After her win, people went to her father's restaurant in hopes of seeing the beauty pageant winner, and also to try her favorite dish. As a result, her father renamed the restaurant Miss Macau Restaurant and the beef dish Miss Macau Beef. Serve this dish with plenty of rice to soak up the sauce.

4 boneless New York strip steaks, or other
    steaks (about 6 ounces each),
    1 inch thick, trimmed
Salt and freshly ground black pepper

FOR THE SAUCE
2 tablespoons heavy cream
1 tablespoon oyster-flavored sauce
1 tablespoon chili garlic sauce
2 teaspoons mustard powder

1 tablespoon vegetable oil

1 tablespoon unsalted butter
8 garlic cloves, thinly sliced
¼ cup thinly sliced ginger
4 button mushrooms, trimmed and thinly sliced
4 fresh shiitake, stems discarded and caps thinly
    sliced
3 oyster mushrooms (optional)
⅓ cup Chinese rice wine or dry sherry

*   *   *

1. Sprinkle both sides of the steak lightly with salt and black pepper.

2. Prepare the sauce: Stir the cream, oyster-flavored sauce, chili garlic sauce, and mustard powder together in a small bowl until thoroughly mixed.

3. Heat a skillet large enough to hold the steaks in a single layer over medium-high heat. Add the oil and swirl to coat the bottom of the pan. Lay the steaks in the pan and cook, turning once halfway through the cooking, for about 3 minutes per side for medium-rare, longer for more well done. Transfer the steaks to a plate and cover them with aluminum foil, shiny side down, to keep them warm.

4. Return the pan to medium-high heat and add the butter. When it is melted, add the garlic and ginger and cook until fragrant, about 30 seconds. Add the mushrooms and rice wine and stir-fry until the mushrooms are tender, 1 to 2 minutes. Add the sauce and bring to a boil.

5. Divide the steaks among four plates and spoon the mushroom sauce over them. Serve immediately.

PEPPER STEAK IN SOY— RED WINE SAUCE

Serves 4 as part of a multicourse meal

White pepper is traditionally used in Chinese cooking, but here's one dish that uses black pepper. Freshly ground black pepper is best. Use any cut of beef suitable for pan-frying, such as New York, rib-eye, or tenderloin steaks.

2 dried black mushrooms

FOR THE SAUCE
¼ cup dry red wine
¼ cup Chicken Stock (page 69) or
    canned chicken broth
2 teaspoons soy sauce
1 teaspoon sugar
1 teaspoon freshly ground black pepper
¼ teaspoon Worcestershire sauce
¼ teaspoon steak sauce (optional)
¼ teaspoon sesame oil

One ¾-pound New York strip steak
    about 1½ inches thick, cut crosswise
    into four pieces at a 45-degree angle
1 teaspoon salt
1 teaspoon freshly ground black pepper

1 tablespoon vegetable oil

¼ cup finely chopped red bell pepper
¼ cup finely chopped green bell pepper
¼ cup finely chopped yellow onion

1 teaspoon cornstarch, dissolved in
    2 teaspoons water

1. Pour enough warm water over the mushrooms in a small bowl to cover completely. Soak until softened, about 20 minutes. Drain the mushrooms, discard the stems, and coarsely chop the caps.

2. Prepare the sauce: Stir the red wine, chicken stock, soy sauce, sugar, black pepper, Worcestershire sauce, steak sauce, if using, and sesame oil together in a bowl until the sugar is dissolved.

3. Season the steak with the salt and black pepper. Heat a large skillet over medium-high heat until hot. Add the oil and swirl to coat the bottom of the pan. Add the steaks and cook, turning once, 3 to 4 minutes on each side for medium-rare, longer for more well done. Transfer the steaks to a serving platter and cover with foil, shiny side down, to keep them warm.

4. Add the bell peppers, onion, and mushrooms to the pan and cook, stirring, until softened, about 2 minutes. Pour in the sauce and bring to a boil. Stir in the dissolved cornstarch and cook, stirring, until the sauce boils and is lightly thickened, about 30 seconds. Spoon the sauce over the steaks and serve.

MACAU

EVERY VISITOR HAS TO POSE BEFORE THE RUINS OF THE CHURCH OF ST. PAUL, THE SYMBOL OF 400 YEARS OF PORTUGUESE INFLUENCE.

Some think of Macau as the last European colony in Asia, the longest-running meeting place between East and West. Others refer to it as a laid-back port, a Chinese banana republic devoted to gaming and food.

I prefer to call Macau the Chinatown on Chinese soil. ❋ In the great age of explorations, Portuguese caravels—three masted ships—first landed here as early as 1535. The town was formally declared a Portuguese possession in 1557. This nub of only twenty-eight kilometers, on the western side of the Pearl River Delta some forty miles from Hong Kong, has been a slow-cooking cultural incubator ever since. The Portuguese gave up their claim to this charming city of nearly half a million in December 1999, but their graceful plazas, baroque churches, sidewalks paved in mosaic waves, and street signs of blue tiles remain. You'll find great Portuguese wines, dishes made with the beloved dried codfish (*bacalhau*), garlic-laced sausages, and egg-rich desserts. Amazing in a place where 99 percent of the citizens are of Chinese descent! ❋ On Macau's two outlying islands, Taipa and Coloane, fishing villages by the calm sea feature pastel houses and colonial libraries beside temples dedicated to Chinese sea gods—and the tiny lanes are filled with the scent of curry-flavored "egg roll" crepes as well as other rare South Chinese street treats. ❋ Preserving the flavors of Macanese cooking, a culinary blend of both cultures, is a priority here. Macau's distinctive cuisine may feature both a wine and a fish sauce, or curry and soy sauce, in some dishes. These combinations, perfected over centuries, are unique. *Minchee* is the Macanese form of minced beef, with garlic and turmeric, while *porco balichao tamarinho* combines a European pork roast with a shrimp paste and the tartness of that Asian classic, tamarind.

LITORAL RESTAURANT

Rua do Almirante Sergio, 261–A, R/C
(853) 967-878
What to order: *porcho tamarinho arroz (stewed pork with shrimp paste); galinha africana (African chicken); camarões recheados (prawns "diable"); pastéis de bacalhau (codfish cake)*

MISS MACAU RESTAURANT

Beco do Goncalo, no. 6 R/C
(853) 827-957
What to order: *Miss Macau beef; clams in butter sauce*

RESTAURANTE CHAN CHI MEI

R. Caetano, No. 1
Coloane
(853) 882-986
What to order: *hanging fish hot pot*

RESTAURANTE PLATAO

Block B, 3 Travessa Sao Domingos
(853) 331-818
What to order: *shrimp patty; duck rice with sausage; clay pot seafood rice*

RESTAURANTE TOU TOU KOI

Travessa do Mastro No. 6–8
(853) 572-629
What to eat: *crispy shrimp puffs; eight treasure duck*

A LOCAL STREET FOOD VENDOR OFFERS NOODLES WITH YOUR CHOICE OF TOPPINGS.

LU'AU STEW

Serves 4 to 6 as part of a multicourse meal

Sam Choy of Hawaii shared this recipe with me, a good example of Hawaiian and Chinese fusion cooking. Sam uses taro leaves in this stew, but since they are hard, if not impossible, to find off the islands, I substitute spinach.

1 tablespoon vegetable oil

1 pound beef tri-tip, cut into 1-inch cubes

1 cup diced onions

3 cups canned beef broth

1 cup water

2 teaspoons Hawaiian sea salt or kosher salt

1 bunch spinach, tough stems discarded, leaves washed well

Steamed Rice (page 285)

1. Heat the oil in a 3-quart saucepan over medium-high heat and swirl to coat the bottom. Add the beef and cook, turning, until browned on all sides, 4 to 5 minutes. Scoop the beef onto a plate.

2. Stir the onions into the oil remaining in the pan. Cook, stirring once or twice, until soft, 3 to 4 minutes. Return the meat to the pan and add the broth, water, and salt. Bring to a boil. Adjust the heat to a simmer, cover the pan, and simmer over low heat until the meat is fork-tender, 1 to 1¼ hours.

3. Stir in the spinach and cook until the spinach is slightly wilted, about 1 minute. Ladle into warm bowls and serve with steamed rice.

MALAY LEMONGRASS BEEF STEW

Serves 6 as part of a multicourse meal

When the Chinese make their beloved stews, they make a big pot to last a few days. With each reheating, the flavors become richer and more intense. This stew is best on a cold winter day.

FOR THE MARINADE

1 tablespoon soy sauce

1 tablespoon dark soy sauce

1 tablespoon cornstarch

1½ pounds boneless beef chuck, cut into 1-inch cubes

4 small dried red chilies (see page 207)

¼ cup warm water

2 tablespoons vegetable oil

2 medium onions, cut into ¼-inch dice

4 cups water

2 stalks lemongrass, bottom 6 inches only, lightly crushed

3 tablespoons fresh lemon juice

2 cinnamon sticks

8 to 10 dried curry leaves or 2 teaspoons curry powder, preferably Madras

2 tablespoons oyster-flavored sauce

1½ tablespoons sugar

* * *

1. Marinate the beef: Stir the soy sauces and cornstarch together in a medium bowl until the cornstarch is dissolved. Toss the beef gently in the marinade until coated. Let stand for 30 minutes.

2. Crumble the dried chilies into a blender jar. Pour in the warm water and let stand for 20 minutes to soften, then blend until smooth.

3. Heat the oil in a 3-quart saucepan over medium-high heat and swirl to coat the bottom. Add as many of the beef cubes to the pan as will fit without touching one another and cook, turning as necessary, until browned on all sides, 4 to 5 minutes. Remove the beef from the pan with a slotted spoon and drain on paper towels. Repeat with the remaining beef.

4. Reduce the heat under the pan to medium. Add the onions and cook, stirring until soft, 4 to 5 minutes. Add the pureed chilies and their liquid and cook for 1 minute, scraping to release any browned bits on the bottom of the pan.

5. Return the meat to the pan and add the water, lemongrass, lemon juice, cinnamon sticks, and curry leaves. Bring to a boil, then adjust the heat so the liquid is simmering, cover the pan, and simmer until the beef is tender, 1 to 1¼ hours.

6. Stir the oyster-flavored sauce and sugar into the stew and simmer, uncovered, until the sauce thickens slightly, 10 to 15 minutes.

7. Ladle the beef and sauce into a warm serving bowl and serve hot.

EMPEROR'S LAMB | *Serves 4 as part of a multicourse meal*

The story goes that China's eighteenth-century emperor Qian Long had his men go hunting for deer. Then the emperor asked his chef to prepare a meal using deer meat and the result was a spicy, sweet dish that caused the emperor to exclaim, "*Ta t'sai mi,*" which means, "It's better than honey." Through the years, lamb has been substituted for deer. Definitely fit for an emperor. Serve with Minted Fried Rice (page 290).

FOR THE MARINADE
1 tablespoon soy sauce
2 teaspoons cornstarch
1/2 teaspoon salt
1/4 teaspoon sugar

3/4 pound boneless lamb (leg or loin),
    thinly sliced

FOR THE SEASONINGS
1 tablespoon soy sauce
1 tablespoon hoisin sauce
2 teaspoons hot bean paste or chili garlic sauce
2 teaspoons Chinese rice wine or dry sherry
1 teaspoon sesame oil
1/4 teaspoon sugar

2 tablespoons vegetable oil
1/2 cup chopped onions
2 tablespoons minced garlic
1 tablespoon chopped red or
    green jalapeño chili

4 to 8 iceberg lettuce cups or Steamed Rice
    (page 285)

1. Marinate the lamb: Stir the soy sauce, cornstarch, salt, and sugar together in a large bowl until the sugar is dissolved. Toss the lamb slices gently in the marinade until coated. Let stand for 10 minutes.

2. Prepare the seasonings: Stir the soy sauce, hoisin sauce, hot bean paste, sesame oil, and sugar together in a small bowl until the sugar is dissolved.

3. Heat a wok over high heat until hot. Add the oil and swirl to coat the sides. Add the onions, garlic, and jalapeño and stir-fry until fragrant, about 30 seconds. Slide the marinated lamb into the wok and stir-fry until the lamb is barely pink, 2 to 2 1/2 minutes. Pour in the seasonings and stir until the lamb is evenly coated.

4. Scoop the lamb and sauce into the lettuce cups, arranged on a platter, or serve with rice.

DEITIES AND SUPERSTITION

asting Chinese beliefs are what have sustained Chinese migrants, and you'll find these beliefs in tangible form on every street of each Chinatown. You might call them a religious faith, except that such labels applied to Chinese people soon get about as hazy as those wisps of clouds on a classic landscape painting, inked with strokes of brush as swift as they are sure. Chinatown's temples do not necessarily placate a single god or represent even a single idea of the universe. In many shrines where incense is lit, you will find several protective figures in whom the migrants placed their faith as they set out across the seas: Kwan Kung, a fearsome god of war, holding a curved blade as sharp as my best set of cleavers, and Kwan Yin, a beneficent goddess of mercy. In worshipping them, however, the Chinese are mainly paying their dues to the forces of nature and the spirits of their ancestors. ✳ Through the long history of China, there were many gods and goddesses that local people worshipped throughout the year. These could be a figurine, an old tree, or even a big rock. Buddhism, which in China has taken numerous forms and led to a cult of a certain contented, well-fed, big-bellied laughing Buddha that you might see beside the cash register in some Chinese restaurants, has been the main influence on religious practice (since Taoism and other Asian concepts are really philosophies of wise living). But the Chinese in general are quite superstitious. Certain numbers and certain colors at certain times of year contain special significance—or danger. One example is that most Chinese will not use sharp objects, such as knives or scissors, on the first day of the Chinese New Year, so most food for the occasion has to be prepared days ahead. That way, people believe, they will not have to "cut off" friendships or family ties. If you see a dingy Chinatown storefront crammed with fanciful paper creations, don't be fooled by the bright colors. These are funereal objects, beautifully crafted only to be burned so the flames can send them to departed spirits who may need them. In some of these shops, you can actually see paper limousines, paper yachts, and, of late, paper computers. The Chinese dead should not lack for anything.

LEMONGRASS LAMB WITH MINTED ORANGE SAUCE

Serves 3 or 4 as part of a multicourse meal

The diverse cultures and regions of any land greatly influence the flavors of its food. Within today's Chinatown restaurants, Western favorites like lamb chops are combined with Asian spices, as in this creative dish from the Harbor Village Restaurant in San Francisco.

FOR THE MARINADE

2 tablespoons water

1 tablespoon soy sauce

1 tablespoon dark soy sauce

1 tablespoon Chinese rice wine or dry sherry

1 tablespoon vegetable oil

1 tablespoon sa cha sauce

2 teaspoons hoisin sauce

1 teaspoon sugar

1/2 teaspoon cornstarch

4 garlic cloves, smashed

1 stalk lemongrass, bottom 6 inches only, finely chopped

1 pound loin or rib lamb chops or one 1-pound rack of lamb, cut between the bones into chops

FOR THE DIPPING SAUCE

4 tablespoons orange marmalade

4 tablespoons rice vinegar

1 tablespoon orange liqueur

1 tablespoon finely chopped mint

2 teaspoons chili garlic sauce

1 tablespoon unsalted butter, cut into small pieces

2 cups shredded napa cabbage or iceberg lettuce (optional)

* * *

1. Marinate the lamb: Combine the water, soy sauces, rice wine, oil, sa cha sauce, hoisin sauce, sugar, cornstarch, garlic, and lemongrass in a blender jar. Blend until smooth, and pour into a large bowl. Toss the lamb gently with the marinade until coated. Cover and refrigerate for at least 2 hours, or as long as overnight.

2. Make the dipping sauce: Stir the orange marmalade, rice vinegar, orange liqueur, mint, and chili garlic sauce together in a small bowl.

3. Preheat the broiler, with the rack about 6 inches from the heat. Line a baking sheet with aluminum foil and set a rack over the foil. Lift the meat from the marinade, shaking the chops over the bowl to allow excess marinade to drip back into the bowl, and place the chops on the rack. Dot them with the butter. Slide the pan under the preheated broiler and broil, turning once, until the chops are nicely browned on both sides but still pink in the center, 6 to 8 minutes. (The cooking time depends on the thickness of the meat.)

4. Serve the lamb over a bed of shredded cabbage, if you like, with the dipping sauce on the side.

FIVE-SPICE CRISPY LAMB LONDON-STYLE

Serves 4 to 6 as part of a multicourse meal

In England, aromatic crispy duck is found on every Chinese menu. Jimmy Jim, owner of the Fung Shing Restaurant, created a version using lamb instead. The balance between the sweet–slightly sour sauce with pickled cucumbers and the aromatic crispy lamb is a match made in heaven. Or at least in London.

FOR THE SPICES

6 quarter-sized slices peeled ginger
6 to 8 whole star anise
2 to 3 cinnamon sticks
4 cardamom pods, crushed
1/2 teaspoon toasted Sichuan peppercorns

6 cups water
One 2-pound boneless leg of lamb

FOR THE DIPPING SAUCE

1/2 cup Chicken Stock (page 69) or
    canned chicken broth
2 tablespoons ketchup
1 tablespoon bottled satay sauce
1 tablespoon minced Chinese pickled
    cucumber
2 teaspoons sugar
1 teaspoon minced salted plum or plum
    preserves
1/2 teaspoon salt

Vegetable oil for deep-frying

1 tablespoon minced garlic
1 tablespoon grated ginger
1 tablespoon minced shallot

6 to 12 iceberg lettuce cups
1 green onion, trimmed and chopped

※　　※　　※

1. Prepare a spice bag: Place the ginger, star anise, cinnamon, cardamom, and peppercorns in the center of an 8-inch square of cheesecloth. Bring the corners of the square together and tie them with a string to form a bag.

2. Pour the water into a 5-quart pot and add the lamb and spice bag. Bring to a boil over medium-high heat. Reduce the heat to low, cover, and simmer until the meat is very tender, about 1 1/2 hours.

3. Meanwhile, prepare the sauce: Stir the chicken stock, ketchup, satay sauce, pickled cucumber, sugar, salted plum, and salt together in a bowl until well blended. Set aside.

4. When the lamb is done, drain it and let stand until cool and dry. Shred the meat with your fingers or by pulling it apart with two forks.

5. Pour enough oil into a 2-quart saucepan to come to a depth of 3 inches. Heat over medium-high to 350° F. Deep-fry the shredded lamb, in

three batches, until crispy, 3 to 4 minutes. Remove the lamb with a slotted spoon and drain on paper towels, then place on a serving plate and drape loosely with foil, shiny side down, to keep warm. Reserve the oil.

6. Heat a wok over high heat until hot. Add 2 tablespoons of the reserved oil and swirl to coat the sides. Add the garlic, ginger, and shallot and cook, stirring, until fragrant, about 30 seconds.

Add the sauce and bring to a boil. Cook until the flavors have blended, about 30 seconds.

7. Serve the lamb in the lettuce cups with the dipping sauce and green onion on the side. Have your guests help themselves to the lettuce cups: show them how to drizzle the sauce over the lamb, sprinkle the green onions over the sauce, and eat out of hand like a burrito.

RICE and NOODLES

No matter how many cookbooks or cooking shows I do, one thing is always at the center, rice! Noodles are great snacks, lunches, or 10-minute dinners, and in northern China, where wheat is plentiful, noodles are a staple. But in southern China, and many other countries around the world, rice is life. It is so simple and it goes with anything.

This chapter is split evenly between rice and noodles, both because the recipes come from all over the world and because we did not want to play starch favorites. As a matter of fact, I make Jia Jiang Mein as a quick meal for my family. Olive Fried Rice is a very interesting dish that uses the unusual Chinese fermented olive. Fried rice also is an excellent way to use up extra ingredients or leftovers. Rice's versatility is limited only by the imagination.

SOMETHING FOR EVERYONE FRIED RICE

Serves 4 as part of a multicourse meal

Avariety of vegetables and meats goes into this fried rice. Fried rice is a great way to use leftovers: keep the ratio of one part vegetable or meat to two parts rice, and the result will make your family happy.

FOR THE SAUCE

2 tablespoons Chicken Stock (page 69) or canned chicken broth
1 tablespoon soy sauce
1 tablespoon oyster-flavored sauce
1 teaspoon sesame oil
1/4 teaspoon salt

1 tablespoon vegetable oil
1 teaspoon minced ginger
1 teaspoon minced garlic
1 cup uncooked meat or seafood cut into 1/2-inch cubes
1 cup assorted vegetables, such as carrots, celery, bok choy, peas, sugar snap peas, long beans, and/or zucchini, cut into 1/2-inch pieces
2 eggs, lightly beaten
4 cups cold cooked long-grain rice, grains separated
1/4 cup chopped macadamia nuts

1. Prepare the sauce: Stir the chicken stock, soy sauce, oyster-flavored sauce, sesame oil, and salt together in a bowl.

2. Heat a wok over high heat until hot. Pour in the oil and swirl to coat the sides. Add the ginger and garlic and stir-fry until fragrant, about 20 seconds. Add the meat and stir-fry until almost cooked through, 1 to 1 1/2 minutes. Scatter the vegetables over the meat and stir-fry until the vegetables are tender-crisp, about 2 minutes.

3. Push the vegetables and meat to the sides of wok and pour in the eggs. Stir until the eggs are lightly scrambled. Add the rice and stir-fry until the eggs and vegetables are mixed throughout the rice and the rice is heated through, about 3 minutes.

4. Pour in the sauce and toss to coat evenly. Scoop onto a warm serving platter, sprinkle with the macadamia nuts, and serve.

STEAMED RICE

No Chinese meal is complete without rice, and no Chinatown restaurant or home kitchen would be complete without an electric rice cooker. Available in many sizes and prices, electric rice cookers guarantee perfect rice every time. If you don't have one, I offer my method for preparing rice. Cold rice is the secret to fried rice, so make enough for leftovers.

Place 2 cups long-grain rice in a sieve and rinse under cold running water until the water runs clear. Drain well. Place the rice and 3 cups water in a 3-quart saucepan. Bring to a boil over high heat and cook uncovered until crater-like holes form and most water has evaporated, about 8 minutes. Cover and reduce the heat to low, and simmer for about 10 minutes. Remove the saucepan from the heat and let the rice stand, covered, for 10 minutes. Remove the cover and fluff the rice with a fork before serving. Makes about 5 cups.

FUJIAN FANCY FRIED RICE

Serves 4 as part of a multicourse meal

Fujian-style fried rice is not like the fried rice you order in Cantonese restaurants in Chinatown. A stir-fry with a great amount of sauce poured over the basic fried rice is a Fujian cuisine classic, and delicious!

4 dried black mushrooms

FOR THE STIR-FRY
2 ounces bay scallops
8 uncooked medium shrimp, shelled and deveined
3 teaspoons cornstarch

FOR THE MARINADE
1 teaspoon minced garlic
1 teaspoon cornstarch
1/2 teaspoon Chinese rice wine or dry sherry
1/2 teaspoon soy sauce
1/2 teaspoon minced ginger

2 ounces boneless, skinless chicken breasts or thighs, cut into 1-inch pieces

FOR THE SAUCE
1 1/2 cups Chicken Stock (page 69) or canned chicken broth
1 tablespoon cornstarch
1 1/2 teaspoons oyster-flavored sauce
1 teaspoon soy sauce
1/2 teaspoon sugar
1/4 teaspoon sesame oil

FOR THE FRIED RICE
5 teaspoons vegetable oil
2 eggs, lightly beaten
3 cups cold cooked long-grain rice, grains separated
1/4 teaspoon sugar
1/4 teaspoon salt
1/8 teaspoon ground white pepper

5 asparagus stalks, trimmed and cut diagonally into 1-inch pieces
1 plum tomato, diced

✳   ✳   ✳

1. Pour enough warm water over the mushrooms in a small bowl to cover them completely. Let stand until softened, about 20 minutes. Drain thoroughly. Remove and discard the stems and cut the caps into quarters.

2. In separate small bowls, toss the scallops with 1 teaspoon of the cornstarch and the shrimp with 2 teaspoons of the cornstarch.

3. Marinate the chicken: Stir the garlic, cornstarch, rice wine, soy sauce, and ginger in another small bowl until the cornstarch is dissolved. Add the chicken and toss gently to coat. Let stand for 10 minutes.

4. Prepare the sauce: Stir the chicken stock, cornstarch, oyster-flavored sauce, soy sauce, sugar, and sesame oil together in a bowl until the cornstarch is dissolved.

5. Make the fried rice: Heat a wok over medium-high heat until hot. Add 2 teaspoons of the oil and swirl to coat the sides. Pour the eggs into the wok and cook, stirring, until the eggs are slightly firm, about 30 seconds. Add the rice, sugar, salt, and pepper and stir constantly until the rice is heated through, 2 to 3 minutes. Transfer to a serving platter and cover with foil, shiny side down, to keep warm.

6. Return the wok to high heat, add the remaining 3 teaspoons oil, and swirl to coat the sides. Add the chicken and stir-fry until the chicken is no longer pink, about 3 minutes. Add the shrimp and scallops and stir-fry until the shrimp turn pink, about 1 minute. Add the asparagus, mushrooms, and tomato and stir-fry until the asparagus is tender-crisp, 1 to 2 minutes.

7. Pour the sauce into the wok and cook, stirring, until the sauce boils and is lightly thickened, about 30 seconds. Scoop the contents of the wok over the fried rice and serve.

* * *

OMELET STRIPS

Instead of adding raw eggs to fried rice, make these omelets instead, cut them into strips, and toss into the rice. Beat 2 eggs with a pinch of salt. Heat an 8-inch nonstick frying pan over medium heat. Add ¼ teaspoon vegetable oil and swirl to coat the bottom of the pan. Pour in one-third of the eggs and swirl to cover the bottom of the pan. Cook until the eggs are lightly browned on the bottom and set on top, about 1 minute. Turn the sheet of eggs over and cook for 5 seconds; slide out of the pan. Repeat to make 2 more omelet sheets. When cool, cut into thin strips.

EMERALD RICE | *Serves 4 as part of a multicourse meal*

An easy way to eat your greens, all chopped up in fried rice. I use spinach, but you can use any of your favorite leafy greens, such as chard, mustard greens, or bok choy. You can even use frozen spinach—just defrost it and squeeze out the excess liquid.

1 large bunch spinach,
   tough stems discarded
2 teaspoons salt

1 tablespoon vegetable oil
2 green onions, trimmed and chopped
4 cups cold cooked long-grain rice,
   grains separated
¼ pound Smithfield ham or Char Siu
   (page 259), cut into ¼-inch cubes
½ cup Omelet Strips (page 287)
1 teaspoon salt
1 teaspoon soy sauce

❋   ❋   ❋

1. Wash, drain, and finely chop the spinach leaves. Toss the spinach together with the 2 teaspoons salt in a bowl. Let stand until the spinach is wilted, about 10 minutes.

2. Squeeze the spinach with your hands to remove the excess water, then chop the spinach again. (To reduce the sodium in this dish, instead of salting the spinach, cook it in a microwave oven until slightly wilted, then squeeze dry and finely chop.)

3. Heat a wok over medium-high heat until hot. Add the oil and swirl to coat the sides. Scatter the green onions into the pan and stir-fry until fragrant, about 20 seconds. Add the rice, ham, omelet strips, and chopped spinach. Sprinkle the salt and soy sauce over the rice. Cook, stirring frequently, until the rice is heated through, 2 to 3 minutes. Pile the rice onto a serving platter and serve.

MINTED FRIED RICE

Serves 4 as part of a multicourse meal

Christina Yau serves this colorful rice dish at YMing, where London's Chinatown and Soho come together.

3 tablespoons vegetable oil
½ red or green jalapeño chili, cut into thin rings
1 teaspoon minced ginger
1 egg, lightly beaten
3 cups cold cooked long-grain rice, grains separated
2 teaspoons oyster-flavored sauce
½ teaspoon salt
¼ teaspoon ground white pepper
¼ cup finely chopped mint

1. Heat a wok over high heat until hot. Add the oil and swirl to coat the sides. Add the chili and ginger, and cook, stirring, until fragrant, about 30 seconds. Add the egg and cook until lightly scrambled. Scatter the rice into the wok and stir until heated through, 2 to 3 minutes.

2. Stirring constantly, add the oyster-flavored sauce, salt, pepper, and mint. Mix well and cook until heated through, 1 to 2 minutes. Scoop the rice onto a warmed platter and serve hot.

FERMENTED CHINESE OLIVE FRIED RICE

Serves 4 as part of a multicourse meal

At Chen Foo Ji Chinese Fried Rice Restaurant in Singapore's Chinatown, the list of fried rice dishes seems endless. I tried as many as I could when I visited there, and this one intrigued me. It may come as a surprise, but Chinese do grow olives. Once harvested, they are fermented and dried, resulting in a concentrated flavor. If you can't locate Chinese olives, substitute any oil-cured black olive.

FOR THE MARINADE

1 tablespoon oyster-flavored sauce

2 teaspoons cornstarch

½ pound boneless, skinless chicken breasts or thighs, minced

FOR THE SEASONINGS

¼ cup Chicken Stock (page 69), Vegetable Stock (page 105), or canned chicken broth

1 teaspoon soy sauce

1 teaspoon sesame oil

1 tablespoon vegetable oil

2 cups cold cooked long-grain rice, grains separated

2 tablespoons chopped Chinese olives or ¼ cup pitted oil-cured black olives

2 tablespoons frozen peas, thawed

4 fresh shiitake, stems discarded and caps diced

2 eggs, lightly beaten

2 green onions, trimmed and minced

1. Marinate the chicken: Stir the oyster-flavored sauce and cornstarch together in a small bowl until the cornstarch is dissolved. Stir the chicken into the marinade, mix well, and let stand for 10 minutes.

2. Prepare the seasonings: Stir the chicken stock, soy sauce, and sesame oil together in a small bowl.

3. Heat a wok over high heat until hot. Add the oil and swirl to coat the sides. Add the chicken and cook, stirring, until no longer pink, about 2 minutes. Sprinkle the rice into the wok and stir-fry until heated through, about 2 minutes. Add the olives, peas, and shiitake. Cook, stirring, for 1 minute.

4. Push the rice and chicken to the sides of the wok and pour the eggs into the center well. Scramble the eggs until set, then stir to combine the rice and eggs. Add the seasonings and green onions and stir-fry until heated through, 1 to 2 minutes. Scoop the rice onto a warm serving platter and serve hot.

SINGAPORE

YUM CHA TIM SUM RESTAURANT—A DIM SUM RESTAURANT THAT'S OPEN TWENTY-FOUR HOURS!

THE RED ROOFS OF SINGAPORE CHINATOWN

This Chinatown is where a world-class, high-tech banking center remembers the best of its past. Lovingly preserved with the smart efficiency and cleanliness for which Singapore is known the world over, Chinatown's narrow godown warehouses, its arcade sidewalks, slatted windows, and elaborate cornices have been repainted in all their glory. All done up in whites and yellows, this is the flower at the heart of a modern "tropical city of excellence." It's a living museum that glows with pride. ✳ But how can a nation-state that most think of as Chinese contain its own Chinatown? There's an Indian town too, and a Malay section as well, in this multicultural port city. And it was the famed British governor Sir Stamford Raffles who ordered the creation of a Chinese "kampong," as the locals called it, way back in 1822. Yet even within this small area, sections were separated by place of origin: Hokkiens or Fujianese living separately from Chiu Chows or Cantonese. ✳ Today, you'll still find many homemade foods reflecting the tastes of these coastal peoples. And plenty of Singapore's famed street hawkers, offering everything from the world's most succulent shrimp to special basil-laced Hakka stir-fries. The world's best—and most expensive—fried rice too. Now, with the internationalization of the workforce and some of the world's finest hotels, have come experienced chefs from every region of China. Singapore is still the crossroads city of Asia, and for Chinese food, the choice of styles is wider and wilder than in any of the other Chinatowns.

CAFÉ AT-SUNRICE

Fort Canning Centre
Fort Canning Park
(65) 336-3307

CHEN FOO JI CHINESE FRIED RICE RESTAURANT

7 Erskine Road
(65) 323-0260
What to order: *seafood-crabmeat fried rice; Chinese olive fried rice; pineapple soybean fried rice with bean curd puffs; golden prawns with shredded egg; Chen Foo Ji special fried rice*

DAMENLOU RESTAURANT

12 Ann Siang Road
(65) 221-1900
What to order: *fish head rice noodle soup; braised fried tofu with fish fillet*

HAI TEN LO CHINESE RESTAURANT

Pan Pacific Hotel Singapore
7 Raffles Boulevard
Marina Square
(65) 336-8111
What to order: *double-boiled whole quail served in coconut; special crispy roast chicken; steamed Vietnamese king water prawns with minced garlic; spring rolls filled with salmon fish and mangoes*

LEE TONG KEE NOODLE RESTAURANT

178 South Bridge Road
(65) 226-0417
What to order: *mushroom hor fun Lee (Tong Kee's special); LTK's KL-style hor fun with chicken feet*

LEUNG SANG HK PASTRIES

18 Sago Street
(65) 221-1344
What to order: *moon cakes; roasted chicken pastry; egg custard*

SOUP RESTAURANT

25A Smith Street
(65) 222-4668
What to order: *steamed boneless chicken with lettuce cups; steamed fish fillet with vegetables; Singapore chili prawn*

YUM CHA TIM SUM RESTAURANT

20 Trengganu Street, 02-01
(65) 372-1717
What to order: *prawn and banana wafers; Shu Zhou vegetable steamed bun; special chicken bun*

ADDING THE FINISHING TOUCH TO A BIG BOWL OF SINGAPORE'S SEAFOOD NOODLE SOUP.

MY FINGERS ARE TRYING TO KEEP UP WITH THESE LADIES, WHO PRODUCE AROUND 300 CHINESE PASTRIES A DAY!

MACAU CLAY POT RICE

Serves 4 as part of a multicourse meal

Rice baked in a clay pot is comfort food all over Southeast Asia. This version is very much a Macanese favorite. Like many Macanese dishes, its unique aroma and flavor come from that golden yellow cousin of ginger, turmeric.

FOR THE SAUCE

2 cups Chicken Stock (page 69) or
    canned chicken broth
1 tablespoon soy sauce
1 tablespoon oyster-flavored sauce
2 teaspoons sugar
1 teaspoon Chinese five-spice powder
1 teaspoon ground bean paste
1 teaspoon garlic powder
1/4 teaspoon turmeric powder

1 cup long-grain rice
1/2 medium carrot, thinly sliced on the bias
1 Chinese sausage (about 2 ounces), thinly
    sliced on the bias
1 1/2 cups shredded Roast Duck meat (page 239)

1. Preheat the oven to 350°F.

2. Prepare the sauce: Bring the chicken stock, soy sauce, oyster-flavored sauce, sugar, five-spice powder, bean paste, and garlic and turmeric powders to a boil in a 1-quart clay pot or oven-proof baking dish over medium heat.

3. Stir in the rice, carrot, and sausage until mixed. Scatter the shredded duck over the rice.

4. Cover the pot and transfer to the oven. Bake for 25 minutes, or until the liquid is absorbed and a light crust has formed on the bottom of the rice. Serve immediately, directly from the clay pot.

CANTONESE CLAY POT RICE

Serves 4 as part of a multicourse meal

Rice baked in a clay pot has two contrasting textures—the soft, fluffy rice and the crispy, lightly browned crust that forms on the bottom of the rice. Chinese sausage, with its sweet, rich flavor, is best when paired with delicately seasoned rice dishes, such as this one served at Bow Hon Restaurant in San Francisco's Chinatown.

2 dried black mushrooms

FOR THE MARINADE
1 tablespoon soy sauce
1 teaspoon cornstarch

6 ounces boneless, skinless chicken breasts or
    thighs, thinly sliced

2 cups Chicken Stock (page 69) or
    canned chicken broth
1 cup long-grain rice
2 quarter-sized slices peeled ginger
1 Chinese sausage (about 2 ounces),
    thinly sliced on the bias
2 ounces preserved pork or
    smoked Canadian bacon, thinly sliced

1 tablespoon chopped cilantro

*   *   *

1. Pour enough warm water over the mushrooms in a small bowl to cover them completely. Let stand until softened, about 20 minutes. Drain, discard the stems, and thinly slice the caps.

2. Marinate the chicken: Stir the soy sauce and cornstarch together in a bowl until the cornstarch is dissolved. Add the chicken and toss gently until coated. Let stand for 10 minutes.

3. Preheat the oven to 350°F.

4. In a 1-quart clay pot, combine the chicken stock, rice, ginger, and mushrooms. Place over medium-high heat and bring to a boil.

5. Lay the chicken, sausage, and preserved pork on top of the rice. Cover the pot and transfer it to the oven. Bake until the liquid is absorbed and a light crust forms on the bottom of the rice, about 25 minutes. Scatter the cilantro over the top and serve right from the pot.

GOLD MEDAL CRAB FRIED RICE

Serves 4 as part of a multicourse meal

This signature dish from Chen Foo Ji Chinese Fried Rice Restaurant in Singapore took first place at the annual fried rice competition a few years ago. Award-winning dishes aren't cheap either—eighteen dollars a plate! The only way this fried rice could be more opulent is if it had gold in it. Thankfully though, the golden color comes from the egg yolks.

2 tablespoons vegetable oil

3 cups cold cooked long-grain rice, grains separated

4 egg yolks, lightly beaten

1/2 teaspoon minced garlic

1/4 pound uncooked medium shrimp, shelled, deveined, and cut into 1/2-inch pieces

1/4 pound crabmeat, flaked and picked over for shells

2 green onions, trimmed, cut into 2-inch lengths, and shredded

2 tablespoons water

1/2 teaspoon salt

1/8 teaspoon ground white pepper

Cooked shelled crabmeat from 2 leg segments (optional)

Cooked meat from 1 lobster tail, cut into bite-sized pieces (optional)

2 teaspoons tobiko caviar, optional

1. Heat a wok over medium heat until hot. Add 1 tablespoon of the oil and swirl to coat the sides. Reduce the heat to low, add the rice and egg yolks, and cook, stirring continuously, until each grain of rice is coated with the yolk and golden, about 2 minutes.

2. Increase the heat to high, make a well in the center of the rice to expose the bottom of the wok, and add the remaining 1 tablespoon oil. Drop the garlic and shrimp into the well and stir constantly until the shrimp turn pink, 1 to 1½ minutes.

3. Stir the shrimp and rice together. Add the flaked crabmeat, half the green onions, the water, salt, and pepper and cook, stirring, until heated through, 1 to 2 minutes.

4. Scoop the rice onto a serving platter, garnish with the remaining green onion and the crab leg meat, lobster, and caviar, if using, and serve immediately.

GINGER AND EGG FRIED RICE

Serves 4 as part of a multicourse meal

Ginger for energy and egg for brain power. This fried rice dish is given to new mothers after they've had a baby. The ginger is said to give the mother energy to recuperate from childbirth and the egg makes the baby smarter. But there's nothing wrong with a little energy and mental boost for the rest of us.

2 tablespoons vegetable oil

2 tablespoons grated ginger

1 egg, lightly beaten

3 cups cold cooked long-grain rice, grains separated

2 tablespoons minced crystallized ginger (optional)

¼ cup diced fresh or canned pineapple

2 tablespoons Chicken Stock (page 69) or canned chicken broth

1 teaspoon sesame oil

¾ teaspoon salt

1. Heat a wok over high heat until hot. Add the oil and swirl to coat the sides. Add the grated ginger and cook until fragrant, about 20 seconds. Pour the egg into the wok and cook, stirring, until lightly scrambled. Add the rice and crystallized ginger, if using and stir-fry until the rice is heated through, 1 to 1½ minutes.

2. Add the pineapple, chicken stock, sesame oil, and salt. Mix well and cook until heated through, about 2 minutes.

3. Mound the rice on a warm serving platter and serve immediately.

CHINESE PHILOSOPHY

Others might argue that our "gods" have been real men. One is Confucius, the paradoxically reclusive philosopher who set down strict rules of conduct for creating a just and harmonious society. No aspect of human life was outside his gentle and considerate view. Confucianism is not really a matter of worship but principles to follow in government, education, and everyday life—even eating. For it was Confucius who formulated the notion that between the two basic drives of man—food and sex—it was food that had to come first. After all, how do humans procreate without first being well fed? Even today, the Chinese like to say that the main test of any set of beliefs is how well it guarantees the greatest number of citizens their shot at health, prosperity, and longevity—giving each of us the most opportunities to, as the saying goes, "live well, dress well, and eat well"—not necessarily in that order. ❋ The second deity of philosophy is Lao Tse, the main formulator of Taoism, a far more ancient concept that permeates the Chinese attitude toward life. Some in the West may see this worldview as passive, stressing an acceptance of nature and the need to work with those forces to achieve harmony and find one's true self. Taoism is the force that causes a general to win a battle by making just the right strategic retreat. It's how a kung fu fighter can defeat a far stronger opponent by harnessing the power generated by his attacker. And it's also how a Chinese banquet can be prepared from a fire using three sticks of straw! Taoism also teaches us to be happy with what we have and to appreciate all that's around us rather than craving things that are not. I always feel fortunate to have been given the opportunity to come to the United States to be educated and to be working in the field that I love. So you might call me one happy surfer on the Way of the Tao.

FUN CHICKEN | *Serves 4 as part of a multicourse meal*

When fresh wide rice noodles are stir-fried, they are called *fun*. Fresh rice noodles have to be pulled apart and fluffed before cooking.

1 pound fresh or dried flat rice noodles
(about ¹/₂ inch wide)

FOR THE MARINADE
¹/₂ tablespoon soy sauce or light soy sauce
1 teaspoon Chinese rice wine or dry sherry
1 teaspoon minced garlic
¹/₂ teaspoon cornstarch
¹/₈ teaspoon ground white pepper

¹/₄ pound boneless, skinless chicken breasts or
thighs, thinly sliced

FOR THE SEASONINGS
2 tablespoons soy sauce or 1 tablespoon each
light and dark soy sauce
1 teaspoon chili garlic sauce
¹/₂ teaspoon sugar

1 tablespoon vegetable oil

¹/₂ yellow onion, thinly sliced
3 green onions, trimmed and cut into
1-inch pieces
1 teaspoon minced ginger
1 cup bean sprouts

¹/₄ cup roasted peanuts

1. If using dried rice noodles, pour enough warm water over them in a medium bowl to cover completely. Let soak until softened, about 30 minutes. Drain thoroughly. If using fresh rice noodles, run under warm water and separate strands.

2. Marinate the chicken: Stir the soy sauce, rice wine, garlic, cornstarch, and pepper together in a bowl until the cornstarch is dissolved. Toss the chicken gently in the marinade until coated. Let stand for 10 minutes.

3. Prepare the seasonings: Stir the soy sauce, chili garlic sauce, and sugar together in a bowl until the sugar is dissolved.

4. Heat a wok over high heat until hot. Add the oil and swirl to coat the sides. Add the soaked or fresh rice noodles and stir-fry until the noodles are lightly browned along the edges, about 2 minutes. Scoop the noodles onto a plate and set aside.

5. Add the chicken to the wok and stir-fry until no longer pink, about 2 minutes. Add both onions and the ginger and stir-fry until fragrant, about 1 minute. Slide the noodles into the wok, scatter the bean sprouts over them, and pour in the seasonings. Toss until the mixture is heated through and the chicken is coated evenly with the seasonings, about 3 minutes.

6. Stir in the peanuts, scoop the contents of the wok onto a warm serving plate, and serve.

MACAU RICE NOODLES

Serves 4 as part of a multicourse meal

This dish is a good example of the centuries-old fusion cuisine of Macau, which is a blend of Chinese and Portuguese. I learned a great deal when I visited Macau's Institute for Tourism Studies. All students are required to master this dish during their time at the school. The combination of barbecued pork, Chinese sausage, and red ginger gives a sweetness to this dish. If you cannot find sweet red ginger, substitute the Japanese-style sushi ginger.

½ package (2 ounces) dried rice vermicelli

1 tablespoon plus ½ teaspoon vegetable oil
1 egg, lightly beaten

2 Chinese sausages (each about 2 ounces), cut into 2-inch-long thin strips
½ white onion cut into strips
2 fresh shiitake, stems removed and caps thickly sliced
½ pound Char Siu (page 259), cut into thin strips
½ cup bean sprouts
1 tablespoon shredded red pickled ginger or pickled ginger
2 teaspoons soy sauce
½ teaspoon salt
⅛ teaspoon ground white pepper

¼ cup thinly sliced green onions
1 teaspoon mixed white and black sesame seeds

1. Pour enough warm water over the noodles in a large bowl to cover completely. Soak until softened, about 10 minutes. Drain thoroughly.

2. Heat a wok over high heat until hot. Add the ½ teaspoon oil and swirl to coat the sides. Pour in the egg and swirl the wok so the egg covers the bottom in a thin layer. Cook until the egg is lightly browned on the underside and set on the top, about 1 minute. Remove from the heat and remove the egg from the wok. Let cool slightly, then cut into strips. Set aside for garnish.

3. Return the wok to high heat until hot. Add the remaining 1 tablespoon oil, swirling to coat the sides. Add the Chinese sausages, onion, and shiitake and stir-fry until the sausage is cooked, about 2 minutes. Add the noodles, char siu, bean sprouts, red ginger, soy sauce, salt, and pepper. Stir-fry until the noodles and other ingredients are heated through and well combined, 1½ to 2 minutes.

4. Scoop the contents of the wok onto a serving platter. Scatter the egg strips, green onions, and sesame seeds over the noodles and serve immediately.

DAIKON WITH BEAN THREAD NOODLES

Serves 4 as part of a multicourse meal

Daikon, the grandfather of the radish family, is used in many different ways in Asian cuisine—soups, salads, stir-fries, or even as an elaborate garnish. Lina Wong in Melbourne passed along her favorite recipe using this large white radish. Crunchy daikon and smooth bean thread noodles are a unique combination.

2 small dried wood ear mushrooms

2 ounces dried bean thread noodles

FOR THE SAUCE

1 cup Vegetable Stock (page 105) or
    canned vegetable broth

1 tablespoon soy sauce

1 tablespoon vegetarian oyster-flavored sauce

1 teaspoon sugar

2 tablespoons vegetable oil

2 quarter-sized slices peeled ginger, cut into
    very thin strips

1 pound daikon, peeled and cut into thin strips
    about 2 inches long (about 2 cups)

2 cups napa cabbage, cut into ½-inch strips

1 leek, cut into thin strips (white part only)
    (about ½ cup)

½ medium carrot, cut into thin strips

2 tablespoons cilantro leaves, plus 1 sprig for
    garnish

1. Pour enough warm water over the wood ear mushrooms in a small bowl to cover them completely. Soak until softened, about 20 minutes. Drain the mushrooms and cut them into thin strips.

2. While the mushrooms are soaking, pour enough warm water over the bean thread noodles in a medium bowl to cover them completely. Soak until softened, about 10 minutes. Drain the noodles, lay them out on a cutting board, and cut them crosswise in half.

3. Prepare the sauce: Stir the vegetable stock, soy sauce, oyster-flavored sauce, and sugar together in a small bowl until the sugar is dissolved.

4. Heat a wok over high heat until hot. Add the oil and swirl to coat the sides. Add the ginger and cook, stirring, until fragrant, about 20 seconds. Add the wood ear, daikon, cabbage, leek, and carrot and stir-fry until the vegetables are tender, about 2 minutes. Add the sauce and noodles, cover, and simmer until the noodles are tender, about 2 to 2½ minutes.

5. Stir in the cilantro leaves and scoop onto a serving platter. Garnish with the cilantro sprig.

BRAISED SEAFOOD MEIN

Serves 4 as part of a multicourse meal

Braising in Asian cooking means that the meat or seafood is cooked in its sauce for a few additional minutes.

FOR THE MARINADE

2 teaspoons cornstarch

2 teaspoons Chinese rice wine or dry sherry

1/4 pound sea scallops, butterflied, sliced almost in half

1/4 pound uncooked medium shrimp, shelled and deveined

1/4 pound firm-fleshed white fish fillets, such as halibut or snapper, cut into 4 pieces

FOR THE SAUCE

1/3 cup Chicken Stock (page 69) or canned chicken broth

2 tablespoons Chinese rice wine or dry sherry

1/2 teaspoon salt

1/4 teaspoon ground white pepper

3 baby bok choy, halved lengthwise

1/2 package (8 ounces) flat Chinese egg noodles

2 tablespoons vegetable oil

1/4 cup thinly sliced carrots

1/4 cup drained canned straw mushrooms

* * *

1. Marinate the seafood: Stir the cornstarch and rice wine together in a small bowl until the cornstarch is dissolved. Add the scallops, shrimp, and fish and stir gently to coat. Let stand for 10 minutes.

2. Prepare the sauce: Stir the chicken stock, rice wine, salt, and pepper together in a bowl until the salt is dissolved. Set aside.

3. Bring a large pot of salted water to a boil. Add the bok choy and cook until tender-crisp, 2 1/2 to 3 minutes. Scoop out with a large wire skimmer and set aside.

4. Cook the noodles according to the package instructions in the same pot of water. Drain well, rinse them under warm water, and drain again. Pile the noodles in the center of a serving bowl. Arrange the bok choy around the noodles, and cover the bowl with aluminum foil, shiny side down, to keep warm.

5. Heat a wok over high heat until hot. Add the oil and swirl to coat the sides. Add the seafood and carrots and stir-fry until the shrimp turn pink, 2 1/2 to 3 minutes. Add the mushrooms and sauce, mix well, and bring to a boil. Scoop the contents of the wok into the center of the noodles and serve immediately.

COLD PEANUT NOODLES WITH CHICKEN

Serves 4 as part of a multicourse meal

This refreshing Sichuan noodle salad is tossed with a spicy peanut dressing. Cut the vegetables into long thin slices to make them easier to eat with the noodles. Enjoy the combination of the chewy noodles and crisp vegetables. If you can't find fresh Chinese egg noodles, substitute angel hair pasta or spaghetti.

1 pound fresh Chinese egg noodles

FOR THE DRESSING

3½ tablespoons soy sauce

2 tablespoons seasoned rice vinegar

2 tablespoons sesame oil

2 tablespoons sesame paste

1 tablespoon creamy peanut butter

1 tablespoon sugar

1 tablespoon minced ginger

2 teaspoons minced garlic

2 teaspoons chili garlic sauce

½ teaspoon ground toasted Sichuan peppercorns

1½ cups (about ½ pound) shredded cooked chicken breasts

½ English cucumber, cut into thin strips about 2 inches long

1 cup bean sprouts

1 medium carrot, peeled and cut into thin strips

3 green onions, trimmed and cut into thin strips

¼ cup chopped roasted peanuts

1. Cook the noodles in a large pot of boiling water according to the package directions. Drain well, rinse them with cold water, and drain again.

2. Make the dressing: Stir the soy sauce, rice vinegar, sesame oil, sesame paste, peanut butter, sugar, ginger, garlic, chili garlic sauce, and Sichuan pepper together in a medium bowl until smooth.

3. Pile the noodles in the center of a serving platter. Arrange the chicken, cucumber, bean sprouts, carrot, and green onions around the noodles. Pour the dressing over the noodles and sprinkle the peanuts over the top. Toss at the table until the noodles are coated with dressing, and serve.

DAN DAN NOODLES

Serves 4 as part of a multicourse meal

Dan dan is the method of balancing baskets or bundles on either end of a thick bamboo stick on the shoulders. A long time ago, that's how these noodles were sold. On one end of the stick would be a bucket containing the noodles and meat, and on the other end would be the heating element with a condiment tray for the peanut sauce.

FOR THE SAUCE

6 tablespoons Chicken Stock (page 69) or canned chicken broth
2 tablespoons creamy peanut butter
2 tablespoons sesame paste or tahini paste
1 tablespoon Chinese black vinegar or balsamic vinegar
1 tablespoon soy sauce
1 tablespoon minced garlic
2 teaspoons sesame oil
2 teaspoons sugar
1 teaspoon dried red chili flakes
½ teaspoon ground toasted Sichuan peppercorns

1 pound fresh Chinese egg noodles

1 green onion, trimmed and thinly sliced
2 tablespoons chopped Sichuan preserved vegetables (optional)
1 tablespoon chopped roasted peanuts

1. Prepare the sauce: Stir the chicken stock, peanut butter, sesame paste, black vinegar, soy sauce, garlic, sesame oil, sugar, chili flakes, and Sichuan peppercorns together in a medium saucepan. Heat the sauce over medium heat until hot, stirring to dissolve the sugar. Cover and set aside.

2. Cook the noodles in a large pot of boiling water according to the package directions. Drain the noodles, rinse them under warm water, and drain again.

3. Mound the noodles on a serving platter and pour the sauce over them. Scatter the green onion, preserved vegetables, if using, and peanuts over the sauce. Serve immediately.

SHANGHAI NOODLES WITH PORK AND BOK CHOY

Serves 4 as part of a multicourse meal

Noodles from Shanghai are thicker and chewier than other Chinese noodles. Try them the next time you see them on the menu—it'll add to your noodle-enjoying experience, and if you like dishes on the sweeter side, you'll enjoy the experience more. Shanghai cuisine is known to be on the sweeter side. If you can find Chinese mustard greens use them in place of the bok choy. The dish can be made without the pork for a vegetarian alternative.

1 pound fresh Shanghai-style thick noodles or Chinese egg noodles

FOR THE SEASONINGS
2 tablespoons sweet bean sauce or hoisin sauce
2 tablespoons soy sauce
2 teaspoons sugar
2 teaspoons sesame oil

FOR THE MARINADE
1 teaspoon soy sauce
1 teaspoon cornstarch

¼ pound ground pork

1 tablespoon vegetable oil
2 quarter-sized slices peeled ginger, cut into thin strips
2 heads baby bok choy, each cut lengthwise into 8 segments
2 green onions, trimmed and cut into thin 2-inch-long strips
⅓ cup Sichuan preserved vegetables, rinsed and chopped (optional)

1. Cook the noodles in a large pot of boiling water according to the package directions. Drain, rinse under cold water, and drain again.

2. Prepare the seasonings: Stir the sweet bean sauce, soy sauce, sugar, and sesame oil together in a small bowl until well blended.

3. Combine the soy sauce, cornstarch, and pork in a bowl, mixing until well coated. Let stand for 10 minutes.

4. Heat a wok over high heat until hot. Add the oil and swirl to coat the sides. Add the ginger and cook, stirring, until fragrant, about 10 seconds. Add the pork and stir-fry until no longer pink, about 2 minutes. Add the bok choy and stir-fry until tender, about 2 minutes. Add the noodles, green onions, and seasonings and toss gently until heated through.

5. Scoop onto a serving platter, sprinkle the preserved vegetables over the noodles, if using, and serve.

JIA JIANG MEIN

Serves 4 as part of a multicourse meal

A comforting meal, jia jiang mein is a Chinatown family favorite. As with any noodle dish, you can use Western noodles, but finding the right kind of Asian noodles for the right dish will pay off with the best flavor and texture.

1 pound fresh Chinese wheat noodles or dried spaghetti

FOR THE SEASONINGS
2 tablespoons hoisin sauce
2 tablespoons hot bean paste or chili garlic sauce
2 teaspoons soy sauce
2 teaspoons dark soy sauce
2 teaspoons sesame oil

2 tablespoons vegetable oil
2 tablespoons minced garlic
½ pound boneless pork, cut into thin strips
¼ cup finely diced bamboo shoots or finely diced water chestnuts

2 teaspoons cornstarch, dissolved in 1 tablespoon water

¼ carrot, cut into very thin 2-inch-long strips
½ English cucumber cut into very thin 2-inch-long strips

* * *

1. Bring a large pot of water to a boil. Cook the noodles according to the package directions. Drain, rinse with warm water, and drain again. Place the noodles in a large serving bowl and cover with foil, shiny side down, to keep warm.

2. Prepare the seasonings: Stir the hoisin sauce, hot bean paste, soy sauces, and sesame oil together in a small bowl until well blended.

3. Heat a wok over high heat until hot. Add the oil and swirl to coat the sides. Add the garlic and cook, stirring, until fragrant, about 10 seconds. Add the pork and stir-fry until lightly browned, about 2 minutes. Add the bamboo shoots and cook for 1 minute.

4. Stir in the seasonings and bring to a boil. Adjust the heat so the sauce is simmering, then stir in the dissolved cornstarch and stir until the sauce thickens slightly, about 30 seconds.

5. Ladle the meat and sauce into the center of the noodles. Scatter the carrot and cucumber around the edges. Bring to the table and toss before serving.

A BALANCE OF FENG SHUI, YIN, AND YANG

Tossed about by elements of wind and fire, walking a tightrope between past ancestors and future ghosts, it's natural that the Chinese should stress the idea of balance. Yin and yang, male and female, good and evil, strong and weak, hot and cold: These are the two sides of every coin, the two answers to every question, the opposites that always contend and must be reconciled. With this in mind, Chinatowns' temples and courtyards tend toward symmetry. And the interiors of all of Chinatowns' enterprises, even restaurants, seek to ensure luck and plenty of business, through the consultation of an expert on feng shui, which means wind and water but actually talks about how the correct placement of a door, mirror, red sash, bed, or even a bathroom can help people gain a better life. ❋ A bit like Chinese food, the concepts of feng shui, at once highly practical and a bit otherworldly, have had to leave China to find full appreciation. These days, Americans and Europeans flock to buy manuals on home design based on these ancient principles, while in China, feng shui masters must be careful about the evil "superstitions" they preach. But is it really so strange to think that people who live in a house in which the front door opens directly into the kitchen may end up with stomachaches? To be honest, I don't know enough about feng shui. Once a feng shui master came to visit my home and commented that it had great feng shui. We have a fishpond with a waterfall that can be viewed from the front entrance. For the Chinese, water is money and prosperity, and a continuous flow of water symbolizes a constant flow of wealth and good fortune. My only reason for having that pond is that landscaping is my hobby. To me, doing things that make you feel good will inevitably breed good feng shui. Check out how the wind and water have been made to flow in the next Chinese restaurant you try. Be assured that no matter how humble, someone has carefully thought about which mirrors should go on which walls. And the plants that give green energy to a dusty corner aren't just leftover gifts from the grand opening.

SPICY-CREAMY NONYA NOODLES

Serves 4 as part of a multicourse meal

In Singapore's Chinatown, you'll often find dishes from its neighbor, Malaysia, and other Southeast Asian countries. These Nonya noodles are a soccer match for the taste buds. You get a kick from the spice, which then gets blocked by the creamy coconut milk. Score one for Malaysian fusion.

4 ounces dried rice stick noodles
8 ounces fresh Chinese egg noodles

½ package (about 7 ounces) firm or regular
    tofu, drained and cut into 1-inch cubes
Vegetable oil for deep-frying

2 eggs, lightly beaten

FOR THE SPICE PASTE
⅓ cup water
2 stalks lemongrass, bottom 6 inches only,
    thinly sliced
4 walnut-sized shallots
3 red or green jalapeño chilies, seeded
4 candlenuts or 8 almonds
1 teaspoon galangal powder (optional)
¾ teaspoon shrimp paste
½ teaspoon turmeric powder

1 cup unsweetened coconut milk
4 cups Chicken Stock (page 69),
    canned chicken broth, or water
3 tablespoons soy sauce

6 ounces bean sprouts, blanched in boiling
    water for 1 minute, then drained

6 ounces cooked medium shrimp, shelled and
    deveined
1 large chicken breast half, cooked, boned, and
    shredded
½ English cucumber, cut into matchstick strips
3 red or green jalapeño chilies, thinly sliced
Lemon or lime wedges

❋   ❋   ❋

1. Pour enough warm water over the rice stick noodles in a bowl to cover them completely. Soak until softened, about 30 minutes. Drain. Mound the noodles in a large serving bowl.

2. Meanwhile, bring a large pot of water to a boil. Cook the egg noodles according to the package directions. Drain, rinse, and drain again. Mound the noodles next to the rice stick noodles in the serving bowl.

3. Deep-fry the tofu: Press the tofu cubes gently between paper towels to remove the excess water. Pour enough oil into a wok to come to a depth of 3 inches. Heat over medium heat to 350°F. Deep-fry the tofu, turning once, until golden on all sides, 3 to 4 minutes. Remove with a slotted spoon and drain on paper towels. Reserve the oil.

4. Heat a nonstick 8- or 9-inch skillet over medium heat until hot. Brush with ½ teaspoon of the reserved oil. Add half the eggs and tilt the pan so the the egg covers the bottom of the skillet. Cook until lightly browned on the bottom and set on the top, about 1 minute. Turn the omelet over and cook for 5 seconds. Slide the omelet out of the pan and repeat with another ½ teaspoon oil and the remaining egg. Roll the omelets into cylinders and cut into ¼-inch-wide strips.

5. Make the spice paste: Combine the water, lemongrass, shallots, jalapeños, nuts, galangal powder, if using, shrimp paste, and turmeric in a food processor. Process until smooth.

6. Heat a wok over medium-low heat until hot. Add 2 tablespoons of the reserved oil and swirl to coat the sides. Add the spice paste and cook, stirring, until fragrant, 6 to 8 minutes. Pour in the coconut milk, bring to a boil, and cook for 3 minutes. Add the 4 cups stock and the soy sauce and return to a boil.

7. Ladle the hot broth over the noodles and arrange the bean sprouts, shrimp, chicken, cucumber, sliced jalapeños, omelet strips, and lemon wedges decoratively over the top. Bring to the table, toss to mix the noodles with the other ingredients, and serve hot.

FORTUNE COOKIES

On Sale

DESSERTS

Dessert is the simplest course of a Chinese meal and runs the gamut. Dressed-up fruit or sweet soups made with nuts or herbs clean the palate and aid in digestion. Because of the vast influences and ingredients available to chefs in Chinatowns all over the world, we have everything from refreshing ice creams to fluffy cakes and classic dim sum favorites. Desserts are especially favored during festival times for their sweet symbolism.

PEANUT BISCUITS | *Makes 2 dozen*

These biscuits are similar to shortbread cookies. Try them with some tea on a weekend afternoon.

1¾ cups all-purpose flour, plus more for the cookie molds

¼ cup sugar

3 tablespoons cornstarch

Pinch salt

¾ cup (1½ sticks) unsalted butter, softened

¼ cup creamy peanut butter

¼ teaspoon sesame oil

¼ cup chopped roasted peanuts

1. Sift the flour, sugar, cornstarch, and salt together into a bowl. With an electric mixer, beat the butter, peanut butter, and sesame oil in a large bowl until creamy. Add the flour mixture and mix at low speed (or by hand) until well blended.

2. To shape the cookies, lightly dust a 2½-inch cookie mold with flour and shake out the excess. Pack enough of the cookie dough into the prepared mold to fill it halfway. Sprinkle a thin layer of chopped peanuts over the dough, then pack in enough dough to fill the mold. Level off the top of the cookie by dragging the back of a butter knife over the mold. Tap the mold firmly on the counter to release the cookie. Repeat with the remaining dough and peanuts, placing the cookies 2 inches apart on a parchment paper–lined baking sheet as you go. Refrigerate the cookies for 30 minutes or up to 1 hour. Meanwhile, preheat the oven to 350°F.

3. Bake the cookies until the edges turn golden brown, 20 to 25 minutes. Cool on the baking sheet for 5 minutes, then transfer to a wire rack to cool completely before serving. Store in an airtight container for up to 2 weeks.

PROGNOSTICATING PASTRIES

No one wants to leave Chinatown, or complete a Chinese meal, without getting their fortune told. And, part of the popularity of fortune cookies is that the fortune you get is almost always good. (Some even include tips on lucky lottery numbers as a bonus.) ❋ Fortune cookies don't exist, there are no such desserts back in China. No, the world's leading prognosticating pastry hails from my adopted home state of California. One version says that David Jung, a baker in Los Angeles Chinatown originally from Guangzhou, wanted to prove his loyalty to the U.S. by putting patriotic slogans inside his biscuits during World War I. Other versions say he was merely trying to cheer up downtrodden locals. ❋ But San Franciscans say Makoto Hagiwara, caretaker at Golden Gate Park's Japanese Tea Garden, made cookies with thank-you notes to grease the palms of local politicos, which later appeared at a 1915 International Exposition. Since I live in the Bay Area, I can't help leaning toward this theory. After all, San Francisco's Chinatown does house the outstanding Golden Gate Fortune Cookie Factory and Lotus Fortune Cookie Company, the maker of the first semi-automated fortune cookie machine. ❋ Or could it all be handed down from twelfth-century China? Supposedly, Chinese monks, hoping to foil Mongol attackers, tucked covert strategy notes in moon cakes, the sweets made for the annual Moon Festival.

CARAMEL DIP
WITH CRACKERS

Serves 4

From Macau's Chinatown comes this caramel sauce made from brown cane sugar, with thin strands of egg running through it. The sauce is served with saltine crackers. It sounds odd, but the sweet-salty flavors work. The dip will thicken as it cools.

6 brown cane sugar slabs
½ teaspoon Chinese five-spice powder
1 cup water
6 tablespoons unsalted butter
1 egg, lightly beaten

20 saltine crackers

❋   ❋   ❋

1. Place the sugar slabs in a resealable plastic bag and whack them with a rolling pin or the bottom of a small saucepan to break them into ¼- to ½-inch pieces.

2. Bring the water, butter, and crushed sugar slabs to a boil in a small saucepan over medium-high heat. Continue boiling until the mixture is thick, foamy, and reduced by one-third, about 5 minutes. Stirring the mixture in a circular motion, slowly drizzle in the beaten egg. Remove from the heat and, using a spoon, break up any large pieces of egg.

3. Pour the caramel dip into a serving bowl and allow to cool slightly. Serve with the crackers.

MOON FESTIVAL

On the fifteenth day of the eighth month of the lunar calendar, when the green hills fade to brown and the days become shorter, the Chinese celebrate the bounty of the fall harvest with three days of festivities. In ancient times, the Moon Festival celebrated the strength of the yin, nature's female force. The bright round moon was worshipped as a female deity. Women arranged pomegranates, grapes, melons, and other round fruits on round plates to represent the moon, nature's abundance, and, by symbolic extension, continuity of family. Through the years, legends have grown up about Yueh Lao-yeh (The Old Man of the Moon) and the Moon Hare, who are like Far Eastern cupids, scheming to tie sweethearts together with invisible red silk thread. ❋ Moon cakes are the edible symbol of the Moon Festival. Small round golden pastries, they are stuffed with various fillings—sweet lotus seeds and bean paste, nuts, candied fruits, and even savories like pork and shrimp.

Whether sweet or savory, moon cakes often contain the yolk of a salted duck egg, which looks like a harvest moon when the cake is sliced in half. The lotus paste cakes filled with salted egg yolks are one of my favorites! These sumptuous delights, too rich to eat every day, are difficult to make at home. Visit an Asian market during the Moon Festival, and you'll often see mile-high stacks of moon cake boxes. Some bakeries, restaurants, and hotels in Hong Kong, Singapore, and other cities start taking orders months in advance. The bakers have to know how many they need to make; the customers have to start putting money in the kitty (moon cakes can be quite expensive) for the dozens, sometimes hundreds, of four-cake boxes they plan to lavish upon friends and family. Come mid-September, the bakeries tap the last cakes out of their wooden molds while hungry customers empty their piggy banks, and moon cakes are enjoyed everywhere in Chinatowns around the world.

LUCKY TREASURE RICE PUDDING

Serves 4 to 6

The number eight is very important to the Chinese culture, especially during special occasions and festivals. In this dish, there are eight treasures, each of which is believed to possess the power of a charm. By offering this pudding to your guests, you are wishing them health and prosperity.

2 cups uncooked glutinous rice

2 tablespoons vegetable oil,
    plus more for oiling the pie plate

¼ cup sugar

THE TREASURES

6 red dates, pitted and sliced in half

4 maraschino cherries

3 dried apricots

2 candied kumquats or candied orange peel
    strips, sliced

2 tablespoons dried cranberries or cherries

2 tablespoons golden raisins

1 tablespoon toasted pine nuts

1 cup sweet lotus seed paste (or a mixture of
    chopped "treasures"; see step 4)

FOR THE SYRUP

1 cup sugar

½ cup water

1 tablespoon fresh lemon juice

2 teaspoons cornstarch, dissolved in
    1 tablespoon water

*   *   *

1. Pour enough water over the rice in a medium bowl to cover completely. Soak for 2 hours. Drain.

2. Combine the drained rice and 2½ cups water in a 2-quart saucepan. Cook uncovered over medium-high heat until little "craters" form on the surface of the rice, 5 to 8 minutes. Reduce the heat to low, cover the pan, and cook until the rice is tender, 15 to 20 minutes. Scrape into a bowl and let cool.

3. Stir 1 tablespoon of the oil and the sugar into the rice. Set aside.

4. Brush the bottom and sides of a 9-inch glass pie plate with vegetable oil. Arrange the dates, maraschino cherries, dried apricots, kumquats, dried cranberries, raisins, and pine nuts in a decorative pattern in the bottom of the pie plate (if you are substituting chopped "treasures" for the lotus seed paste, chop enough of the treasures to measure 1 cup and set aside, then arrange the remaining treasures in the pie plate). Cover the treasures with an even layer of half the rice. Spread the lotus seed paste (or reserved mixed chopped treasures) over the center of the rice. Top with an even layer of the remaining rice.

Cover the rice with a sheet of plastic wrap and press down firmly with your hands to pack the ingredients tightly into the plate.

5. Prepare a wok for steaming according to the directions on page xxvi. Set the pie plate in the steamer, cover, and steam the pudding for 10 minutes. Immediately invert the pie plate onto a plate.

6. Heat a wide nonstick skillet over medium heat until hot. Add the remaining 1 tablespoon oil and swirl to coat the bottom. Slide the pudding into the pan, decorative side down. Fry until the underside is golden, about 2 minutes. Carefully slide the pudding onto a plate, invert it onto a second plate, and slide it back into the pan. Cook until the second side is golden, about 2 minutes. Slide the pudding onto a rimmed serving plate.

7. Make the syrup: Bring the sugar, water, and lemon juice to a boil in a small saucepan. Cook, stirring, until the sugar is dissolved. Add the dissolved cornstarch and cook, stirring, until the sauce thickens, about 30 seconds.

8. Pour the syrup over the warm pudding and serve.

FLUFFY SNOW CLOUD IN LIME SYRUP

Serves 4

I love the refreshing taste of lime and the unique fragrance of kaffir lime leaves. The crunchy texture of the snow fungus is distinctive. Snow fungus doubles in size and absorbs all the flavors. In China, it is believed that the combination of snow fungus and rock sugar brightens the eyes and refreshes the palate. If you can't find kaffir lime leaves, use a bit more lime zest.

2 pieces dried snow fungus (about 2 ounces)

2½ cups water
1 cup sugar
3 ounces (about ¼ cup) rock sugar
1 teaspoon chopped crystallized ginger
Grated zest and juice of 1 lime
1 kaffir lime leaf, cut into thin strips

⅓ cup toasted, sliced almonds
Lime slices

✳ ✳ ✳

1. Pour enough warm water over the snow fungus in a medium bowl to cover completely. Soak until softened, about 20 minutes. Using scissors, remove and discard the hard core from each piece, then cut the snow fungus into bite-sized pieces.

2. Combine the water, granulated sugar, rock sugar, and ginger in a 2-quart saucepan and bring to a simmer over medium heat. Cook, stirring, until the sugar is dissolved. Stir in the lime zest, lime juice, and lime leaf. Stir in the snow fungus and mix well. Let cool to room temperature, then cover and refrigerate for 1 hour.

3. To serve, spoon the snow fungus and syrup into dessert bowls, sprinkle with the almonds, and garnish with the lime slices.

FRIED LYCHEE CUSTARD BARS

This is a delicious dessert that can even be eaten right out of the steamer. The pureed lychee fruit has a lovely texture and fragrance that blends well with the creamy custard.

Vegetable oil cooking spray
Cornstarch for dusting

¾ cup whole milk
½ cup tightly packed canned lychees
¼ cup sugar
1 tablespoon cornstarch

3 egg yolks
1 whole egg
1 teaspoon white sesame seeds
½ teaspoon black sesame seeds

Vegetable oil for deep-frying
All purpose flour for dusting
¼ cup confectioners' sugar

❋   ❋   ❋

1. Spray an 8-inch square glass baking dish with the cooking spray. Lightly dust the bottom and sides of the dish with cornstarch.

2. In a blender combine the milk, lychees, sugar, and cornstarch. Blend on high until smooth, about 20 seconds.

3. Lightly beat the egg yolks, whole egg, and sesame seeds in a medium bowl. Slowly stir in the milk mixture, avoiding a whisking motion, which would create bubbles.

4. Pour the mixture into the prepared dish and cover snugly with plastic wrap. Place the custard in a steamer, cover, and cook over medium-high heat until the custard is firm in the center, about 25 minutes.

5. Remove the custard from the steamer and carefully discard the plastic wrap, not allowing any of the condensation to fall into the custard. Set aside until the custard cools to room temperature, then refrigerate until cold, about 30 minutes. This can be done up to 2 days ahead.

6. Cut the custard into sixteen 4 x 1-inch bars.

7. Pour enough oil into a wok to come to a depth of 3 inches. Heat over medium-low heat to 180°F. Carefully remove the custard bars from the dish, a few at a time, and dust lightly with flour. Gently slide the flour-coated bars into the oil. Fry, turning occasionally, until golden brown, about 1½ minutes. Drain on paper towels. Sprinkle the fried custard with the confectioners' sugar and serve warm.

CHINESE PEANUT PANCAKES | *Serves 4*

Tofu is China's fun food. It is used for so many different purposes, both savory and sweet. Here it is paired with crunchy peanuts in delicate pancakes. A dish like this is not at all what a Westerner has in mind when you say tofu can be healthy and delicious.

1 cup mashed drained firm or regular tofu
1 cup finely chopped roasted peanuts
½ cup sugar
⅓ cup chopped candied winter melon or
    candied pineapple

FOR THE BATTER
⅔ cup water
⅓ cup milk
1 egg
1 tablespoon vegetable oil
1 cup all-purpose flour

About 2 tablespoons vegetable oil

1. Stir the tofu, peanuts, sugar, and winter melon together in a bowl until well blended.

2. Make the batter: Whisk the water, milk, egg, and oil together in a medium bowl until blended. Add the flour and mix until smooth.

3. Heat a nonstick 8-inch skillet over medium-high heat until hot. Add 1 to 2 teaspoons of the oil and swirl to coat the bottom of the pan. Add ¼ cup of the batter to the pan, tilting the pan so the batter covers the bottom in an even layer. Cook until the pancake is set and the bottom is light brown, 1½ to 2 minutes. Turn the pancake and cook until it begins to brown, about 30 seconds. Spread one-quarter of the tofu mixture in a 1-inch band slightly below the center of the pancake. Fold the bottom of the pancake over the filling, then roll up the pancake into a neat, slightly flattened cylinder. Slide the filled pancake onto a warm plate and cover with aluminum foil, shiny side down, to keep warm. Make and fill three more pancakes, adding more oil to the pan as needed. (Leftover pancake batter, if any, can be refrigerated for up to 2 days.)

4. Cut each pancake into thirds and serve warm.

MELBOURNE

A CHINESE GENERAL STORE IN THE 1860S AT MEL-BOURNE'S MUSEUM OF CHINESE HISTORY

Say "Gold Rush," and people think California. But Australia had its own Gold Rush, in the hills of Victoria, hours from Melbourne. And once the mines had run dry, immigrant Chinese workers came to the city to settle, just as they did in San Francisco, making Melbourne's one of the oldest, truest, and most historic Chinatowns. For decades, however, the place survived a hostile "Whites Only" atmosphere. But today the must-see Chinese Museum, founded in 1995, and the best of all Chinatowns, re-creates and celebrates Chinese immigration, life in the mining camps and the city, in video, audio, and 3-D. But most of the Chinese have left for green pastures in sprawling suburbs. So

this is a Chinatown without the crowds and the tumult—very nearly a Chinatown without Chinese. Red-brick alleys like Heffernan Lance seem to echo with the cries of peddlers long gone. Few holes-in-the-wall still find a niche amid the stolid, prim facades. With touches of the Gothic, this virtual exhibit of Victorian architecture is best for viewing distinguished churches, not temples. The Nam Poon and Sze Yap Associations still stand, though, and on Sunday, some of the best dim sum houses on earth fill with Chinese and Aussies and, those lucky, plucky heirs of the Gold Rush, the Australian-Chinese. This charming showplace Chinatown sports renewed pride and a cavalcade of elegant eateries along Russell and Little Bourke Streets. Who can miss the superbly posh Flower Drum, masterminded by Gilbert Lau? Come see this newly polished gem of a multicultural Australia.

FLOWER DRUM RESTAURANT
17 Market Lane
(61-3) 9662-3655
What to order: *baked stuffed king crab with cream and butter; braised fish tail with mushrooms and lily buds*

POST-DENG CAFÉ
214 Little Bourke Street
(61-3) 9663-9866
What to order: *green onion pancakes; Sichuan wonton soup; Sichuan dan dan noodles; Sichuan double-cooked pork; Sichuan chili duck in beer*

SUPPER INN CAFÉ
15–17 Celestial Avenue
(61-3) 9663-4759
What to order: *sweet-and-sour sliced fish; Chinese doughnuts with prawns and scallops*

BANANA WONTONS WITH COCONUT CREAM SAUCE

Makes 16 wontons; serves 4

A dessert version of wontons.

FOR THE FILLING
2 bananas, peeled and coarsely chopped
2 tablespoons sugar
$1/2$ teaspoon ground cinnamon
1 tablespoon flaked sweetened coconut

FOR THE SAUCE
$1^1/2$ cups whole milk
$1/2$ cup unsweetened coconut milk
4 egg yolks
$1/2$ cup sugar
$1/2$ cup flaked sweetened coconut (optional)

16 wonton wrappers

Vegetable oil for deep-frying

*   *   *

1. Make the filling: Stir the bananas, sugar, cinnamon, and coconut together in a small bowl, lightly mashing the bananas as you mix. The mixture should still be a little chunky.

2. Make the sauce: Bring the milk and coconut milk to a boil in a small saucepan. Remove from the heat and set aside. Beat the egg yolks and sugar together in a medium bowl until pale yellow and smooth, 2 to 3 minutes. Stirring constantly, gradually pour half of the hot milk mixture into the egg yolk mixture, then stir the yolk mixture into the milk mixture remaining in the pan. Return the saucepan to medium heat and cook, stirring constantly, until the sauce thickens, about 2 minutes. Strain the sauce into a medium bowl. For extra coconut flavor, add the $1/2$ cup coconut flakes. Let cool to room temperature, then cover the bowl and chill until cold.

3. Place a heaping teaspoonful of the filling in the center of one of the wonton wrappers. (Keep the remaining wrappers covered with a damp kitchen towel to prevent them from drying out.) Moisten the edges of the wrapper with a fingertip dipped in water, then fold the wrapper in half to form a triangle. Pinch the edges firmly to seal. Pull the opposite corners of the base of the triangle together, moisten one of the corners with water, and press the two corners firmly together to seal. Repeat with the remaining wontons and filling, keeping the folded wontons covered with a damp kitchen towel to prevent them from drying out.

4. Pour enough vegetable oil into a wok or 2-quart saucepan to come to a depth of 3 inches. Heat the oil over medium heat to 350°F. Slip a few of the wontons into the oil and fry, turning occasionally, until golden brown, 2 to 3 minutes. Remove with a slotted spoon and drain on paper towels. Repeat with the remaining wontons. Serve hot or cold, with the coconut cream sauce.

CITRUS–WATER CHESTNUT CAKE

Serves 8

This translucent cold Cantonese dessert is ideal on a hot summer day. You can use a variety of citrus to flavor the dish such as orange or lemon.

1 tablespoon vegetable oil, or vegetable oil
   cooking spray
3 cups water
1 cup cornstarch
½ cup wheat starch
1 cup sugar
¾ cup sliced water chestnuts (preferably fresh)
1 tablespoon grated lime zest
2 tablespoons fresh lime juice
1 tablespoon crystallized ginger cut into thin
   strips

＊　　＊　　＊

1. Using the oil or cooking spray, grease a 9-inch glass pie plate.

2. Stir 1½ cups of the water, the cornstarch, and wheat starch together in a bowl until the starches are dissolved.

3. Bring the remaining 1½ cups water, the sugar, water chestnuts, lime zest, lime juice, and crystallized ginger to a boil in a medium saucepan, stirring occasionally. Add the cornstarch mixture

and cook, stirring, until lightly thickened, 3 to 4 minutes. Remove from the heat.

4. Prepare a wok for steaming according to the directions on page xxvi. Set the prepared pie plate into the steamer and ladle the batter into the plate. Cover and steam over medium-high heat until the cake is translucent at the center, about 20 minutes.

5. Remove the cake from the steamer basket and let cool to room temperature, then refrigerate until chilled through.

6. To serve, unmold the cake onto a platter. Serve chilled.

TO PREPARE SEVERAL SMALLER CAKES: Prepare the batter and a wok for steaming as described above. Grease 20 to 25 small (about 3 tablespoons each) tartlet pans. Set as many of the prepared tartlet pans at a time into the steamer as will fit without touching one another. Spoon the batter into the pans to fill them about two-thirds full. Steam until the cakes are translucent, about 20 minutes.

CHINATOWN-STYLE SPONGE CAKE WITH BERRIES AND CREAM

Serves 6 to 8

I am surprised that steamed cakes are not more popular in the United States. They are so fluffy and moist. It is best to use an electric mixer to make this cake or your arm will get quite tired with all the beating. Cakes like this can be found on the sweets cart in many dim sum restaurants.

Vegetable shortening or vegetable oil cooking spray for greasing the pan

4 large eggs
1½ cups cake flour
1 cup sugar
¾ cup whole or lowfat milk
1½ teaspoons baking powder
½ teaspoon baking soda
1½ teaspoons water
½ cup lard or vegetable shortening
1 teaspoon vanilla extract

Fresh berries
Whipped cream

* * *

1. Grease a 6-inch steamer basket or a 1-quart soufflé dish with the shortening or cooking spray. If using a steamer basket, line with parchment paper and trim the paper so it does not extend above the top of the steamer.

2. Beat the eggs in a large bowl with an electric mixer until thick and doubled in volume, 4 to 5 minutes. Stir the flour and sugar together in a small bowl. Beat the flour-sugar mixture into the eggs 2 tablespoons at a time. Continue to beat until light, about 10 minutes. Add the milk and baking powder and beat for 2 minutes.

3. Dissolve the baking soda in the water and pour into the batter. Beat in the lard and vanilla extract and continue to beat until thoroughly incorporated, about 2 minutes. Pour the batter into the prepared container.

4. Prepare a wok for steaming according to the directions on page xvii. Set the container in the steamer, cover tightly, and steam over high heat, about 30 minutes, until a wooden pick inserted in the center of the cake comes out clean.

5. Remove the cake from the steaming basket and cool slightly. Cut into wedges with a serrated knife. Serve with berries and whipped cream, or plain.

CHINESE BAKERIES

Chinese cuisine isn't known for the quality of its baked goods, but don't tell that to the folks in Chinatown. What would any Chinatown today be without its crowded Chinese bakeries? Many Chinatown bakeries provide tables and stools for older folks to while away the hours over a sweet roll, or even some soup and noodles on the side, and to chat with friends. As much as Chinese teahouses have traditionally been popular places to eat and socialize, Chinese bakeries now hold a similar role. They're casual, convenient places to gather—the equivalent of the American coffee shop or French café. Walk on in and try the variety of tasty Chinese bakery items: egg custard tarts (*don tot*), pineapple buns (*baw law bao*), or my favorite, cocktail buns (*guy may bao*).

SWEET BRIDE'S DELIGHT CAKES

Traditionally, "Wife's Delight" is filled with sweet winter melon. These baked buns are often stamped, using red food color, with the Chinese characters for double happiness or prosperity. The two doughs give the buns different layers of texture and flavor, but if you don't have the time to make both, you can purchase puff pastry dough.

FOR THE FILLING
3 slices candied pineapple
4 strips candied papaya
4 dried figs
¾ cup glutinous rice flour
¼ cup sugar
¼ cup water
3 tablespoons toasted white sesame seeds
1 tablespoons vegetable oil

FOR THE OUTER DOUGH
1 cup bread flour
1 cup all-purpose flour
¼ cup sugar
½ cup chilled vegetable shortening or lard
¼ cup water

FOR THE INNER DOUGH
¾ cup all-purpose flour
1 tablespoon wheat starch
⅓ cup chilled vegetable shortening or lard

1 egg yolk, beaten

❋   ❋   ❋

1. Make the filling: Place the candied pineapple and papaya and the dried figs in a food processor and process until the fruit is chopped. Scrape the fruit into a medium bowl. Add the glutinous rice flour, sugar, water, sesame seeds, and oil and mix until the flour is well blended.

2. Make the outer dough: Sift the bread flour, all-purpose flour, and sugar together into a bowl. With a pastry blender or two table knives, cut the shortening into the flour until the mixture is the size of small peas. Stir in the water and knead briefly to form a soft dough.

3. Divide the dough in half on a floured work surface. Roll each half into a 15-inch cylinder. Cut each cylinder crosswise into 1-inch pieces. Cover the dough with plastic wrap to prevent it from drying out.

4. Make the inner dough: Sift the all-purpose flour and wheat starch together into a bowl. With a pastry blender or two table knives, cut the shortening into the flour until the mixture is the size of small peas. Knead briefly to form a smooth dough. Divide the dough in half, roll into cylinders, and cut into 30 pieces. Cover with plastic wrap as described above.

5. Preheat the oven to 300°F. Line two baking sheets with parchment paper.

6. Shape the pastries: Flatten a piece of the outer dough into a 3- to 4-inch circle. Flatten a piece of inner dough to the same size and place it on top of the outer dough. Roll the stacked doughs up into a cylinder and roll the cylinder out with the palms of your hands to 4 inches long. Coil the dough into a round patty, then flatten the patty with your hand or a rolling pin to make a 4-inch circle about ⅛ inch thick. Place 1 heaping tablespoon of the filling in the center. Bring the edges of the dough up over the filling to enclose it and pinch the edges together to seal. Place the bun seam side down on the prepared baking sheet. With the palm of your hand, flatten the circle slightly. With a paring knife, make two ½-inch slits in the top of the dough. Brush with the egg yolk. Repeat with the remaining dough and filling.

7. Bake the buns until golden brown, 25 to 30 minutes. Let cool slightly before serving.

FRIED ICE CREAM WITH GINGER-CARAMEL SAUCE

Serves 6

The secret to this dessert is that the ice cream must be very cold, and go directly from the freezer to the fryer, or you will end up with a mess. The contrast of the ice cream and the crispy coating with the hot and cold temperatures is a delight.

1 quart vanilla ice cream

2 eggs, lightly beaten
¼ cup milk
½ cup all-purpose flour
2 cups (about 6 ounces) crushed Ritz crackers
    or other butter crackers

FOR THE CARAMEL SAUCE
1 cup packed light brown sugar or 2 sticks slab
    brown sugar, crusted
4 tablespoons unsalted butter
½ cup water
2 tablespoons orange liqueur
1 tablespoon thinly sliced crystallized ginger
    (optional)
1 teaspoon finely chopped dried
    tangerine peel

Vegetable oil for deep-frying

❋ ❋ ❋

1. Chill a rimmed baking sheet in the freezer. Once it is chilled, with an ice cream scoop, form rounds of ice cream about the size of tennis balls, placing them on the chilled baking sheet as you do so. Freeze until the ice cream is very hard, at least 4 hours.

2. Beat the eggs and milk in a wide shallow bowl until thoroughly blended. Spread the flour and cracker crumbs in separate bowls. Working quickly, roll an ice cream ball in flour to coat it completely, dip in the egg-milk mixture, and then roll in the cracker crumbs, pressing the crumbs onto the ice cream ball. Return the coated ice cream ball to the cold baking sheet and repeat with the remaining balls. Return the pan to the freezer and chill until the ice cream is very hard, at least 4 hours, or up to a day. Refrigerate the remaining egg-milk mixture and set the flour and crumbs aside.

3. Repeat the coating process, and return the coated ice cream balls to the freezer until you are ready to cook and serve them. (The coated ice cream balls can be kept in an airtight container in the freezer for up to a month.)

4. Prepare the caramel sauce: Place the brown sugar and butter in a 2-quart saucepan and cook over medium heat until the butter is melted, about 2 minutes. Add the water, orange liqueur, crystallized ginger, and dried tangerine peel, reduce the heat to low, and stir until the brown sugar dissolves and the mixture comes to a boil. Simmer, stirring constantly, until the sauce has thickened, about 3 minutes. Remove from the heat and cover the pan to keep the sauce warm.

5. Pour enough oil into a wok or 2-quart saucepan to come to a depth of 3 or 4 inches; there should be enough oil to completely submerge the ice cream balls. Heat the oil over medium-high heat to 350°F. Deep-fry the ice cream balls two at a time until golden brown, 45 seconds to 1 minute. Remove with a slotted spoon and drain briefly on paper towels. Place in serving bowls. Spoon the warm caramel sauce over the ice cream balls and serve immediately.

FROZEN TOFU FRUIT SMOOTHIE | *Makes 5½ cups*

Because of the volumes of research about the soybean and its positive effects, soymilk and tofu are finally gaining greater acceptance in the American diet. You will find several kinds of soymilk and tofu in your local supermarket. Creamy-style soymilk and frozen soft tofu yield the best texture and consistency in a smoothie. Adjust the amount of sugar to your liking.

One 14-ounce package soft tofu, frozen

3 cups assorted fresh or frozen fruit—including
    1 banana, cut up

3 tablespoons sugar, or to taste

1¾ cups creamy soymilk

*   *   *

1. Thaw the tofu in a microwave set on defrost for about 5 minutes, or thaw in the refrigerator, until just soft enough to cut into 8 pieces. Place in a blender.

2. Add the fruit and sugar, and pour in the soymilk to reach the 3-cup mark.

3. Blend on the highest speed until smooth, adding more soymilk if necessary to reach the desired consistency, 30 seconds to 1 minute. Serve in cold glasses.

SWEET CHINESE HERBAL TEA | *Serves 4*

This tea, as nutritious as it is delicious, can be served as a dessert soup. The snow fungus is said to brighten the eyes and refresh the palate. The red dates are purifying and are believed to build strength, provide energy, calm nerves, and improve circulation. Gingko nuts are a symbol of good luck as well as said to be a cleanser of the body's systems. Who knew food as medicine could be so sweet?

1 piece (about 1 ounce) dried snow fungus
3½ cups water
⅔ cup (2½ to 3 ounces) rock sugar or
　　packed light brown sugar
⅓ cup dried red dates
¼ cup canned gingko nuts
¼ cup canned lotus seeds

❋　　❋　　❋

1. Pour enough warm water over the snow fungus in a small bowl to cover it completely. Soak until softened, about 20 minutes; drain. Using scissors, remove and discard the hard core, then cut the snow fungus into bite-sized pieces.

2. Place the snow fungus, water, rock sugar, dates, gingko nuts, and lotus seeds in a 1½-quart heatproof bowl. Prepare a wok for steaming according to the directions on page xxvi. Set the bowl in the steamer basket, cover the wok, and steam over low heat, replenishing the water in the wok as necessary, until the tea has a pleasant, sweet flavor, about 1½ hours. Serve in small soup bowls.

Chinese Pantry

ALUM: A powder commonly used for pickling or baking. Found in the spice section of most grocery stores in 2-ounce bottles.

BABY CORN: Very young and tender sweet corn. The 2- to 3-inch ears are entirely edible. Typically found canned; drain and rinse before using. Once opened, cover with cool water and refrigerate for up to a week in a tightly sealed container.

BAMBOO SHOOTS: Most markets carry canned bamboo shoots; Asian markets carry the fresh in water-filled tubs in the produce section. The canned shoots are available in different forms: whole tips, young tips, slices, or thin strips. Texture varies with age; the younger shoots are the most tender. Before using, drain and rinse. Store fresh or opened canned bamboo shoots in a sealed container covered with water in the refrigerator for up to 2 weeks.

BARLEY: A hardy grain; beige, slightly flattened, oval-shaped barley can be found in any supermarket in plastic packages or sold in bulk. Store in a tightly sealed container in a cool, dry place.

BEAN CURD SKINS—SHEETS AND STICKS: This off-white dried bean curd skin is a by-product of the tofu-making process. It is the thin layer of film that forms on the top of the heated soybean milk, which is removed and dried. If completely dried while flat it forms the bean curd sheets; if rolled while cooling it forms the bean curd sticks. The sheets need to be briefly soaked to soften prior to use; typically used as a wrapper which can be deep-fried or steamed. The sticks require a longer soaking period before use; often used in vegetarian dishes that are braised.

BEAN SAUCE AND PASTE: The many types available include yellow bean sauce, hot bean sauce, and brown bean paste, all made from soybeans fermented with salt. Those called bean sauces contain whole beans in a thick sauce; pastes are thick purees of mashed beans. All add a salty flavor to stir-fries and stews. Miso can be used as a substitute. Hot bean sauce or paste, also called chili bean paste, is infused with mashed chili peppers, which give it an intense fiery flavor. Many other hot bean pastes include broad beans. Chili garlic sauce can be used as a substitute. Once opened, store the jars in the refrigerator for up to a year. Sweet bean paste is fermented soybeans with a touch of sweetness; hoisin sauce is a suitable substitute.

BEAN SPROUTS: Two popular varieties of sprouts are used in this book: mung bean and soybean. Mung bean are the most common; pale yellow with thin white 2-inch stems, they have a slightly sweet nutty flavor. Fresh mung bean sprouts are widely available in produce sections. Soybean sprouts are more difficult to find—look for them in Asian markets. They have large pale greenish heads with long firm white stems. Soybean sprouts have a nuttier flavor than mung bean sprouts and are usually added at the end of cooking. Both will keep for a day or two in the refrigerator, but are best used the day they are purchased; rinse before using.

BEAN THREAD NOODLES: Also referred to as mung bean noodles, cellophane noodles, and vermicelli. These semi-transparent noodles are made from the starch of mung beans. Packaged in small plastic bags, bean thread noodles can be used in soups or stir-fries or deep-fried.

BITTER MELON: Also known as bitter gourd. Resembles a wrinkled cucumber with bumpy ridged skin, light green to yellowish green in color. The chemical quinine gives it its sharp bitter taste. In traditional Asian medicine, bitter

SOYBEAN SPROUTS

BITTER MELON

melon is considered a "cooling" fruit that purifies the blood. Can be stir-fried or steamed.

BLACK BEAN SAUCE: Sauce made from salted black beans and wine. Some varieties contain garlic or hot chilies. Black bean sauce can be used to flavor anything from dipping sauces to stir-fries to braised dishes. Store opened jars in the refrigerator for up to a year.

BLACK MOSS: Also known as hair vegetable. This is a dried algae that is harvested in the Mongolian desert. Typically sold in small plastic bags, it looks like a mass of black hair. Black moss is used in Chinese New Year celebration dishes because its Cantonese name, *fat choy,* sounds like the last two words in the Lunar New Year greeting *"Gung hei fat choy,"* meaning, "Wishing you happiness and prosperity."

BROWN CANE SUGAR: These 3- to 5-inch rectangular caramel-colored slabs of compressed layers of partially refined brown sugar, white sugar, and honey are typically sold in 1-pound packages. Light brown sugar can be used as a substitute.

CANDIED FRUIT: Cooked in sugar syrup, then dried and coated in granulated sugar, good-quality candied fruit has a delicate sweet flavor. A large variety of candied fruit is available, including pineapple, ginger, papaya, and mango. Store in tightly sealed containers in a cool, dry place.

CARDAMOM: A flavorful spice native to India. The large black pods are commonly used in stews and slow cooking items. Found in the spice section of most supermarkets.

CHAR SIU SAUCE: Chinese barbecue sauce, made from a blend of fermented soybeans, vinegar, garlic, sugar, honey, and spices, with a bit of tomato paste and chilies. Use char siu sauce as you would any other barbecue sauce, especially for pork and pork spareribs. Store opened jars in the refrigerator for up to a year.

CHILI PASTE AND SAUCE: Usually a blend of fresh and dried chilies and vinegar. Some varieties also contain garlic, ginger, sugar, and/or sesame oil. Can be used as a dipping sauce or added to stir-fries or other dishes. Sold in plastic and glass bottles and jars. Try a few different brands, as they vary significantly in flavor and intensity. Store opened containers in the refrigerator for up to a year.

SPICY MUSTARD AND CHILI SAUCE

CHINESE BLACK MUSHROOMS

CHINESE BROCCOLI

CHINESE BLACK MUSHROOMS: Dried mushrooms with brownish-black caps and gills, these have an earthy flavor and meaty texture. Can be used interchangeably with dried shiitake mushrooms. Store in an airtight container in a cool, dry place. To use soak in hot water for about 20 minutes. Discard the stems.

CHINESE BLACK VINEGAR: Made from a mixture of fermented rice, wheat, and millet or sorghum, with a deep, sweet-smoky flavor and tanginess. Also referred to as Chinkiang vinegar, the name of the region in eastern China where it is produced. Can be used for dipping or to add character to a variety of dishes. Intensity diminishes with time, but it will keep for several months to a year. Balsamic vinegar can be used as a substitute.

CHINESE BROCCOLI: Also known by its Chinese name, *gai lan*. Has thin smooth dusty-green stems with large oval leaves and small white flowers. It looks something like broccoli rabe, and it has a slightly bitter taste. Used in stir-fries, soups, or simply steamed. Available year-round.

CHINESE CELERY: Sold in bunches, Chinese celery has long slender hollow crisp stems and flat leaves that look something like cilantro; it ranges in color from almost white to deep green. The leaves have a very strong celery flavor and are used as a flavoring in soups or fillings. The stems are often sliced and added to stir-fries. Regular celery can be used as a substitute in stir-fries.

CHINESE CHIVES: Also called garlic chives. There are three types: green, yellow, and flowering green. Green chives look like long blades of grass; yellow chives are shorter and less fibrous; and flowering green chives have firm stalks with small edible buds. All have a pungent garlic-and-onion flavor.

CHINESE CHIVES

CHINESE LONG BEANS

Highly perishable, they are a seasonal delicacy. Used in fillings, noodle recipes, and soups. Wrap in a damp paper towel and refrigerate in a plastic bag.

CHINESE EGG NOODLES (OR MEIN): Available both fresh and dried, made from wheat, water, and eggs. Shanghai-style noodles are the thickest with a hearty texture that makes them good for soups and home-style dishes. Slightly thinner are the regular Chinese egg noodles, typically used for chow mein. The thinnest are the Hong Kong–style noodles, similar to angel hair pasta; these are served in light broths or fried up into crisp pancakes. Found in the refrigerated section of Asian grocery stores. Dried varieties are also available in a variety of shapes and sizes. Italian pastas can be substituted.

CHINESE EGGPLANT: Long and slender, varying from white to lavender in color. Milder than purple eggplant, with a sweeter taste, Chinese eggplant does not require seeding, salting, soaking, or peeling. The darker Japanese eggplant can be substituted. Store in the refrigerator for up to a week.

CHINESE FIVE-SPICE POWDER: A combination of ground star anise, fennel, cinnamon, clove, Sichuan peppercorns, and sometimes other spices. Adds a slightly sweet spicy flavor to braised meats, roasts, sauces, and other dishes. Found in the spice section of most grocery stores.

CHINESE LONG BEANS: Also referred to as yard-long beans, so called because this vegetable can grow up to 3 feet long. These pencil-thin green beans have a bumpy surface with a crunchy bite and a slightly sweet flavor. Look for unblemished beans with no wrinkles. Cut into shorter lengths, these can be used in place of common green beans.

CHINESE RICE WINE

CHINESE SAUSAGE

CHINESE OKRA: Also known as luffa, silk melon, or accordion squash. It has long, bumpy ridges that run along the side of the elongated cylindrical gourd. The bitter ridges should be peeled before use. It can be stir-fried, braised, or steamed. It has a flavor similar to common okra, but the flesh has a texture closer to zucchini, which can be used as a substitute.

CHINESE OLIVES: Chinese olives come in two types: honey olives preserved with salt, licorice, and honey, and a more savory salt-cured version, the only kind used in this book. Salt-cured Chinese olives are tart, green, and slightly chewy. Black oil-cured olives make a good substitute. Look for Chinese olives in the dried foods section of Asian markets; add them to salads and stir-fried dishes for a salty tang.

CHINESE PICKLES: A wide range of vegetables, including cucumbers, garlic, ginger, bamboo shoots, daikon, and carrots, are often pickled. The brine usually consists of dark soy sauce, sugar, and spices; you also might find chilies and vinegar included. Typically found in small glass jars; once opened the pickles should be refrigerated.

CHINESE RICE WINE: Also called Shaoxing wine, for the eastern Chinese city famous for this wine. Made from fermented glutinous rice and millet, Chinese rice wine is aged from 10 to 100 years. Amber in color with a strong aromatic flavor, it can be used in stir-fries, fillings, and braised dishes as well as for marinating meats and seafood. Dry sherry is a suitable substitute.

CHINESE SAUSAGE: Known as *lop chong* in Chinese. Most Chinese sausages are made with pork,

pork fat, duck, or beef seasoned lightly with salt, rice wine, and sugar. They are about 6 inches in length with red or brownish skin and a salami-like texture. Unlike salami, they must be cooked. Used in rice and noodle dishes, fillings, stir-fries, and clay pot dishes. Sold in strings of two in 1-pound vacuum sealed packages in the refrigerated section of Asian markets. Wrapped air tight, Chinese sausages will keep in the refrigerator for a few weeks and for months in the freezer.

CILANTRO: Fresh coriander, sometimes called Chinese parsley. In Chinese cuisine, the leaves are most often used, but the stems can be chopped and added to filling for a more intense flavor.

COCONUT MILK: Unsweetened coconut milk, sold in cans. As it stands, it separates into two layers: the coconut cream floats on top, and the milk below it; always shake the can prior to using. Store leftover coconut milk in a tightly sealed container in the refrigerator for several days. Or freeze in ice cube trays, then transfer the cubes to a tightly sealed container and store for up to 3 months.

CORNSTARCH: Cornstarch is the most common starch used to thicken sauces and marinades in the Chinese kitchen. Dissolved in a cold liquid to form what is called a slurry, it is added shortly before a dish is finished. It is also blended with other ingredients and used for marinating meat, poultry, or fish, sealing in moisture in the marinated food. Deep-fried foods dusted with cornstarch are crisper than those coated with flour. Cornstarch is found in the baking aisle of any supermarket; store it in a tightly sealed container in a cool, dry place.

CURRY POWDER: A blend of many spices ground to a powder. Although the blend varies, it usually includes coriander, cumin, mustard seeds, red and black peppercorns, cardamom, cinnamon, cloves, and turmeric, which gives the powder its characteristic yellow color. Can be used to flavor vegetables, meat dishes, noodles, and dumplings.

CUSTARD POWDER/MIX: Also labeled "dessert mix." Custard powder is usually an egg- and sugar-free powder that is blended with milk and sugar and stirred into heated cream or milk to make a smooth, pudding-like custard. It comes in small boxes of individual packets; look for it in the supermarket with other pudding mixes. Store opened packets in a tightly sealed container in a cool, dry place.

DAIKON: A member of the radish family, this large white root is usually about 1 foot long and 2 to 3 inches in diameter. It has crisp flesh with a peppery bite. Used in stews, clay pot dishes, and stir-fries.

DARK SOY SAUCE: A thick soy sauce with added molasses and cornstarch. This has a richer, sweeter, more full-bodied flavor than regular soy sauce. Used in braised and red-cooked dishes. Store in a cool, dark place for several months.

DRIED SHRIMP: Tiny shrimp that have been preserved in brine and dried. Because they have a strong flavor, they should be used sparingly. Can be added directly to soups and braised dishes, but should be soaked in hot water, drained, and rinsed before being added to stir-fries. Look for packages of plump, bright orange shrimp that are uniform in size. Store in the refrigerator for several months.

FERMENTED BEAN CURD

FISH SAUCE, OYSTER SAUCE, AND SOY SAUCE

DRIED TANGERINE PEEL: Wrinkled, burnt-looking orange strips of dried citrus peel, used to season braised dishes, soups, and sauces. Soak in hot water before using and remove any remaining white pith. Found in small packages in the dried foods section of Asian markets. Fresh tangerine peel is a suitable substitute.

ENGLISH CUCUMBER: Sometimes called hothouse cucumbers, as that is where they are grown. Virtually seedless, English cucumbers have edible bright green skin and can grow up to a foot in length. Use them interchangeably with the smaller Japanese cucumber. If unavailable, substitute peeled and seeded regular cucumber.

FERMENTED BEAN CURD: Comes in two varieties: white and red. The red contains annatto seeds, which give it a deep red color, and may include additional flavorings such as red wine, rice wine, or chiles. Red bean curd is best in clay pot or braised dishes. The white, which is saltier, is used as a condiment or to season stir-fried greens. Both come in glass jars and should be refrigerated after opening; they will keep for several months.

FERMENTED RICE: Fermented cooked grains of glutinous rice, this porridge-like substance is packaged in glass or plastic jars. Sold in the refrigerated section of Asian markets and some specialty grocery stores, it has a slightly fermented, sweet-starchy flavor.

FISH SAUCE: Made from the extract of salted, fermented anchovies; a thin, caramel-colored liquid that has a very pungent odor. Typically combined with citrus juice, vinegar, sugar, and chilies to provide richness and fragrance. Fish sauce is used throughout Southeast Asia; nam pla is the Thai version, nuoc nam (or mam) is the Vietnamese.

FRIED SHALLOTS: Found in plastic jars in Asian groceries. A popular item used for flavoring oil and as a garnish.

FUZZY MELON: Also called hairy squash. Long and cylindrical, fuzzy melon has a taste similar to cucumber or zucchini. Its pale green hairy skin should be peeled before eating. Cook as you would zucchini: steamed, braised, or stir-fried.

GINGKO NUT: Small elliptical-shaped ivory colored nut with a slightly bitter taste. Usually parboiled with salt and then canned. Used in vegetarian soups and stews, as well as in Chinese New Year desserts.

GINSENG: A root that is thought to boost the immune system, sharpen intelligence, and cleanse the internal organs. It's added to teas, soups, and steamed dishes. Available in health food stores and Chinese groceries.

GLUTINOUS RICE FLOUR: Made from ground glutinous rice, typically used to make dim sum dough. Boiled, it produces a smooth, chewy dough; fried, it develops an outer crispy shell and sticky inside; when steamed, it has a sticky texture. Sold in small boxes and plastic pouches.

HAW: A pear or oval-shaped dark red fruit that is about 1 inch in diameter with a sweet juicy taste and grown only in China. Used to make moke and haw flakes. The haw flakes are made from the fruit that is cooked and combined with sugar, then dehydrated and ground into a powder. The powder is then used to make a 1-inch diameter circular cake that is cut into very thin disks. These are sold as haw flakes in most Chinese groceries in the snack section. They have a sweet-sour fresh taste. See also *moke stick*.

HOISIN SAUCE: A slightly sweet dark chocolate brown sauce with a thick grainy texture, made from a blend of fermented soybeans, vinegar, sugar, and spices. Used in stir-fry sauces and marinades, or as a condiment. Store opened bottles in the refrigerator.

HOT CHILI OIL: Vegetable oil infused with dried red chilies. A flavor enhancer for sauces as well as a table condiment. Store in a cool, dry place for several months.

JAPANESE BREAD CRUMBS: Called panko; coarse, irregular crumbs that absorb less grease than ordinary dried bread crumbs when fried. They give fried foods a golden-brown, crisp texture and a slight toasted flavor. Coarsely ground dried bread crumbs are a suitable substitute.

JICAMA: A starchy root vegetable with crisp ivory flesh and a tough brown skin that should be removed before using. Used raw or cooked. A good substitute for water chestnuts.

KAFFIR LIME LEAVES: Bright green, bumpy, double-lobed leaves. Available fresh and frozen in Asian and specialty markets. Whole leaves should be removed from a dish after cooking. Thinly shredded leaves can be added to salads, soups, and syrups to impart a lemon-lime flavor. Lime zest can be substituted if necessary.

KECAP MANIS: A thick sweet Indonesian sauce made with soy sauce, palm sugar, star anise, and garlic. Added to stews and braised meats and used as a condiment. Store in a cool, dry place.

KUMQUAT: A grape-sized citrus fruit with an edible rind. Used as a garnish, added to desserts, and eaten as a snack. In season from early fall through spring. Some Asian groceries and specialty stores sell canned kumquats preserved in syrup as well as the fresh ones.

LEMONGRASS: An herb with a long, pale-green stalk, distinguished by its lemony, slightly floral flavor. Only the bottom 6 inches of the stalks are used. Remove the tough outer layers before using. Sliced, minced, or crushed, lemongrass is added to soups, sauces, or curries. Can be refrigerated for a week or so or frozen for months.

LILY BUDS: The unopened flowers of the day lily, lily buds, 2 to 3 inches long, are sold dried. They add a sweet earthy fragrance to soups, vegetables, and steamed dishes. They should be soaked in hot water until softened and the hard stems removed before using; they are often tied in knots before they are added to a dish.

LONGAN: A small oval fruit between the size of a large grape and a small plum. The white flesh has an appearance, taste, and texture similar to that of a lychee. Found in Asian markets, canned, dried, crystallized, or fresh (remove the shell before cooking). Used in herbal soups and desserts.

LOTUS LEAVES: The leaves of the water lily, these are sold dried and may be almost 2 feet in diameter. Used as a wrapper for savory fillings and rice or meat dishes, they impart a tea-like flavor to

LEMONGRASS

LONGAN

food. The stiff dried leaves are softened before using. Sold in plastic packages in the dried foods section of Asian markets.

LOTUS ROOT: Fresh, it resembles a linked series of thick irregularly shaped off-white sausages. Lotus root has a mild, sweet, nutty flavor. A cross section reveals a ring of holes that run the length of the root. Peeled and sliced, fresh lotus root is added to stir-fries and to salads, or deep-fried as chips. Fresh lotus root is found in the produce section of Asian and some specialty food markets; or look for it vacuum-packed and peeled in the refrigerated section.

LOTUS SEEDS: Lotus seeds are available fresh, canned, or dried. The beige, dried seeds, which are the size of an olive, need to be soaked in boiling water for about an hour before use. They must also be peeled and the dark central core at their tip removed (poke it out with a toothpick). Canned lotus seeds are peeled, cored, soft, and ready to use. Add them to savory soups and stews, or mash them to a paste to use as a filling in sweet buns or in desserts.

LYCHEE: A fruit with a semi-translucent flesh that tastes like grapes. Found canned, fresh, and dried. Canned lychees are usually packed in syrup. Fresh lychees have a red bumpy skin that is easily removed. Used in a variety of dishes from stir-fries to desserts, or eaten as a snack.

MALTOSE: A type of malt sugar made from barley. Used in Chinese cooking to coat the skin of roast duck, giving it a deep rich flavor and color (as seen in the ducks hanging in the windows of Chinese delis). Sold in glass jars or plastic tubs. Chinese honey is a suitable substitute.

MOKE STICK: A brownish-red stick about 2 inches long and 1/4 inch thick that is made from pureed haw fruit and sugar. It has a tangy sweet flavor. Moke is softened with liquid before use. Haw flakes or tamarind paste and sugar can be used as a substitute. Moke stick is usually found with the candied fruit in Chinese groceries. Store in a cool, dry place in a tightly sealed bag.

MUSTARD POWDER: This powder is mixed with a liquid to make a spicy mustard condiment for dipping spring rolls and wontons. Found in small jars or tins in the spice section.

NAPA CABBAGE: Oval-shaped mild-flavored cabbage with ruffled, pale-green leaves and firm white ribs. Used in soups, salads, stir-fries, and other dishes; it is also pickled. Found year-round in most produce sections.

NORI: The paper-thin sheets of dried seaweed used to make sushi. Sheets are generally 7½ by 8½ inches; shredded nori is also available. Primarily used in Japanese cuisine but has been incorporated in some Chinese dishes.

OYSTER-FLAVORED SAUCE: A thick, dark brown seasoning made from oyster extract, sugar, seasonings, and cornstarch; has a sweet-smoky complex flavor. Can be used in sauces or as a dip. Mushroom-based "oyster-flavored" sauce is a vegetarian option. Keep opened bottles in the refrigerator for up to a year.

PALM SUGAR: Made from the sap of palm trees, it is boiled down to a thick paste, which is formed into hard round disks. The tan sugar has a mild flavor with a distinctive almost coconut-like fragrance. Often sold under the name "coconut sugar," it can be found in any market that carries Southeast Asian foods. Use a knife to cut off a portion of the slab and coarsely chop to measure. Light brown sugar can be substituted. Store in a tightly sealed container.

PEA SHOOTS: Tender stems about 2½ inches long with tiny green leaves, from the snow pea plant. Added to stir-fries, salads, soups, and noodle dishes. Pea shoots are quite perishable; refrigerate for only a day or two.

PICKLED GINGER: Pieces of ginger that have been pickled in salt, sugar, and vinegar with a pink dye. Found sliced, shredded, or in chunks. Commonly served with sushi, but its sharp clean taste also works in stir-fries and salads. Can be found in the refrigerated section of most supermarkets. See also *red pickled ginger*.

PINE NUTS: Nuts found inside the cones of the pinion pine tree. The small ivory-colored nuts have a buttery flavor and slight crunch. Usually toasted or fried, they are added to stir-fries, desserts, and other dishes.

PLUM SAUCE: Golden jam-like condiment made from salted plums and apricots, rice wine vinegar, and pureed yams, with a touch of red chili flakes. It has a sweet, tangy, and salty balance that works well with roasted and barbecued meats and fried finger foods. Store opened bottles in the refrigerator for up to a year.

PRESERVED PORK: Also known as Chinese bacon, preserved pork is salt-cured but not smoked; since it's not smoked, it must be cooked.

The slender slabs of pink meat with a thick layer of fat have a sweet-salty flavor (similar to Chinese sausage). Look for plastic shrink-wrapped packages in the dried foods sections of Asian markets. Add it to soups, stir-fries, and noodle dishes. Store it, tightly wrapped in plastic wrap, in the refrigerator for up to 3 weeks.

PRESERVED VEGETABLES, SICHUAN PRESERVED VEGETABLES: Can be turnips, radishes, napa cabbage, mustard greens, or bok choy, to name just a few types. Preserved vegetables come vacuum-sealed, canned, or in small crockery pots. Rinse before using to remove excess salt. After opening, store in the refrigerator for up to a month.

PRESSED TOFU, OR PRESSED BEAN CURD: Pressed during processing to remove excess liquid, this has a dense, chewy texture. Typically found in plastic packages in the refrigerated section. Available in a variety of flavors. Use as you would regular or firm tofu, or use in place of meat in stir-fries. Refrigerate opened packages for up to a week.

QUAIL EGGS: These bite-sized eggs are sold hard-boiled, peeled, and canned in brine. Look for small and medium-sized cans in the canned goods sections of Asian markets. Use quail eggs in stews, soups, or dumpling fillings, or deep-fry and eat them as a snack.

RED DATES: Also known as Chinese jujubes, sold dried or preserved. The dried dates resemble wrinkled red raisins. They have a sweet-tart apple flavor; dried cranberries are the best substitute. Look for them in bulk or plastic packages in the dried foods section of Asian markets.

RED DATES

RICE

RED PICKLED GINGER: Pieces of ginger cured in a salt brine, then soaked in a sugar and vinegar solution and colored red. Red ginger has a sweet tangy taste. Used primarily in sauces and dips.

RICE: The three main varieties are long-grain, medium-grain, and short-grain. Long-grain rice, such as jasmine, lacks the starchiness of the other two types, allowing it to cook up dry and fluffy; use it for fried rice dishes. Medium-grain rice, slightly shorter, is used primarily in Japan, for sushi especially, and in Korea. Short-grain rices include sweet or sticky rice, also called glutinous rice. When cooked, glutinous rice becomes sticky and translucent.

RICE NOODLES, FRESH AND DRIED: Fresh rice noodles come in sheets and cut into strips. Made from rice flour and water, they have a smooth, chewy texture. They are found in the refrigerated section of Asian markets. Pull the sheets of noodles apart prior to stir-frying. Dried rice noodles are a suitable substitute if fresh are not available. They should be soaked prior to using, unless they will be used for deep-frying. Dried rice noodles come in a variety of widths. The thin variety is also called rice sticks or rice vermicelli.

RICE VINEGAR: Less tart than distilled white vinegar, Chinese rice vinegar is available in seasoned and unseasoned varieties. The unseasoned variety is preferred for most recipes; it's not as sweet as the seasoned rice vinegar.

ROCK SUGAR: Lumps of crystallized sugar with a yellowish tint. Used in braised dishes, soups, and sauces, and for dessert soups. Rock sugar has a richer flavor than refined sugar. Sold in 1-pound boxes. Light brown sugar or granulated sugar are suitable substitutes.

SA CHA SAUCE: A pungent blend of shrimp, brill fish, and chilies. Used as a dipping sauce or added to sauces and noodle dishes. Store opened bottles in the refrigerator for several months.

SALTED BLACK BEANS: Fermented and dried black beans, these have a smoky, pungent flavor. Also referred to as preserved or fermented black beans. Rinse and lightly mash before using. Sold in plastic bags in the dried foods section of Asian markets. Black bean sauce is a suitable substitute.

SALTED PLUM: This firm light-colored plum has a sweet, tart taste with a soft but firm texture. It is made by soaking the plum in a salt brine, then in a sugar solution, and finally drying it. It is thought to stimulate the appetite. It is found with other preserved fruits in most Asian groceries. Store in a cool, dry place in an airtight container.

SESAME OIL: Golden-amber oil with a toasty, nutty flavor. Very different from the light sesame oil made from unroasted sesame seeds found in Middle Eastern stores. Used for flavoring rather than cooking, it should be added toward the end of the cooking process. Pure sesame oils are the best, but those blended with soybean oil are acceptable. Store at room temperature for several months, or refrigerate for longer storage.

SESAME PASTE: Made from finely ground toasted white sesame seeds, sesame paste has a roasted nutty flavor and a texture similar to peanut butter. Stir to incorporate the oil that pools on top prior to using. Suitable substitutes are peanut butter and tahini (which is made from untoasted sesame seeds). Store opened jars in the refrigerator for up to a month.

SESAME SEEDS: White sesame seeds should be toasted to bring out their sweet nutty flavor; use in salads, appetizers, and desserts. Black sesame seeds don't need to be toasted; they have a slightly bitter flavor, so it's best to use them sparingly.

SHRIMP PASTE: A thick, pinkish-gray paste made from salted and fermented shrimp. Has a pungent aroma and flavor that mellows when cooked. Available in bottles and jars; store opened containers in the refrigerator for up to a year.

SALTED BLACK BEANS

SICHUAN PEPPERCORNS: Not in fact peppercorns, but the dried reddish-brown berries of the prickly ash tree. They have a slightly medicinal woodsy fragrance. Available whole and in powdered form. Whole peppercorns should be toasted in a dry skillet before use. If unavailable, substitute a pinch or so of Chinese five-spice powder. Also labeled "red" or "wild" pepper.

SIU MAI WRAPPERS: Made from a wheat noodle dough, these round wrappers are the thinnest of the noodle wrappers available. If you cannot find them, cut square wonton wrappers into circles. Refrigerate or freeze any extra wrappers.

SMITHFIELD HAM: A dark red, highly salty ham; usually available sliced at Asian and specialty markets. Referred to as Virginia ham in Asian markets. If unavailable, substitute smoked ham.

SNOW FUNGUS: Also known as white fungus, looks like a small, golden-beige sponge. With little or no flavor of its own, it takes on the flavors of the dish it is cooked in. Sold in plastic bags or decorative boxes. Before using, soak in warm water to soften, then trim off the yellow core. Used in stir-fries, stews, and desserts.

SNOW PEAS: Flat, bright green pods with a mild flavor and gentle crunch. The ends and the strings running down the sides should be removed before using raw or cooked. Added to a wide variety of dishes, but pair especially well with seafood.

SOY SAUCE: Fundamental seasoning in Chinese cuisine, a dark brown, slightly salty liquid made from fermented soybeans and wheat. A primary ingredient in braising liquids, stir-fries, roasting sauces, and salad dressings, soy sauce is also used as a dipping sauce and in marinades. See also *dark soy sauce*.

SPRING ROLL WRAPPERS: Thin delicate wrappers made from a wheat-flour-and-water batter. (Egg roll wrappers are made from a noodle dough.) When fried, the paper-thin wrappers become light and crispy. Spring roll wrappers are found in the refrigerated section of Asian markets and some supermarkets.

STAR ANISE: A spice whose pods are about 1 inch across, with eight pointed rays each containing a shiny, mahogany-brown seed; has a licorice-like flavor. Added to stews, braised dishes, and marinades.

STRAW MUSHROOMS: Small mushrooms with dark brown caps and tender white stems, a delicate sweet flavor, and a firm texture. Usually found canned, peeled, or unpeeled (which look similar to little brown eggs). Blanch briefly to remove the tinny flavor.

SUGAR SNAP PEAS: Bright green peas with an edible pod containing tiny peas. Snap off the ends and remove the strings, and add whole or sliced to soups, stir-fries, or salads.

SWEET CHILI SAUCE: The thick, red, spicy, sweet, and tangy sauce made from ground red chilies, sugar, garlic, and salt. It is primarily used as a dipping sauce but can be used as a glaze for chicken or added to a sweet-and-sour sauce for some extra punch in flavor. Keep open bottles in the refrigerator.

TAPIOCA STARCH: A fine white powder that comes from the cassava root, used for thickening sauces and to give strength to dim sum doughs. Sometimes labeled "tapioca flour." Also used to make tapioca balls for desserts and drinks.

TARO ROOT: A tuber with a dark brown, rough skin and pale speckled flesh; ranges in size from as small as a golf ball to as big as a melon. When cooked, it has a sweet, nutty flavor. Can be used like potatoes.

THAI SWEET BASIL: An herb with angular green leaves, purplish stems, and a crown of purplish flowers. It adds a pungent, slightly minty-licorice flavor to curries, soups, stews, and stir-fries. Can be used shredded, fresh or cooked. If not available, use regular basil, although the taste will not be the same.

TOBIKO: Also known as flying fish roe. These tiny, bright orange eggs add a crunchy texture and burst of flavor. First popularized by sushi chefs, it is a versatile ingredient that can be used as a garnish, in a salad, or even mixed in with scrambled eggs. Found in jars on the shelves in specialty grocery stores or in the refrigerated section of Asian markets. Store the unused portion in the freezer for up to 6 months.

TOFU: Made from soybeans and water. Also called bean curd, it can be found in a variety of textures and forms. Soft or silken tofu has a smooth, custard-like texture; its best in sauces, soups, and pudding-like desserts. Regular or firm tofu is denser, with a spongy interior (more liquid is squeezed out during processing). It can be used in stir-fries or long-cooked dishes or stuffed.

Dense extra-firm tofu is also used in stir-fries or long-cooked dishes and stuffed.

TOFU PUFFS OR BEAN CURD PUFFS: Light, crispy, golden brown, deep-fried cubes of tofu with soft, dry spongy centers. Found with other types of tofu in the refrigerated section, packaged in plastic bags, or in large tubs in Asian markets. Store any unused puffs in a tightly sealed container in the refrigerator for up to a week.

TURMERIC: A bright, rusty-orange powder that comes from the turmeric root, used primarily for color. A member of the ginger family, the root has a pungent, bitter flavor.

WASABI: Sometimes called Japanese horseradish. Available as a powder, in cans or jars, or as a paste, in tubes. It has a sharp bite.

WATER CHESTNUTS: Available both fresh and canned. Fresh are walnut-sized with a dark skin that should be peeled before use. They have a mild sweet taste but are primarily used for texture. The canned version has a slightly tinny taste and should briefly be blanched before using. Jicama is an acceptable substitute.

WHEAT STARCH: The fine off-white powder left after all the glutinous proteins are removed from wheat flour, used to make translucent dim sum doughs. Sold in cellophane-wrapped packages or sturdy paper bags.

WINTER MELON: A very large pale-green gourd with milky-white flesh and a mild flavor. Most Asian markets offer it cut into slices and wrapped in plastic. Can be used in soups or stews or

WATER CHESTNUTS

steamed; it's best paired with more strongly flavored ingredients. *Not to be eaten raw.*

WOLFBERRIES: Small, deep red oval fruit of the medlar tree, with a slightly spiced apple flavor. Found in the dried foods section of Asian markets. Used in soups, desserts, and steamed dishes. Dried cranberries can be substituted.

WONTON WRAPPERS: Made from a dough of wheat flour, eggs, and water, these are square wrappers of medium thickness. Used to make wontons that are fried or boiled, they are also cut into thin strips and deep-fried for garnish. Store extra wrappers in the refrigerator or freezer.

XO SAUCE: Originated in Hong Kong, a sauce made of dried scallops and shrimp, chili peppers, and spices, with a pleasantly fishy, salty, spicy flavor. Used as a condiment or to add complexity to many dishes. Found in most Asian markets.

WINTER MELON

Index

chicken-mushroom, for golden baked buns, 27
custard, for pineapple buns, 33
for duck-filled sweet sesame balls, 59
for Hakka-style stuffed tofu, 140–41
for jade scallop dumplings, 13–14
for Shanghai sticky rice siu mai, 6
shrimp-scallop, for golden baked buns, 27
for surefire siu mai, 4
for vegetarian "faux" fish, 137
for wontons in hot-and-sour chili sauce, 61
fish:
    ahi tuna, in beer-battered rolls, 44–45
    ahi tuna, in okey doke poke, 109
    bacalhau Macau, 41–42
    braised, fillets with tofu puffs, 169
    chowder, good fortune, 71
    chrysanthemum, in sweet vinegar sauce, 157–58
    crispy halibut with miso vinaigrette, 160–61
    crispy seafood and mango packets, 43
    custard, comfort-food, 139
    double ginger, 148
    family-style, with bean sprouts, 146
    Hakkasan salmon and sea bass in champagne sauce, 173
    -head soup, Singapore's, 70
    mousse, 152
    nori-dusted flounder bundles, 163
    oven-baked salmon in spicy chili-bean sauce, 171
    salad, year of good fortune, 112
    Sam Choy's whole, with fruit salsa, 159
    Shanghai lacquered bass, 170
    Shanghainese wok-seared, in wine sauce, 149
    steamed, with mushrooms and baby bok choy, 164–65

steamed whole, with ginger and green onions, 167
sweet and tangy catfish fillets, 153
tail, red-cooked, 168
trout stuffed with fish mousse, 150–51
five-flavor chicken and eggplant, 216
five-spice crispy lamb London-style, 280–81
flounder bundles, nori-dusted, 163
flower drum crab baked in the shell, 197
fluffy snow cloud in lime syrup, 323
four-mushroom beef, 265
fried:
    garlic, mushrooms and baby bok choy with, 97
    ice cream with ginger-caramel sauce, 334–35
    lychee custard bars, 324
fritters, broccoli, in Sichuan pepper-salt, 103
frozen tofu fruit smoothie, 336
fruit:
    salsa, Sam Choy's whole fish with, 159
    and shrimp rolls, tropical, 11
    smoothie, frozen tofu, 336
    see also specific fruits
Fujian fancy fried rice, 286–87
fun chicken, 301

G

game hen, three-pepper, 227
ginger:
    -chili clams with brothy glass noodles, 185
    and egg fried rice, 298
golden baked buns, 25
golden pancake, beef stir-fry over, 268–69
golden shrimp puffs, 10
gold medal crab fried rice, 297
good fortune fish chowder, 71
grapes and kiwi, emerald chicken with, 209

green beans, dry-fried, 88
green onion(s):
    -ginger sauce, velvet oysters with, 188
    pancakes, mandarin, 39
    steamed whole fish with ginger and, 167
gum-lo wontons with seafood sweet-and-sour sauce, 50–51

H

Hakka:
    cuisine, 141
    shrimp-stuffed peppers and eggplant, 101–2
    -style stuffed tofu, 140–41
Hakkasan salmon and sea bass in champagne sauce, 173
halibut, crispy, with miso vinaigrette, 160–61
hidden-treasure omelet, 130–31
honeydew melon bowl soup, eight-treasure, 75
Hong Kong wonton noodle bowl, 78
hot-and-sour egg flower soup, 83
Hunan chicken with nuts, 217

I

ingredients, 338–55

J

jia jiang mein, 310
jook, 9
    chicken, 8

K

Kung Pao:
    chicken, 206–7
    lobster tails, fiery, 201

L

lamb:
emperor's, 276
five-spice crispy, London-style, 280–81
lemongrass, with minted orange sauce, 279
lemongrass:
beef stew, Malay, 275
egg-flower soup with mushrooms and, 68–69
lamb with minted orange sauce, 279
lettuce cups, pepper-salt squid in, 191
light and tender mushroom-steamed chicken, 220
lobster:
steamed whole, with dried tangerine peel, 199–200
tails, fiery Kung Pao, 201
tails, wok-braised, in creamy rum sauce, 203
long beans, tofu puffs with mushrooms and, 127
lotus blossom omelet in broth, 223
lotus root salad, sweet and tangy, 111
lu'au stew, 274
lucky duck melon salad, 121
lucky treasure rice pudding, 320–21

M

Macau:
bacalhau, 41–42
clay pot rice, 294
minchee minced pork, 250
rice noodles, 302
shrimp and rice noodle soup, 77
spicy grilled chicken thighs à la, 225
-style stuffed prawns, 54
Malay lemongrass beef stew, 275
mandarin green onion pancakes, 39
mango packets, crispy seafood and, 43

ma po bean curd, 134
marinade(s):
for big pot wor wonton soup, 84–85
for crispy seafood and mango packets, 43
for lemongrass lamb with minted orange sauce, 279
for ma po bean curd, 134
for oven-baked salmon in spicy chili-bean sauce, 171
for seven-flavor slow-cooked pork, 258
for Shandong stir-fry soup noodles, 81–82
for spicy grilled chicken thighs à la Macau, 225
for tomato beef, 264
master sauce squab, 244–45
meat, 246–81
see also specific meats
meatballs, double-harmony, in sweet-and-sour sauce, 63
melon:
bitter, stir-fried beef with, 262–63
eight-treasure honeydew, bowl soup, 75
salad, lucky duck, 121
seafood-stuffed fuzzy, 106
tricolor, salad with coconut prawns, 114–15
minted fried rice, 290
miso vinaigrette, crispy halibut with, 160–61
Mongolian beef, 261
mousse, fish, 152
mushroom(s):
beef, four-, 265
button, and baby bok choy with fried garlic, 97
dried, in market basket vegetable stir-fry, 93
dried and button, in Buddha's feast, 104–5
egg-flower soup with lemongrass and, 68
parchment-baked squab with, 242

soft tofu with black vinegar sauce and, 125
-steamed chicken, light and tender, 220
steamed fish with baby bok choy and, 164–65
tofu puffs with long beans and, 127
mu shu:
duck wraps, 229
pork, 248

N

nachos, roast duck, 60
Nanjing "surf and turf" stir-fry, 267
napa cabbage, duck soup with, 79
Nonya noodles, spicy-creamy, 312–13
noodle(s), 300–313
bean thread, daikon with, 303
bean thread, stir-fried soybean sprouts with, 96
bean thread brothy, ginger-chili clams with, 185
beef stir-fry over golden pancake, 268–69
bowl, Hong Kong wonton, 78
braised seafood mein, 305
cold peanut, with chicken, 306
dan dan, 307
fun chicken, 301
jia jiang mein, 310
Macau rice, 302
Macau shrimp and rice noodle soup, 77
rice, 18
rice, beef-filled pillows, 15
salad with black bean and mint dressing, 108
Shandong stir-fry soup, 81–82
Shanghai, with pork and bok choy, 309
spicy-creamy Nonya, 312–13
in steamed oysters on the half-shell, 57